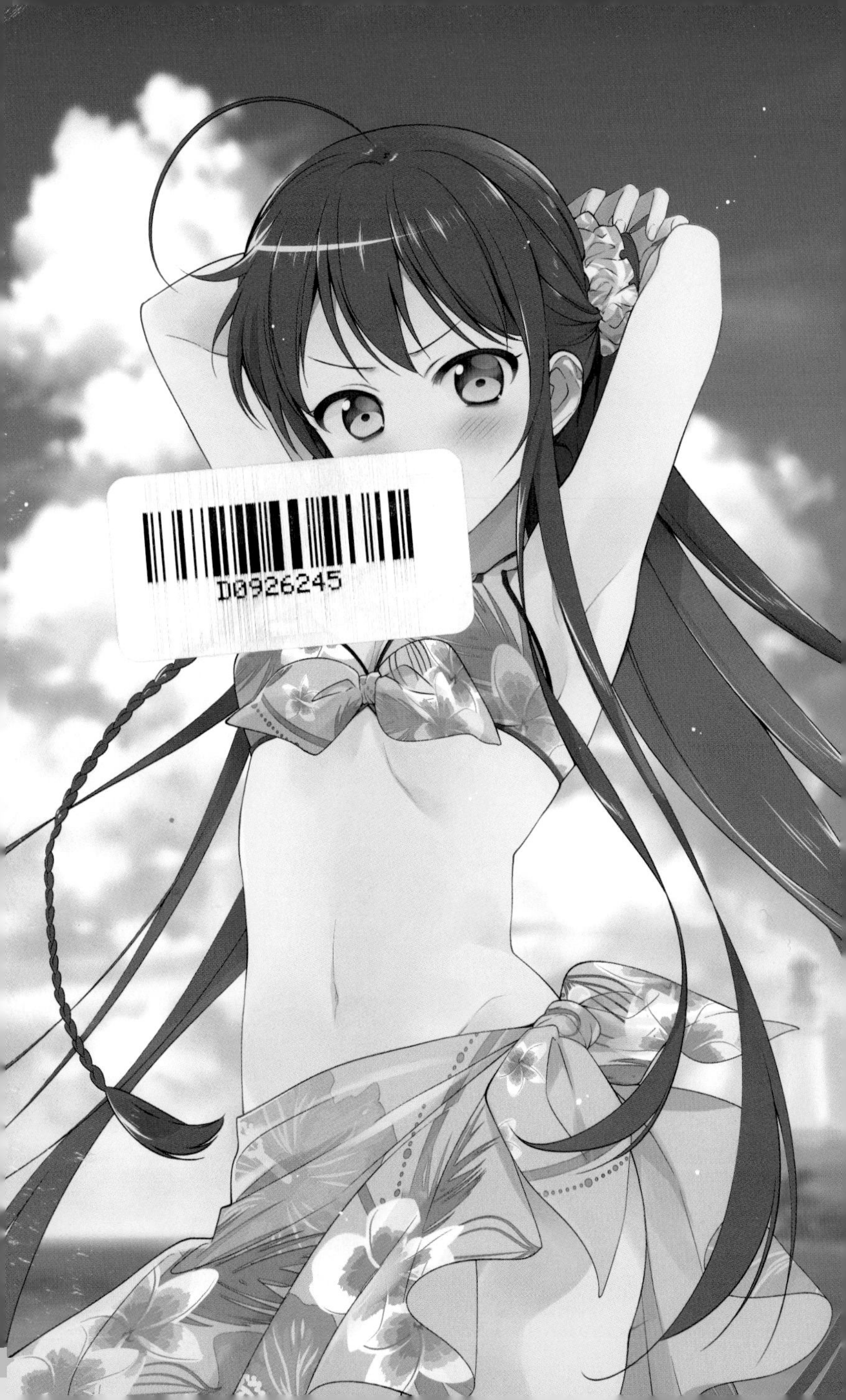

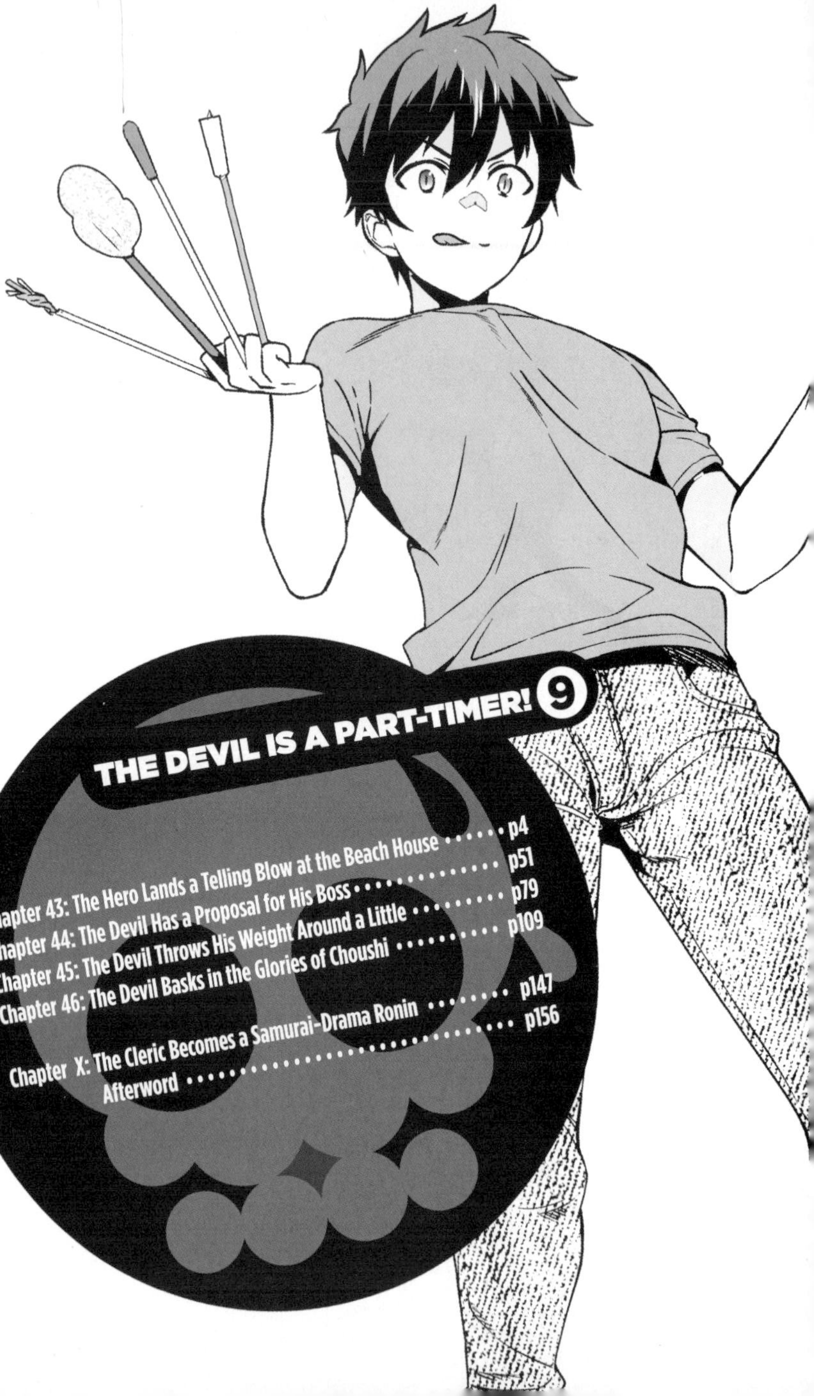

THE DEVIL IS A PART-TIMER! 9

Amane
Ohguro

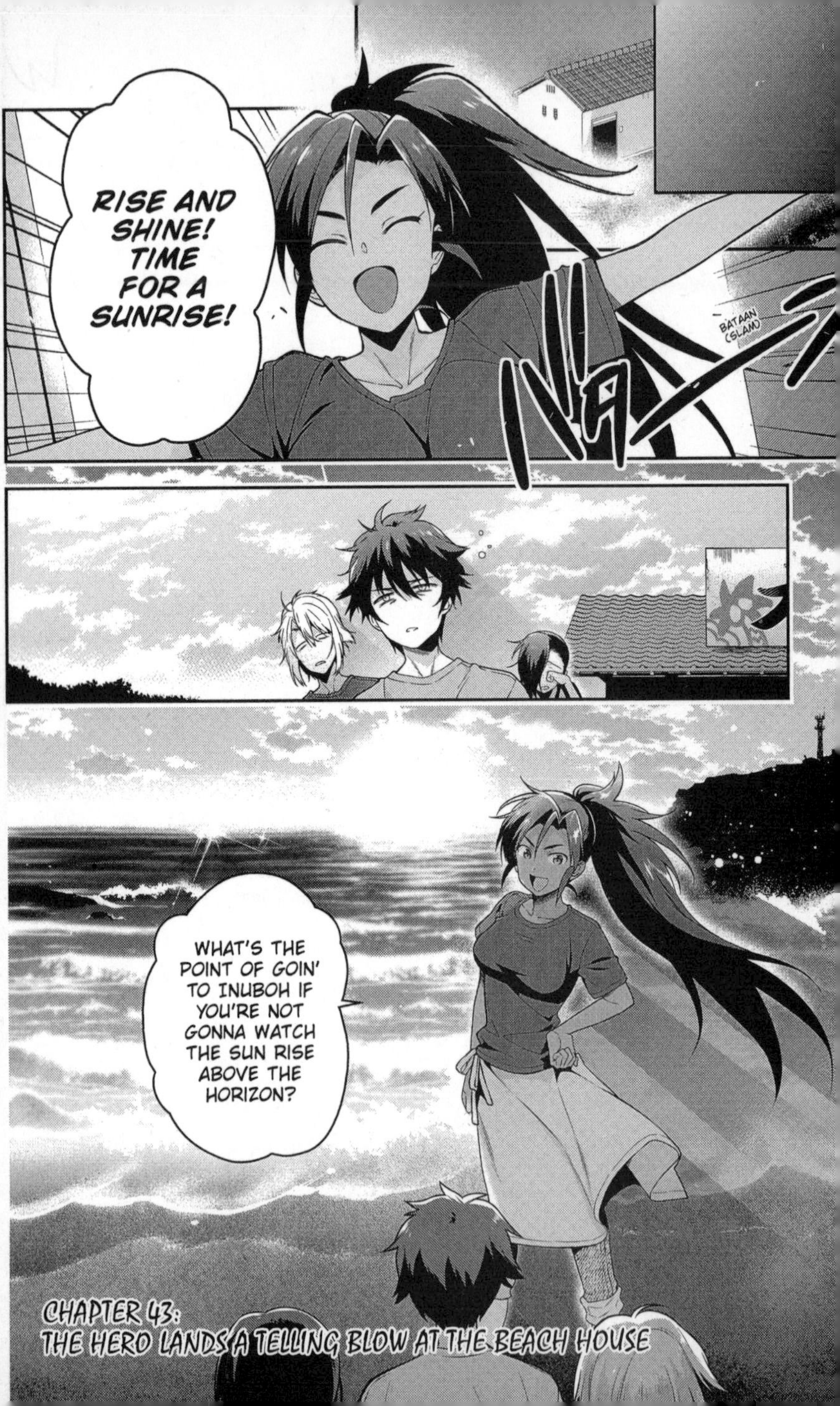
BATAAN (SLAM)
RISE AND SHINE! TIME FOR A SUNRISE!
WHAT'S THE POINT OF GOIN' TO INUBOH IF YOU'RE NOT GONNA WATCH THE SUN RISE ABOVE THE HORIZON?

CHAPTER 43:
THE HERO LANDS A TELLING BLOW AT THE BEACH HOUSE

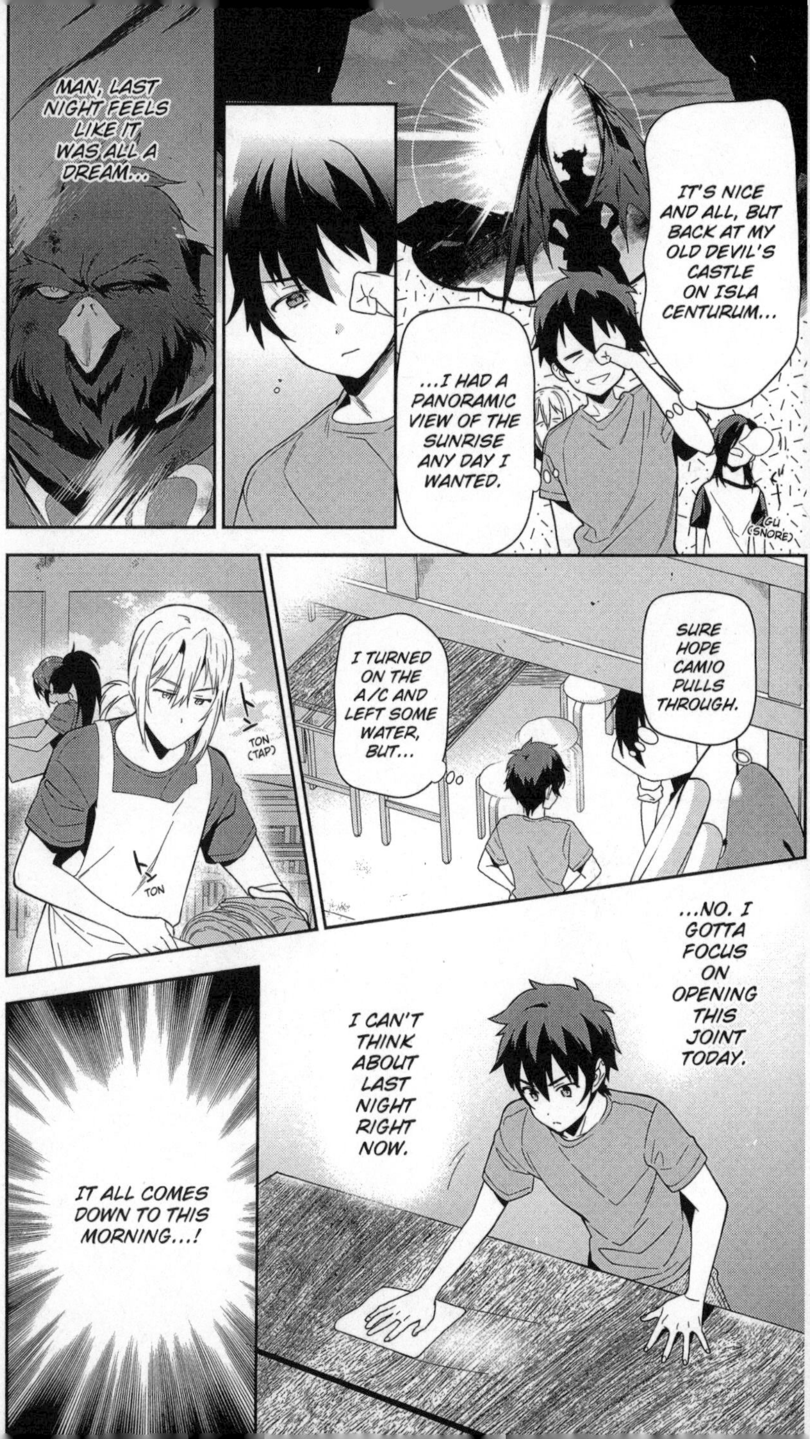
IT'S NICE AND ALL, BUT BACK AT MY OLD DEVIL'S CASTLE ON ISLA CENTURUM...
...I HAD A PANORAMIC VIEW OF THE SUNRISE ANY DAY I WANTED.
GU (SNORE)
MAN, LAST NIGHT FEELS LIKE IT WAS ALL A DREAM...
SURE HOPE CAMIO PULLS THROUGH.
I TURNED ON THE A/C AND LEFT SOME WATER, BUT...
TON (TAP)
TON
...NO. I GOTTA FOCUS ON OPENING THIS JOINT TODAY.
I CAN'T THINK ABOUT LAST NIGHT RIGHT NOW.
IT ALL COMES DOWN TO THIS MORNING...!

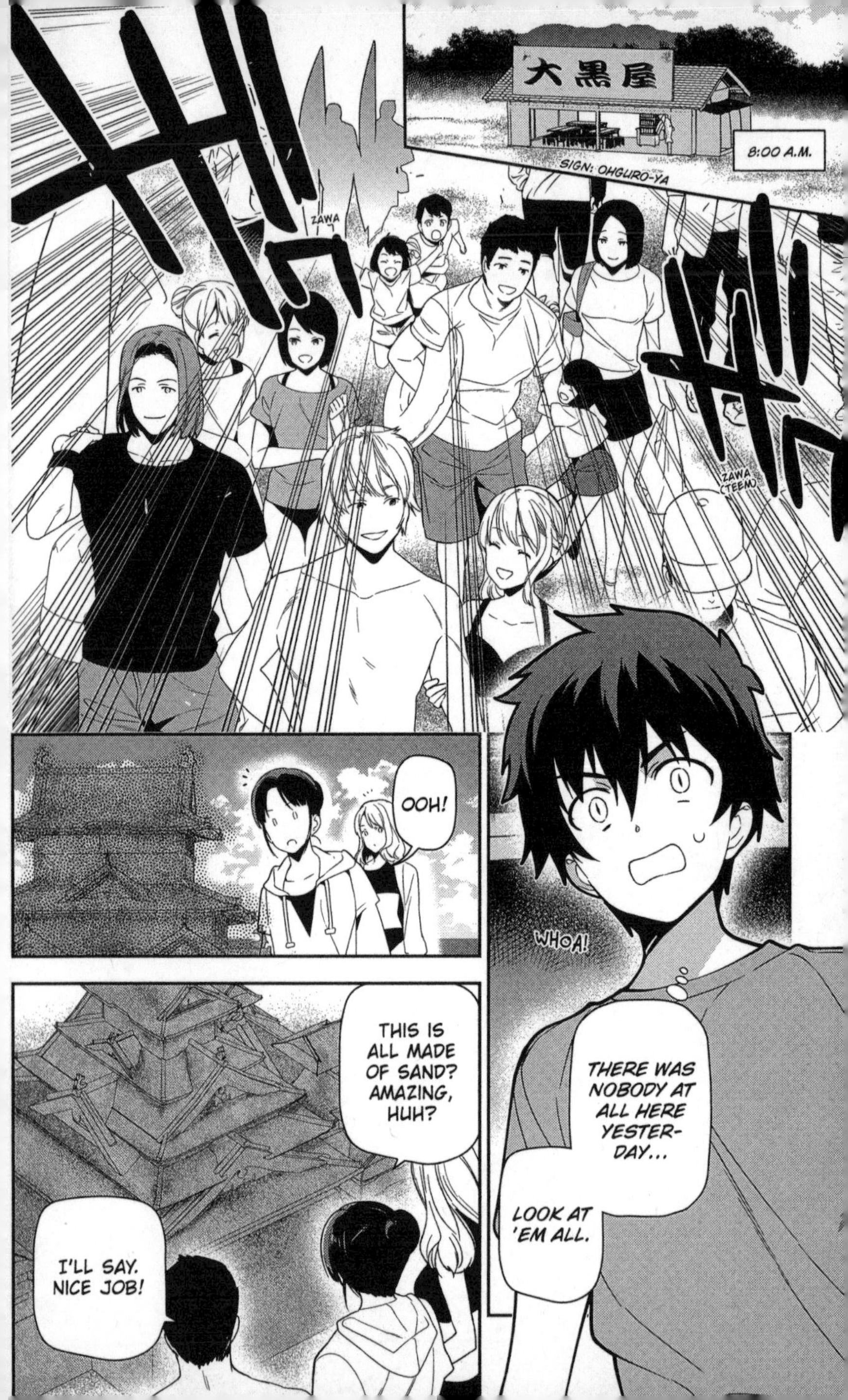
大黒屋
8:00 A.M.
SIGN: OHGURO-YA
ZAWA
ZAWA (TEEM)
WHOA!
THERE WAS NOBODY AT ALL HERE YESTER-DAY...
LOOK AT 'EM ALL.
OOH!
THIS IS ALL MADE OF SAND? AMAZING, HUH?
I'LL SAY. NICE JOB!

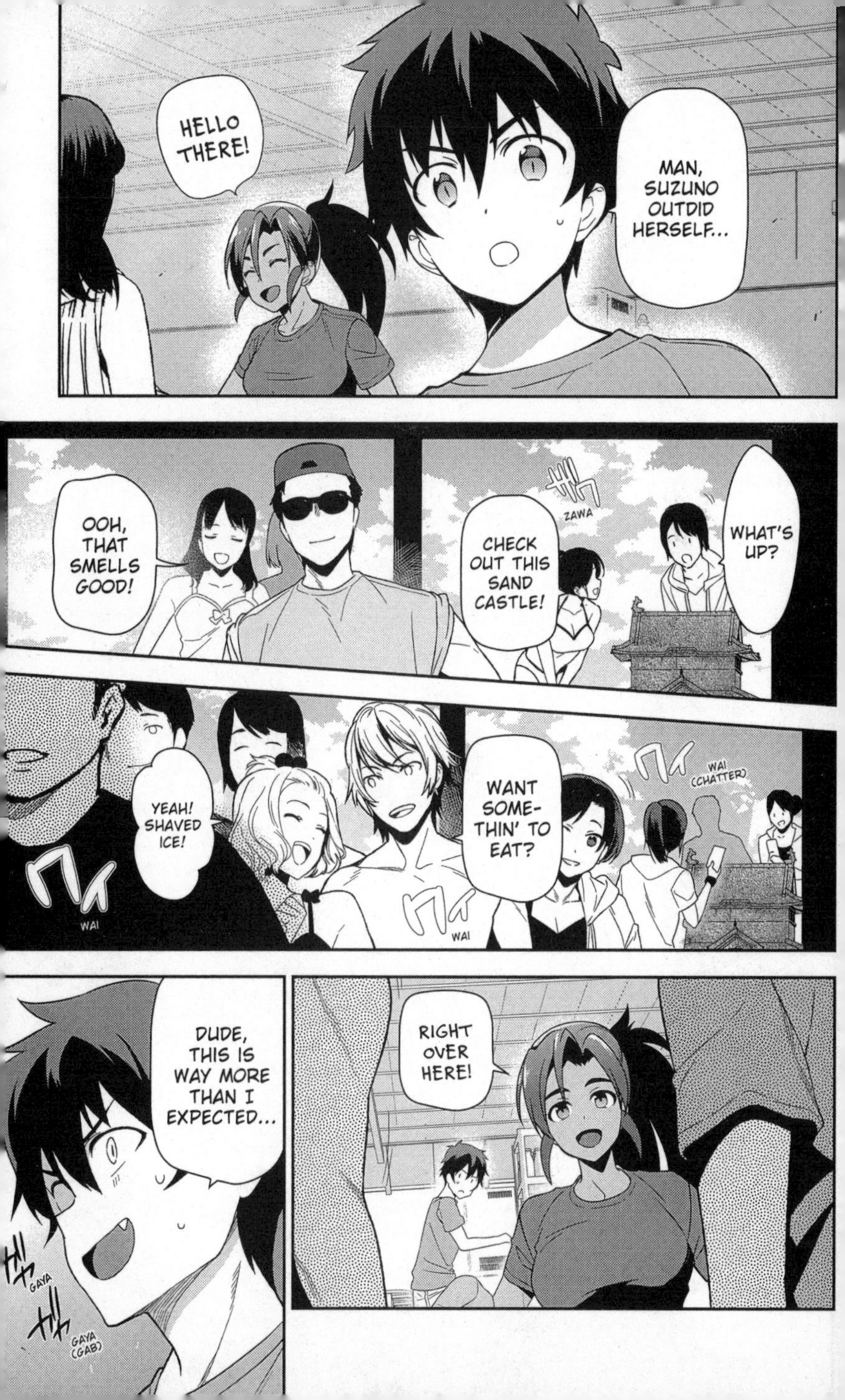
MAN, SUZUNO OUTDID HERSELF...
HELLO THERE!
WHAT'S UP?
ZAWA
CHECK OUT THIS SAND CASTLE!
OOH, THAT SMELLS GOOD!
WAI (CHATTER)
WANT SOME-THIN' TO EAT?
WAI
YEAH! SHAVED ICE!
WAI
RIGHT OVER HERE!
DUDE, THIS IS WAY MORE THAN I EXPECTED...
GAYA
GAYA (GAB)

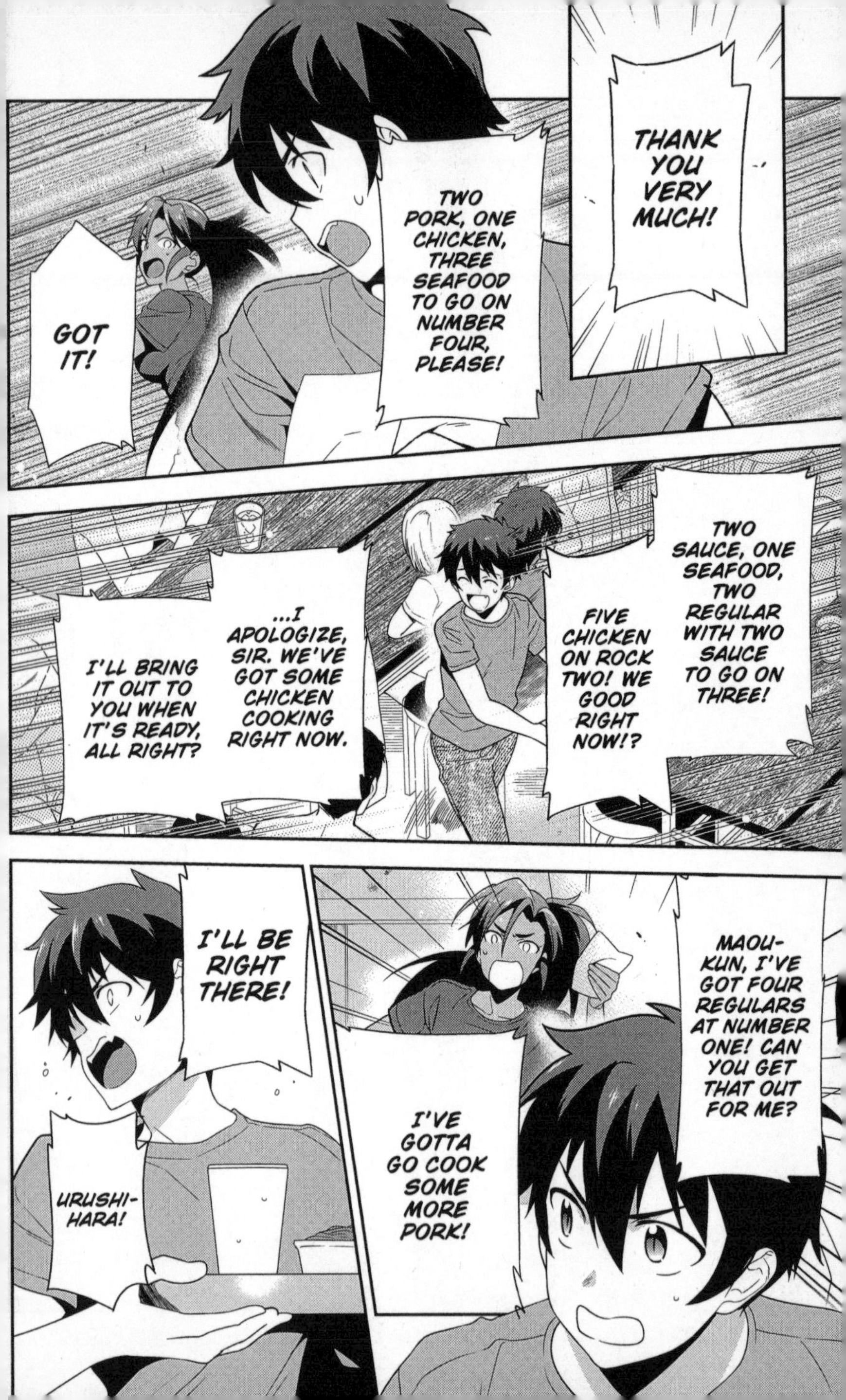
THANK YOU VERY MUCH!
TWO PORK, ONE CHICKEN, THREE SEAFOOD TO GO ON NUMBER FOUR, PLEASE!
GOT IT!
TWO SAUCE, ONE SEAFOOD, TWO REGULAR WITH TWO SAUCE TO GO ON THREE!
FIVE CHICKEN ON ROCK TWO! WE GOOD RIGHT NOW!?
...I APOLOGIZE, SIR. WE'VE GOT SOME CHICKEN COOKING RIGHT NOW.
I'LL BRING IT OUT TO YOU WHEN IT'S READY, ALL RIGHT?
MAOU-KUN, I'VE GOT FOUR REGULARS AT NUMBER ONE! CAN YOU GET THAT OUT FOR ME?
I'VE GOTTA GO COOK SOME MORE PORK!
I'LL BE RIGHT THERE!
URUSHI-HARA!

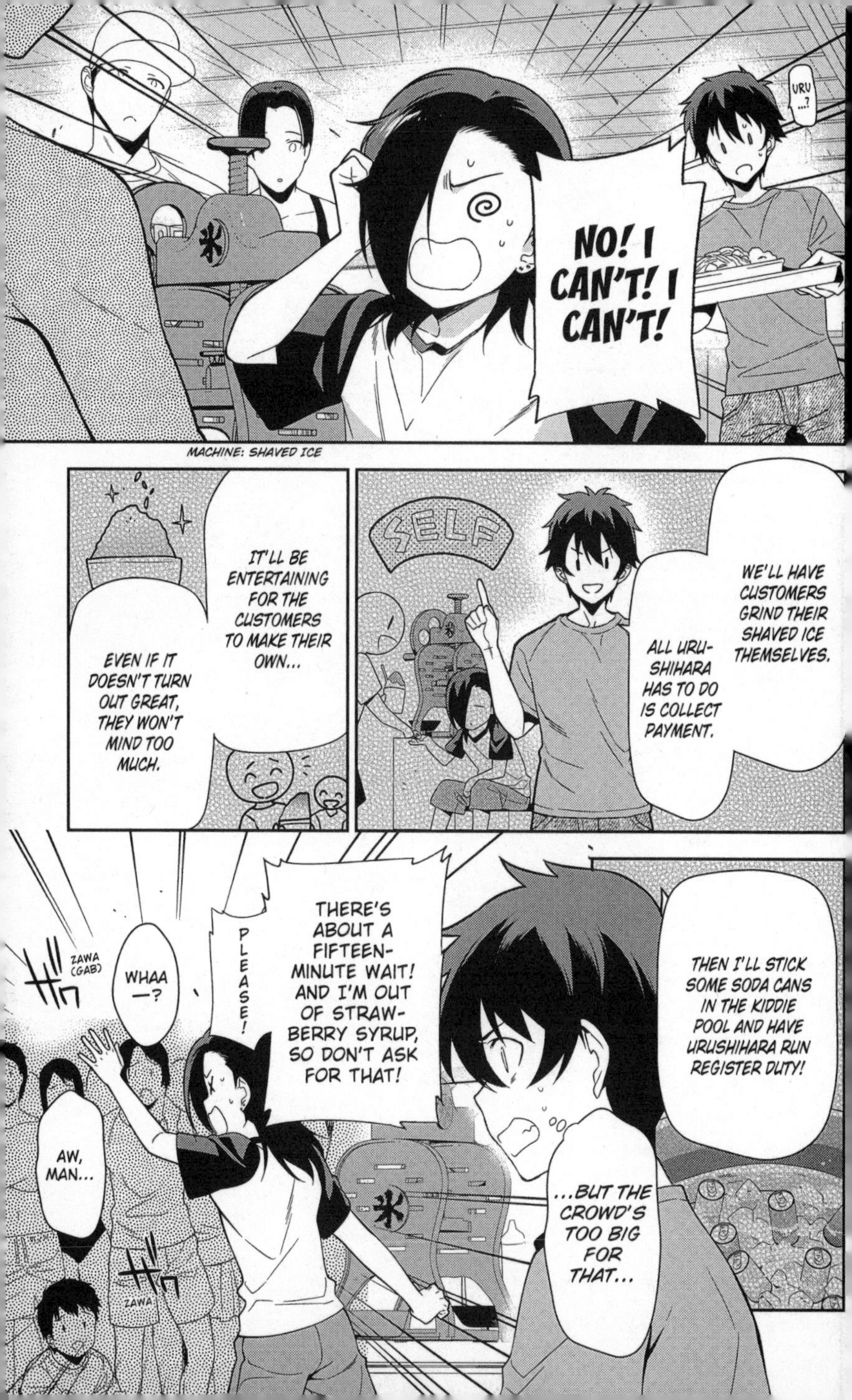
URU ...?
NO! I CAN'T! I CAN'T!
MACHINE: SHAVED ICE
WE'LL HAVE CUSTOMERS GRIND THEIR SHAVED ICE THEMSELVES.
ALL URU-SHIHARA HAS TO DO IS COLLECT PAYMENT.
IT'LL BE ENTERTAINING FOR THE CUSTOMERS TO MAKE THEIR OWN...
EVEN IF IT DOESN'T TURN OUT GREAT, THEY WON'T MIND TOO MUCH.
THEN I'LL STICK SOME SODA CANS IN THE KIDDIE POOL AND HAVE URUSHIHARA RUN REGISTER DUTY!
...BUT THE CROWD'S TOO BIG FOR THAT...
THERE'S ABOUT A FIFTEEN-MINUTE WAIT! AND I'M OUT OF STRAW-BERRY SYRUP, SO DON'T ASK FOR THAT!
PLEASE!
WHAA—?
ZAWA (GAB)
AW, MAN...
ZAWA

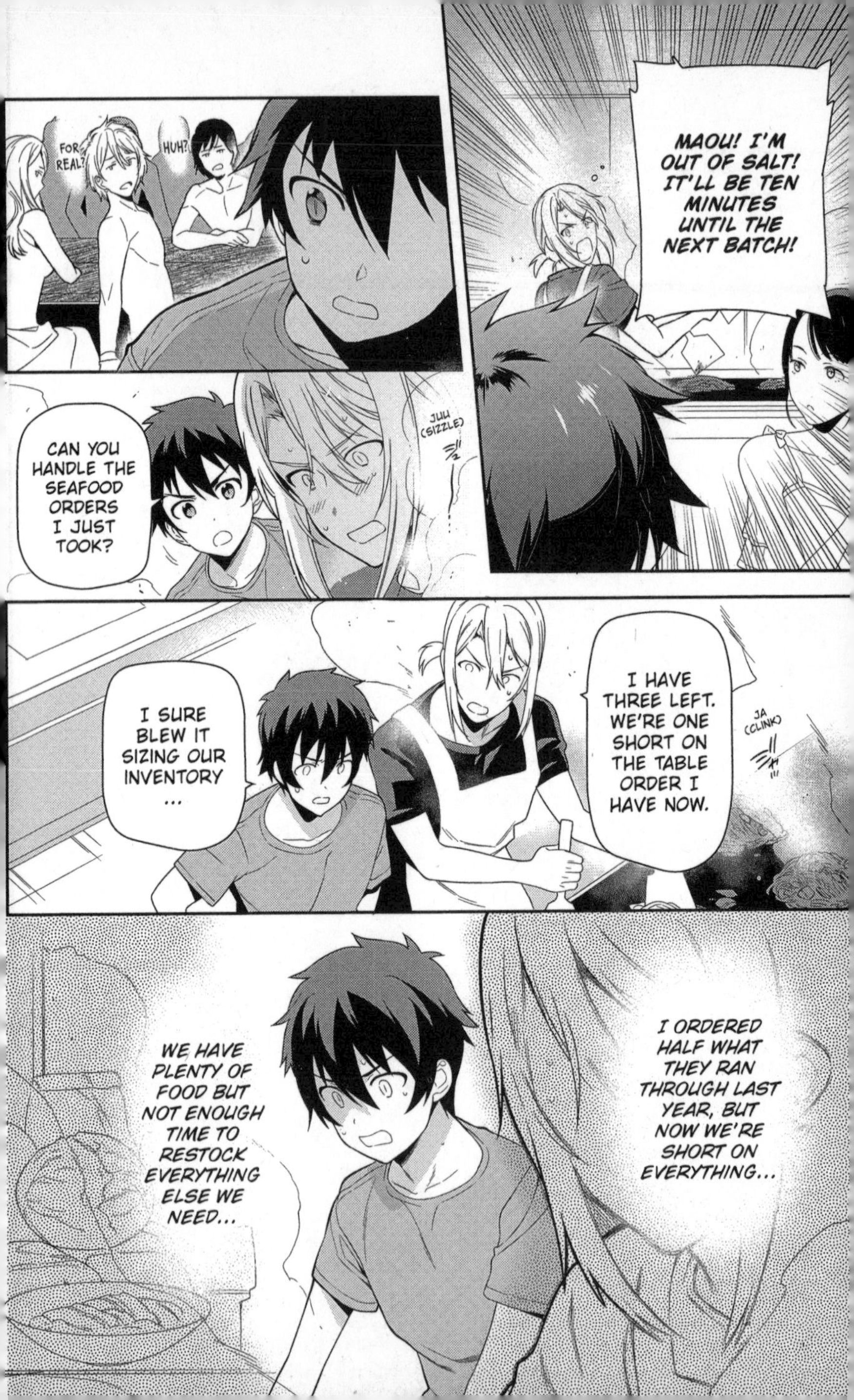
MAOU! I'M OUT OF SALT! IT'LL BE TEN MINUTES UNTIL THE NEXT BATCH!
HUH?
FOR REAL?
JUU (SIZZLE)
CAN YOU HANDLE THE SEAFOOD ORDERS I JUST TOOK?
JA (CLINK)
I HAVE THREE LEFT. WE'RE ONE SHORT ON THE TABLE ORDER I HAVE NOW.
I SURE BLEW IT SIZING OUR INVENTORY ...
I ORDERED HALF WHAT THEY RAN THROUGH LAST YEAR, BUT NOW WE'RE SHORT ON EVERYTHING...
WE HAVE PLENTY OF FOOD BUT NOT ENOUGH TIME TO RESTOCK EVERYTHING ELSE WE NEED...

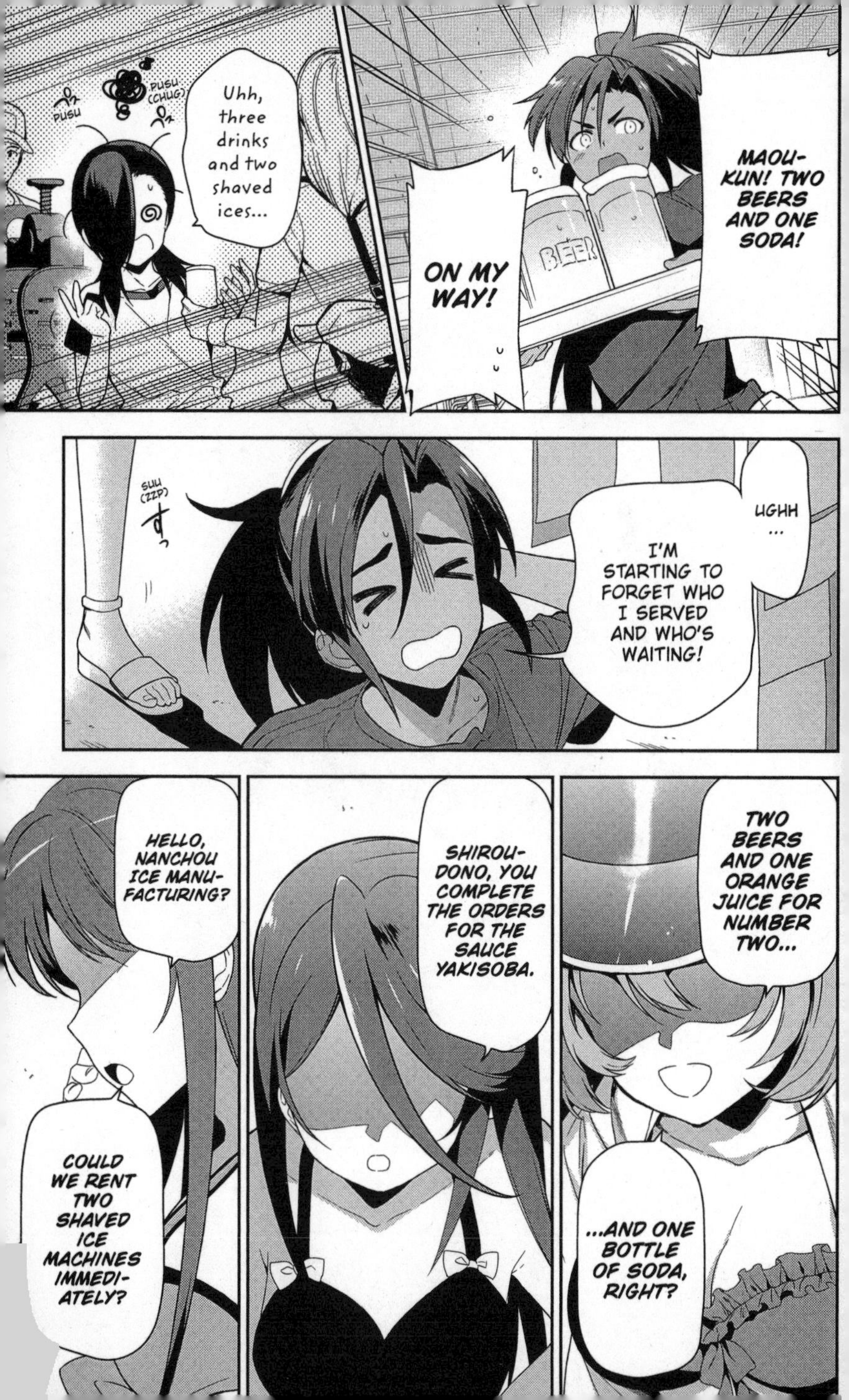
MAOU-KUN! TWO BEERS AND ONE SODA!
ON MY WAY!
BEER
PUSU (CHUG)
PUSU
Uhh, three drinks and two shaved ices...
UGHH ...
I'M STARTING TO FORGET WHO I SERVED AND WHO'S WAITING!
SUU (ZZP)
TWO BEERS AND ONE ORANGE JUICE FOR NUMBER TWO...
...AND ONE BOTTLE OF SODA, RIGHT?
SHIROU-DONO, YOU COMPLETE THE ORDERS FOR THE SAUCE YAKISOBA.
HELLO, NANCHOU ICE MANUFACTURING?
COULD WE RENT TWO SHAVED ICE MACHINES IMMEDIATELY?

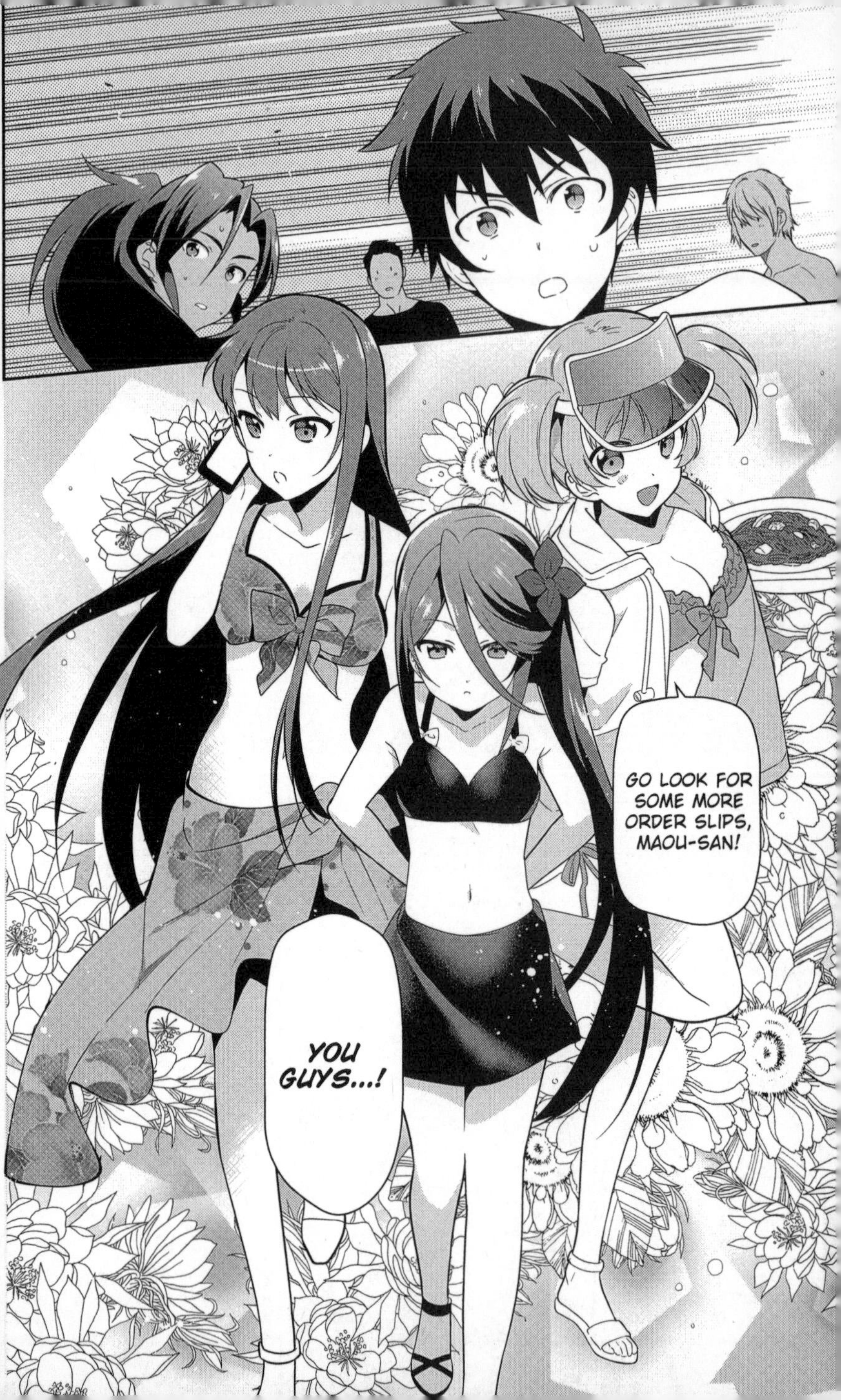
GO LOOK FOR SOME MORE ORDER SLIPS, MAOU-SAN!
YOU GUYS...!

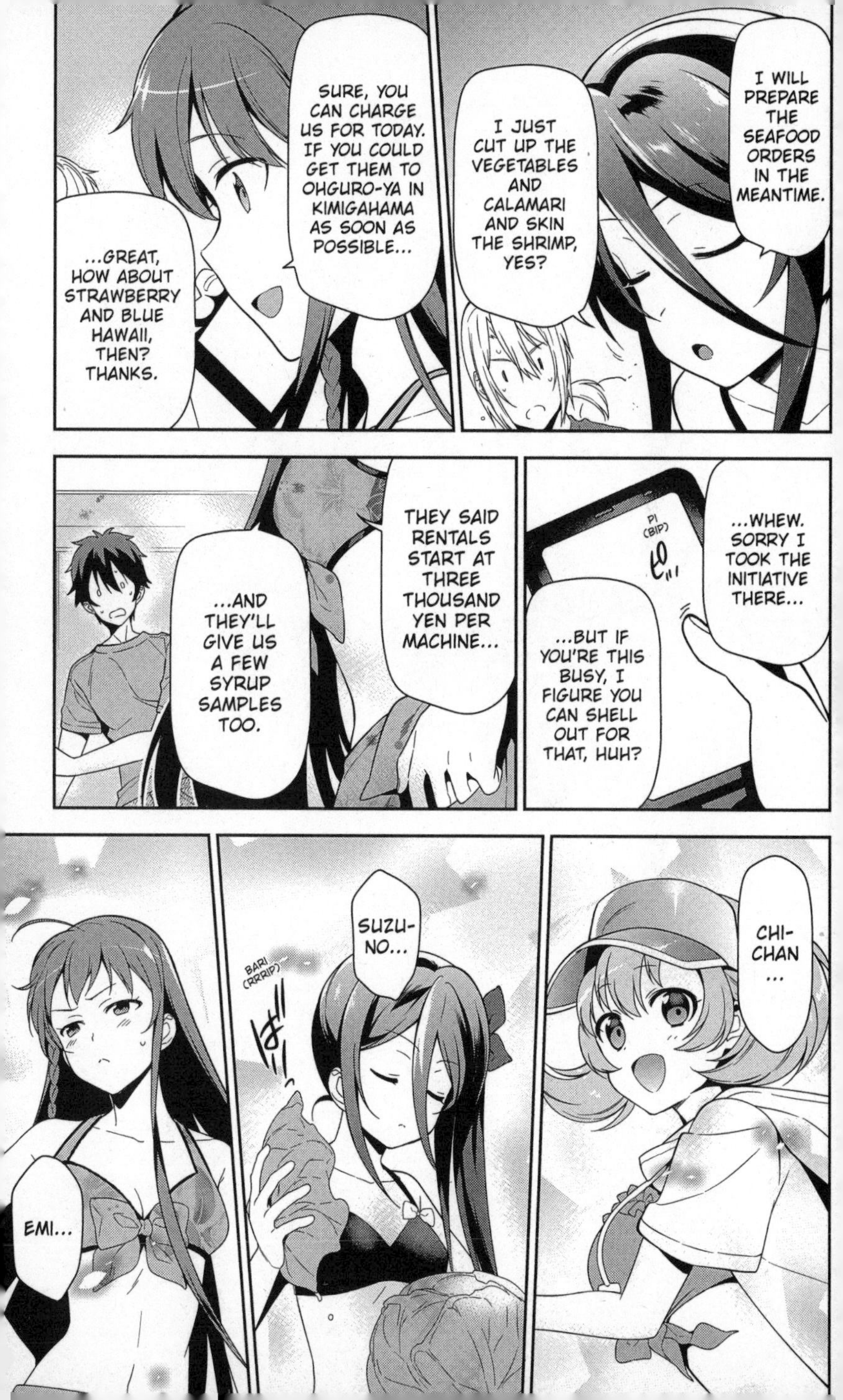
I WILL PREPARE THE SEAFOOD ORDERS IN THE MEANTIME.
I JUST CUT UP THE VEGETABLES AND CALAMARI AND SKIN THE SHRIMP, YES?
SURE, YOU CAN CHARGE US FOR TODAY. IF YOU COULD GET THEM TO OHGURO-YA IN KIMIGAHAMA AS SOON AS POSSIBLE...
...GREAT, HOW ABOUT STRAWBERRY AND BLUE HAWAII, THEN? THANKS.
...WHEW. SORRY I TOOK THE INITIATIVE THERE...
PI (BIP)
...BUT IF YOU'RE THIS BUSY, I FIGURE YOU CAN SHELL OUT FOR THAT, HUH?
THEY SAID RENTALS START AT THREE THOUSAND YEN PER MACHINE...
...AND THEY'LL GIVE US A FEW SYRUP SAMPLES TOO.
CHI-CHAN...
SUZU-NO...
BARI (RRRIP)
EMI...

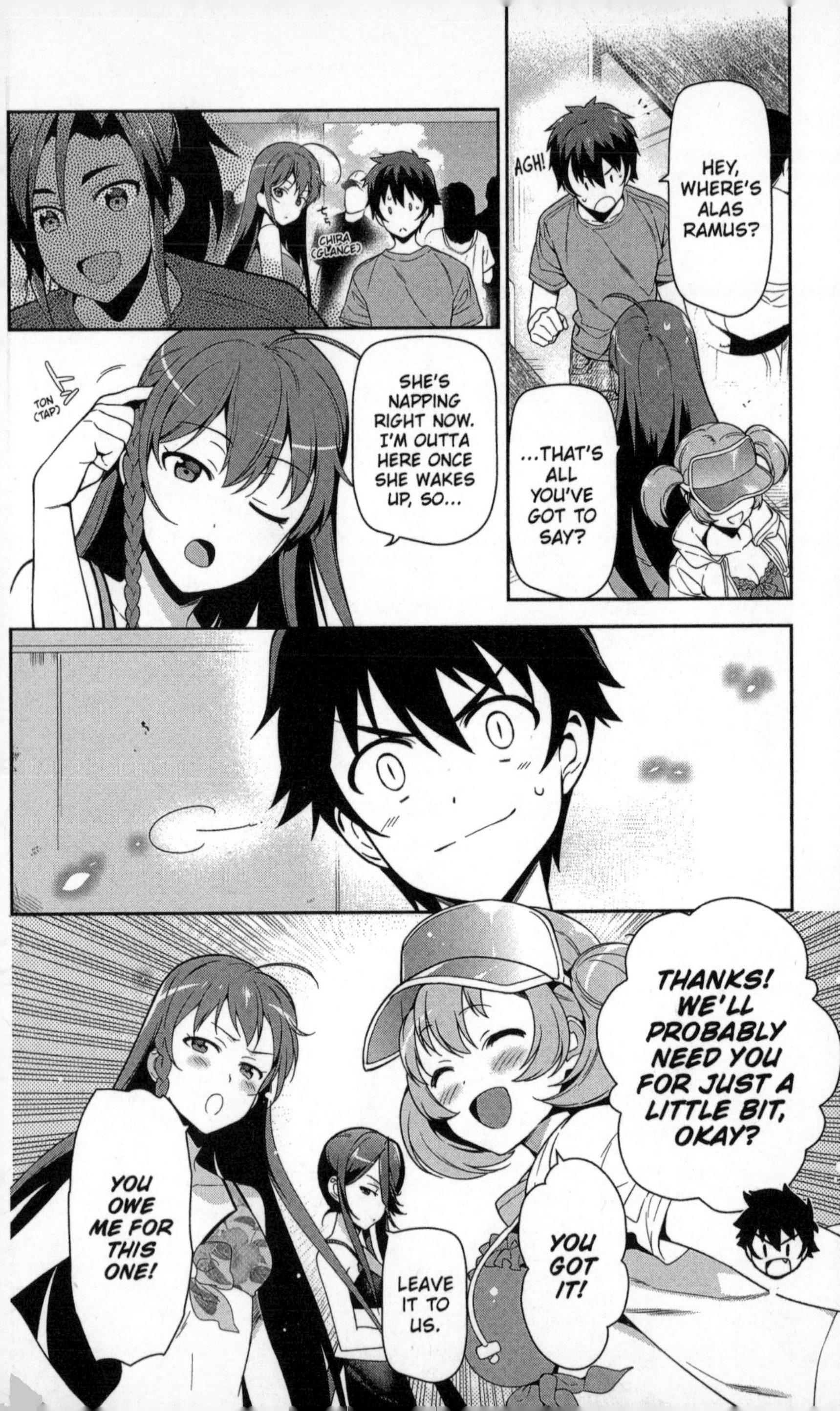
HEY, WHERE'S ALAS RAMUS?
AGH!
...THAT'S ALL YOU'VE GOT TO SAY?
CHIRA (GLANCE)
SHE'S NAPPING RIGHT NOW. I'M OUTTA HERE ONCE SHE WAKES UP, SO...
TON (TAP)
THANKS! WE'LL PROBABLY NEED YOU FOR JUST A LITTLE BIT, OKAY?
YOU GOT IT!
LEAVE IT TO US.
YOU OWE ME FOR THIS ONE!

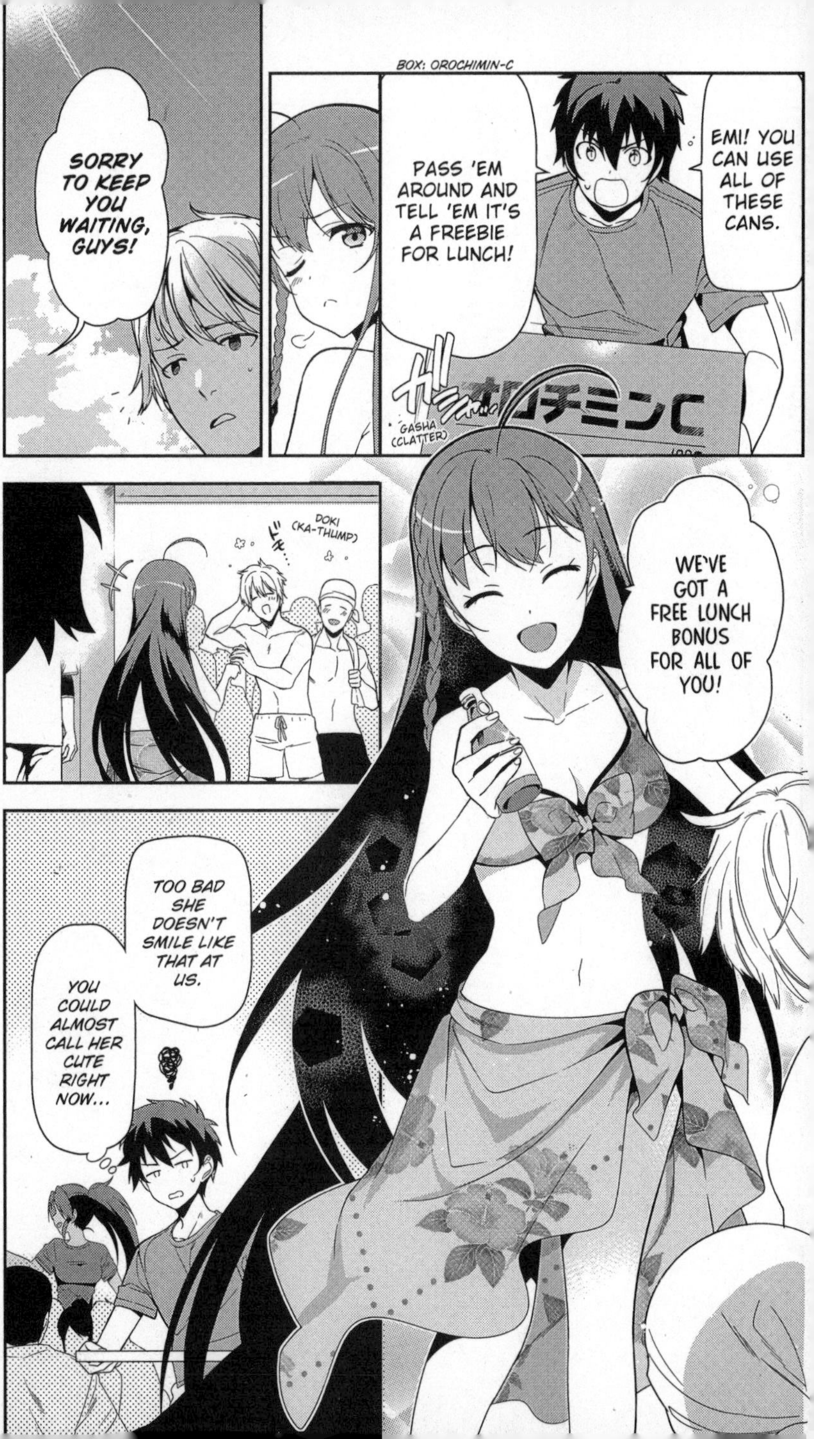
BOX: OROCHIMIN-C
EMI! YOU CAN USE ALL OF THESE CANS.
PASS 'EM AROUND AND TELL 'EM IT'S A FREEBIE FOR LUNCH!
GASHA (CLATTER)
SORRY TO KEEP YOU WAITING, GUYS!
WE'VE GOT A FREE LUNCH BONUS FOR ALL OF YOU!
DOKI (KA-THUMP)
TOO BAD SHE DOESN'T SMILE LIKE THAT AT US.
YOU COULD ALMOST CALL HER CUTE RIGHT NOW...

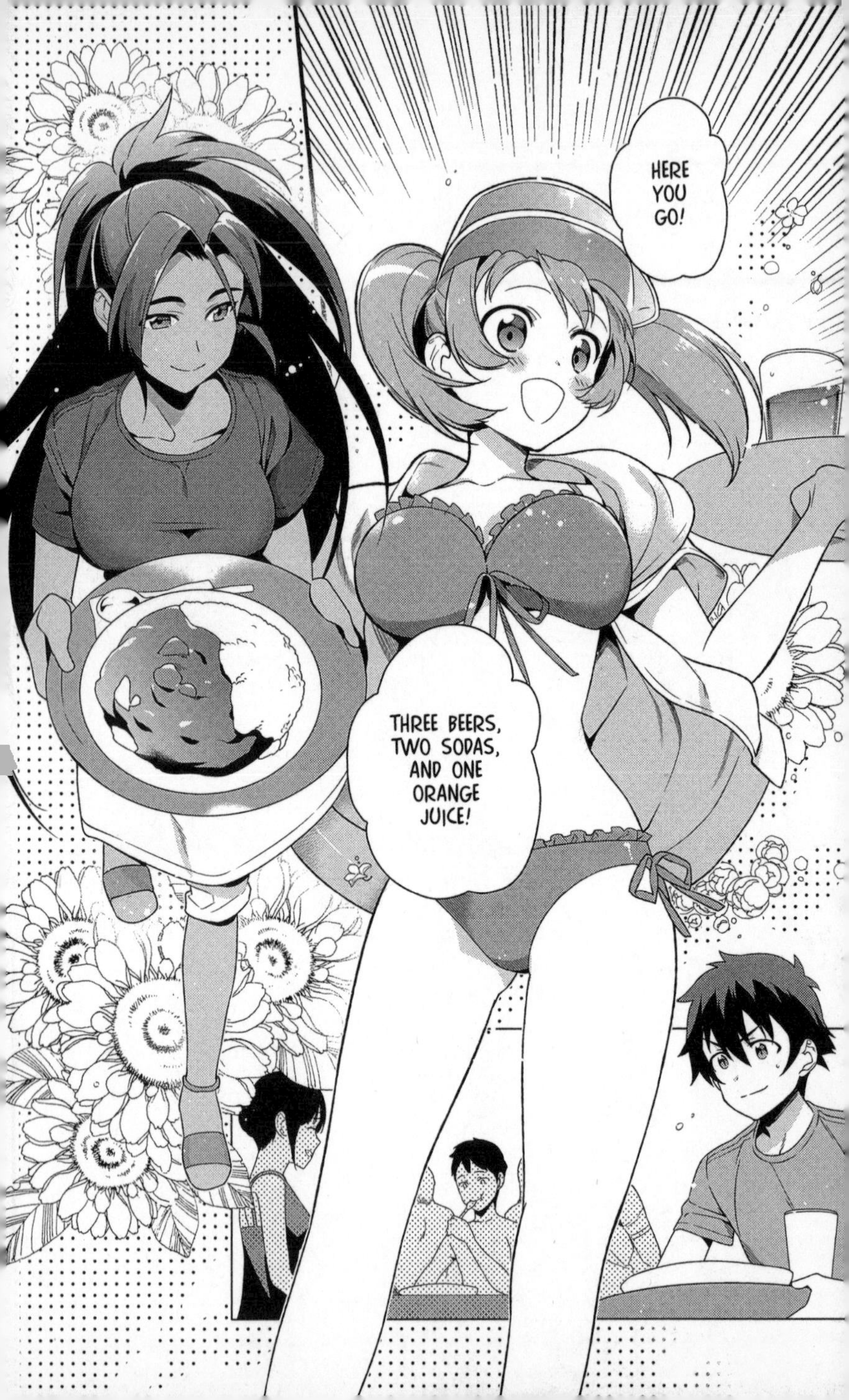
HERE YOU GO!
THREE BEERS, TWO SODAS, AND ONE ORANGE JUICE!

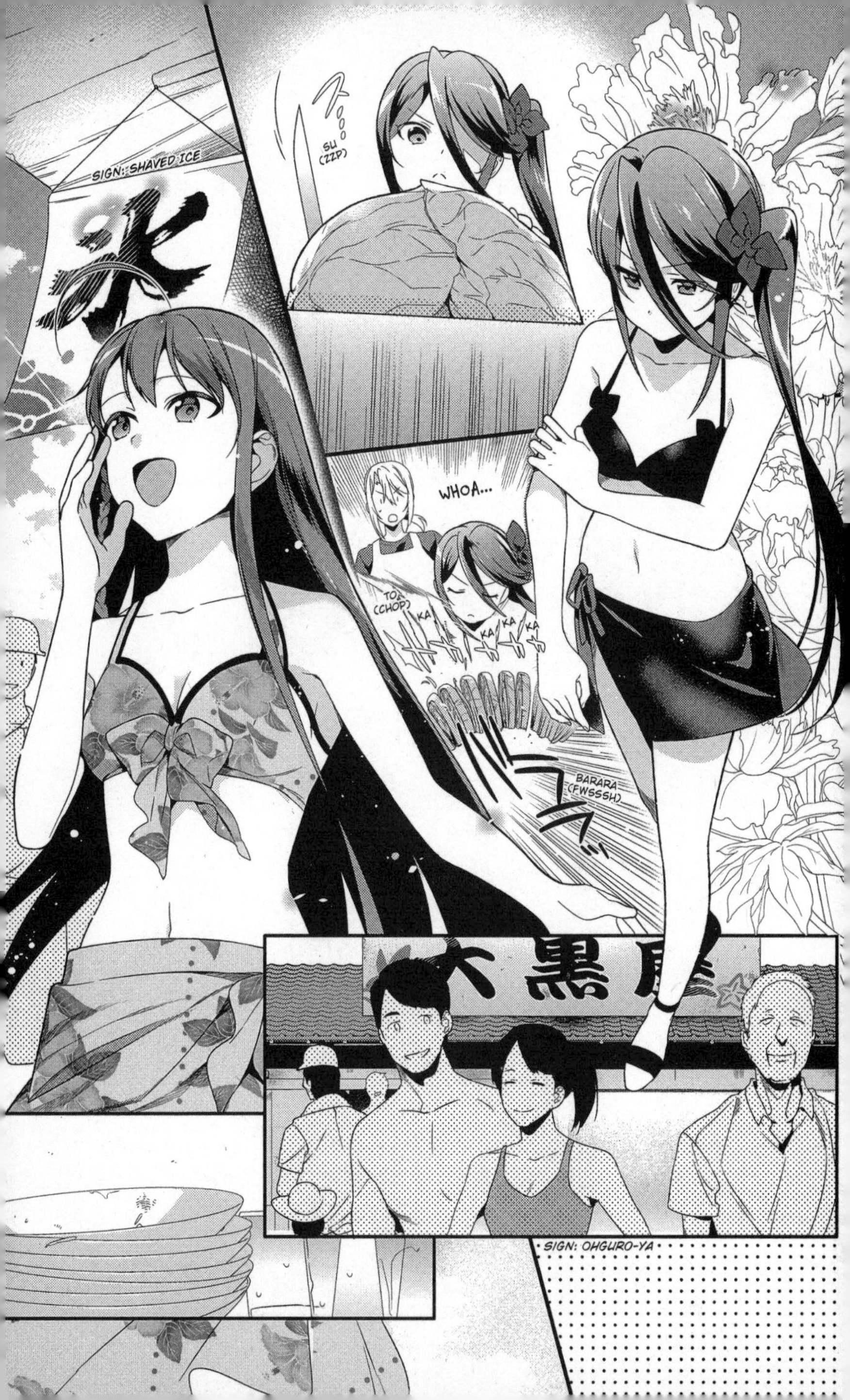
SU
(ZZP)
SIGN: SHAVED ICE
WHOA...
TO
(CHOP)
KA
KA
KA
KA
BARARA
(FWSSSH)
SIGN: OHGURO-YA

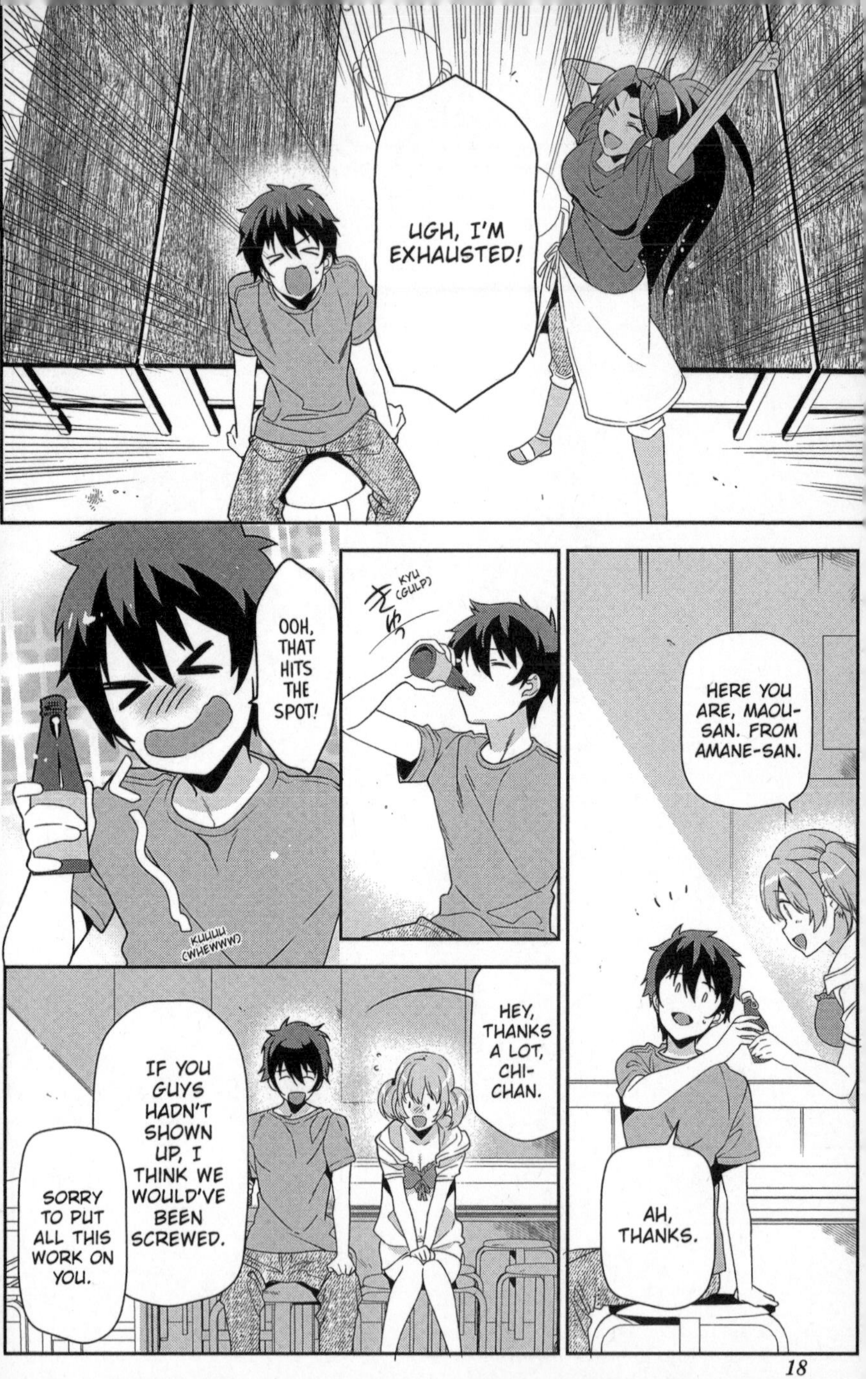
UGH, I'M EXHAUSTED!
HERE YOU ARE, MAOU-SAN. FROM AMANE-SAN.
AH, THANKS.
KYU (GULP)
OOH, THAT HITS THE SPOT!
KUUUU (WHEWWW)
HEY, THANKS A LOT, CHI-CHAN.
IF YOU GUYS HADN'T SHOWN UP, I THINK WE WOULD'VE BEEN SCREWED.
SORRY TO PUT ALL THIS WORK ON YOU.

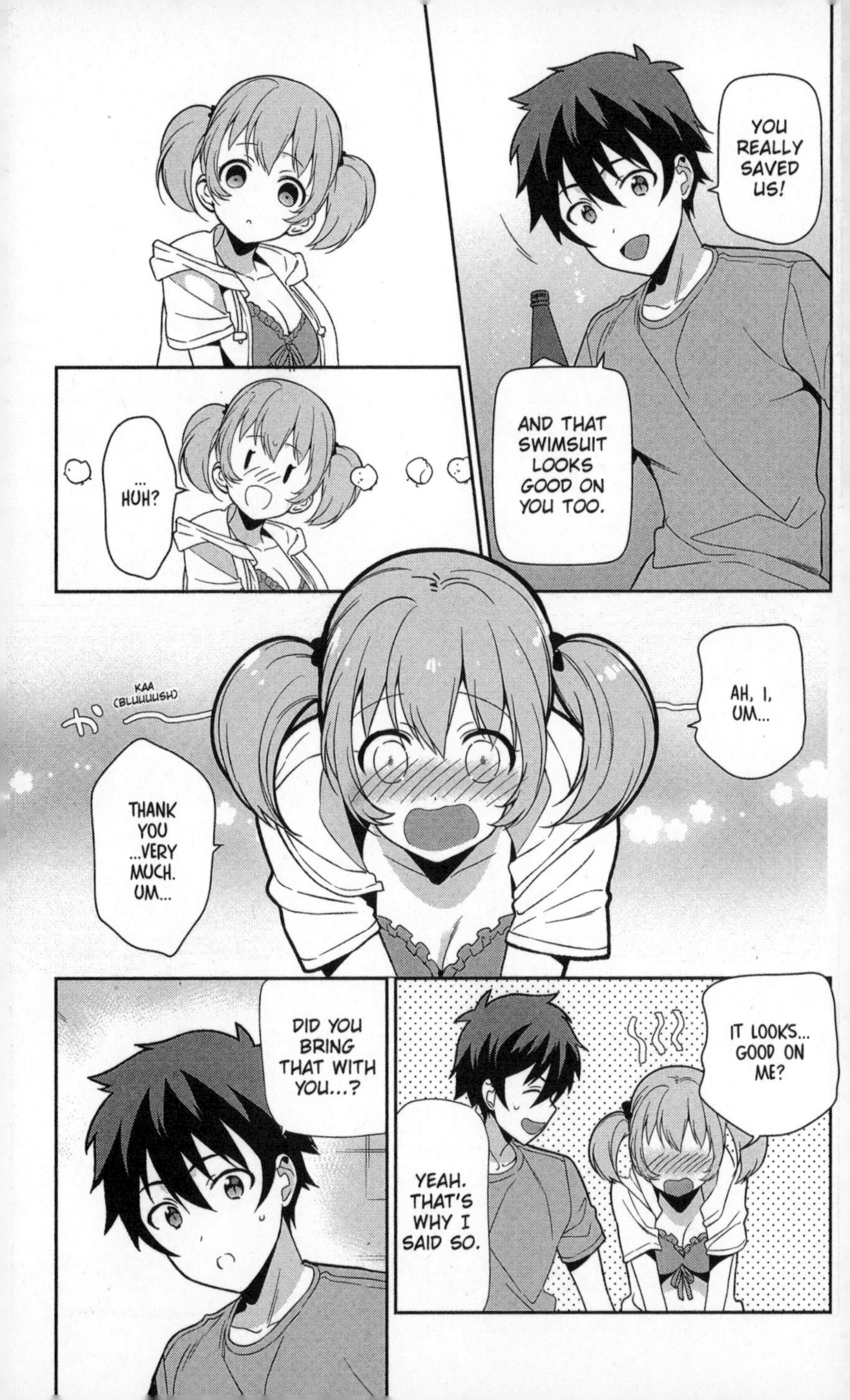
YOU REALLY SAVED US!
AND THAT SWIMSUIT LOOKS GOOD ON YOU TOO.
... HUH?
AH, I, UM...
KAA (BLUUUUSH)
THANK YOU ...VERY MUCH. UM...
IT LOOKS... GOOD ON ME?
YEAH. THAT'S WHY I SAID SO.
DID YOU BRING THAT WITH YOU...?

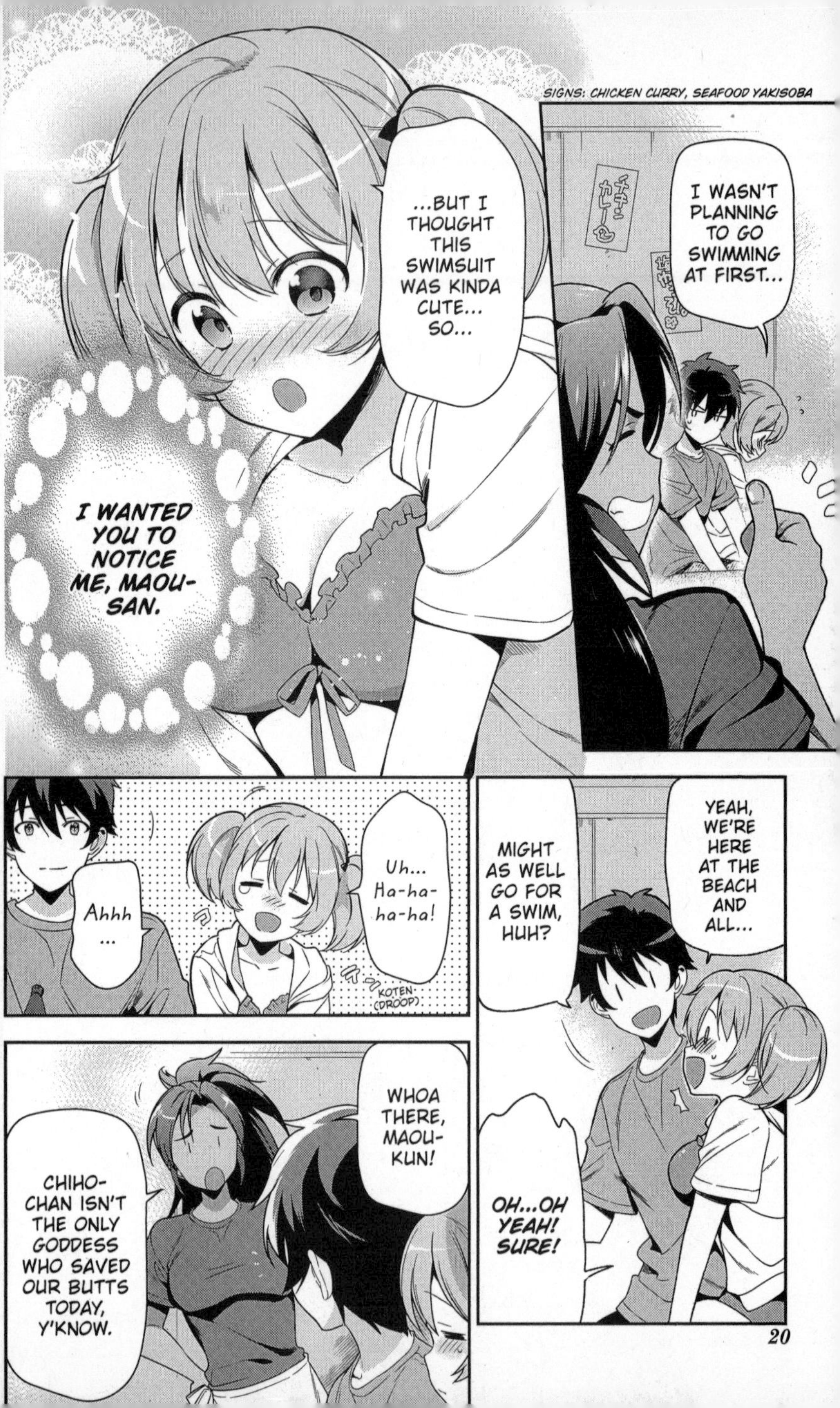
SIGNS: CHICKEN CURRY, SEAFOOD YAKISOBA
I WASN'T PLANNING TO GO SWIMMING AT FIRST...
...BUT I THOUGHT THIS SWIMSUIT WAS KINDA CUTE... SO...
I WANTED YOU TO NOTICE ME, MAOU-SAN.
YEAH, WE'RE HERE AT THE BEACH AND ALL...
MIGHT AS WELL GO FOR A SWIM, HUH?
OH...OH YEAH! SURE!
Uh... Ha-ha-ha-ha!
Ahhh ...
KOTEN (DROOP)
WHOA THERE, MAOU-KUN!
CHIHO-CHAN ISN'T THE ONLY GODDESS WHO SAVED OUR BUTTS TODAY, Y'KNOW.

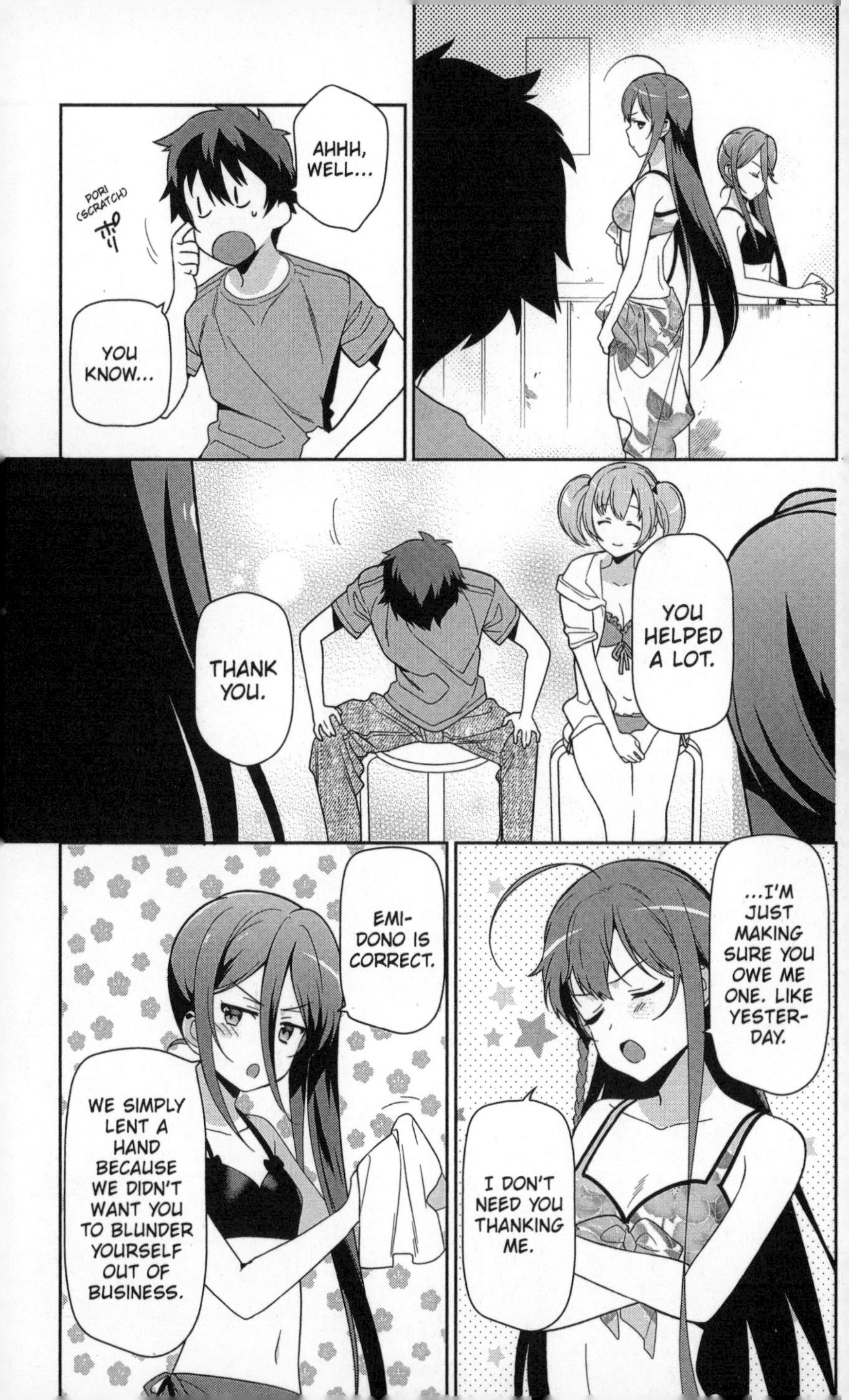
AHHH, WELL...
PORI (SCRATCH)
YOU KNOW...
YOU HELPED A LOT.
THANK YOU.
...I'M JUST MAKING SURE YOU OWE ME ONE. LIKE YESTERDAY.
I DON'T NEED YOU THANKING ME.
EMI-DONO IS CORRECT.
WE SIMPLY LENT A HAND BECAUSE WE DIDN'T WANT YOU TO BLUNDER YOURSELF OUT OF BUSINESS.

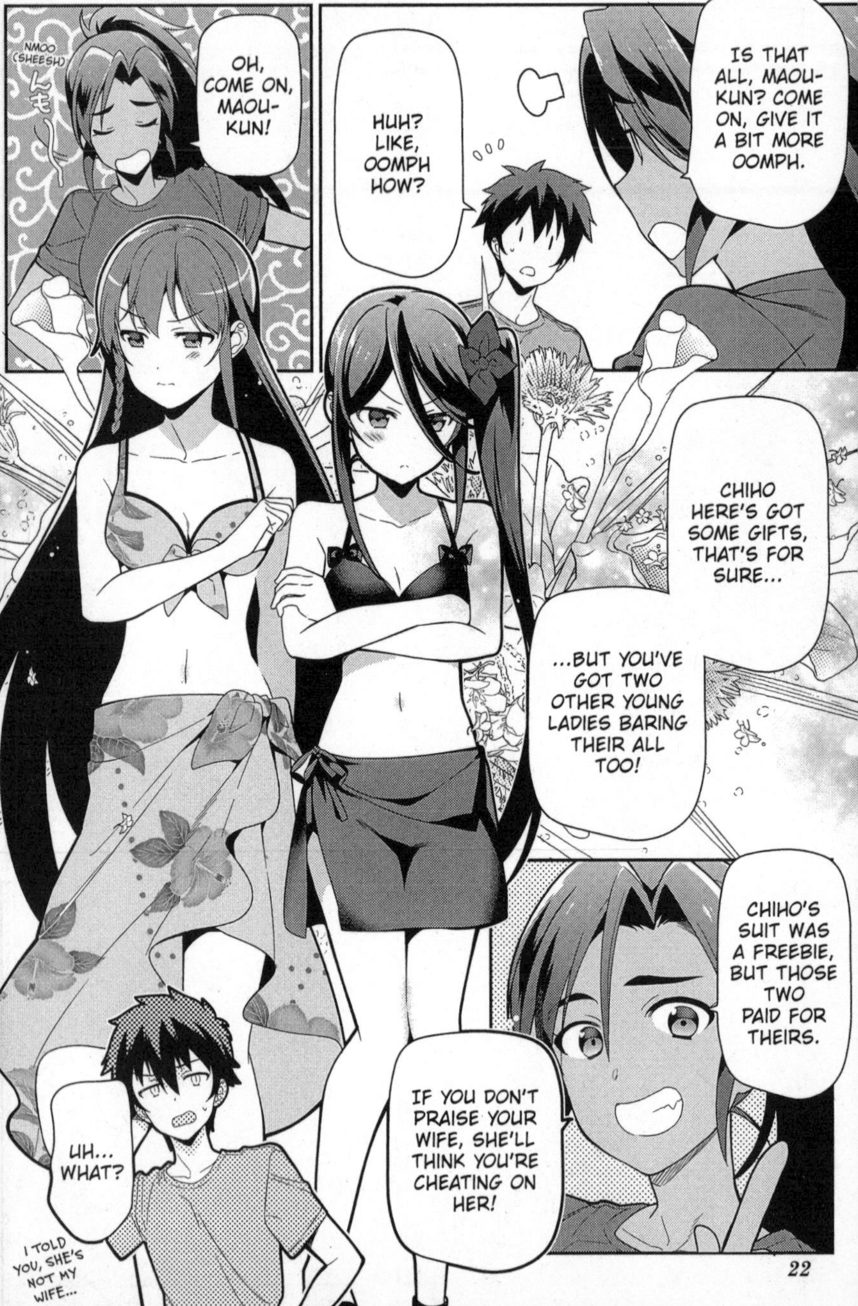
IS THAT ALL, MAOU-KUN? COME ON, GIVE IT A BIT MORE OOMPH.
HUH? LIKE, OOMPH HOW?
NMOO (SHEESH)
OH, COME ON, MAOU-KUN!
CHIHO HERE'S GOT SOME GIFTS, THAT'S FOR SURE...
...BUT YOU'VE GOT TWO OTHER YOUNG LADIES BARING THEIR ALL TOO!
CHIHO'S SUIT WAS A FREEBIE, BUT THOSE TWO PAID FOR THEIRS.
IF YOU DON'T PRAISE YOUR WIFE, SHE'LL THINK YOU'RE CHEATING ON HER!
UH... WHAT?
I TOLD YOU, SHE'S NOT MY WIFE...

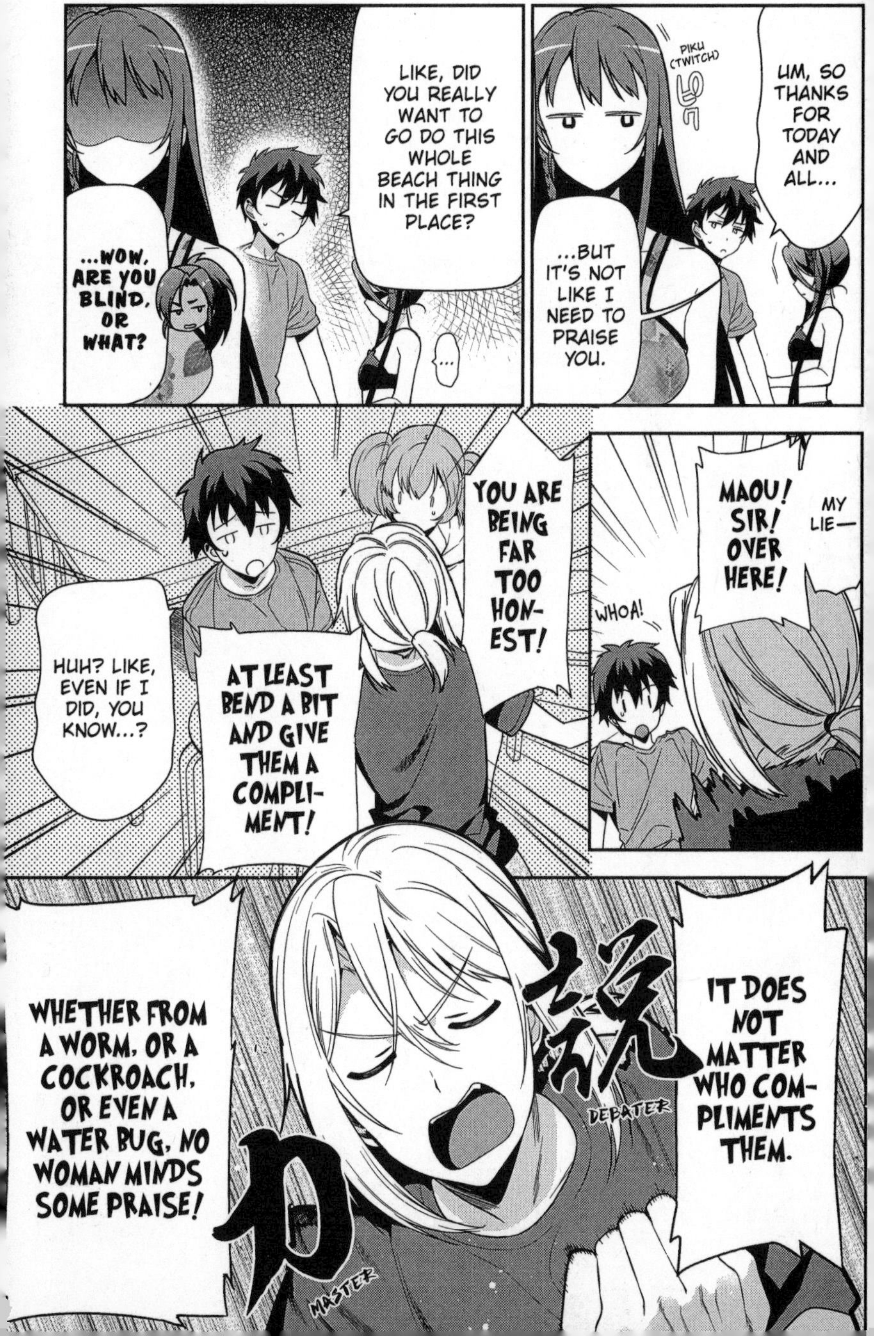
UM, SO THANKS FOR TODAY AND ALL...
PIKU (TWITCH)
...BUT IT'S NOT LIKE I NEED TO PRAISE YOU.
LIKE, DID YOU REALLY WANT TO GO DO THIS WHOLE BEACH THING IN THE FIRST PLACE?
...WOW, ARE YOU BLIND, OR WHAT?
...
MY LIE—
MAOU! SIR! OVER HERE!
WHOA!
YOU ARE BEING FAR TOO HON-EST!
AT LEAST BEND A BIT AND GIVE THEM A COMPLI-MENT!
HUH? LIKE, EVEN IF I DID, YOU KNOW...?
IT DOES NOT MATTER WHO COM-PLIMENTS THEM.
DEBATER
MASTER
WHETHER FROM A WORM, OR A COCKROACH, OR EVEN A WATER BUG, NO WOMAN MINDS SOME PRAISE!

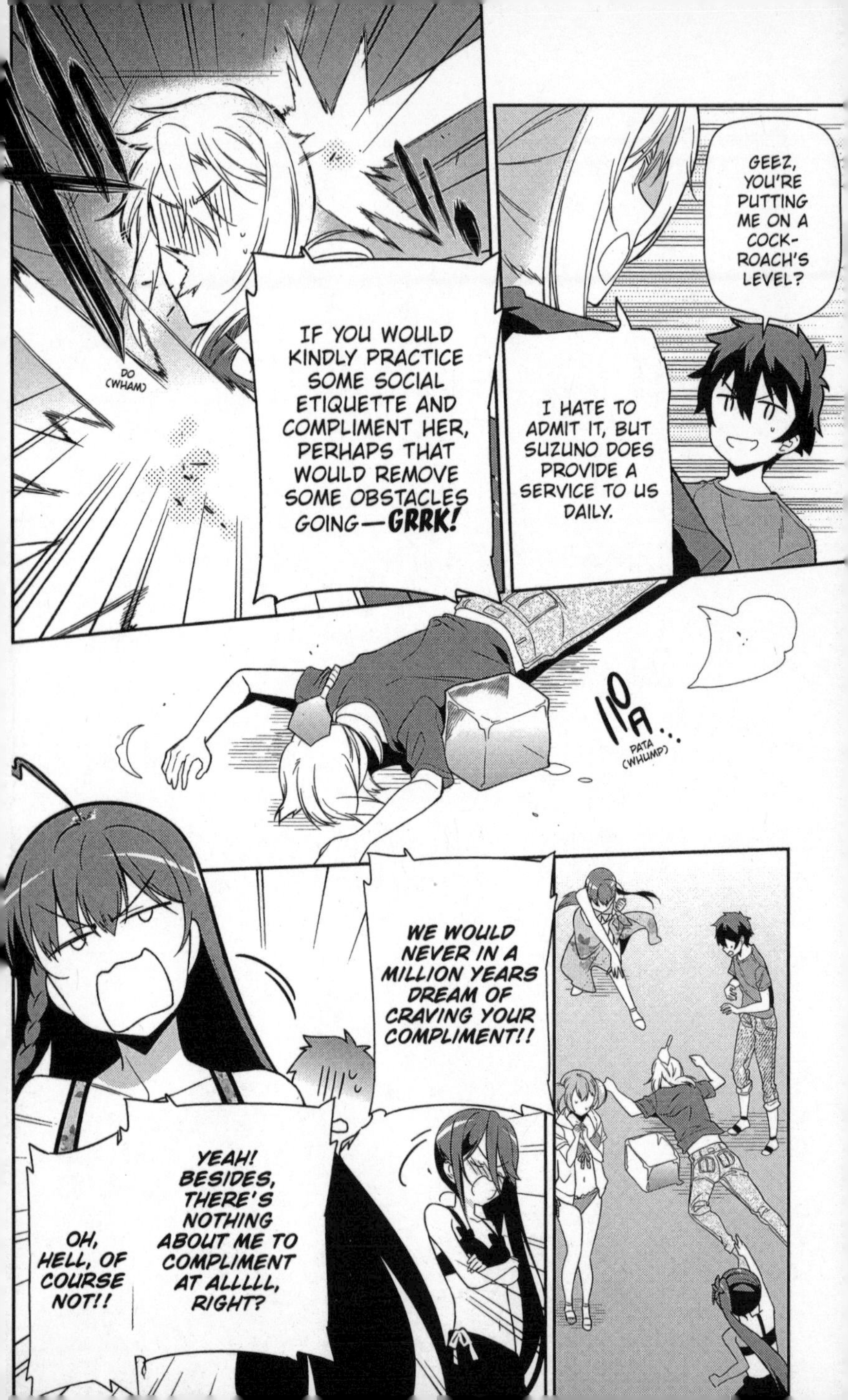
GEEZ, YOU'RE PUTTING ME ON A COCK-ROACH'S LEVEL?
I HATE TO ADMIT IT, BUT SUZUNO DOES PROVIDE A SERVICE TO US DAILY.
IF YOU WOULD KINDLY PRACTICE SOME SOCIAL ETIQUETTE AND COMPLIMENT HER, PERHAPS THAT WOULD REMOVE SOME OBSTACLES GOING—GRRK!
DO (WHAM)
PATA (WHUMP)
WE WOULD NEVER IN A MILLION YEARS DREAM OF CRAVING YOUR COMPLIMENT!!
YEAH! BESIDES, THERE'S NOTHING ABOUT ME TO COMPLIMENT AT ALLLLL, RIGHT?
OH, HELL, OF COURSE NOT!!

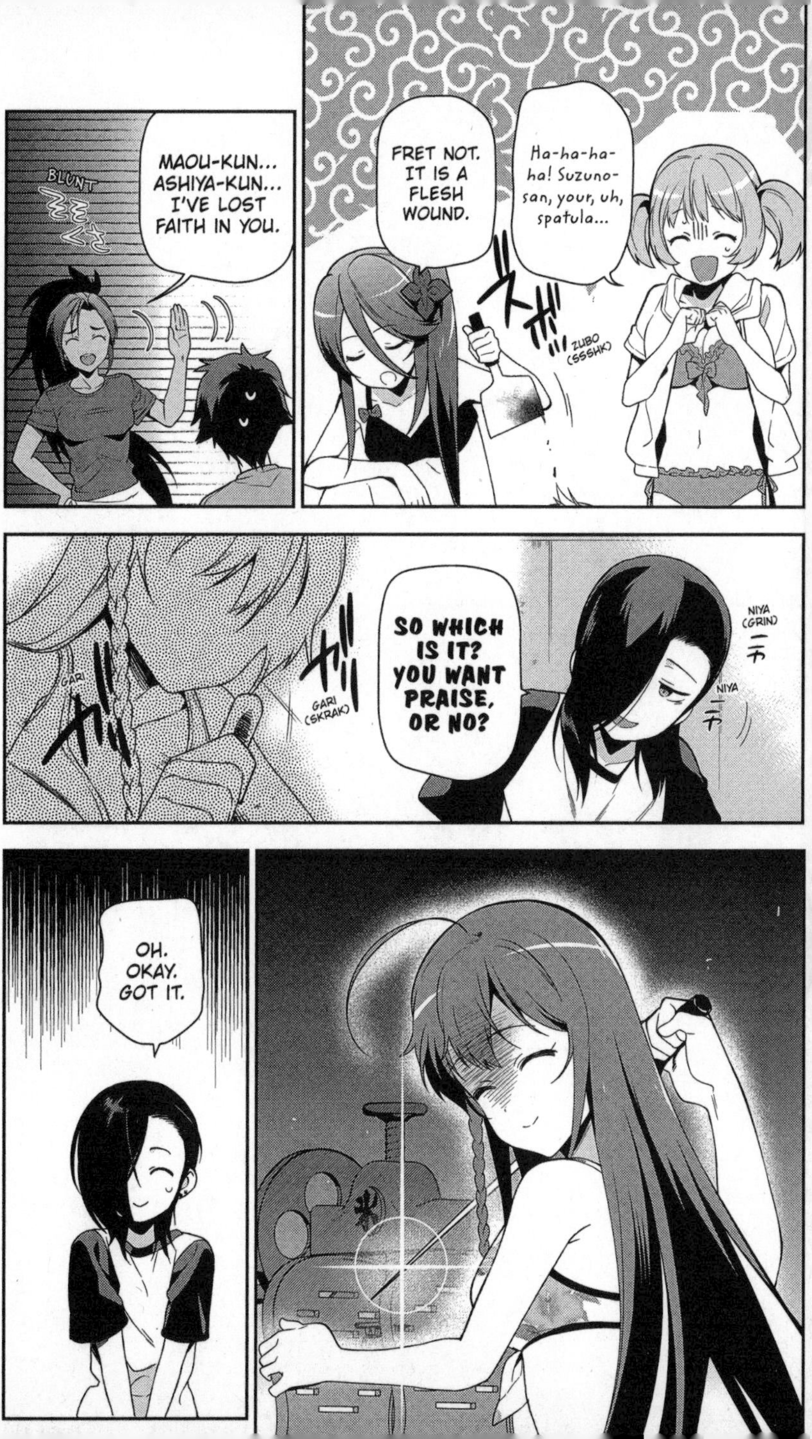
Ha-ha-ha-ha! Suzuno-san, your, uh, spatula...
FRET NOT. IT IS A FLESH WOUND.
ZUBO (SSSHK)
BLUNT
MAOU-KUN... ASHIYA-KUN... I'VE LOST FAITH IN YOU.
NIYA (GRIN)
NIYA
SO WHICH IS IT? YOU WANT PRAISE, OR NO?
GARI (SKRAK)
GARI
OH. OKAY. GOT IT.

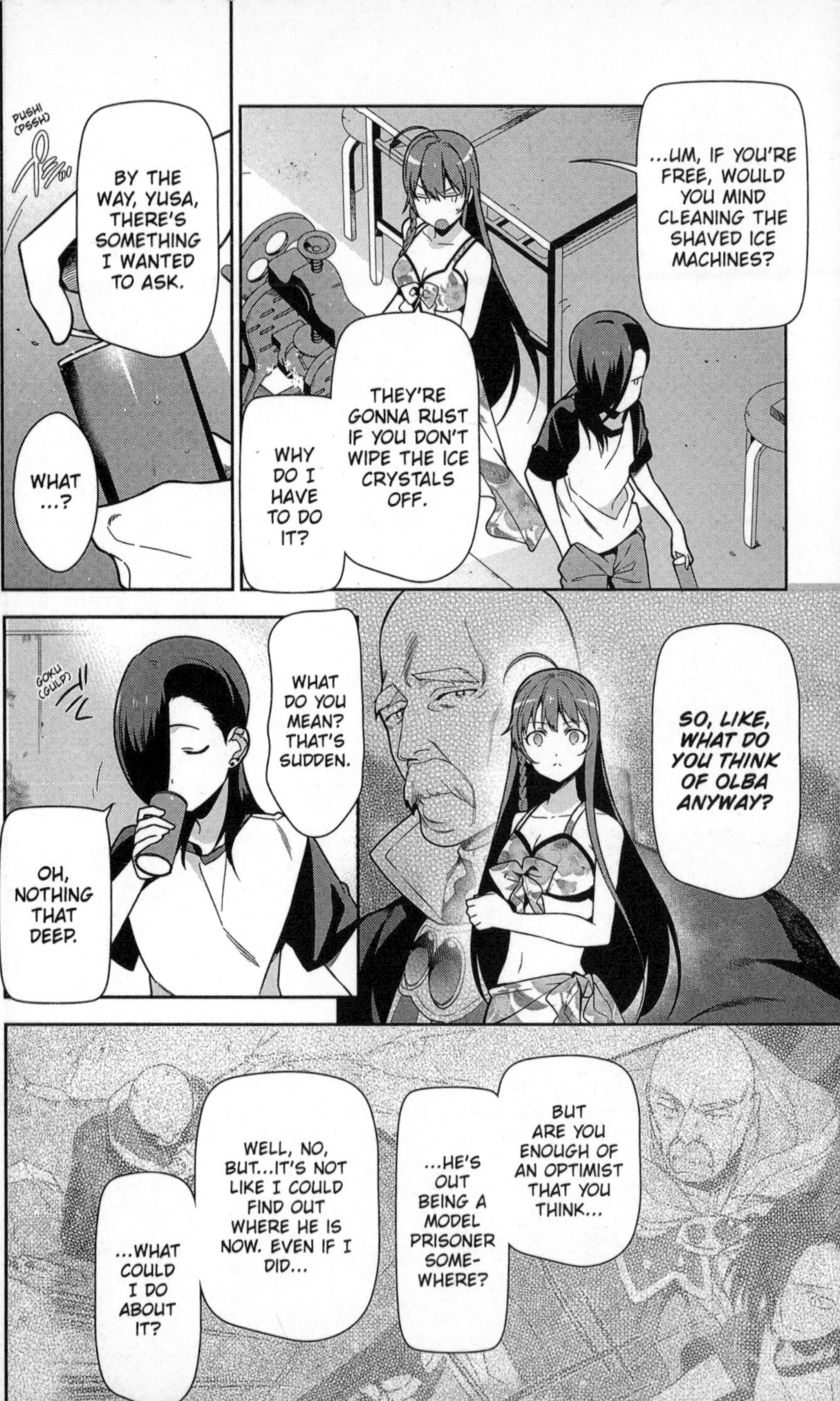
...UM, IF YOU'RE FREE, WOULD YOU MIND CLEANING THE SHAVED ICE MACHINES?
THEY'RE GONNA RUST IF YOU DON'T WIPE THE ICE CRYSTALS OFF.
WHY DO I HAVE TO DO IT?
PUSHI (PSSH)
BY THE WAY, YUSA, THERE'S SOMETHING I WANTED TO ASK.
WHAT ...?
SO, LIKE, WHAT DO YOU THINK OF OLBA ANYWAY?
WHAT DO YOU MEAN? THAT'S SUDDEN.
GOKU (GULP)
OH, NOTHING THAT DEEP.
BUT ARE YOU ENOUGH OF AN OPTIMIST THAT YOU THINK...
...HE'S OUT BEING A MODEL PRISONER SOME-WHERE?
WELL, NO, BUT...IT'S NOT LIKE I COULD FIND OUT WHERE HE IS NOW. EVEN IF I DID...
...WHAT COULD I DO ABOUT IT?

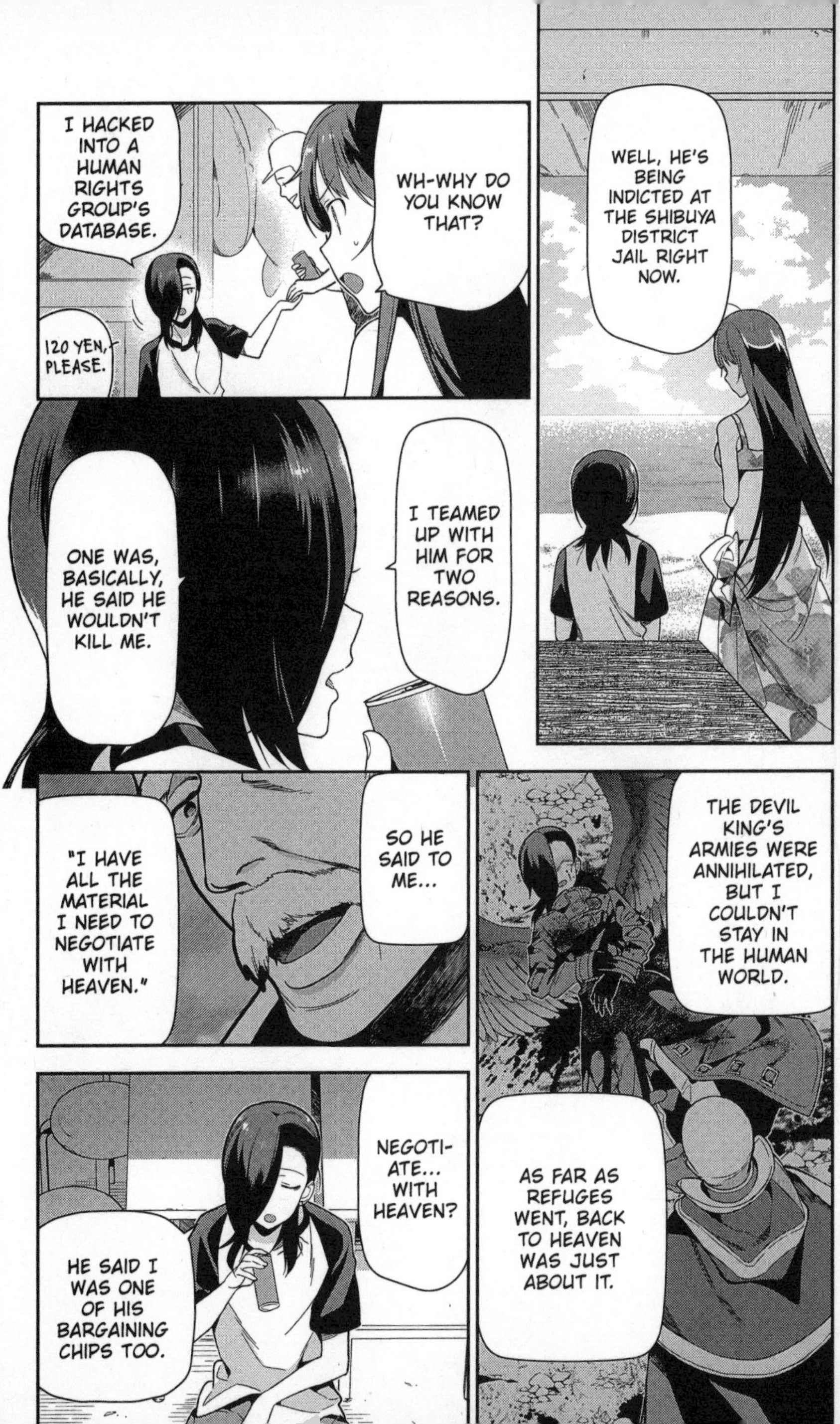
WELL, HE'S BEING INDICTED AT THE SHIBUYA DISTRICT JAIL RIGHT NOW.
WH-WHY DO YOU KNOW THAT?
I HACKED INTO A HUMAN RIGHTS GROUP'S DATABASE.
120 YEN, PLEASE.
I TEAMED UP WITH HIM FOR TWO REASONS.
ONE WAS, BASICALLY, HE SAID HE WOULDN'T KILL ME.
THE DEVIL KING'S ARMIES WERE ANNIHILATED, BUT I COULDN'T STAY IN THE HUMAN WORLD.
AS FAR AS REFUGES WENT, BACK TO HEAVEN WAS JUST ABOUT IT.
SO HE SAID TO ME...
"I HAVE ALL THE MATERIAL I NEED TO NEGOTIATE WITH HEAVEN."
NEGOTI-ATE... WITH HEAVEN?
HE SAID I WAS ONE OF HIS BARGAINING CHIPS TOO.

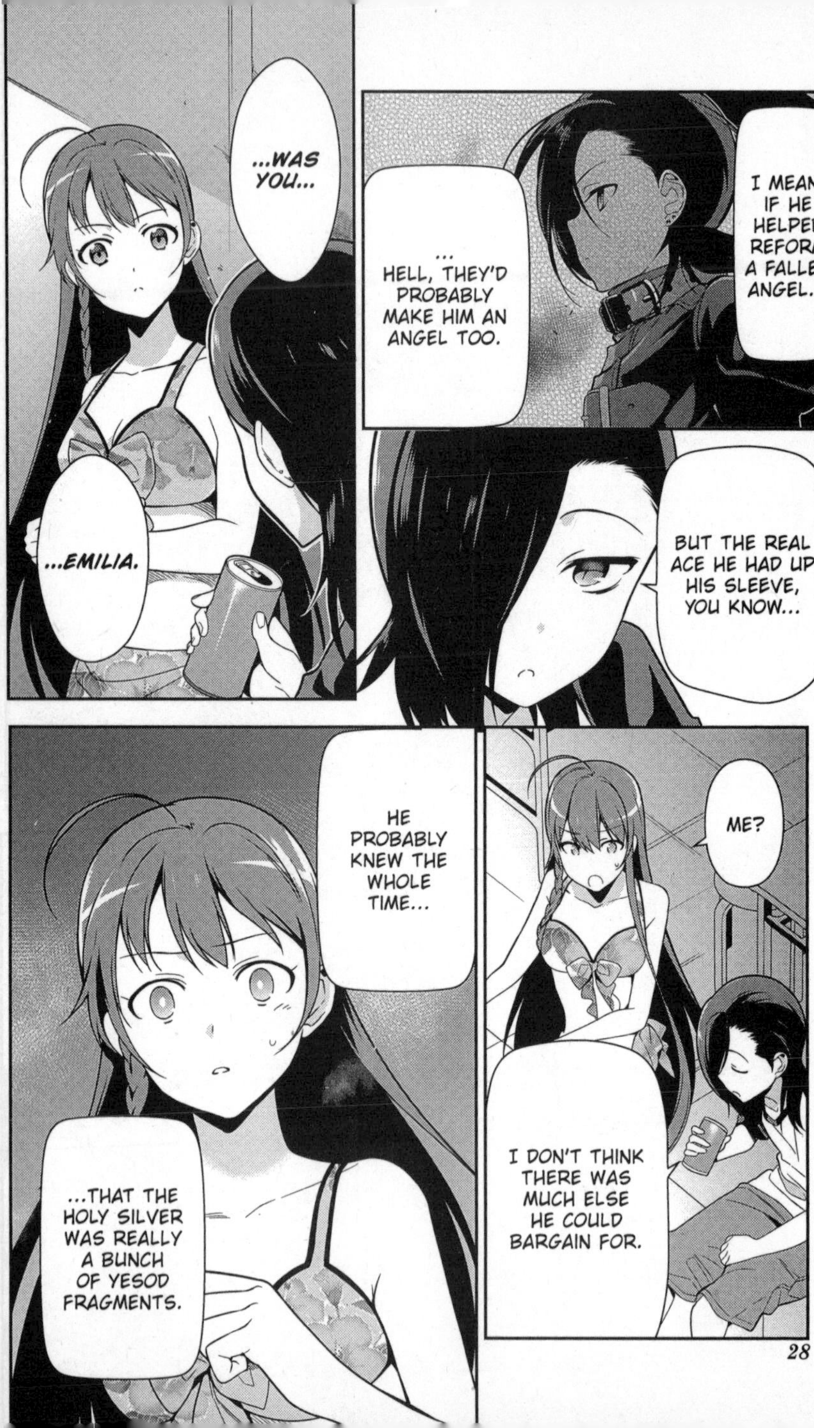
I MEAN, IF HE HELPED REFORM A FALLEN ANGEL...
... HELL, THEY'D PROBABLY MAKE HIM AN ANGEL TOO.
BUT THE REAL ACE HE HAD UP HIS SLEEVE, YOU KNOW...
...WAS YOU...
...EMILIA.
ME?
I DON'T THINK THERE WAS MUCH ELSE HE COULD BARGAIN FOR.
HE PROBABLY KNEW THE WHOLE TIME...
...THAT THE HOLY SILVER WAS REALLY A BUNCH OF YESOD FRAGMENTS.

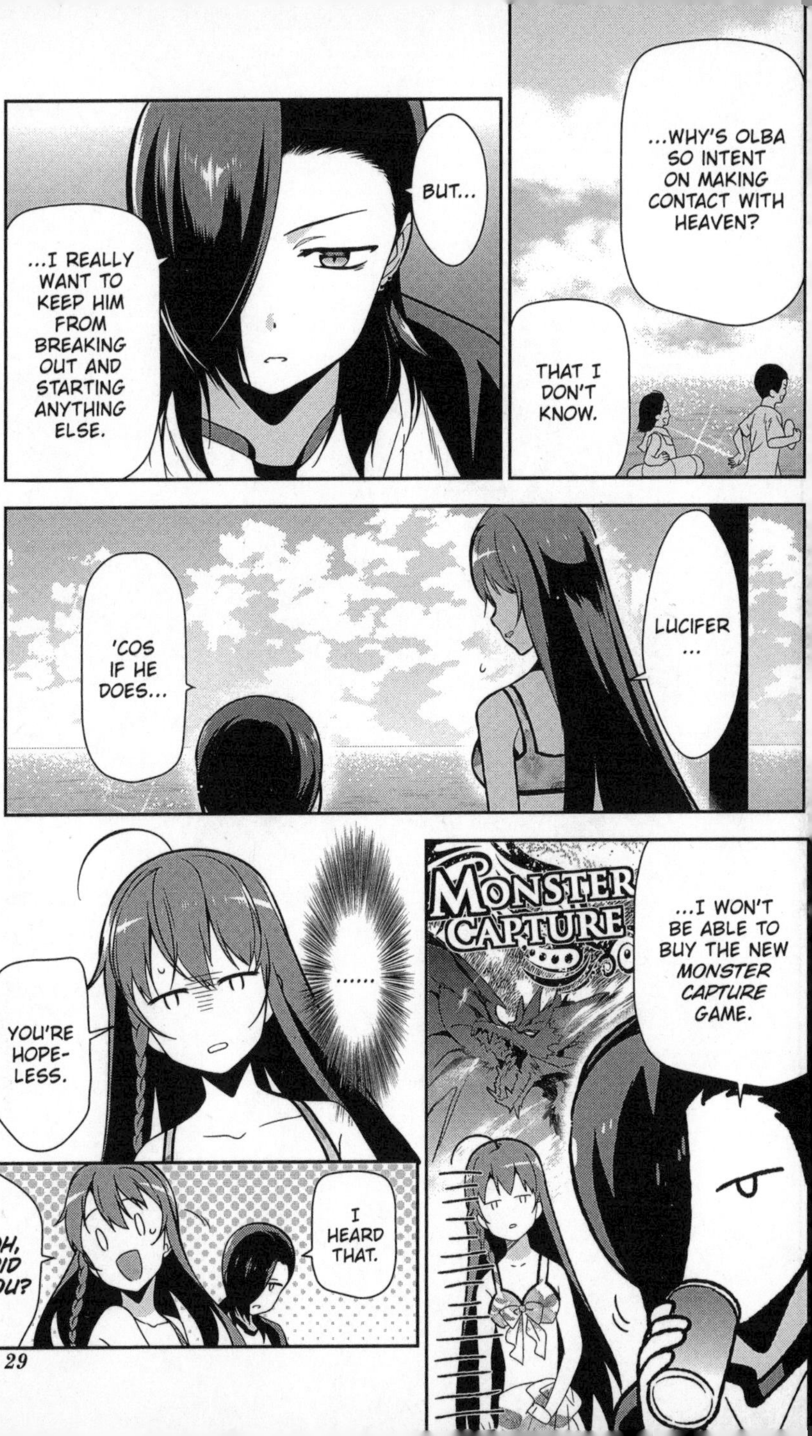
...WHY'S OLBA SO INTENT ON MAKING CONTACT WITH HEAVEN?
THAT I DON'T KNOW.
BUT...
...I REALLY WANT TO KEEP HIM FROM BREAKING OUT AND STARTING ANYTHING ELSE.
LUCIFER...
'COS IF HE DOES...
...I WON'T BE ABLE TO BUY THE NEW *MONSTER CAPTURE* GAME.
MONSTER CAPTURE
......
YOU'RE HOPE-LESS.
I HEARD THAT.
OH, DID YOU?

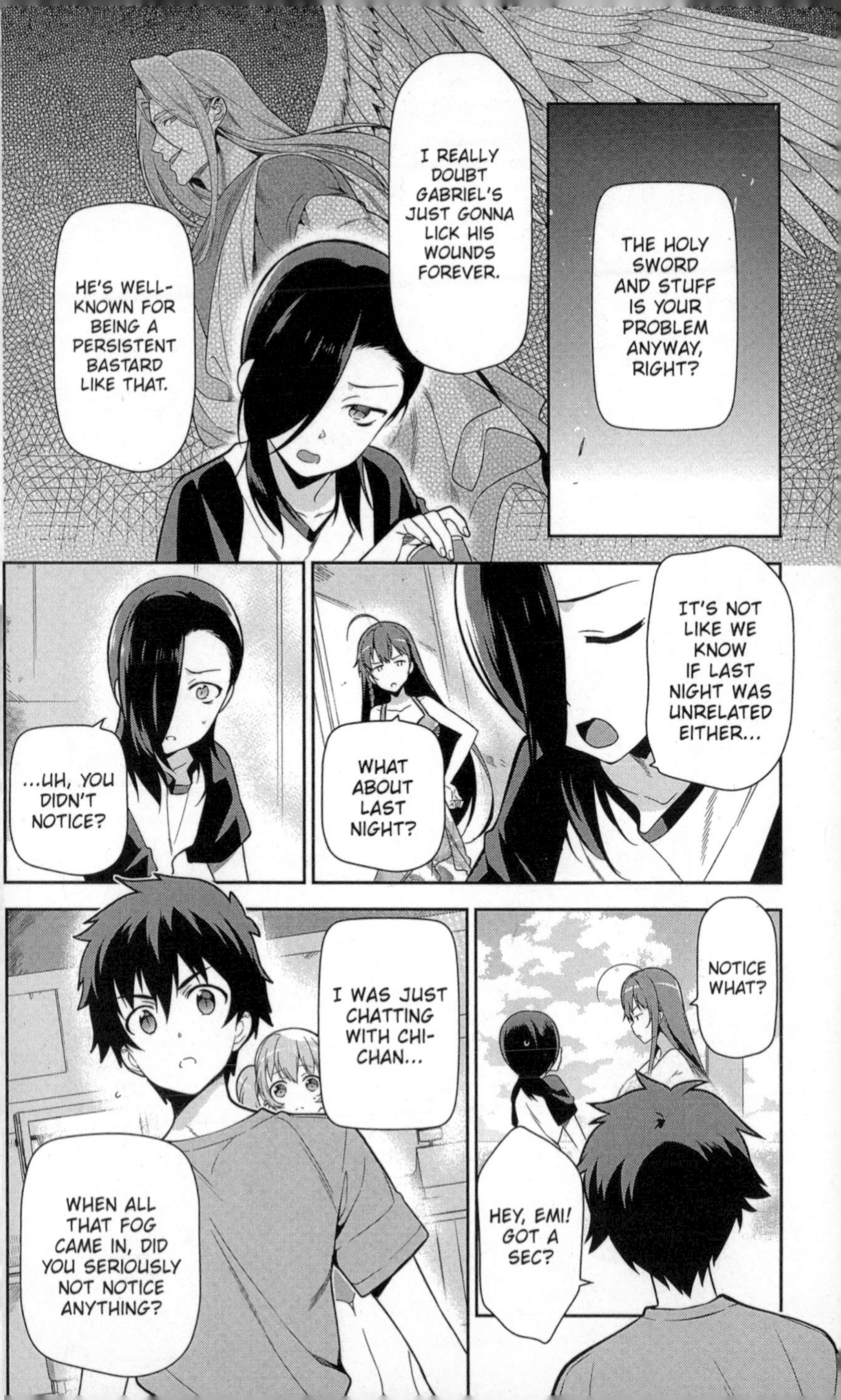
THE HOLY SWORD AND STUFF IS YOUR PROBLEM ANYWAY, RIGHT?
I REALLY DOUBT GABRIEL'S JUST GONNA LICK HIS WOUNDS FOREVER.
HE'S WELL-KNOWN FOR BEING A PERSISTENT BASTARD LIKE THAT.
IT'S NOT LIKE WE KNOW IF LAST NIGHT WAS UNRELATED EITHER...
WHAT ABOUT LAST NIGHT?
...UH, YOU DIDN'T NOTICE?
NOTICE WHAT?
HEY, EMI! GOT A SEC?
I WAS JUST CHATTING WITH CHI-CHAN...
WHEN ALL THAT FOG CAME IN, DID YOU SERIOUSLY NOT NOTICE ANYTHING?

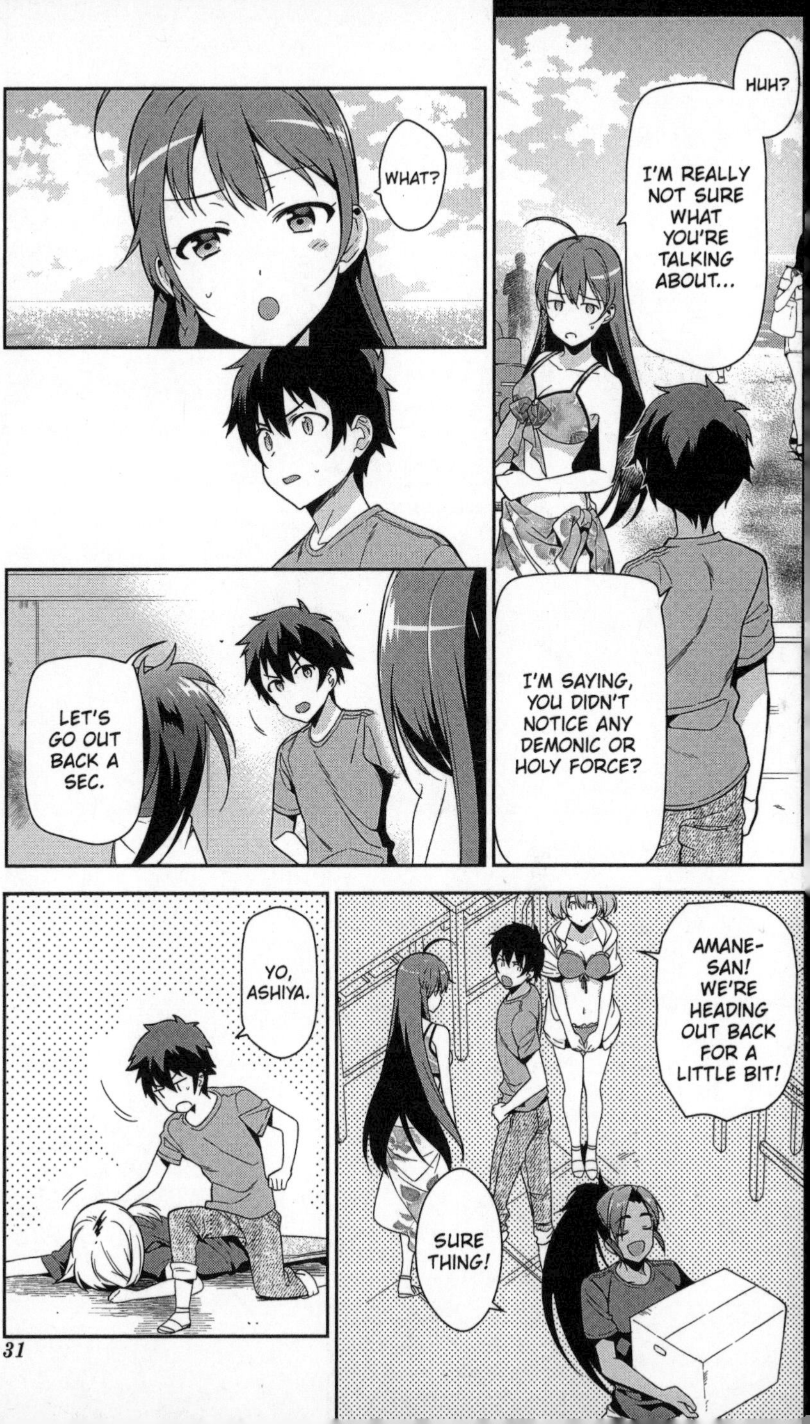
HUH?
I'M REALLY NOT SURE WHAT YOU'RE TALKING ABOUT...
I'M SAYING, YOU DIDN'T NOTICE ANY DEMONIC OR HOLY FORCE?
WHAT?
LET'S GO OUT BACK A SEC.
AMANE-SAN! WE'RE HEADING OUT BACK FOR A LITTLE BIT!
SURE THING!
YO, ASHIYA.

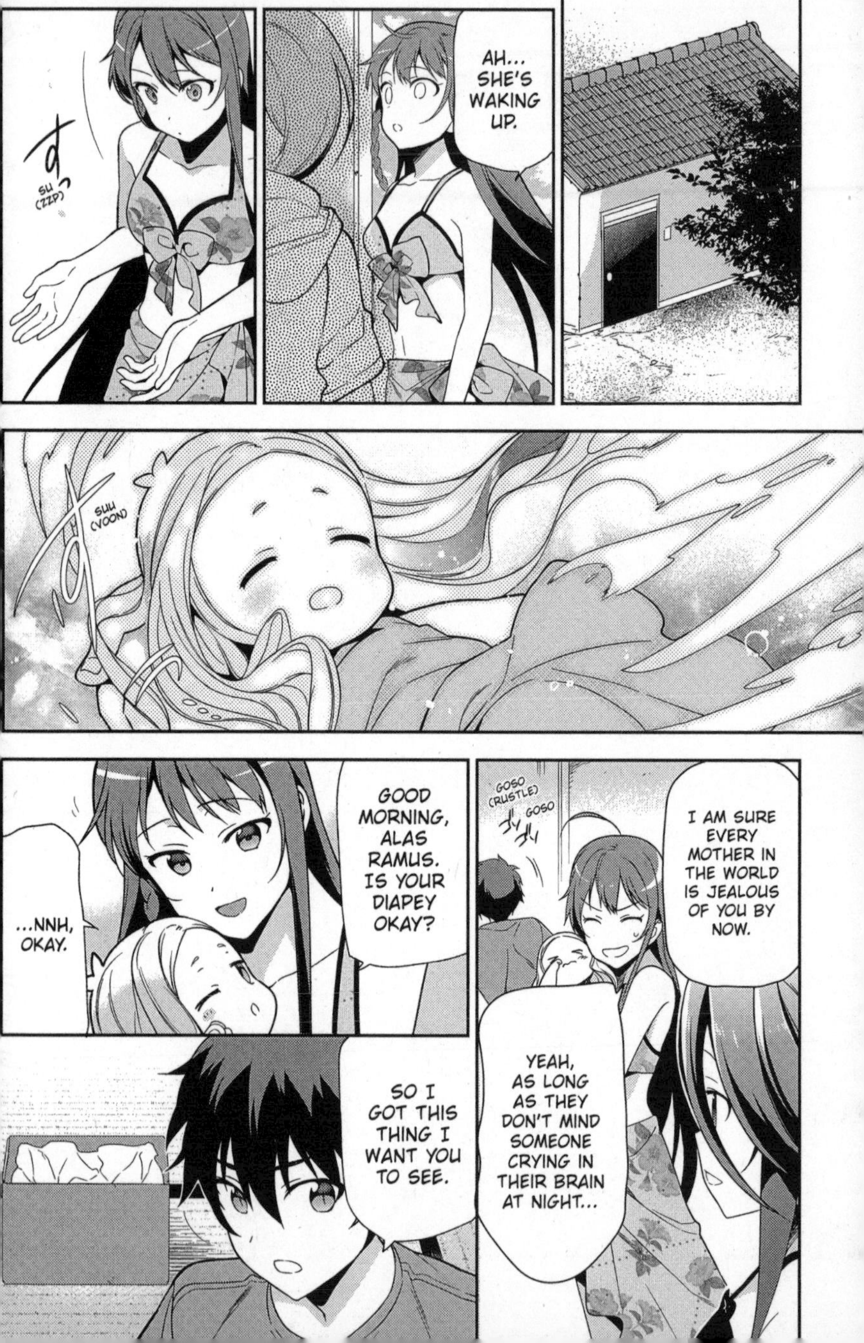

AH... SHE'S WAKING UP.
SU (ZZP)
SUU (VOON)
I AM SURE EVERY MOTHER IN THE WORLD IS JEALOUS OF YOU BY NOW.
GOSO (RUSTLE) GOSO
YEAH, AS LONG AS THEY DON'T MIND SOMEONE CRYING IN THEIR BRAIN AT NIGHT...
GOOD MORNING, ALAS RAMUS. IS YOUR DIAPEY OKAY?
...NNH, OKAY.
SO I GOT THIS THING I WANT YOU TO SEE.

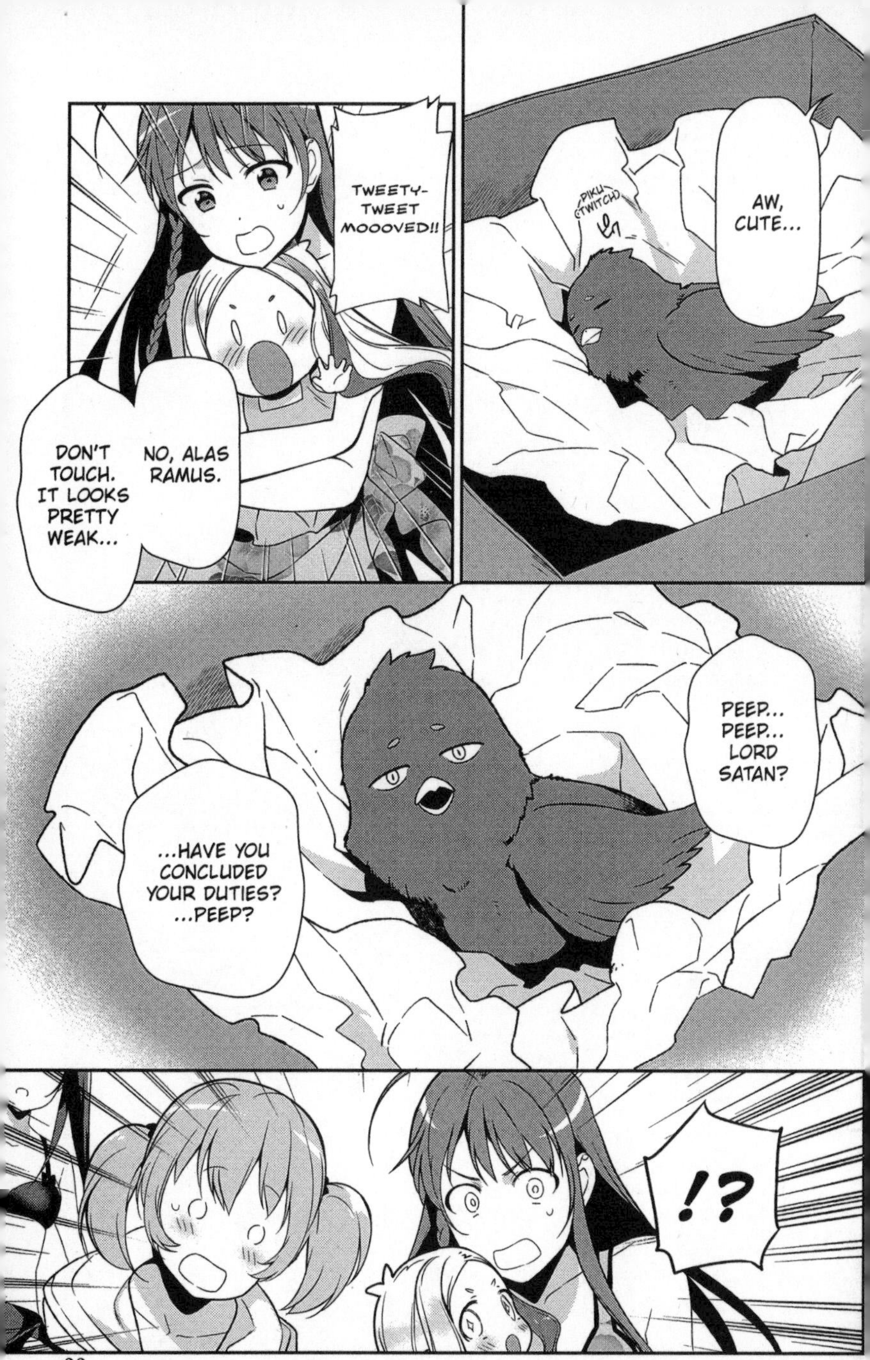
AW, CUTE...
PIKU (TWITCH)
TWEETY-TWEET MOOOVED!!
NO, ALAS RAMUS.
DON'T TOUCH. IT LOOKS PRETTY WEAK...
PEEP... PEEP... LORD SATAN?
...HAVE YOU CONCLUDED YOUR DUTIES? ...PEEP?
!?

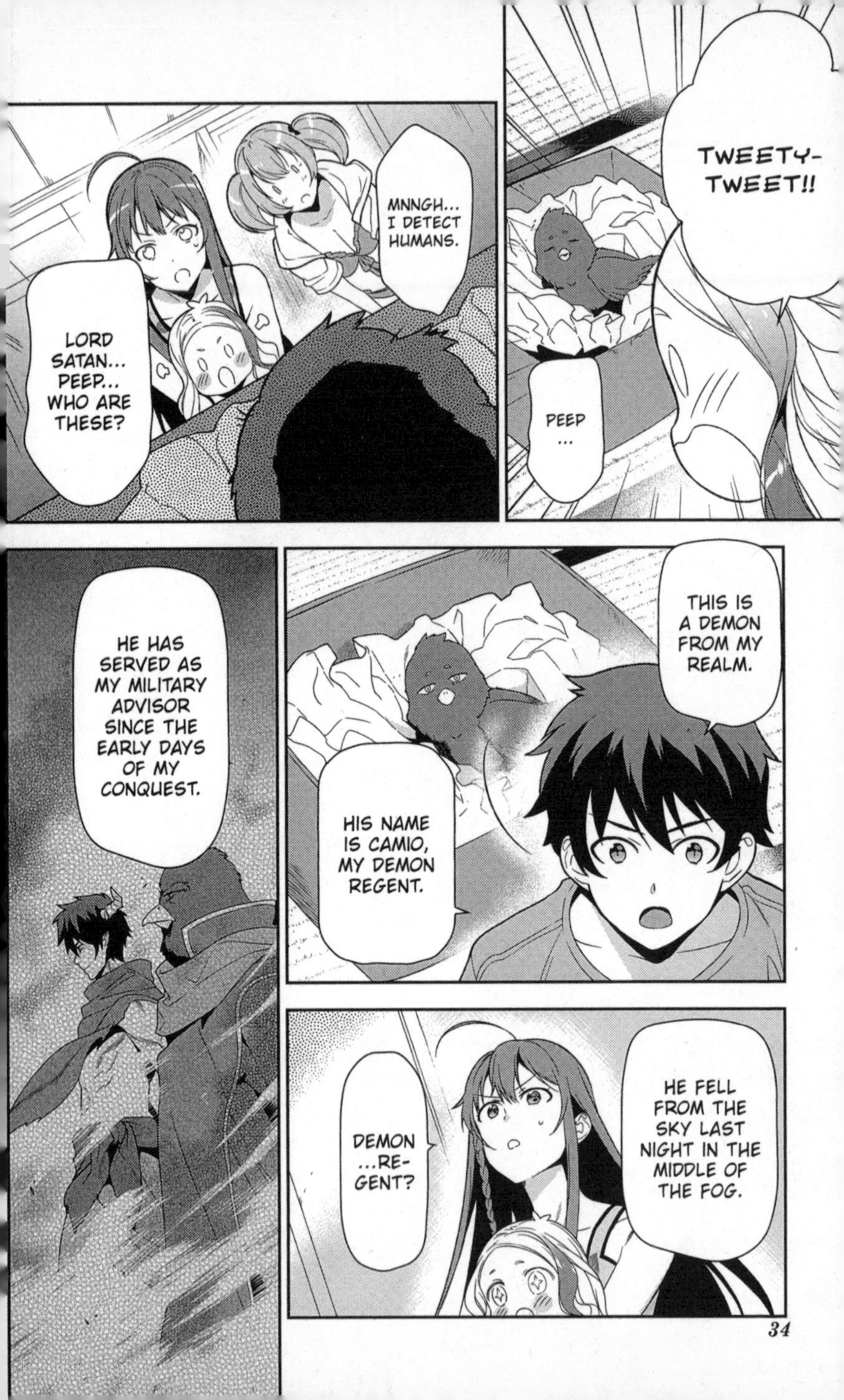
TWEETY-TWEET!!
PEEP ...
MNNGH... I DETECT HUMANS.
LORD SATAN... PEEP... WHO ARE THESE?
THIS IS A DEMON FROM MY REALM.
HIS NAME IS CAMIO, MY DEMON REGENT.
HE FELL FROM THE SKY LAST NIGHT IN THE MIDDLE OF THE FOG.
DEMON ...RE-GENT?
HE HAS SERVED AS MY MILITARY ADVISOR SINCE THE EARLY DAYS OF MY CONQUEST.

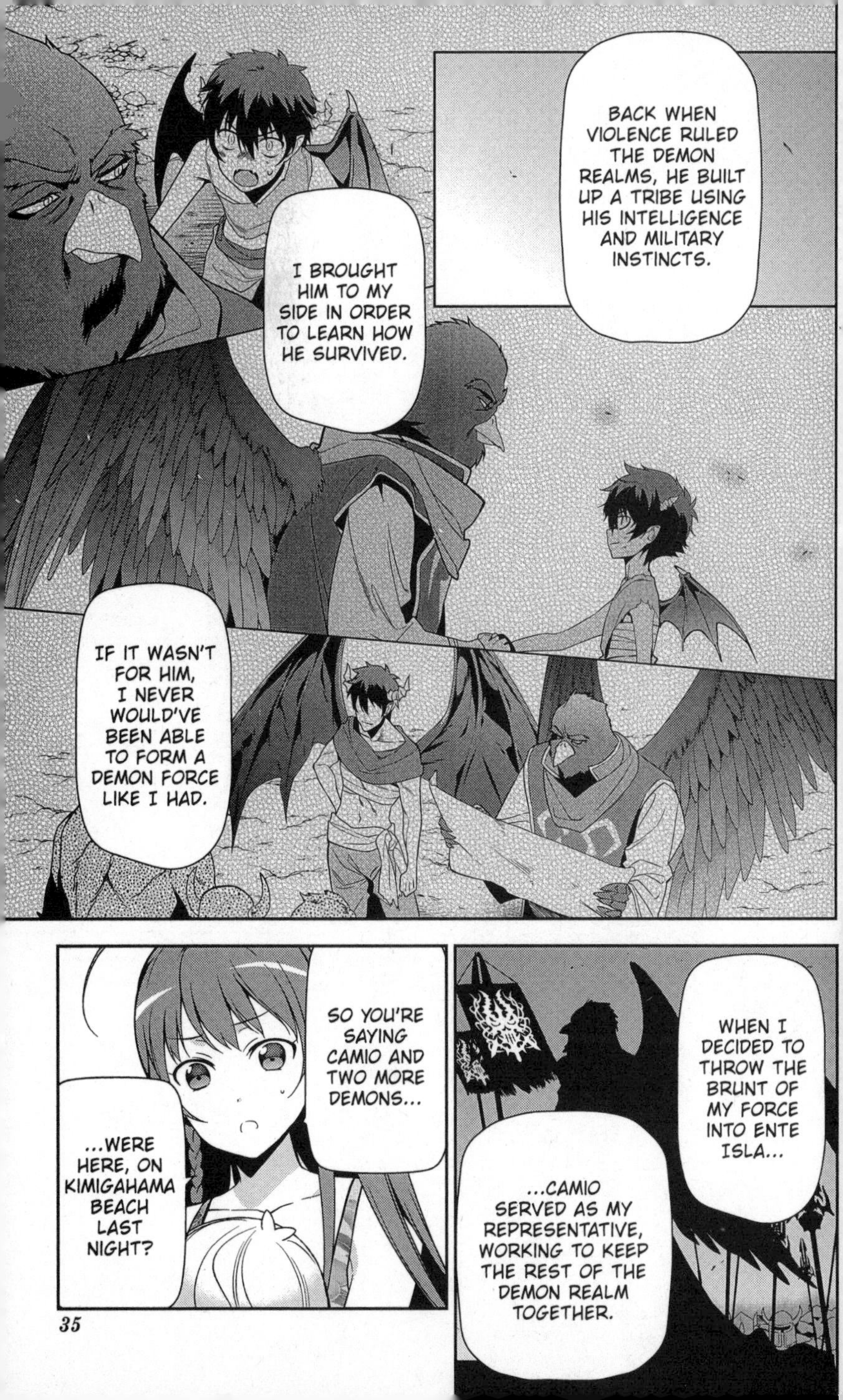
BACK WHEN VIOLENCE RULED THE DEMON REALMS, HE BUILT UP A TRIBE USING HIS INTELLIGENCE AND MILITARY INSTINCTS.
I BROUGHT HIM TO MY SIDE IN ORDER TO LEARN HOW HE SURVIVED.
IF IT WASN'T FOR HIM, I NEVER WOULD'VE BEEN ABLE TO FORM A DEMON FORCE LIKE I HAD.
WHEN I DECIDED TO THROW THE BRUNT OF MY FORCE INTO ENTE ISLA...
...CAMIO SERVED AS MY REPRESENTATIVE, WORKING TO KEEP THE REST OF THE DEMON REALM TOGETHER.
SO YOU'RE SAYING CAMIO AND TWO MORE DEMONS...
...WERE HERE, ON KIMIGAHAMA BEACH LAST NIGHT?

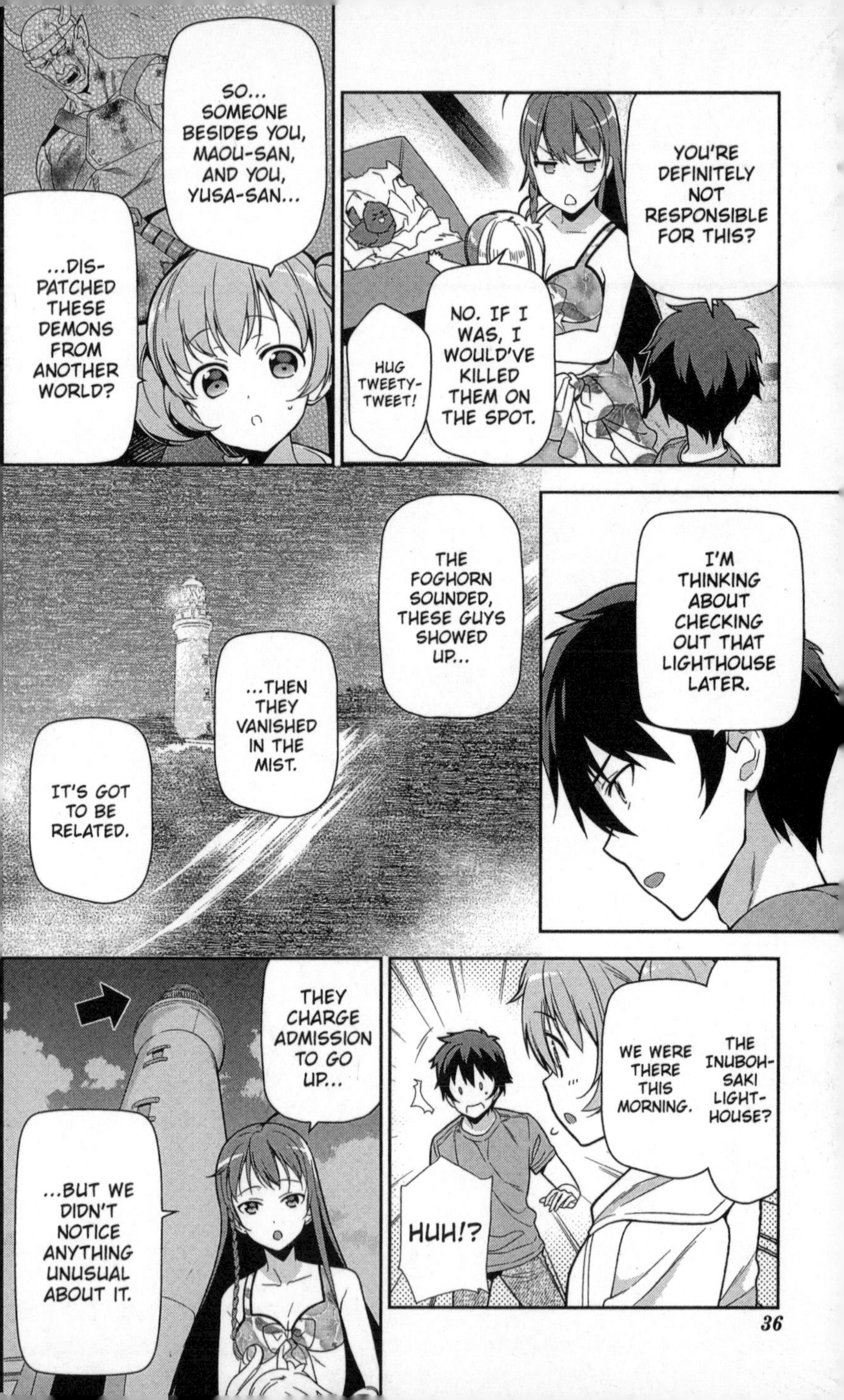
YOU'RE DEFINITELY NOT RESPONSIBLE FOR THIS?
NO. IF I WAS, I WOULD'VE KILLED THEM ON THE SPOT.
HUG TWEETY-TWEET!
SO... SOMEONE BESIDES YOU, MAOU-SAN, AND YOU, YUSA-SAN...
...DIS-PATCHED THESE DEMONS FROM ANOTHER WORLD?
I'M THINKING ABOUT CHECKING OUT THAT LIGHTHOUSE LATER.
THE FOGHORN SOUNDED, THESE GUYS SHOWED UP...
...THEN THEY VANISHED IN THE MIST.
IT'S GOT TO BE RELATED.
THE INUBOH-SAKI LIGHT-HOUSE?
WE WERE THERE THIS MORNING.
HUH!?
THEY CHARGE ADMISSION TO GO UP...
...BUT WE DIDN'T NOTICE ANYTHING UNUSUAL ABOUT IT.

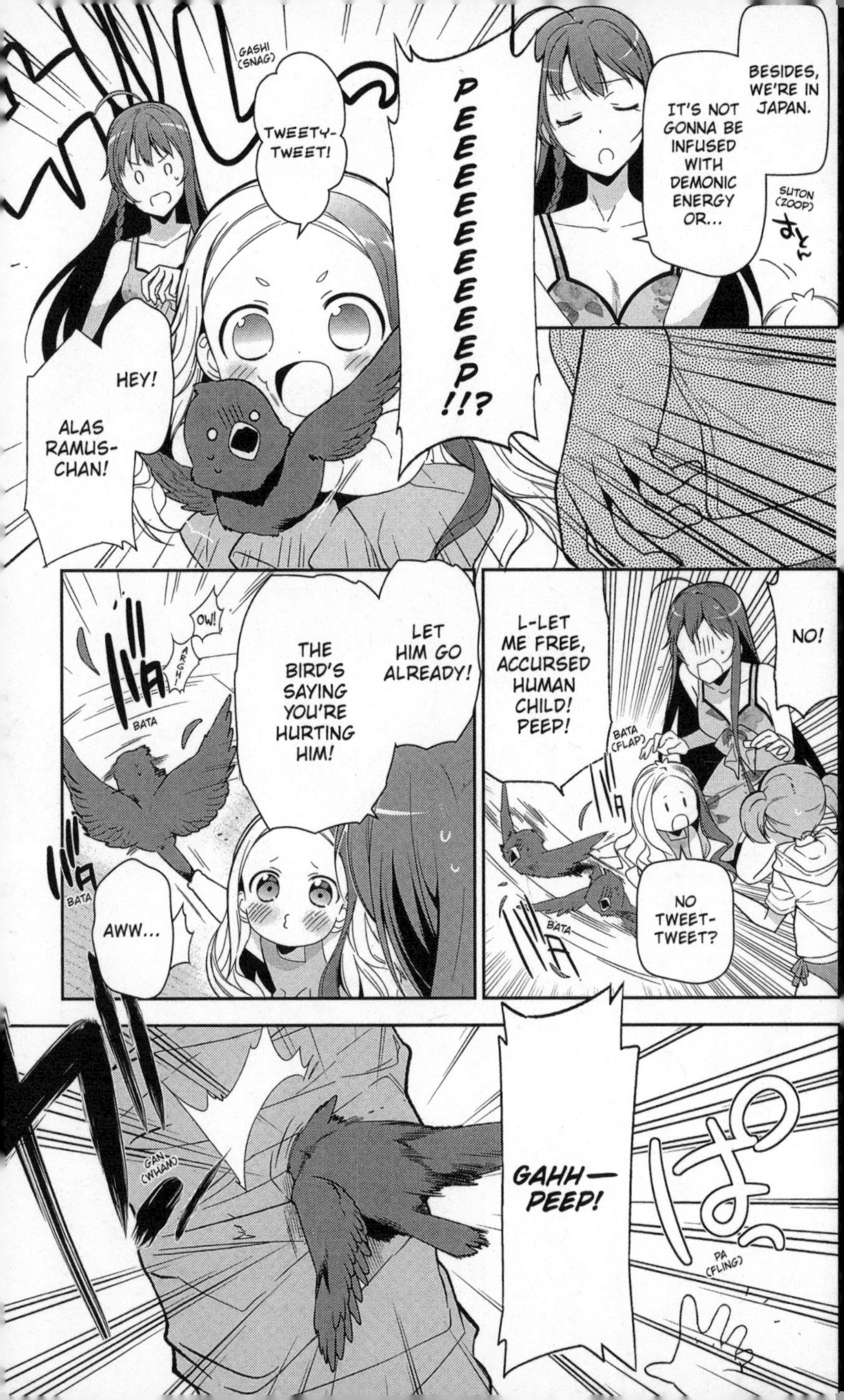
BESIDES, WE'RE IN JAPAN.
IT'S NOT GONNA BE INFUSED WITH DEMONIC ENERGY OR...
SUTON (ZOOP)
PEEEEEEEEEEP!!?
TWEETY-TWEET!
GASHI (SNAG)
HEY!
ALAS RAMUS-CHAN!
NO!
L-LET ME FREE, ACCURSED HUMAN CHILD! PEEP!
BATA (FLAP)
NO TWEET-TWEET?
BATA
LET HIM GO ALREADY!
THE BIRD'S SAYING YOU'RE HURTING HIM!
OW!
ARGH!
BATA
BATA
AWW...
PA (FLING)
GAHH—PEEP!
GAN (WHAM)

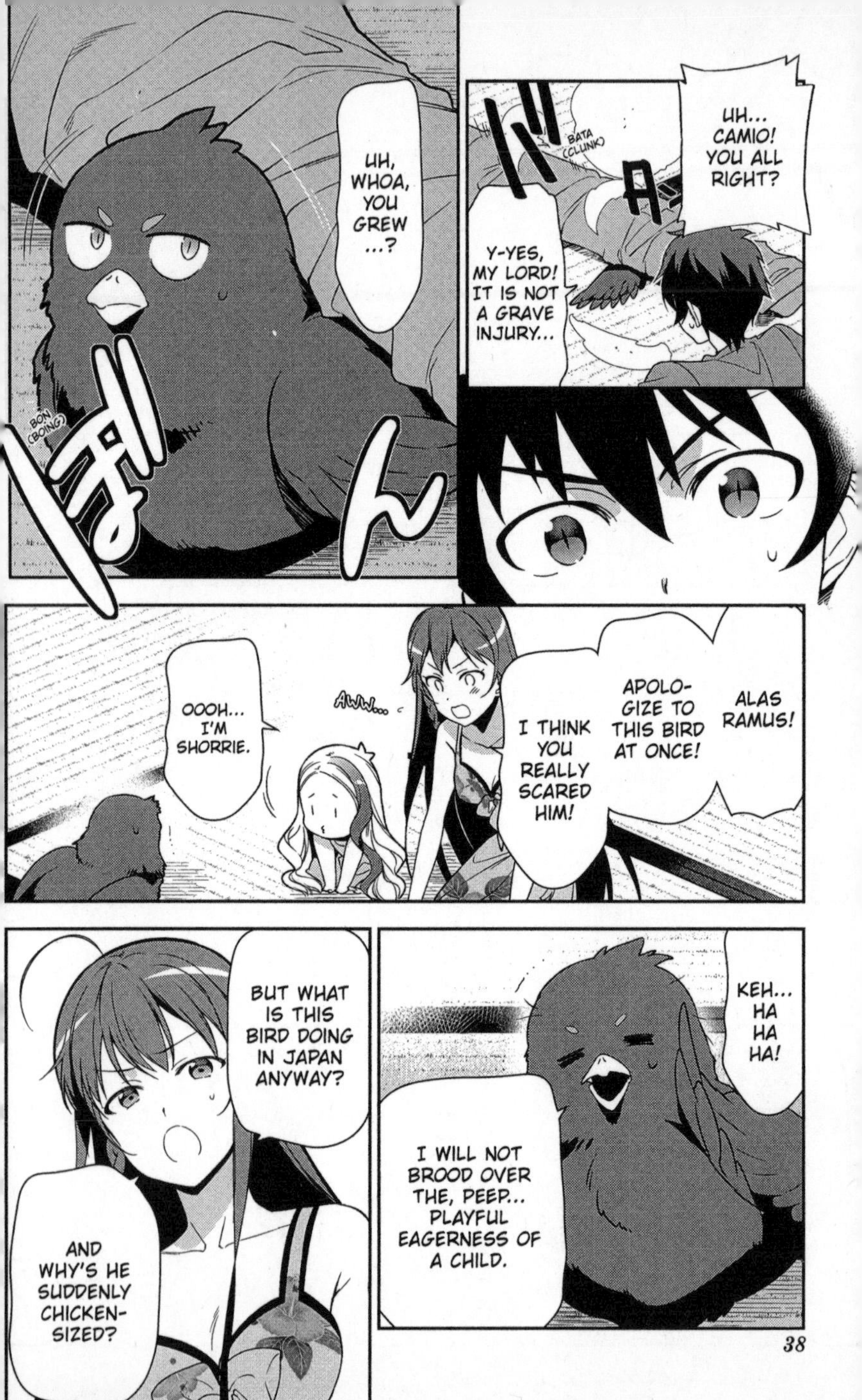
UH... CAMIO! YOU ALL RIGHT?
BATA (CLUNK)
Y-YES, MY LORD! IT IS NOT A GRAVE INJURY...
UH, WHOA, YOU GREW ...?
BON (BOING)
ALAS RAMUS!
APOLO-GIZE TO THIS BIRD AT ONCE!
I THINK YOU REALLY SCARED HIM!
AWW...
OOOH... I'M SHORRIE.
KEH... HA HA HA!
I WILL NOT BROOD OVER THE, PEEP... PLAYFUL EAGERNESS OF A CHILD.
BUT WHAT IS THIS BIRD DOING IN JAPAN ANYWAY?
AND WHY'S HE SUDDENLY CHICKEN-SIZED?

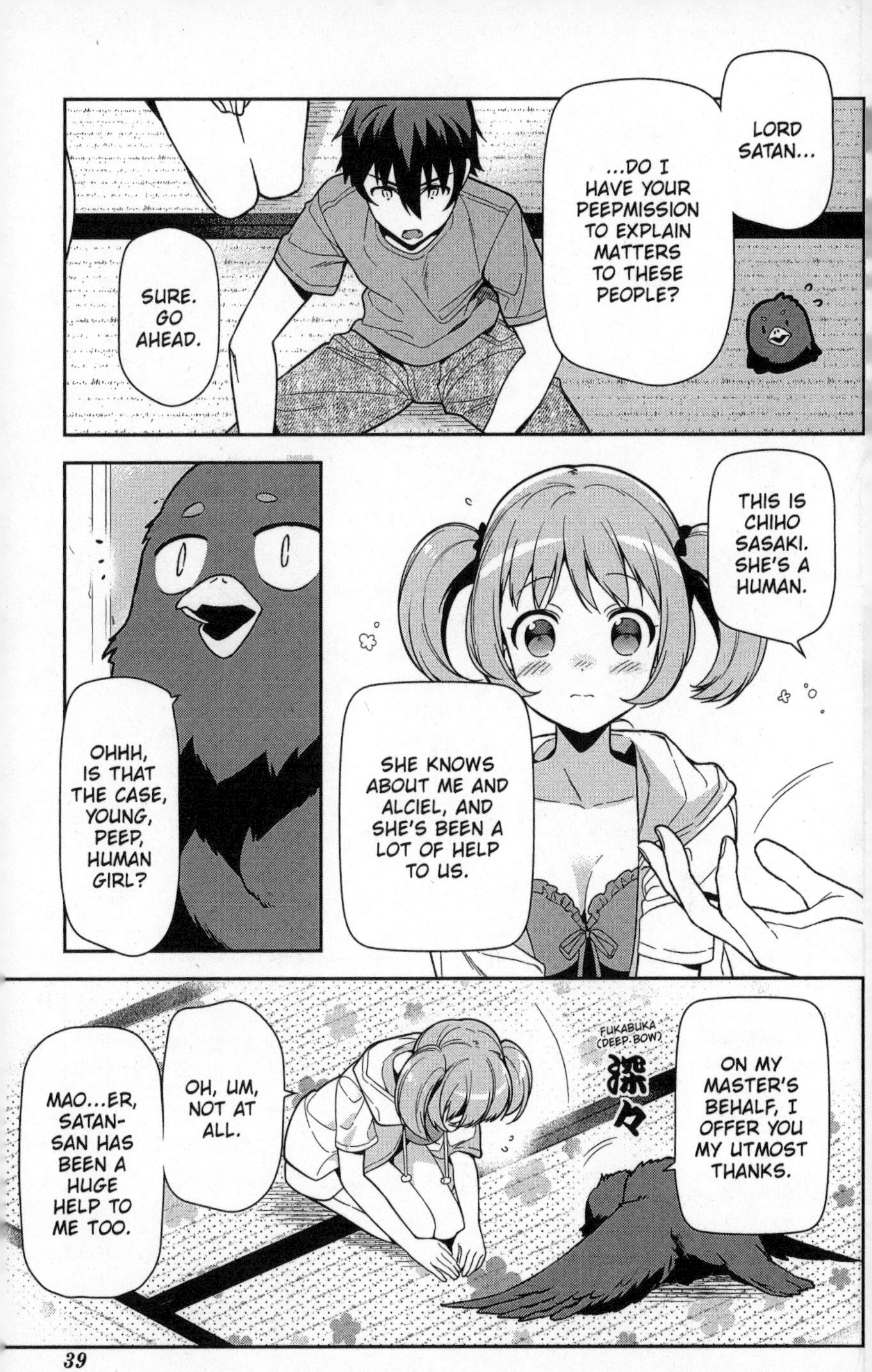
LORD SATAN...
...DO I HAVE YOUR PEEPMISSION TO EXPLAIN MATTERS TO THESE PEOPLE?
SURE. GO AHEAD.
THIS IS CHIHO SASAKI. SHE'S A HUMAN.
SHE KNOWS ABOUT ME AND ALCIEL, AND SHE'S BEEN A LOT OF HELP TO US.
OHHH, IS THAT THE CASE, YOUNG, PEEP, HUMAN GIRL?
深々
FUKABUKA (DEEP BOW)
ON MY MASTER'S BEHALF, I OFFER YOU MY UTMOST THANKS.
OH, UM, NOT AT ALL.
MAO...ER, SATAN-SAN HAS BEEN A HUGE HELP TO ME TOO.

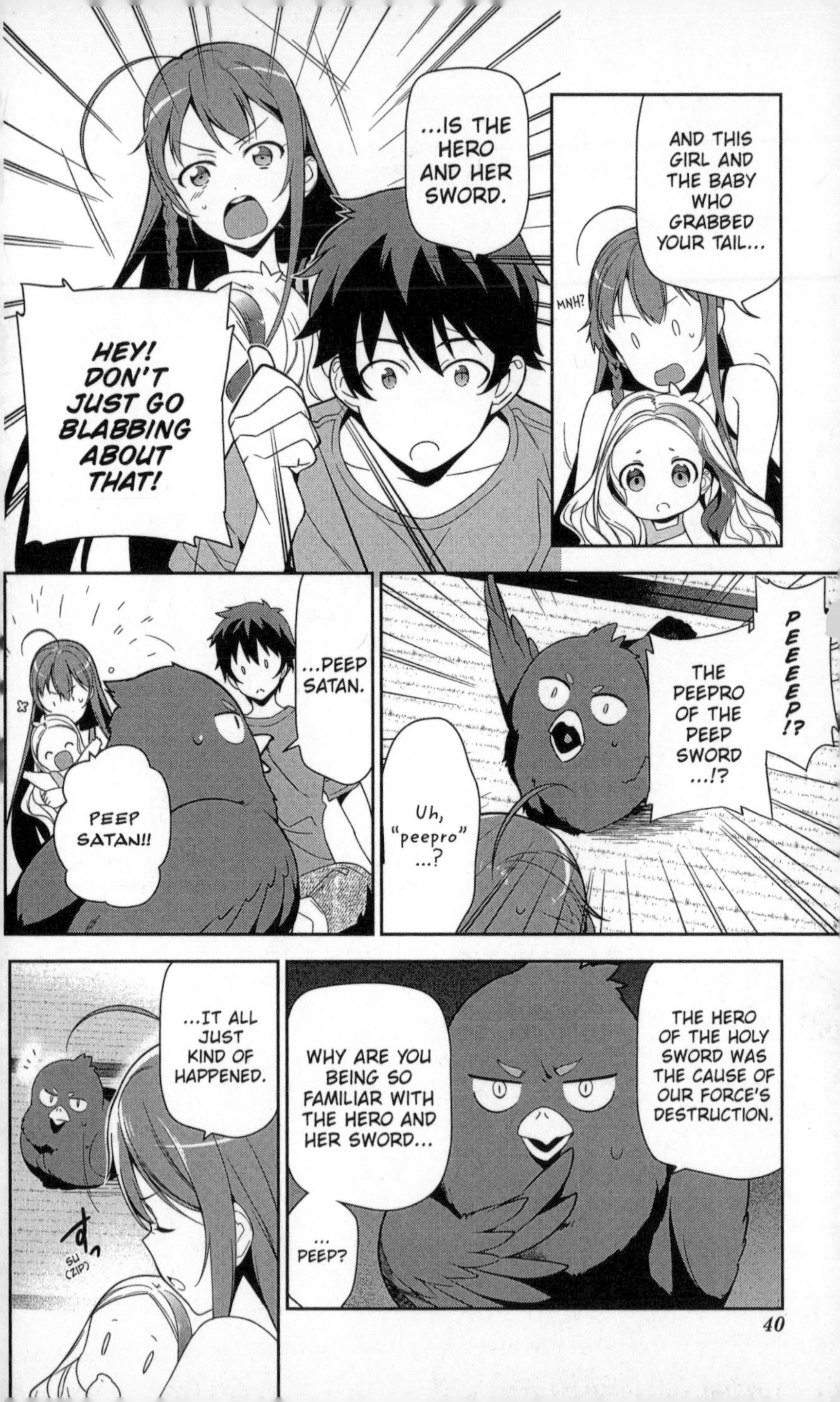
AND THIS GIRL AND THE BABY WHO GRABBED YOUR TAIL...
MNH?
...IS THE HERO AND HER SWORD.
HEY! DON'T JUST GO BLABBING ABOUT THAT!
PEEEEEP!?
THE PEEPRO OF THE PEEP SWORD ...!?
Uh, "peepro" ...?
...PEEP SATAN.
PEEP SATAN!!
THE HERO OF THE HOLY SWORD WAS THE CAUSE OF OUR FORCE'S DESTRUCTION.
WHY ARE YOU BEING SO FAMILIAR WITH THE HERO AND HER SWORD...
... PEEP?
...IT ALL JUST KIND OF HAPPENED.
SU (ZIP)

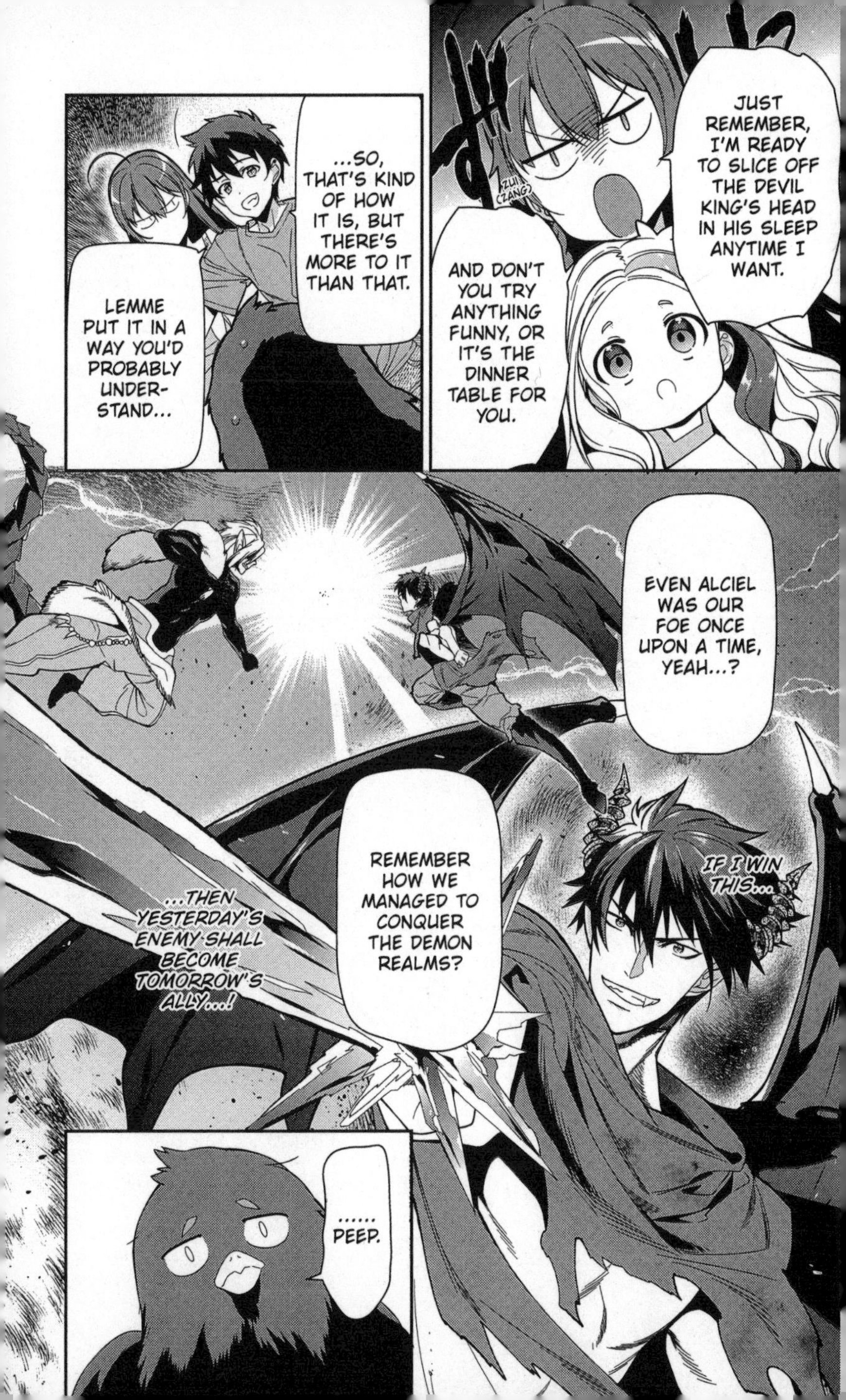
JUST REMEMBER, I'M READY TO SLICE OFF THE DEVIL KING'S HEAD IN HIS SLEEP ANYTIME I WANT.
ZUI (ZANG)
AND DON'T YOU TRY ANYTHING FUNNY, OR IT'S THE DINNER TABLE FOR YOU.
...SO, THAT'S KIND OF HOW IT IS, BUT THERE'S MORE TO IT THAN THAT.
LEMME PUT IT IN A WAY YOU'D PROBABLY UNDER-STAND...
EVEN ALCIEL WAS OUR FOE ONCE UPON A TIME, YEAH...?
IF I WIN THIS...
REMEMBER HOW WE MANAGED TO CONQUER THE DEMON REALMS?
...THEN YESTERDAY'S ENEMY SHALL BECOME TOMORROW'S ALLY...!
......PEEP.

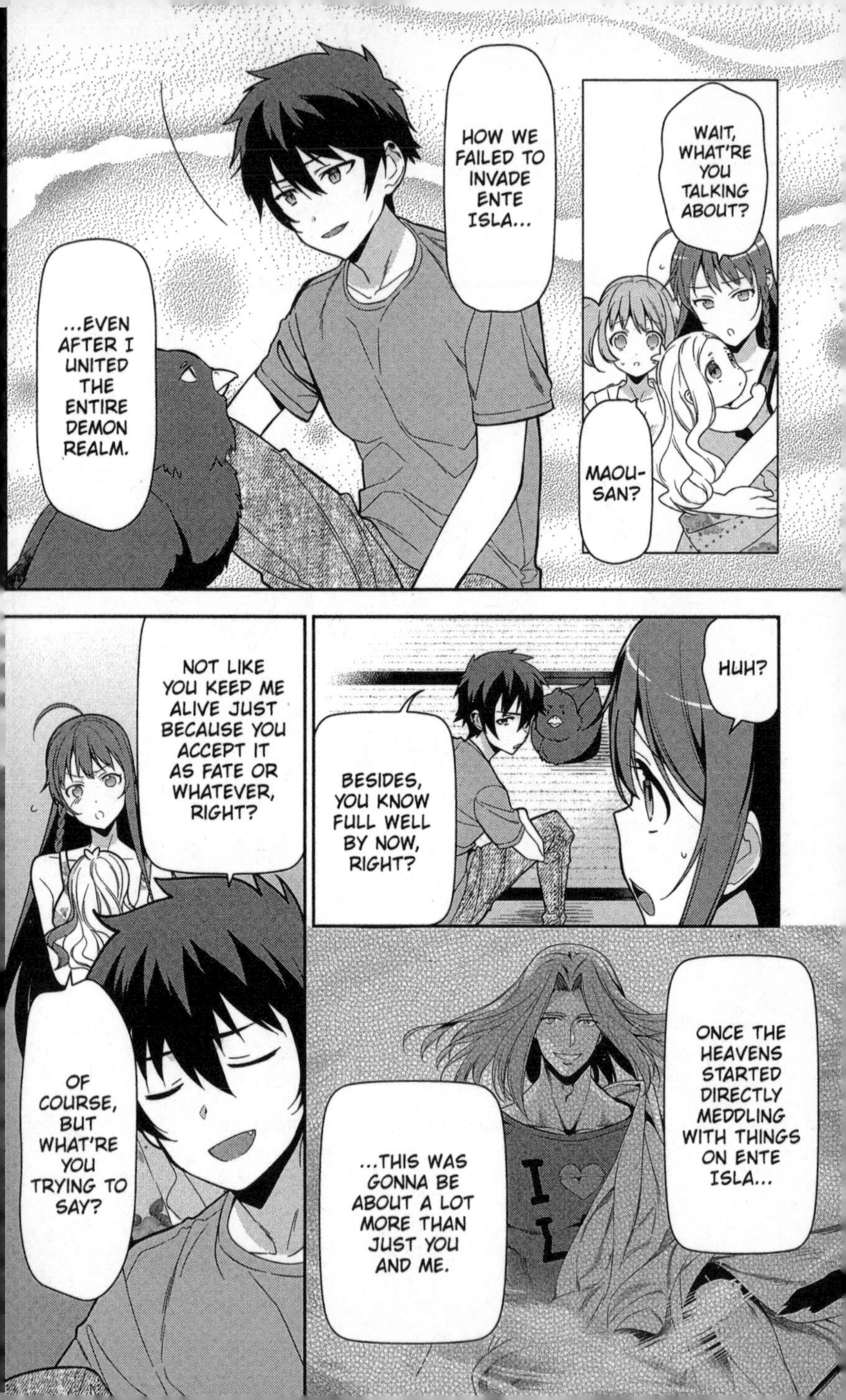
WAIT, WHAT'RE YOU TALKING ABOUT?
MAOU-SAN?
HOW WE FAILED TO INVADE ENTE ISLA...
...EVEN AFTER I UNITED THE ENTIRE DEMON REALM.
HUH?
BESIDES, YOU KNOW FULL WELL BY NOW, RIGHT?
ONCE THE HEAVENS STARTED DIRECTLY MEDDLING WITH THINGS ON ENTE ISLA...
...THIS WAS GONNA BE ABOUT A LOT MORE THAN JUST YOU AND ME.
NOT LIKE YOU KEEP ME ALIVE JUST BECAUSE YOU ACCEPT IT AS FATE OR WHATEVER, RIGHT?
OF COURSE, BUT WHAT'RE YOU TRYING TO SAY?

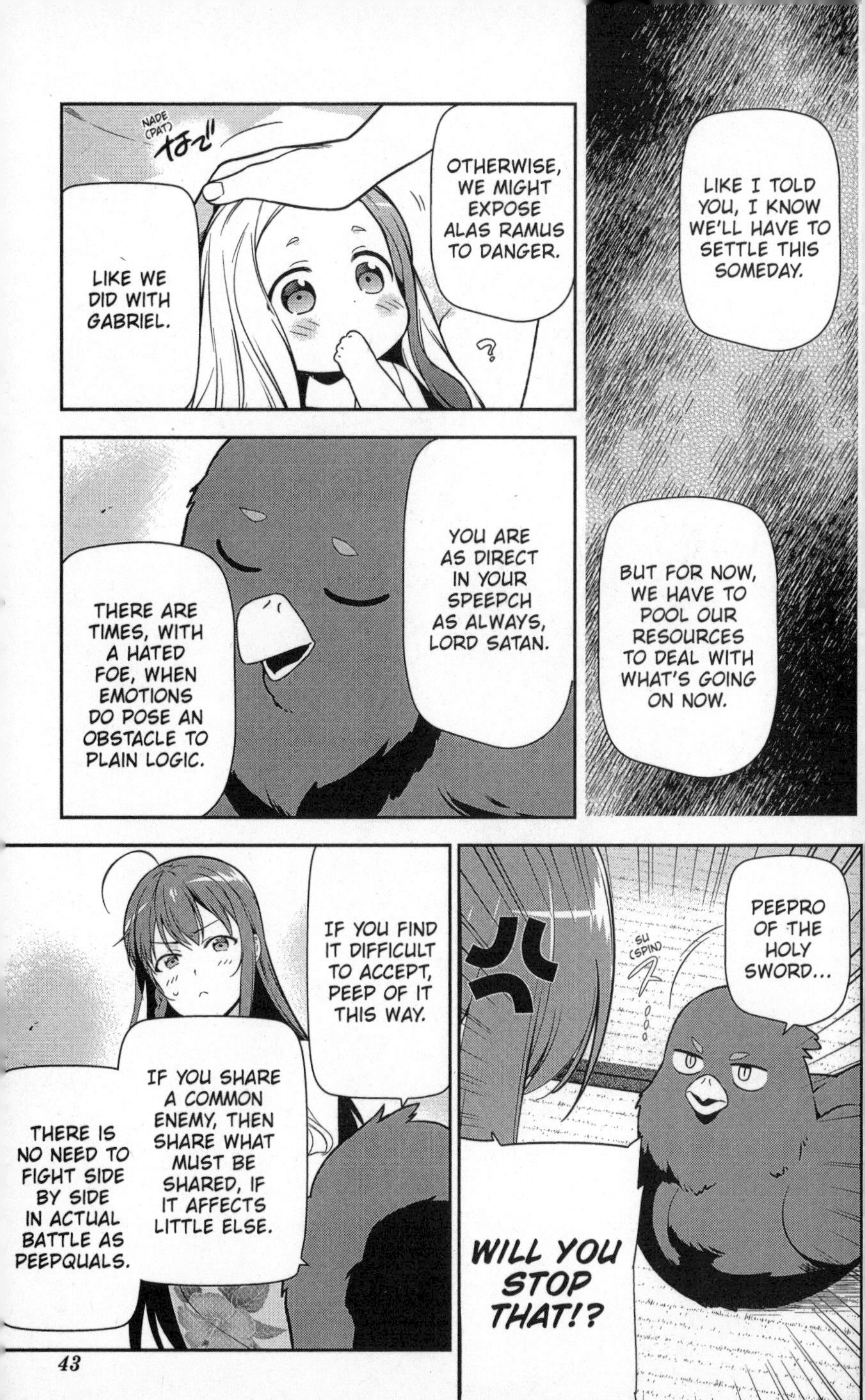

LIKE I TOLD YOU, I KNOW WE'LL HAVE TO SETTLE THIS SOMEDAY.
BUT FOR NOW, WE HAVE TO POOL OUR RESOURCES TO DEAL WITH WHAT'S GOING ON NOW.
NADE (PAT)
なで
OTHERWISE, WE MIGHT EXPOSE ALAS RAMUS TO DANGER.
LIKE WE DID WITH GABRIEL.
?
YOU ARE AS DIRECT IN YOUR SPEEPCH AS ALWAYS, LORD SATAN.
THERE ARE TIMES, WITH A HATED FOE, WHEN EMOTIONS DO POSE AN OBSTACLE TO PLAIN LOGIC.
PEEPRO OF THE HOLY SWORD...
SU (SPIN)
WILL YOU STOP THAT!?
IF YOU FIND IT DIFFICULT TO ACCEPT, PEEP OF IT THIS WAY.
IF YOU SHARE A COMMON ENEMY, THEN SHARE WHAT MUST BE SHARED, IF IT AFFECTS LITTLE ELSE.
THERE IS NO NEED TO FIGHT SIDE BY SIDE IN ACTUAL BATTLE AS PEEPQUALS.

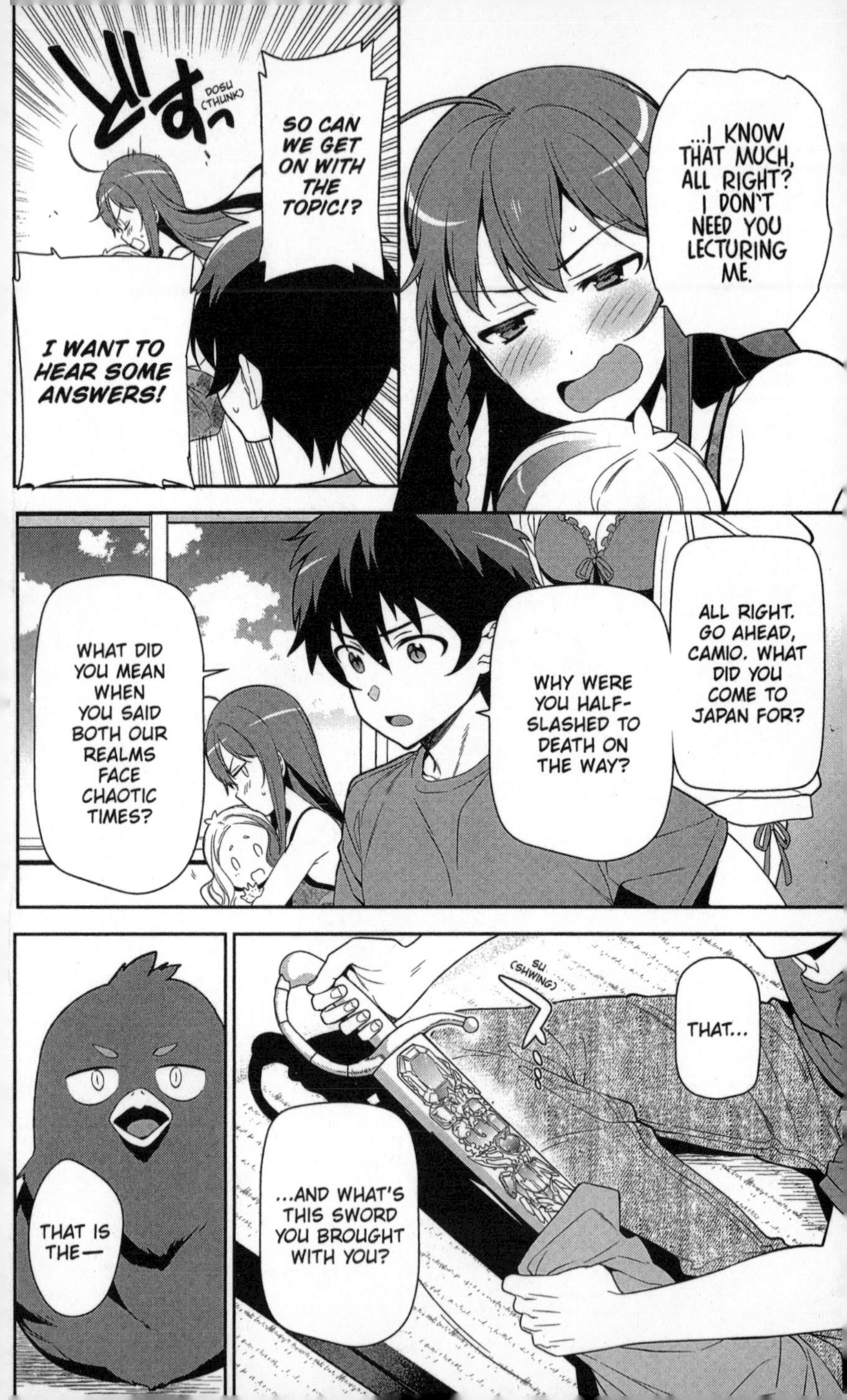
...I KNOW THAT MUCH, ALL RIGHT? I DON'T NEED YOU LECTURING ME.
どすっ
DOSU (THUNK)
SO CAN WE GET ON WITH THE TOPIC!?
I WANT TO HEAR SOME ANSWERS!
ALL RIGHT. GO AHEAD, CAMIO. WHAT DID YOU COME TO JAPAN FOR?
WHY WERE YOU HALF-SLASHED TO DEATH ON THE WAY?
WHAT DID YOU MEAN WHEN YOU SAID BOTH OUR REALMS FACE CHAOTIC TIMES?
THAT...
SU (SHWING)
...AND WHAT'S THIS SWORD YOU BROUGHT WITH YOU?
THAT IS THE—

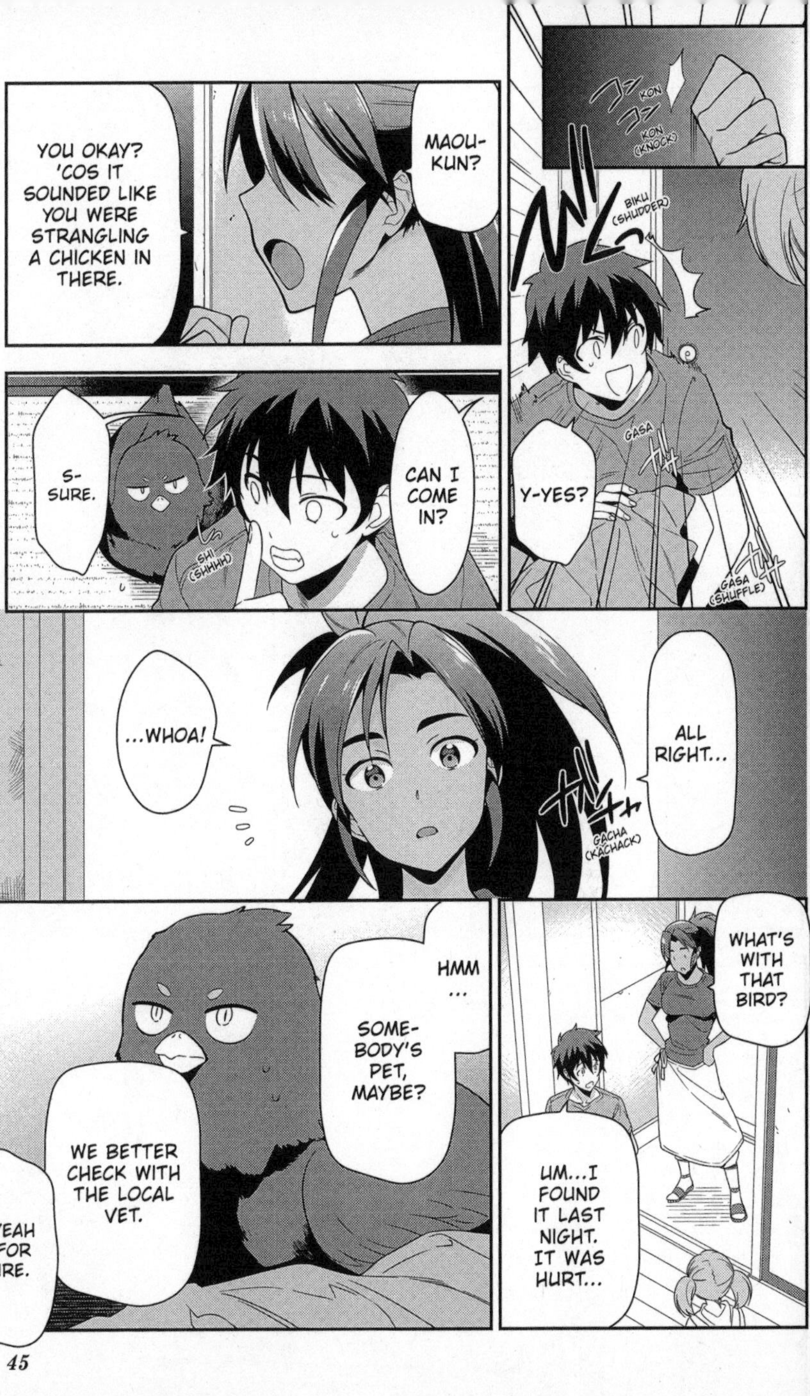
KON
KON (KNOCK)
BIKU (SHUDDER)
Y-YES?
GASA
GASA (SHUFFLE)
MAOU-KUN?
YOU OKAY? 'COS IT SOUNDED LIKE YOU WERE STRANGLING A CHICKEN IN THERE.
CAN I COME IN?
S-SURE.
SHI (SHHHH)
ALL RIGHT...
GACHA (KACHACK)
...WHOA!
WHAT'S WITH THAT BIRD?
UM...I FOUND IT LAST NIGHT. IT WAS HURT...
HMM ...
SOME-BODY'S PET, MAYBE?
WE BETTER CHECK WITH THE LOCAL VET.
Y-YEAH ...FOR SURE.

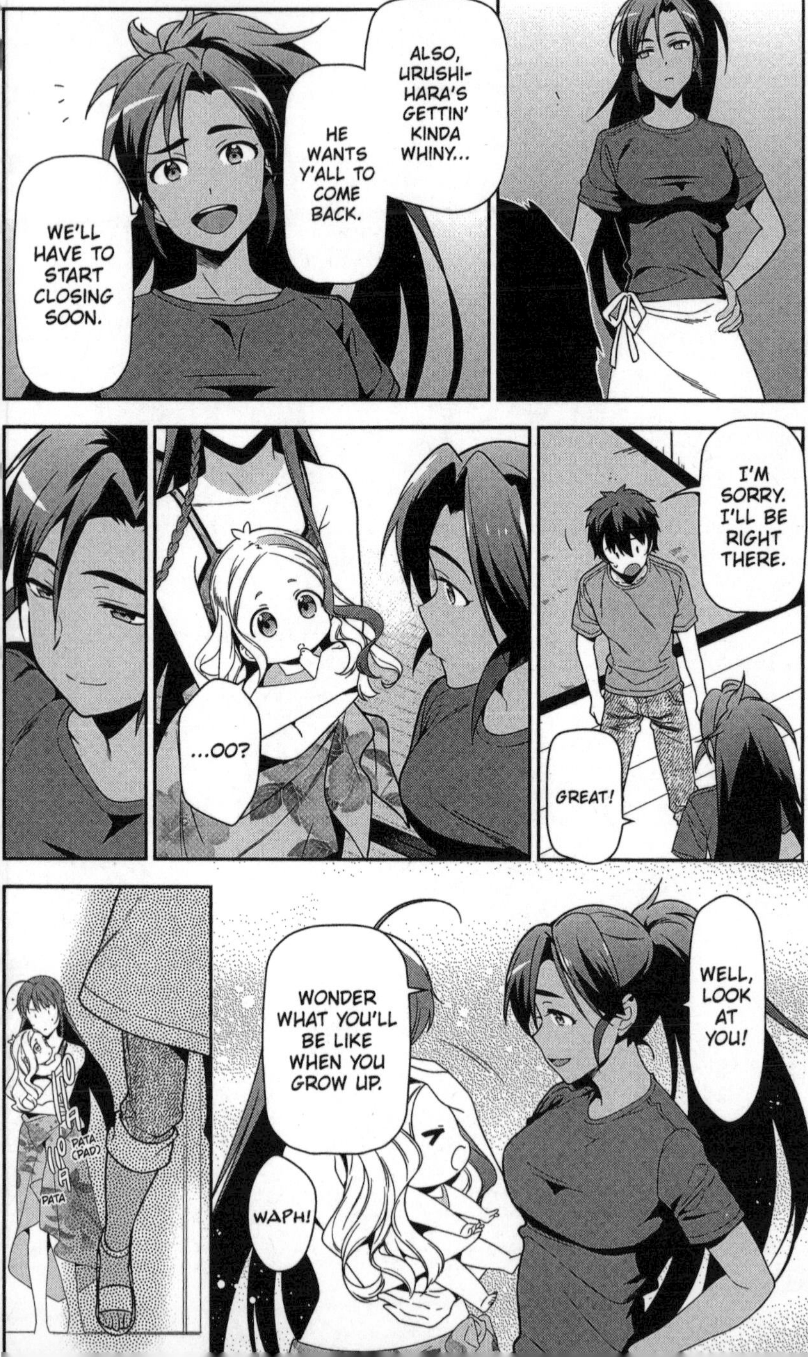
ALSO, URUSHI-HARA'S GETTIN' KINDA WHINY...
HE WANTS Y'ALL TO COME BACK.
WE'LL HAVE TO START CLOSING SOON.
I'M SORRY. I'LL BE RIGHT THERE.
GREAT!
...OO?
WELL, LOOK AT YOU!
WONDER WHAT YOU'LL BE LIKE WHEN YOU GROW UP.
WAPH!
PATA (PAD)
PATA

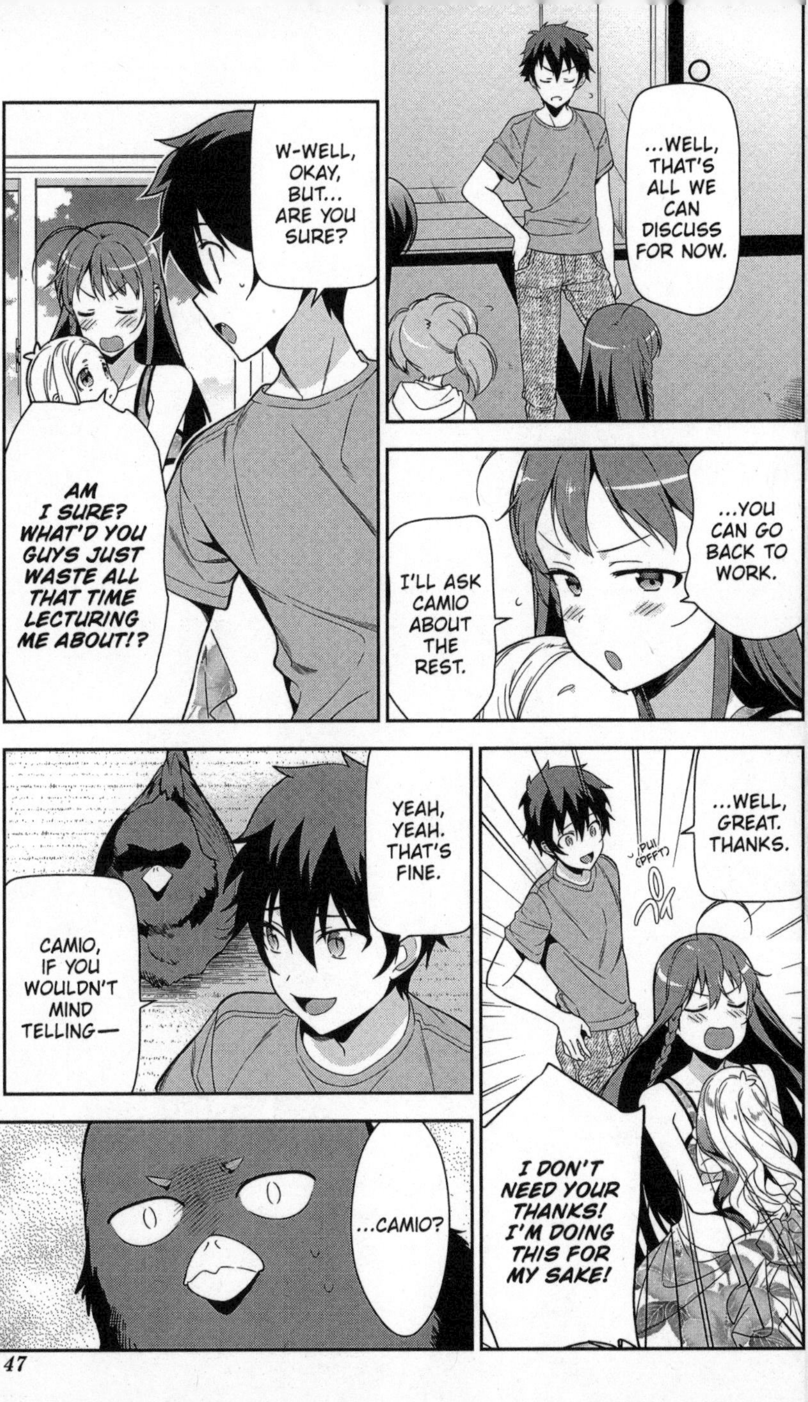
...WELL, THAT'S ALL WE CAN DISCUSS FOR NOW.
...YOU CAN GO BACK TO WORK.
I'LL ASK CAMIO ABOUT THE REST.
W-WELL, OKAY, BUT... ARE YOU SURE?
AM I SURE? WHAT'D YOU GUYS JUST WASTE ALL THAT TIME LECTURING ME ABOUT!?
...WELL, GREAT. THANKS.
PUI (PFFT)
I DON'T NEED YOUR THANKS! I'M DOING THIS FOR MY SAKE!
YEAH, YEAH. THAT'S FINE.
CAMIO, IF YOU WOULDN'T MIND TELLING—
...CAMIO?

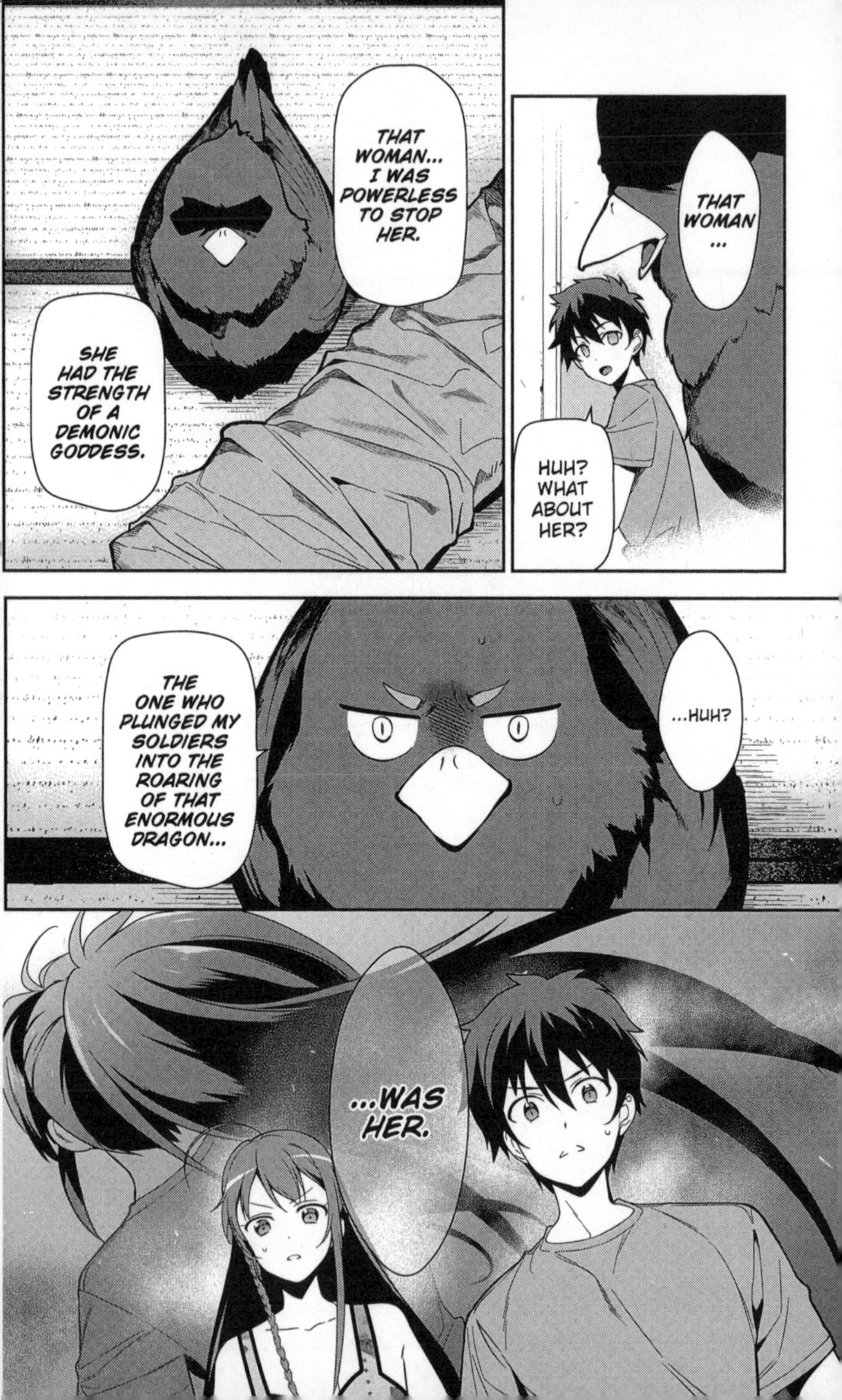
THAT WOMAN...
HUH? WHAT ABOUT HER?
THAT WOMAN... I WAS POWERLESS TO STOP HER.
SHE HAD THE STRENGTH OF A DEMONIC GODDESS.
...HUH?
THE ONE WHO PLUNGED MY SOLDIERS INTO THE ROARING OF THAT ENORMOUS DRAGON...
...WAS HER.

Camio

THE DEVIL IS A PART-TIMER!

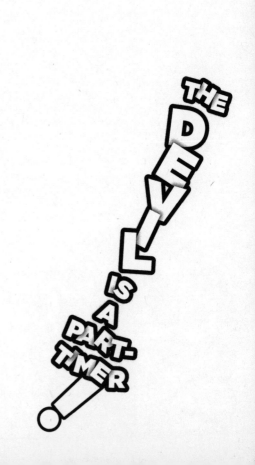

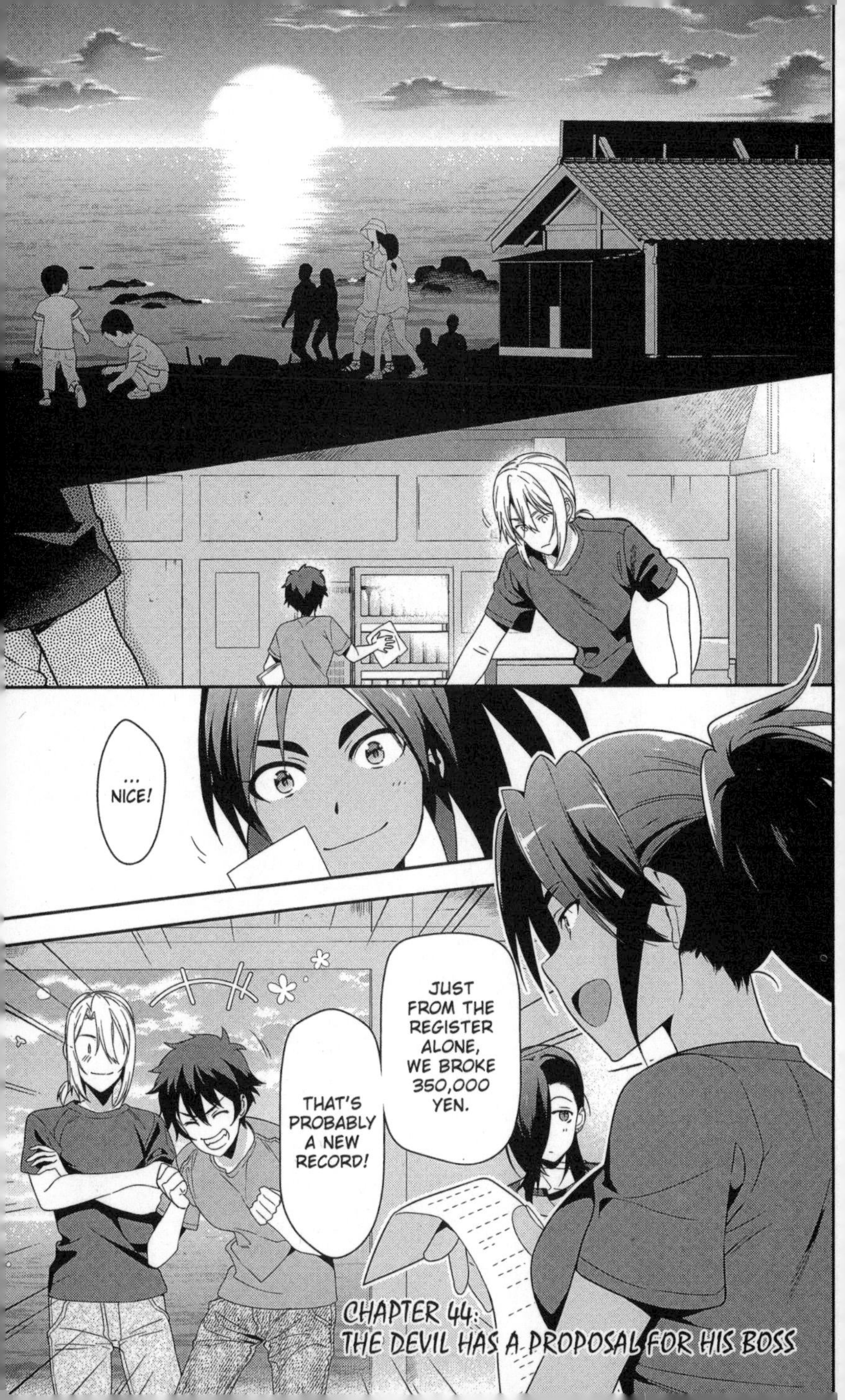

...NICE!
JUST FROM THE REGISTER ALONE, WE BROKE 350,000 YEN.
THAT'S PROBABLY A NEW RECORD!
CHAPTER 44:
THE DEVIL HAS A PROPOSAL FOR HIS BOSS

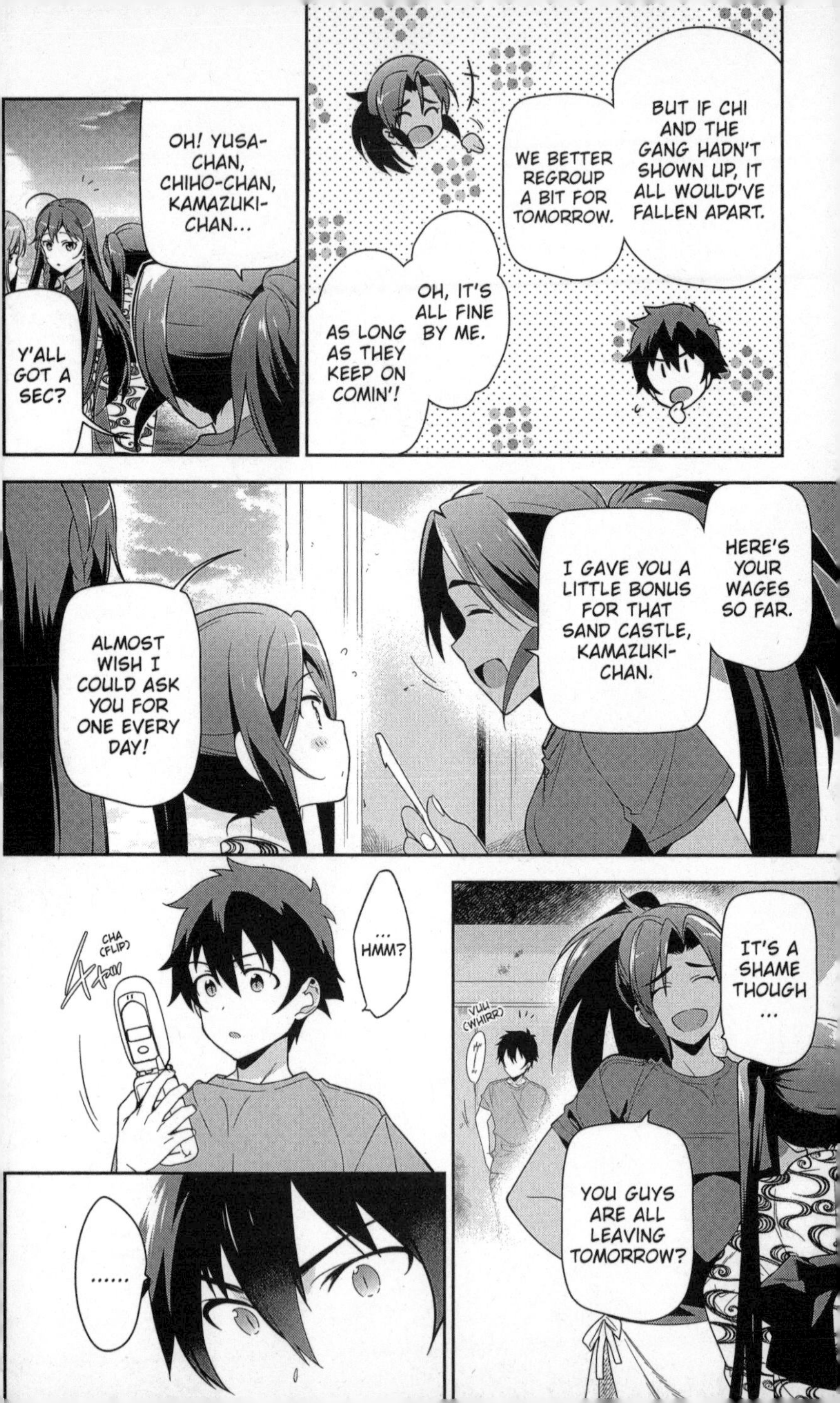
BUT IF CHI AND THE GANG HADN'T SHOWN UP, IT ALL WOULD'VE FALLEN APART.
WE BETTER REGROUP A BIT FOR TOMORROW.
OH, IT'S ALL FINE BY ME.
AS LONG AS THEY KEEP ON COMIN'!
OH! YUSA-CHAN, CHIHO-CHAN, KAMAZUKI-CHAN...
Y'ALL GOT A SEC?
HERE'S YOUR WAGES SO FAR.
I GAVE YOU A LITTLE BONUS FOR THAT SAND CASTLE, KAMAZUKI-CHAN.
ALMOST WISH I COULD ASK YOU FOR ONE EVERY DAY!
IT'S A SHAME THOUGH...
VUU (WHIRR)
YOU GUYS ARE ALL LEAVING TOMORROW?
...HMM?
CHA (FLIP)
......

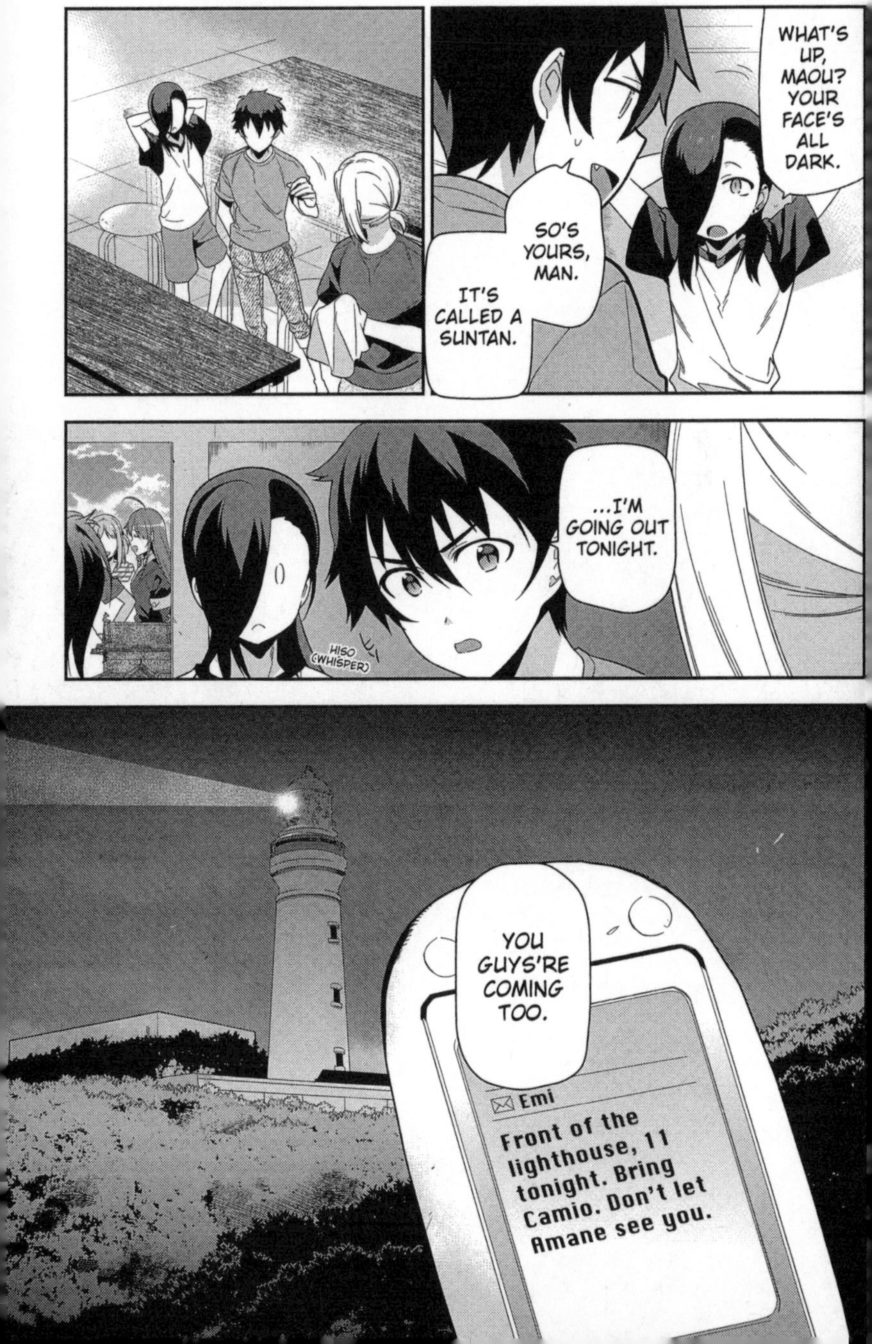
WHAT'S UP, MAOU? YOUR FACE'S ALL DARK.
SO'S YOURS, MAN.
IT'S CALLED A SUNTAN.
...I'M GOING OUT TONIGHT.
HISO (WHISPER)
YOU GUYS'RE COMING TOO.
Emi
Front of the lighthouse, 11 tonight. Bring Camio. Don't let Amane see you.

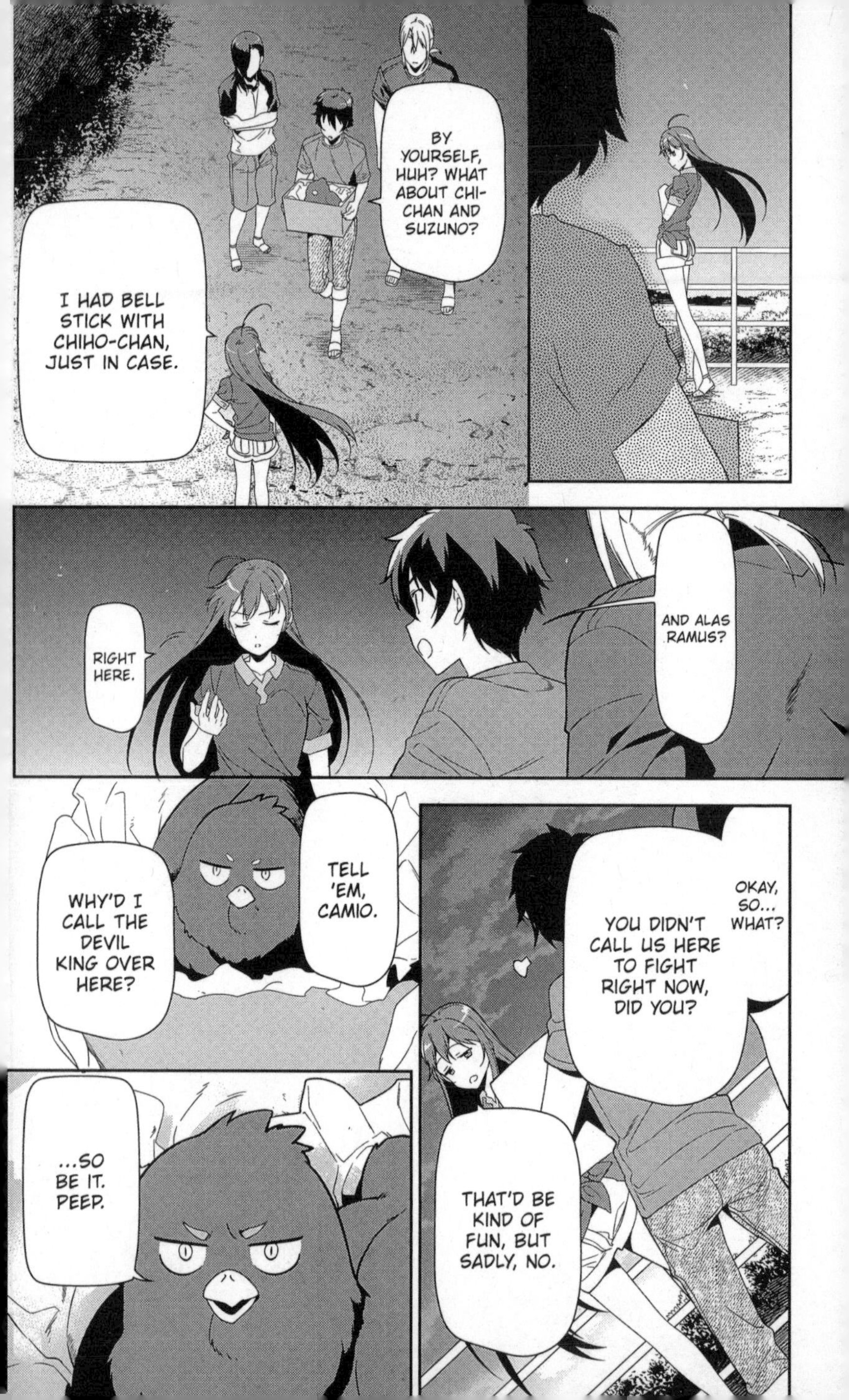
BY YOURSELF, HUH? WHAT ABOUT CHI-CHAN AND SUZUNO?
I HAD BELL STICK WITH CHIHO-CHAN, JUST IN CASE.
AND ALAS RAMUS?
RIGHT HERE.
OKAY, SO... WHAT?
YOU DIDN'T CALL US HERE TO FIGHT RIGHT NOW, DID YOU?
THAT'D BE KIND OF FUN, BUT SADLY, NO.
TELL 'EM, CAMIO.
WHY'D I CALL THE DEVIL KING OVER HERE?
...SO BE IT. PEEP.

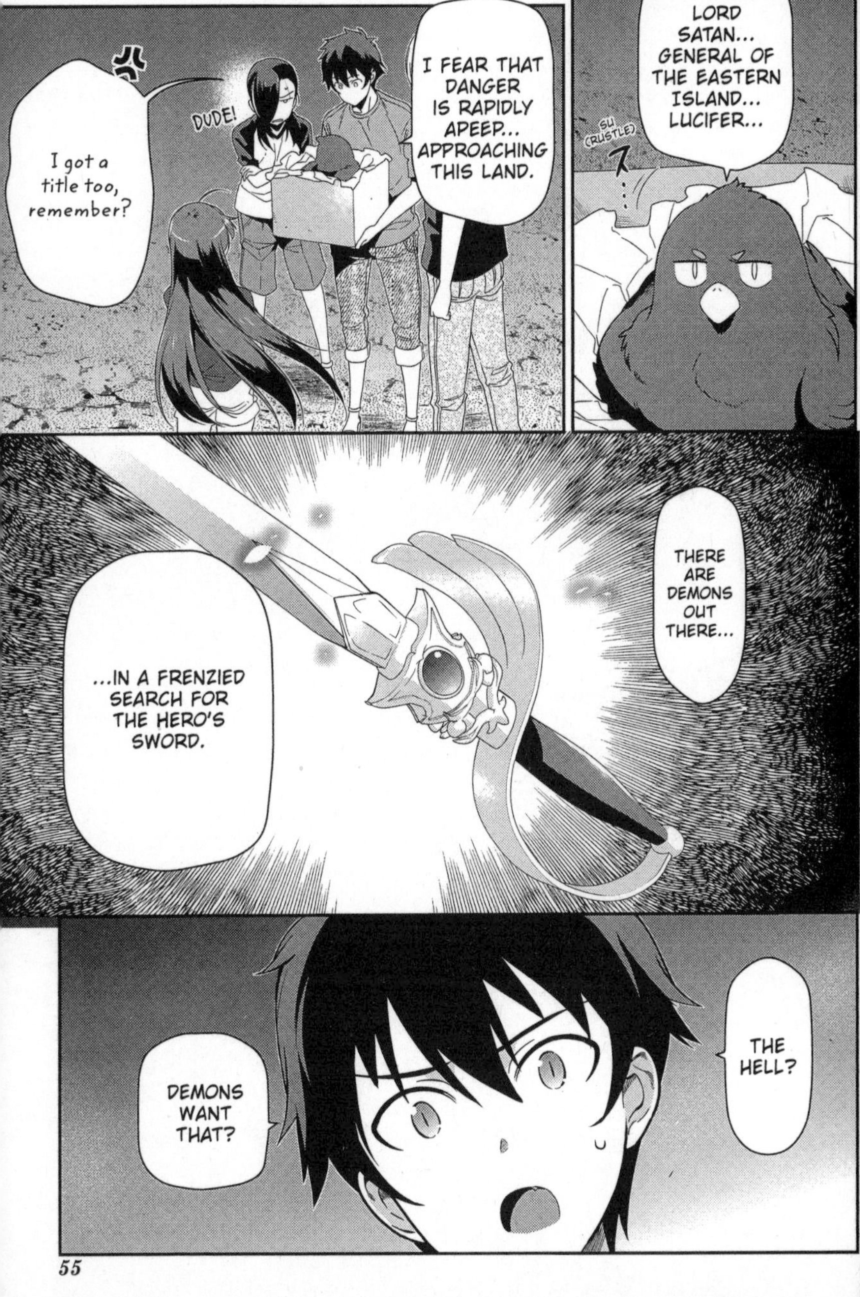
LORD SATAN... GENERAL OF THE EASTERN ISLAND... LUCIFER...
SU (RUSTLE)
I FEAR THAT DANGER IS RAPIDLY APEEP... APPROACHING THIS LAND.
DUDE!
I got a title too, remember?
THERE ARE DEMONS OUT THERE...
...IN A FRENZIED SEARCH FOR THE HERO'S SWORD.
THE HELL?
DEMONS WANT THAT?

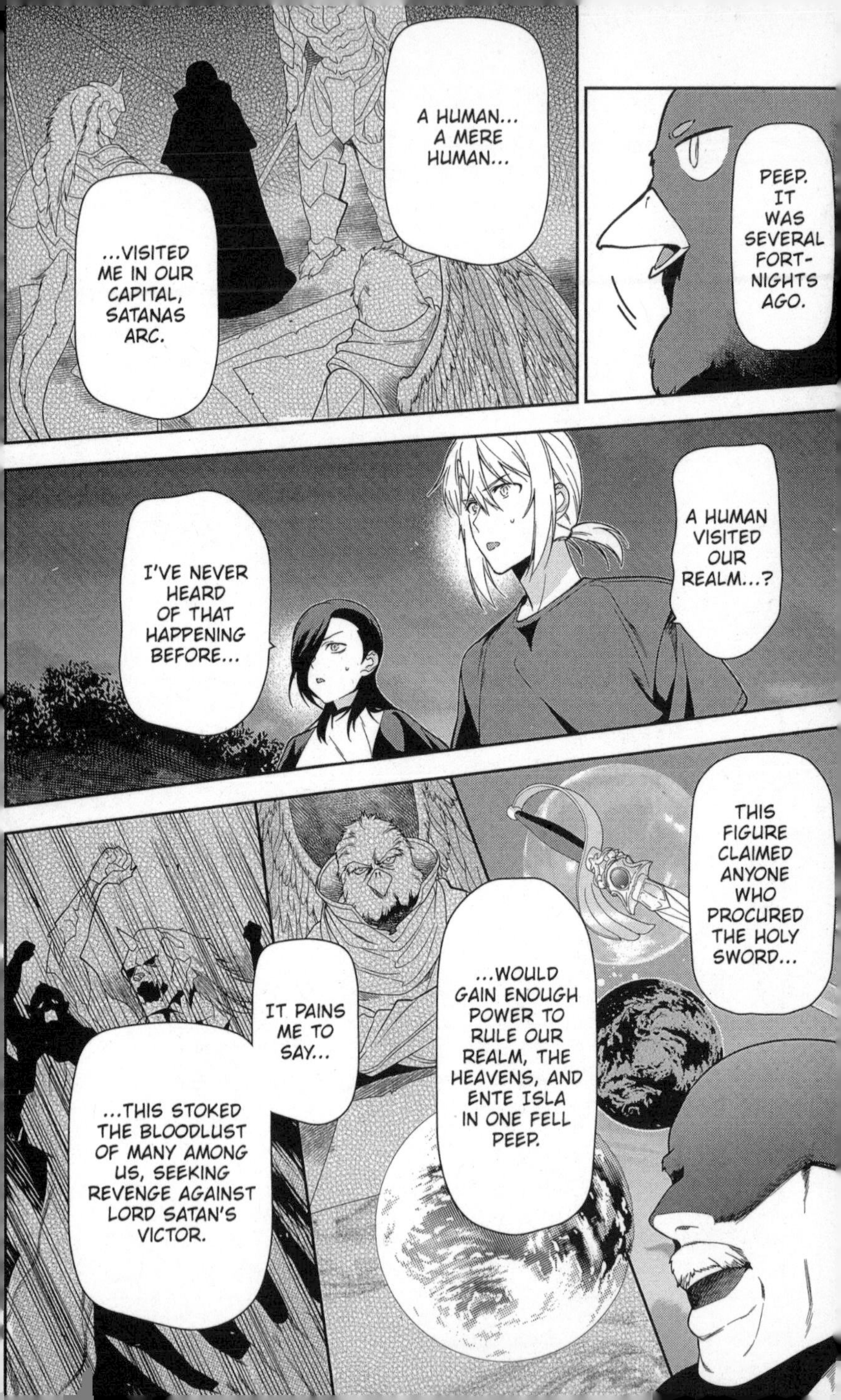
PEEP. IT WAS SEVERAL FORT-NIGHTS AGO.
A HUMAN... A MERE HUMAN...
...VISITED ME IN OUR CAPITAL, SATANAS ARC.
A HUMAN VISITED OUR REALM...?
I'VE NEVER HEARD OF THAT HAPPENING BEFORE...
THIS FIGURE CLAIMED ANYONE WHO PROCURED THE HOLY SWORD...
...WOULD GAIN ENOUGH POWER TO RULE OUR REALM, THE HEAVENS, AND ENTE ISLA IN ONE FELL PEEP.
IT PAINS ME TO SAY...
...THIS STOKED THE BLOODLUST OF MANY AMONG US, SEEKING REVENGE AGAINST LORD SATAN'S VICTOR.

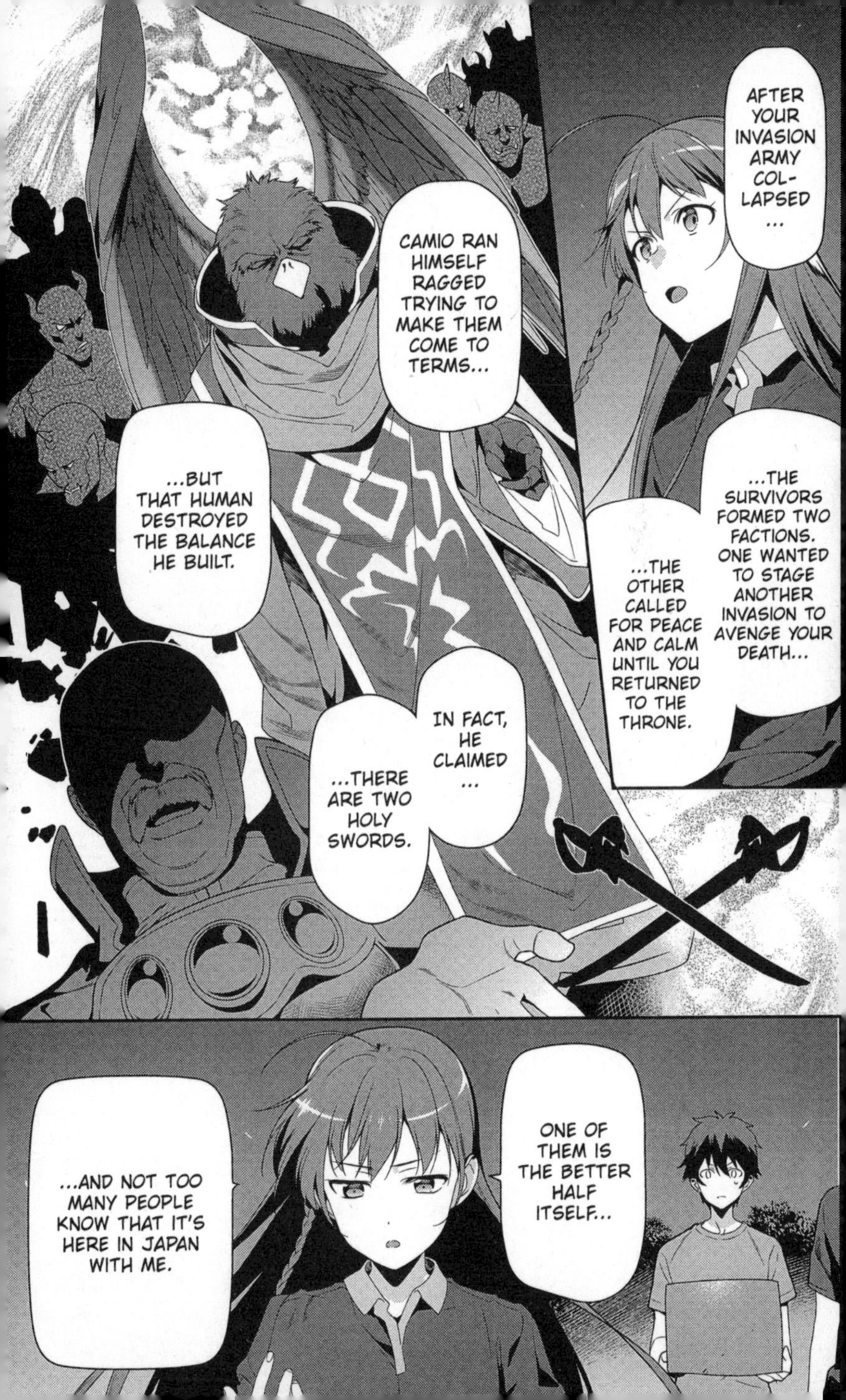
AFTER YOUR INVASION ARMY COL-LAPSED...
...THE SURVIVORS FORMED TWO FACTIONS. ONE WANTED TO STAGE ANOTHER INVASION TO AVENGE YOUR DEATH...
...THE OTHER CALLED FOR PEACE AND CALM UNTIL YOU RETURNED TO THE THRONE.
CAMIO RAN HIMSELF RAGGED TRYING TO MAKE THEM COME TO TERMS...
...BUT THAT HUMAN DESTROYED THE BALANCE HE BUILT.
IN FACT, HE CLAIMED...
...THERE ARE TWO HOLY SWORDS.
ONE OF THEM IS THE BETTER HALF ITSELF...
...AND NOT TOO MANY PEOPLE KNOW THAT IT'S HERE IN JAPAN WITH ME.

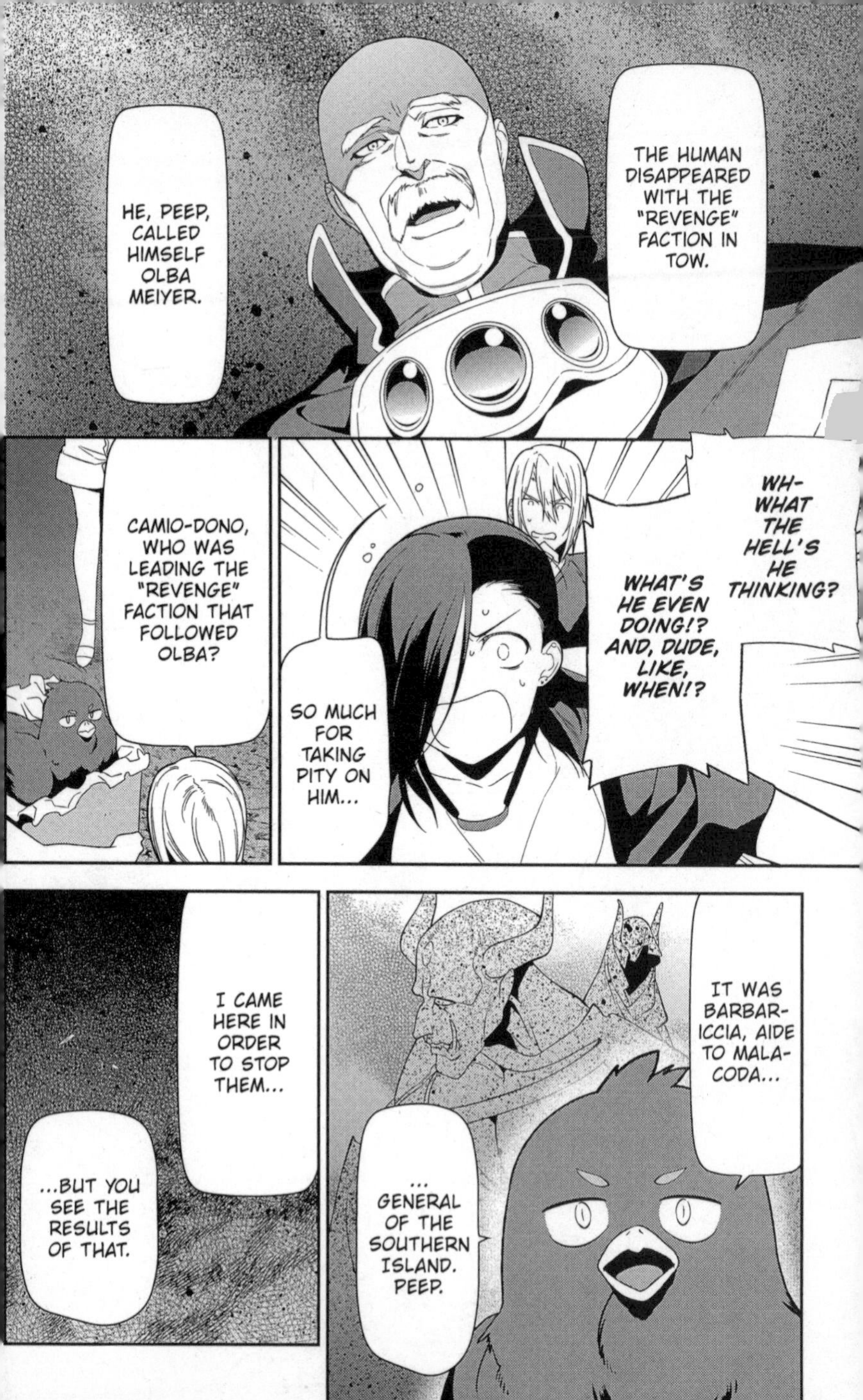
THE HUMAN DISAPPEARED WITH THE "REVENGE" FACTION IN TOW.
HE, PEEP, CALLED HIMSELF OLBA MEIYER.
WH-WHAT THE HELL'S HE THINKING?
WHAT'S HE EVEN DOING!? AND, DUDE, LIKE, WHEN!?
SO MUCH FOR TAKING PITY ON HIM...
CAMIO-DONO, WHO WAS LEADING THE "REVENGE" FACTION THAT FOLLOWED OLBA?
IT WAS BARBARICCIA, AIDE TO MALACODA...
...GENERAL OF THE SOUTHERN ISLAND. PEEP.
I CAME HERE IN ORDER TO STOP THEM...
...BUT YOU SEE THE RESULTS OF THAT.

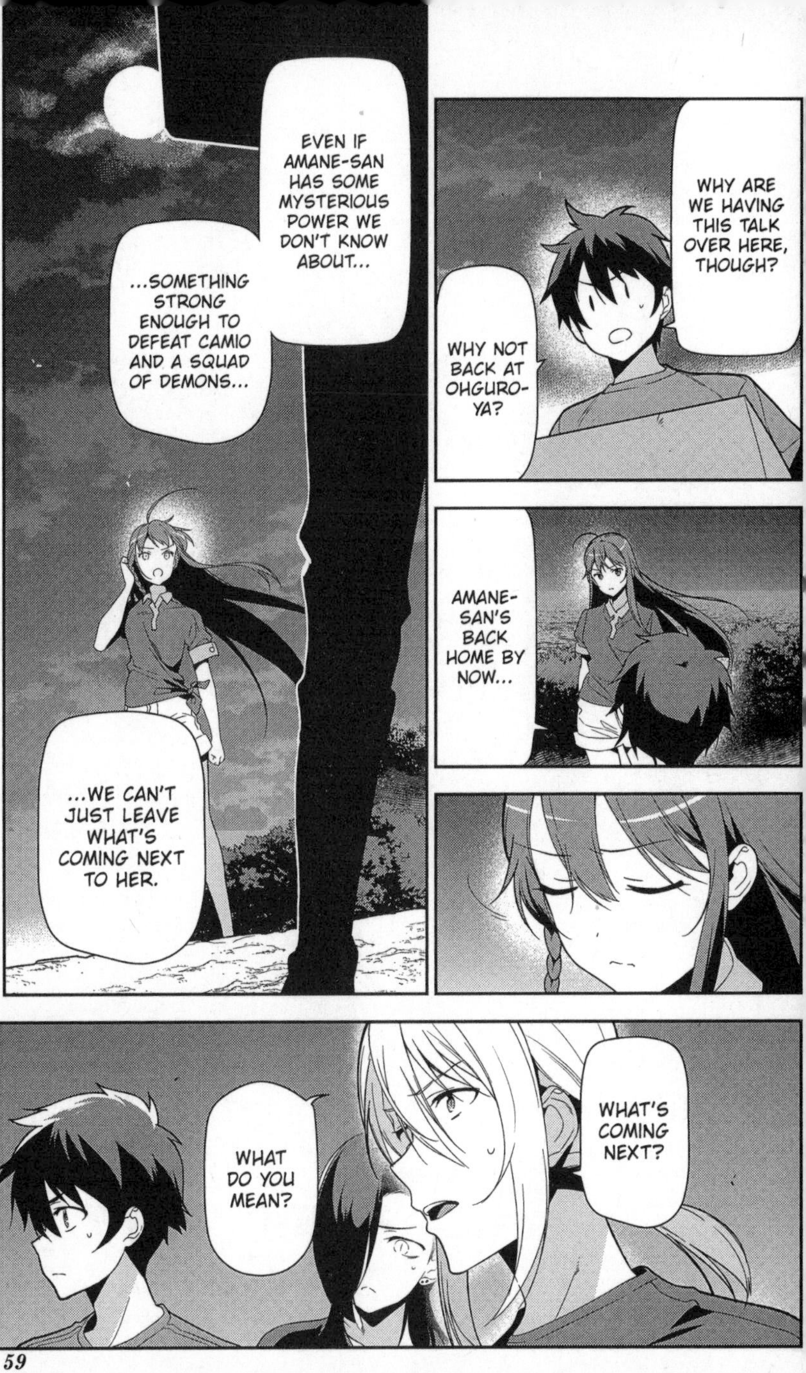
WHY ARE WE HAVING THIS TALK OVER HERE, THOUGH?
WHY NOT BACK AT OHGURO-YA?
AMANE-SAN'S BACK HOME BY NOW...
EVEN IF AMANE-SAN HAS SOME MYSTERIOUS POWER WE DON'T KNOW ABOUT...
...SOMETHING STRONG ENOUGH TO DEFEAT CAMIO AND A SQUAD OF DEMONS...
...WE CAN'T JUST LEAVE WHAT'S COMING NEXT TO HER.
WHAT'S COMING NEXT?
WHAT DO YOU MEAN?

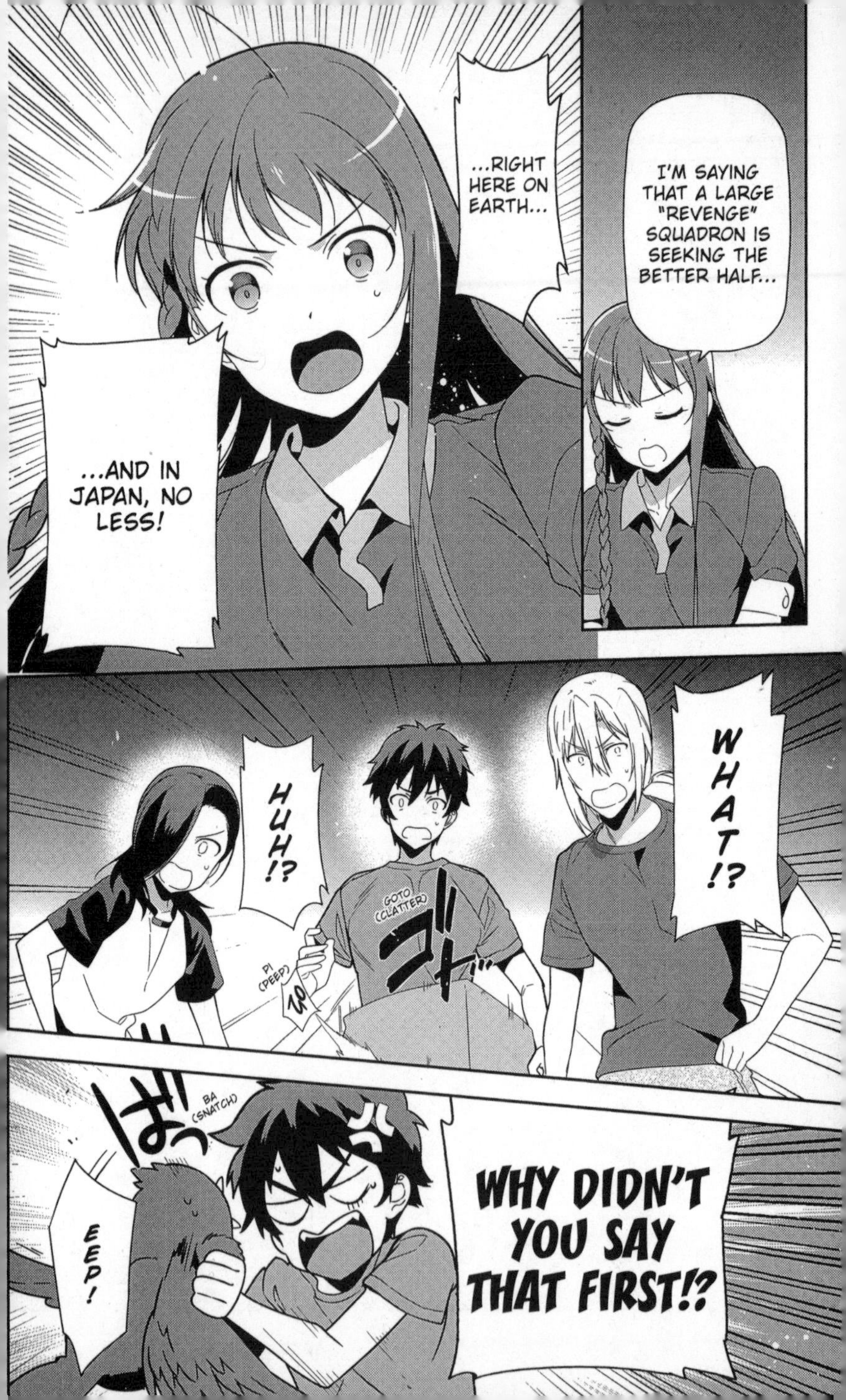
I'M SAYING THAT A LARGE "REVENGE" SQUADRON IS SEEKING THE BETTER HALF...
...RIGHT HERE ON EARTH...
...AND IN JAPAN, NO LESS!
WHAT!?
GOTO (CLATTER)
HUH!?
PI (PEEP)
WHY DIDN'T YOU SAY THAT FIRST!?
BA (SNATCH)
EEP!

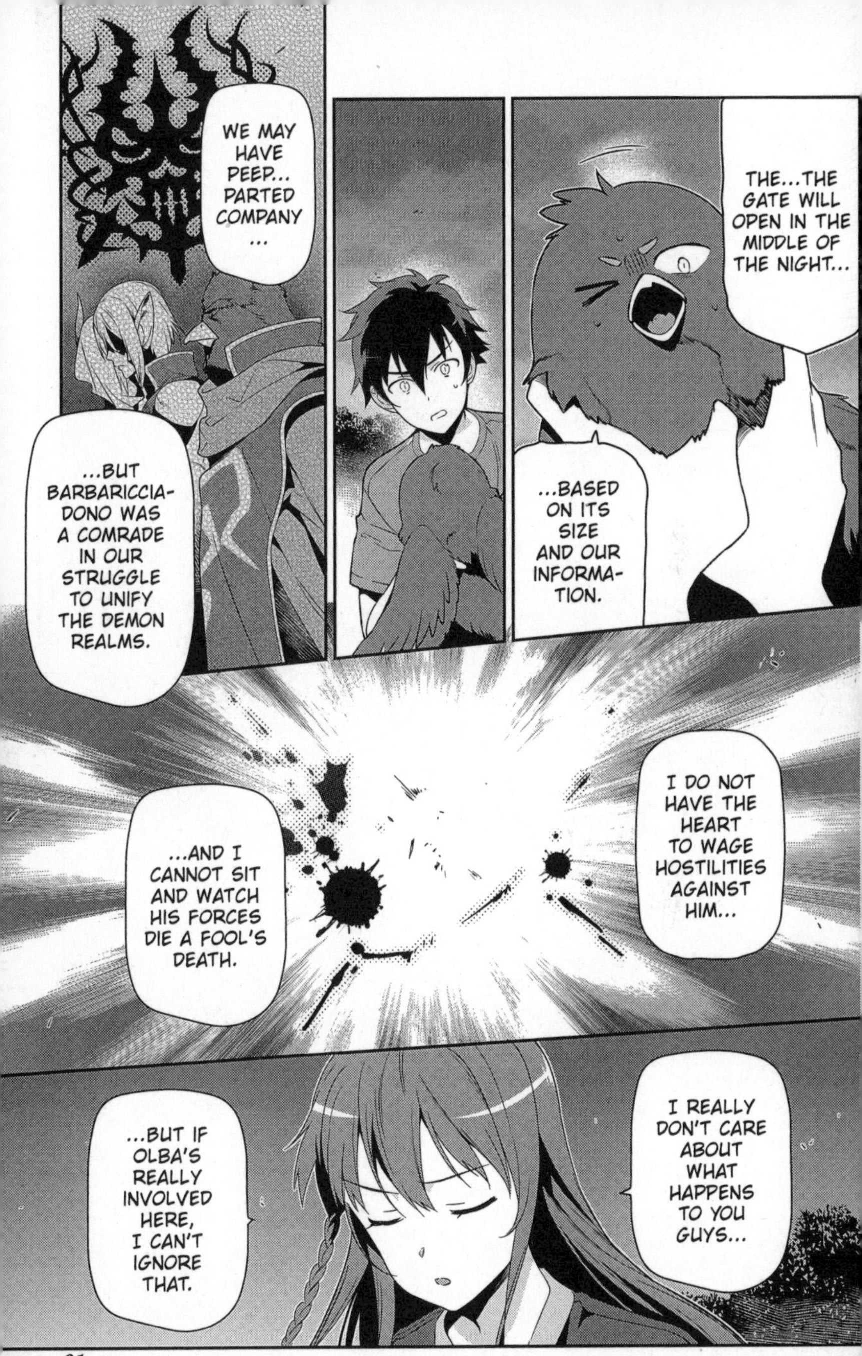
THE...THE GATE WILL OPEN IN THE MIDDLE OF THE NIGHT...
...BASED ON ITS SIZE AND OUR INFORMATION.
WE MAY HAVE PEEP... PARTED COMPANY ...
...BUT BARBARICCIA-DONO WAS A COMRADE IN OUR STRUGGLE TO UNIFY THE DEMON REALMS.
I DO NOT HAVE THE HEART TO WAGE HOSTILITIES AGAINST HIM...
...AND I CANNOT SIT AND WATCH HIS FORCES DIE A FOOL'S DEATH.
I REALLY DON'T CARE ABOUT WHAT HAPPENS TO YOU GUYS...
...BUT IF OLBA'S REALLY INVOLVED HERE, I CAN'T IGNORE THAT.

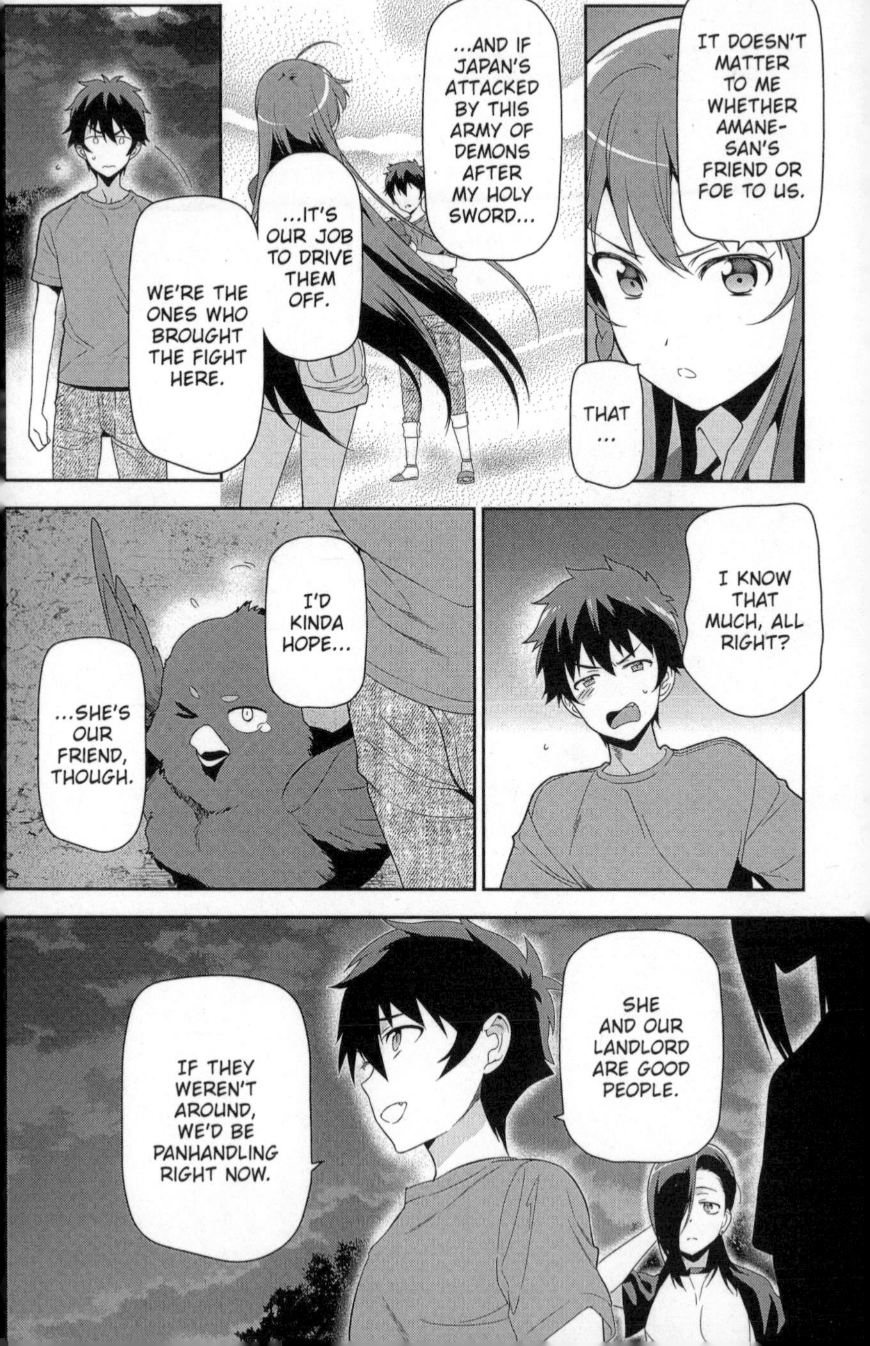
IT DOESN'T MATTER TO ME WHETHER AMANE-SAN'S FRIEND OR FOE TO US.
THAT...
...AND IF JAPAN'S ATTACKED BY THIS ARMY OF DEMONS AFTER MY HOLY SWORD...
...IT'S OUR JOB TO DRIVE THEM OFF.
WE'RE THE ONES WHO BROUGHT THE FIGHT HERE.
I KNOW THAT MUCH, ALL RIGHT?
I'D KINDA HOPE...
...SHE'S OUR FRIEND, THOUGH.
SHE AND OUR LANDLORD ARE GOOD PEOPLE.
IF THEY WEREN'T AROUND, WE'D BE PANHANDLING RIGHT NOW.

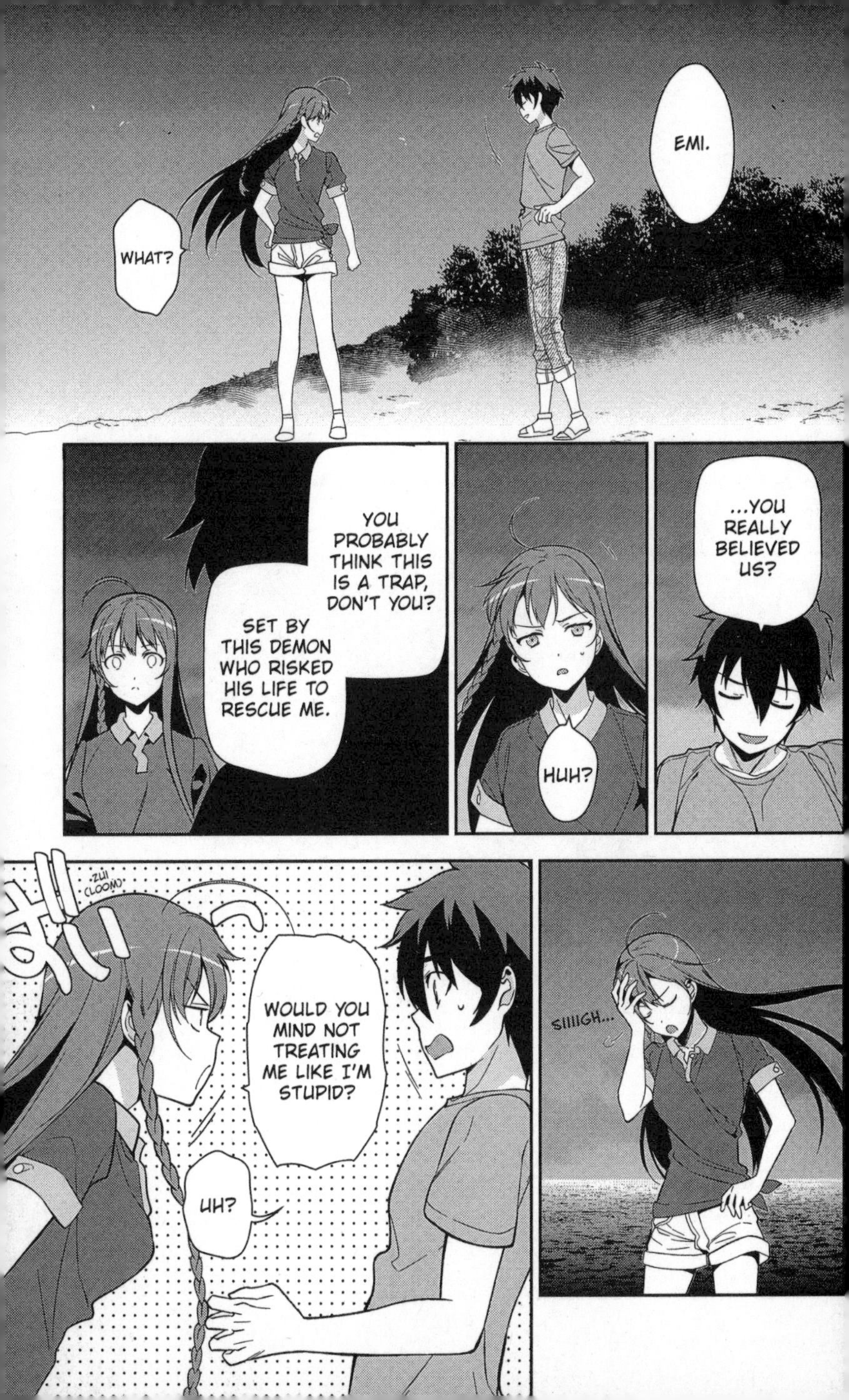
EMI.
WHAT?
...YOU REALLY BELIEVED US?
HUH?
YOU PROBABLY THINK THIS IS A TRAP, DON'T YOU?
SET BY THIS DEMON WHO RISKED HIS LIFE TO RESCUE ME.
SIIIGH...
ZUI (LOOM)
WOULD YOU MIND NOT TREATING ME LIKE I'M STUPID?
UH?

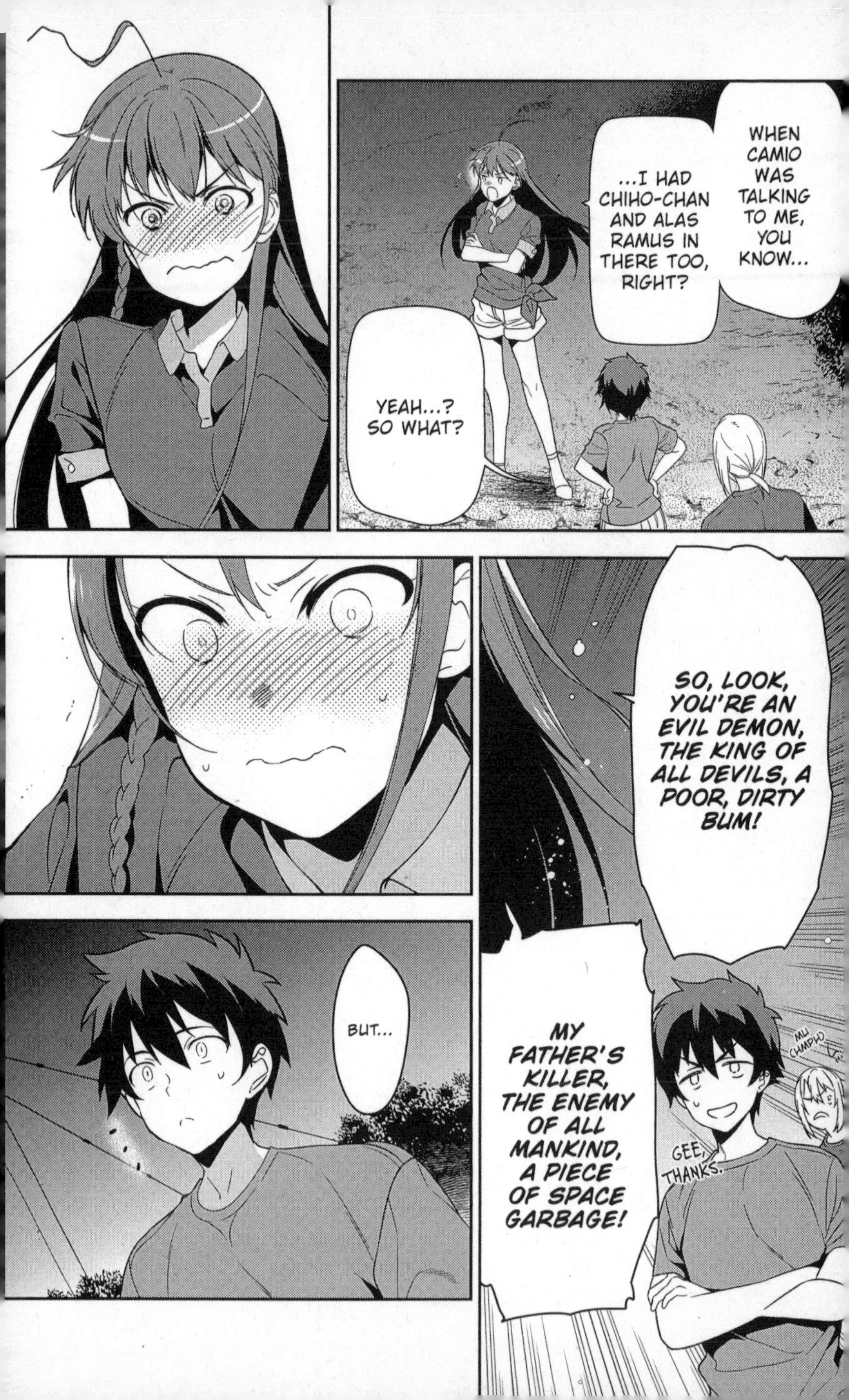
WHEN CAMIO WAS TALKING TO ME, YOU KNOW...
...I HAD CHIHO-CHAN AND ALAS RAMUS IN THERE TOO, RIGHT?
YEAH...? SO WHAT?
SO, LOOK, YOU'RE AN EVIL DEMON, THE KING OF ALL DEVILS, A POOR, DIRTY BUM!
MY FATHER'S KILLER, THE ENEMY OF ALL MANKIND, A PIECE OF SPACE GARBAGE!
MU CHMPH
GEE, THANKS.
BUT...

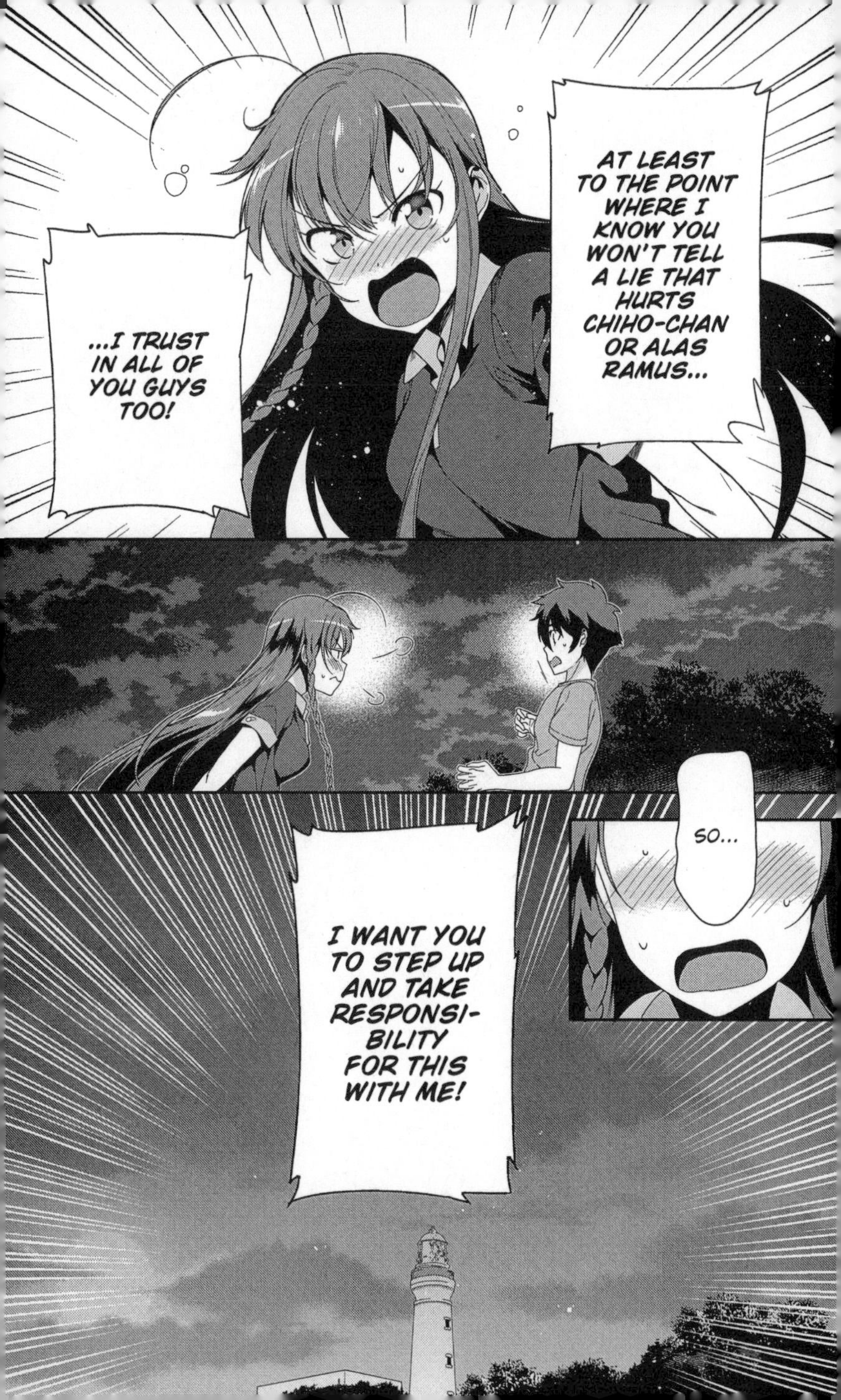
AT LEAST TO THE POINT WHERE I KNOW YOU WON'T TELL A LIE THAT HURTS CHIHO-CHAN OR ALAS RAMUS...
...I TRUST IN ALL OF YOU GUYS TOO!
SO...
I WANT YOU TO STEP UP AND TAKE RESPONSI-BILITY FOR THIS WITH ME!

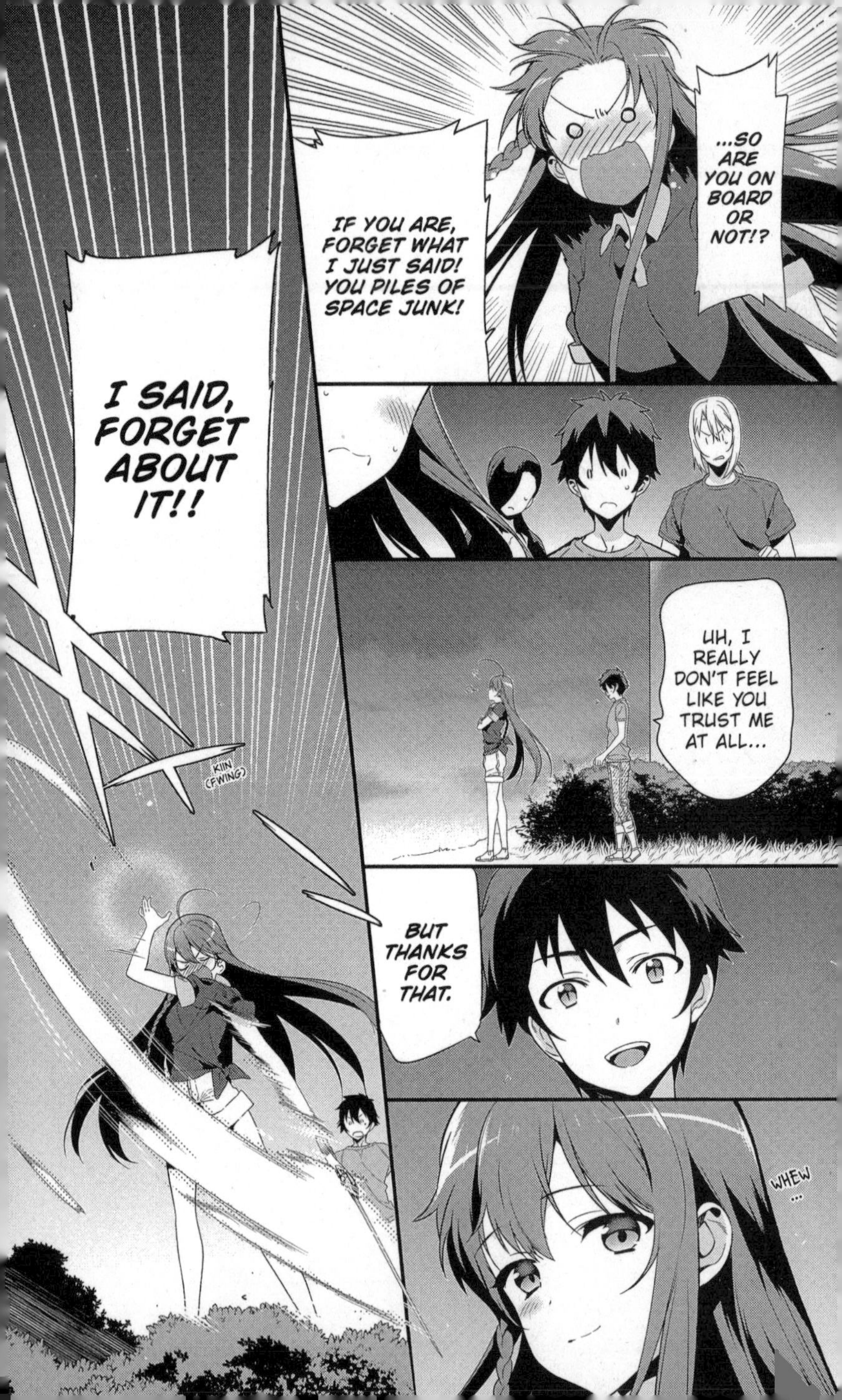
...SO ARE YOU ON BOARD OR NOT!?
IF YOU ARE, FORGET WHAT I JUST SAID! YOU PILES OF SPACE JUNK!
UH, I REALLY DON'T FEEL LIKE YOU TRUST ME AT ALL...
BUT THANKS FOR THAT.
WHEW ...
I SAID, FORGET ABOUT IT!!
KIIN (FWING)

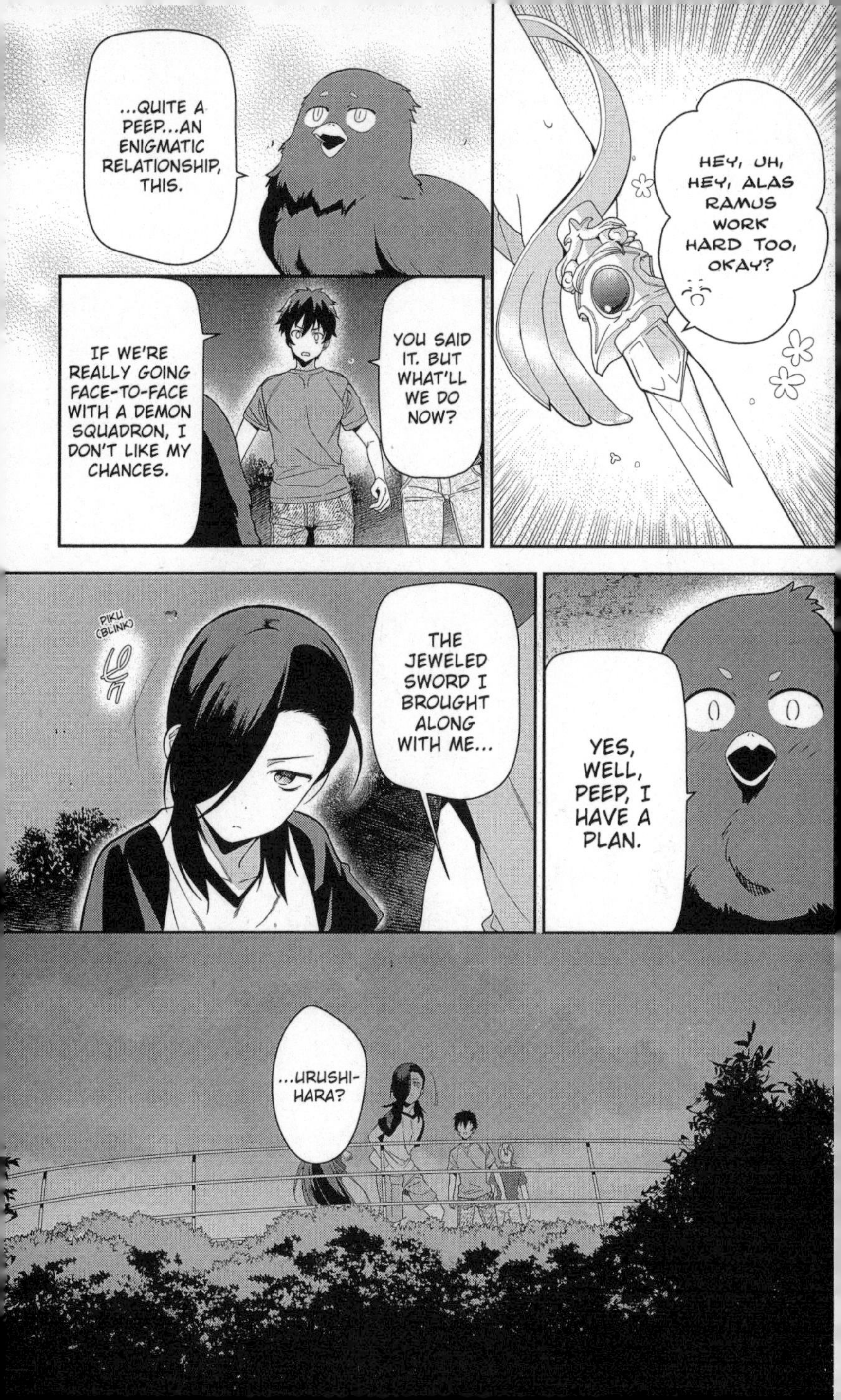
HEY, UH, HEY, ALAS RAMUS WORK HARD TOO, OKAY?
...QUITE A PEEP...AN ENIGMATIC RELATIONSHIP, THIS.
YOU SAID IT. BUT WHAT'LL WE DO NOW?
IF WE'RE REALLY GOING FACE-TO-FACE WITH A DEMON SQUADRON, I DON'T LIKE MY CHANCES.
YES, WELL, PEEP, I HAVE A PLAN.
THE JEWELED SWORD I BROUGHT ALONG WITH ME...
PIKU (BLINK)
...URUSHI-HARA?

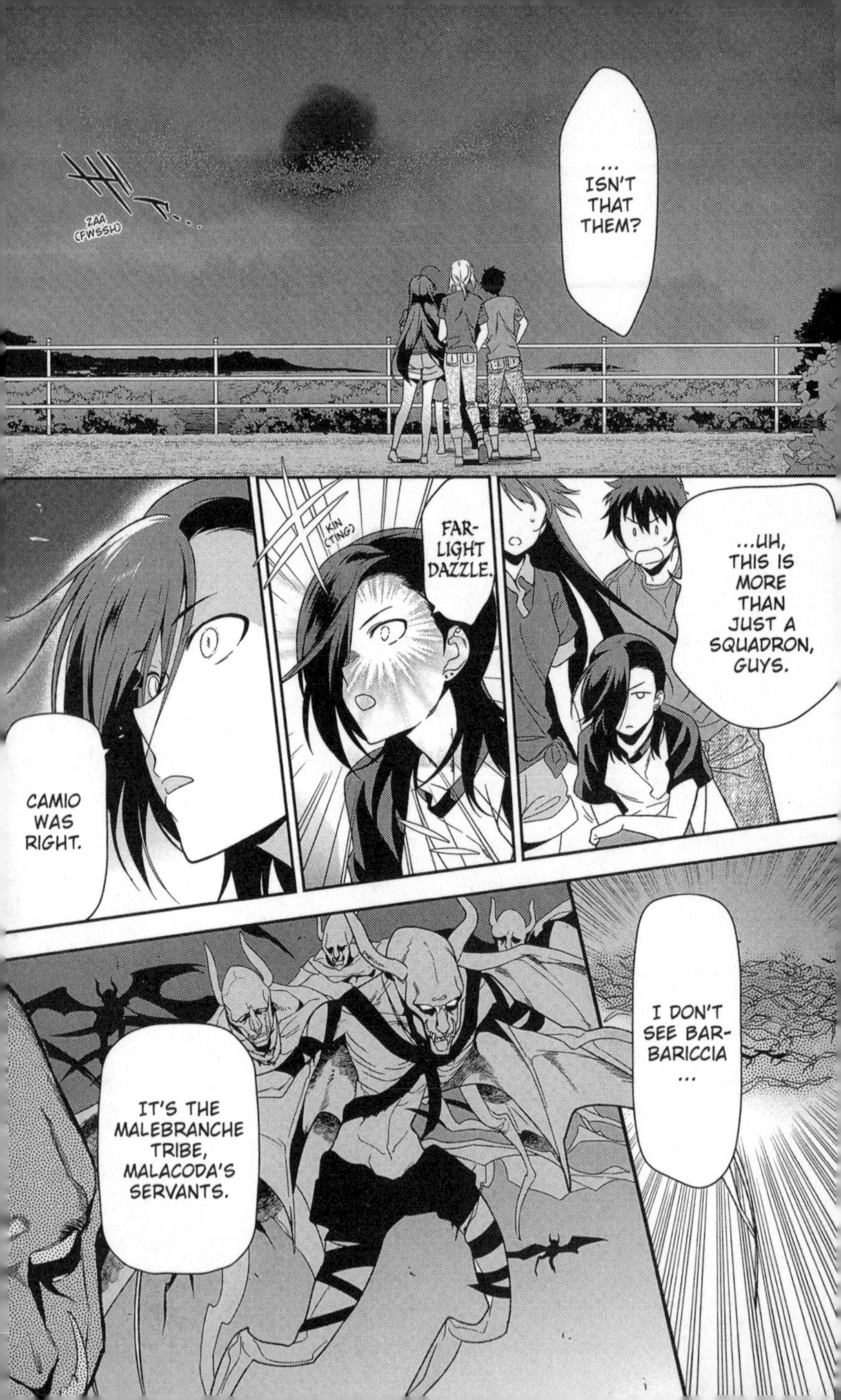
...ISN'T THAT THEM?
ZAA (FWSSH)
...UH, THIS IS MORE THAN JUST A SQUADRON, GUYS.
FAR-LIGHT DAZZLE.
KIN (TING)
CAMIO WAS RIGHT.
I DON'T SEE BAR-BARICCIA...
IT'S THE MALEBRANCHE TRIBE, MALACODA'S SERVANTS.

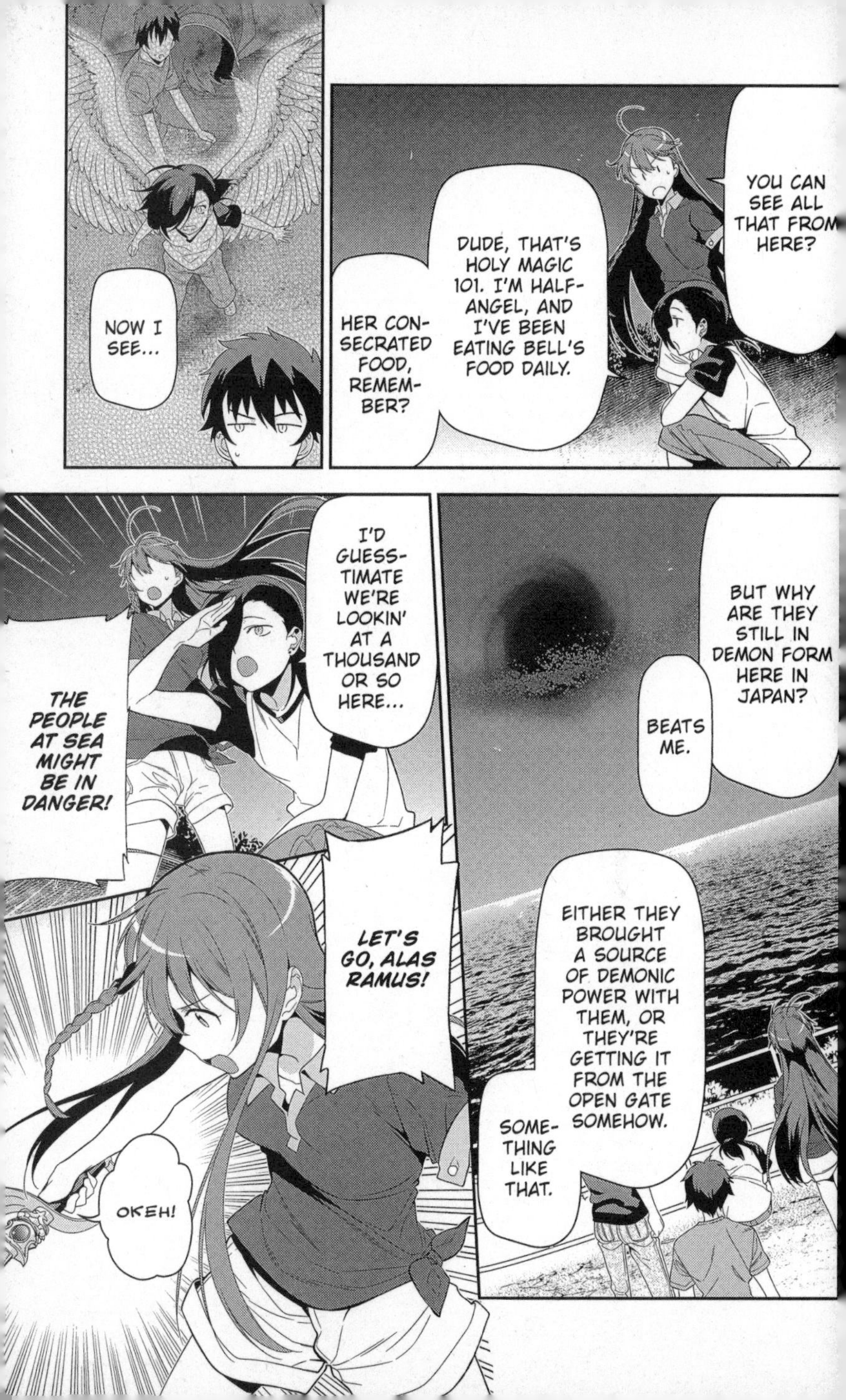
YOU CAN SEE ALL THAT FROM HERE?
DUDE, THAT'S HOLY MAGIC 101. I'M HALF-ANGEL, AND I'VE BEEN EATING BELL'S FOOD DAILY.
HER CONSECRATED FOOD, REMEMBER?
NOW I SEE...
BUT WHY ARE THEY STILL IN DEMON FORM HERE IN JAPAN?
BEATS ME.
EITHER THEY BROUGHT A SOURCE OF DEMONIC POWER WITH THEM, OR THEY'RE GETTING IT FROM THE OPEN GATE SOMEHOW.
SOMETHING LIKE THAT.
I'D GUESSTIMATE WE'RE LOOKIN' AT A THOUSAND OR SO HERE...
THE PEOPLE AT SEA MIGHT BE IN DANGER!
LET'S GO, ALAS RAMUS!
OKEH!

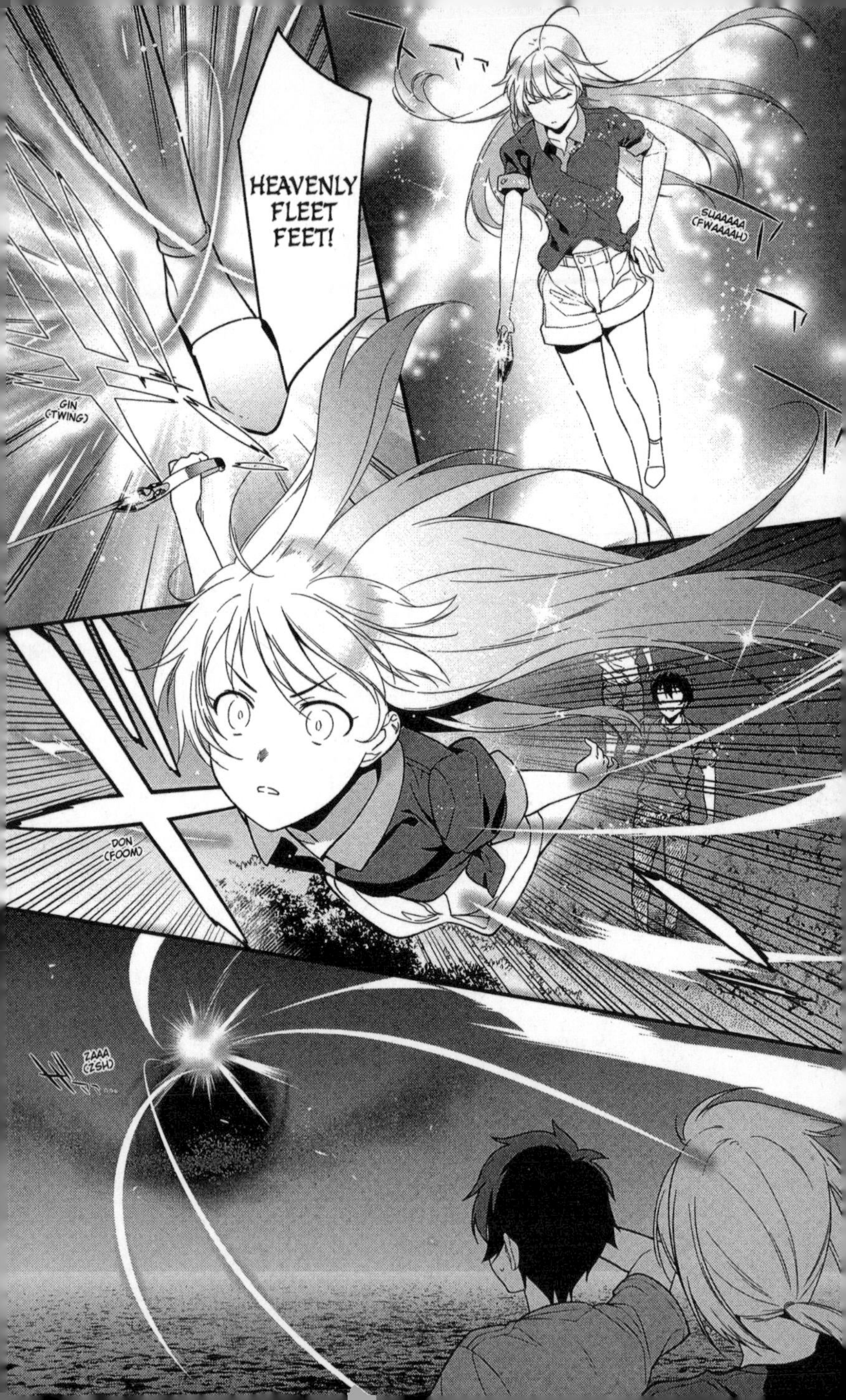
SUAAAAA (FWAAAAH)
HEAVENLY FLEET FEET!
GIN (TWING)
DON (FOOM)
ZAAA (ZSH)

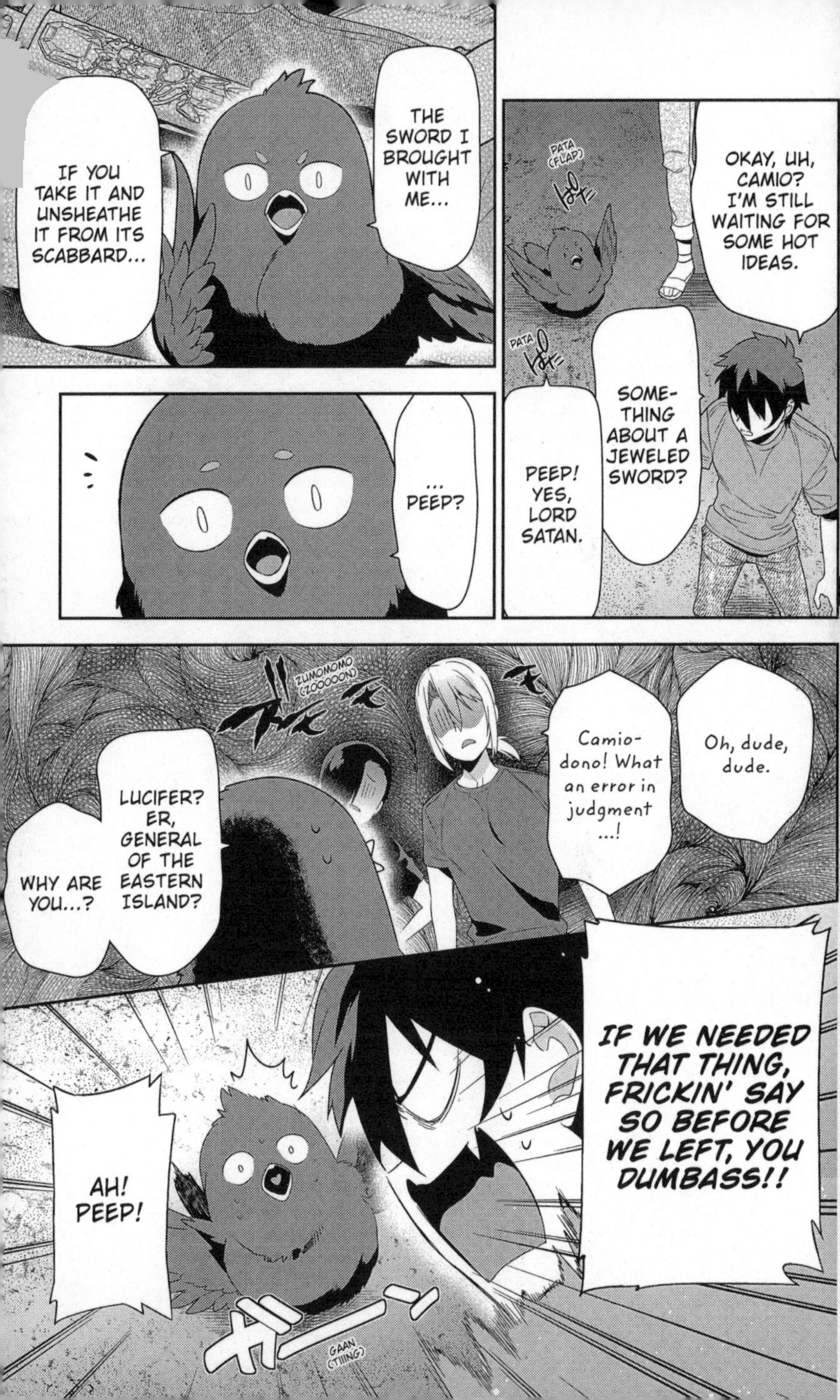

OKAY, UH, CAMIO? I'M STILL WAITING FOR SOME HOT IDEAS.
PATA (FLAP)
PATA
SOME-THING ABOUT A JEWELED SWORD?
PEEP! YES, LORD SATAN.
THE SWORD I BROUGHT WITH ME...
IF YOU TAKE IT AND UNSHEATHE IT FROM ITS SCABBARD...
... PEEP?
Oh, dude, dude.
Camio-dono! What an error in judgment ...!
ZUMOMOMO (ZOOOOON)
LUCIFER? ER, GENERAL OF THE EASTERN ISLAND?
WHY ARE YOU...?
IF WE NEEDED THAT THING, FRICKIN' SAY SO BEFORE WE LEFT, YOU DUMBASS!!
AH! PEEP!
GAAN (TIIING)

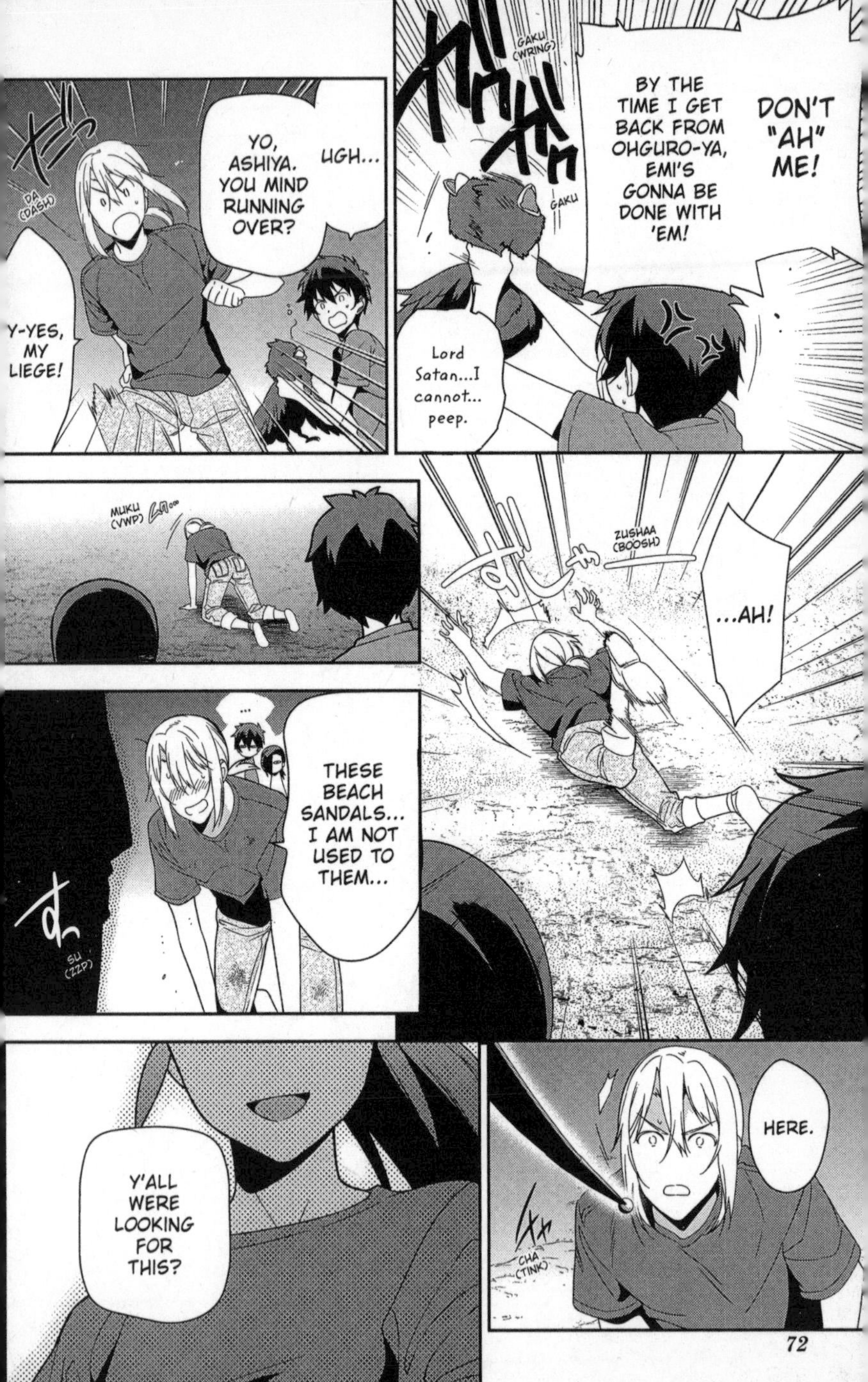
DON'T "AH" ME!
BY THE TIME I GET BACK FROM OHGURO-YA, EMI'S GONNA BE DONE WITH 'EM!
GAKU (WRING)
GAKU
Lord Satan...I cannot... peep.
UGH...
YO, ASHIYA. YOU MIND RUNNING OVER?
DA (DASH)
Y-YES, MY LIEGE!
...AH!
ZUSHAA (BOOSH)
MUKU (VWP)
...
THESE BEACH SANDALS... I AM NOT USED TO THEM...
SU (ZZP)
HERE.
CHA (TINK)
Y'ALL WERE LOOKING FOR THIS?

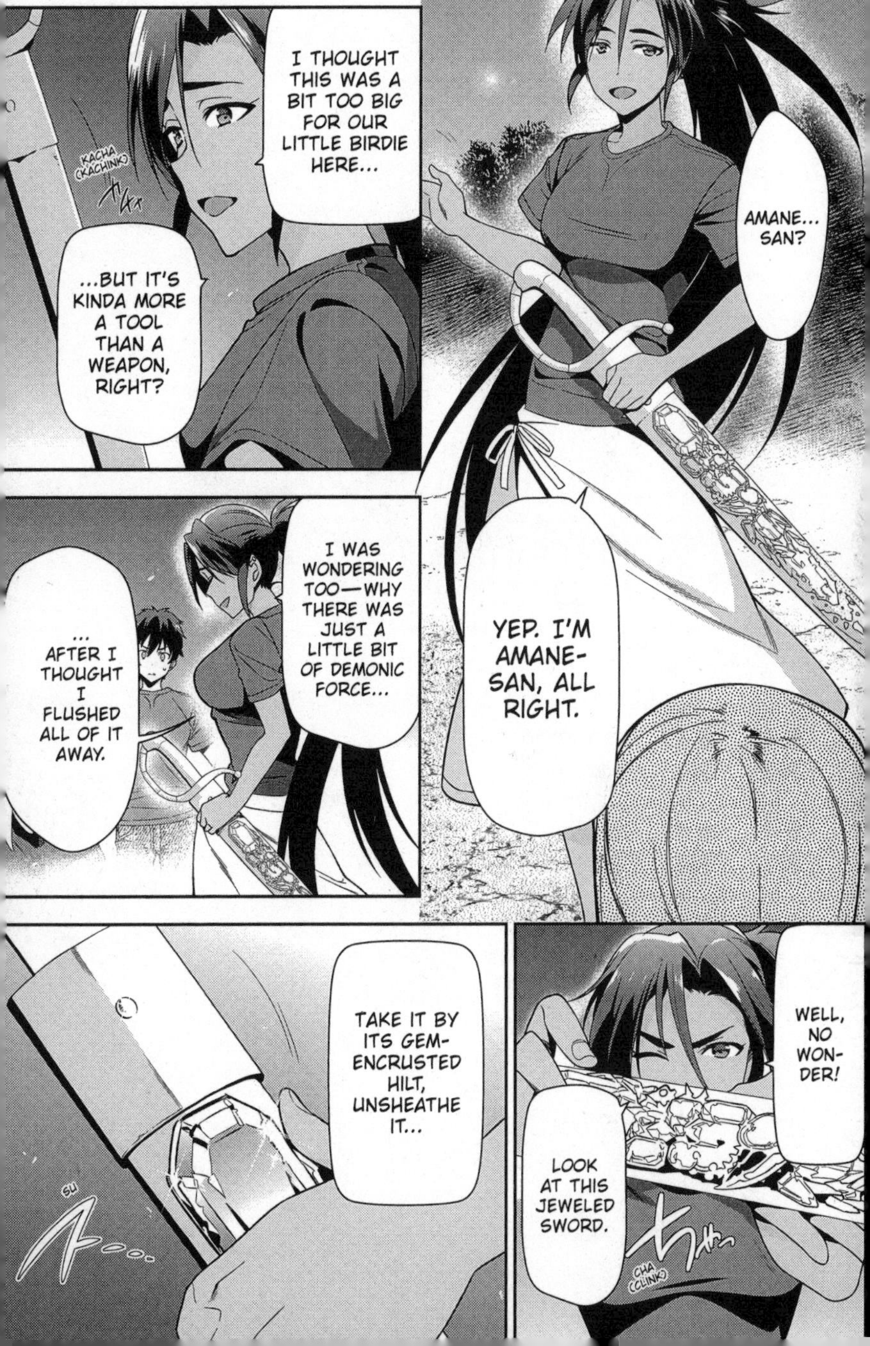
AMANE... SAN?
YEP. I'M AMANE-SAN, ALL RIGHT.
I THOUGHT THIS WAS A BIT TOO BIG FOR OUR LITTLE BIRDIE HERE...
KACHA (KACHINK)
...BUT IT'S KINDA MORE A TOOL THAN A WEAPON, RIGHT?
I WAS WONDERING TOO—WHY THERE WAS JUST A LITTLE BIT OF DEMONIC FORCE...
...AFTER I THOUGHT I FLUSHED ALL OF IT AWAY.
WELL, NO WON-DER!
LOOK AT THIS JEWELED SWORD.
CHA (CLINK)
TAKE IT BY ITS GEM-ENCRUSTED HILT, UNSHEATHE IT...
SU

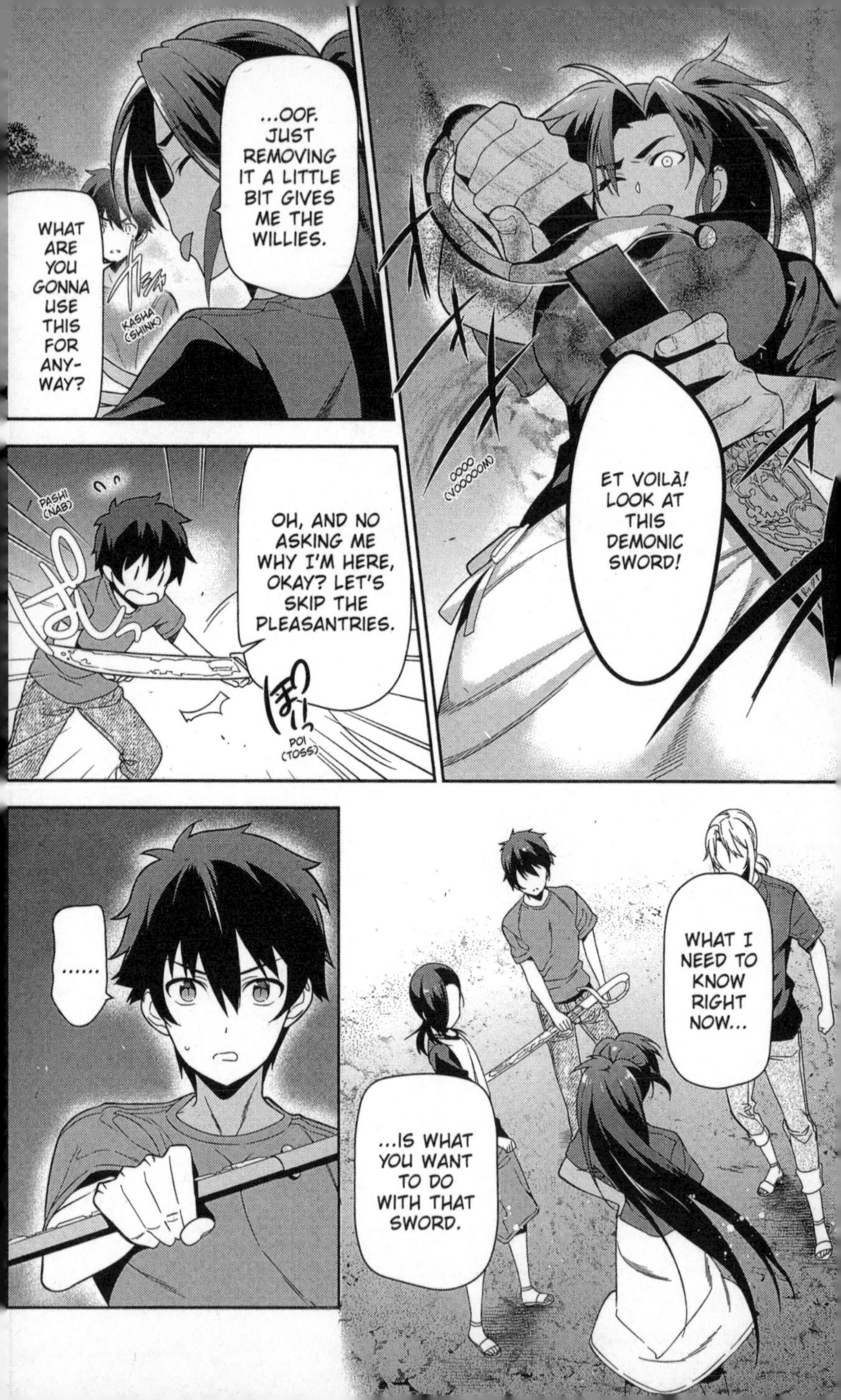ET VOILÀ! LOOK AT THIS DEMONIC SWORD!
OOOO (VOOOOOM)
...OOF. JUST REMOVING IT A LITTLE BIT GIVES ME THE WILLIES.
KASHA (SHINK)
WHAT ARE YOU GONNA USE THIS FOR ANY-WAY?
OH, AND NO ASKING ME WHY I'M HERE, OKAY? LET'S SKIP THE PLEASANTRIES.
POI (TOSS)
PASHI (NAB)
WHAT I NEED TO KNOW RIGHT NOW...
...IS WHAT YOU WANT TO DO WITH THAT SWORD.
......

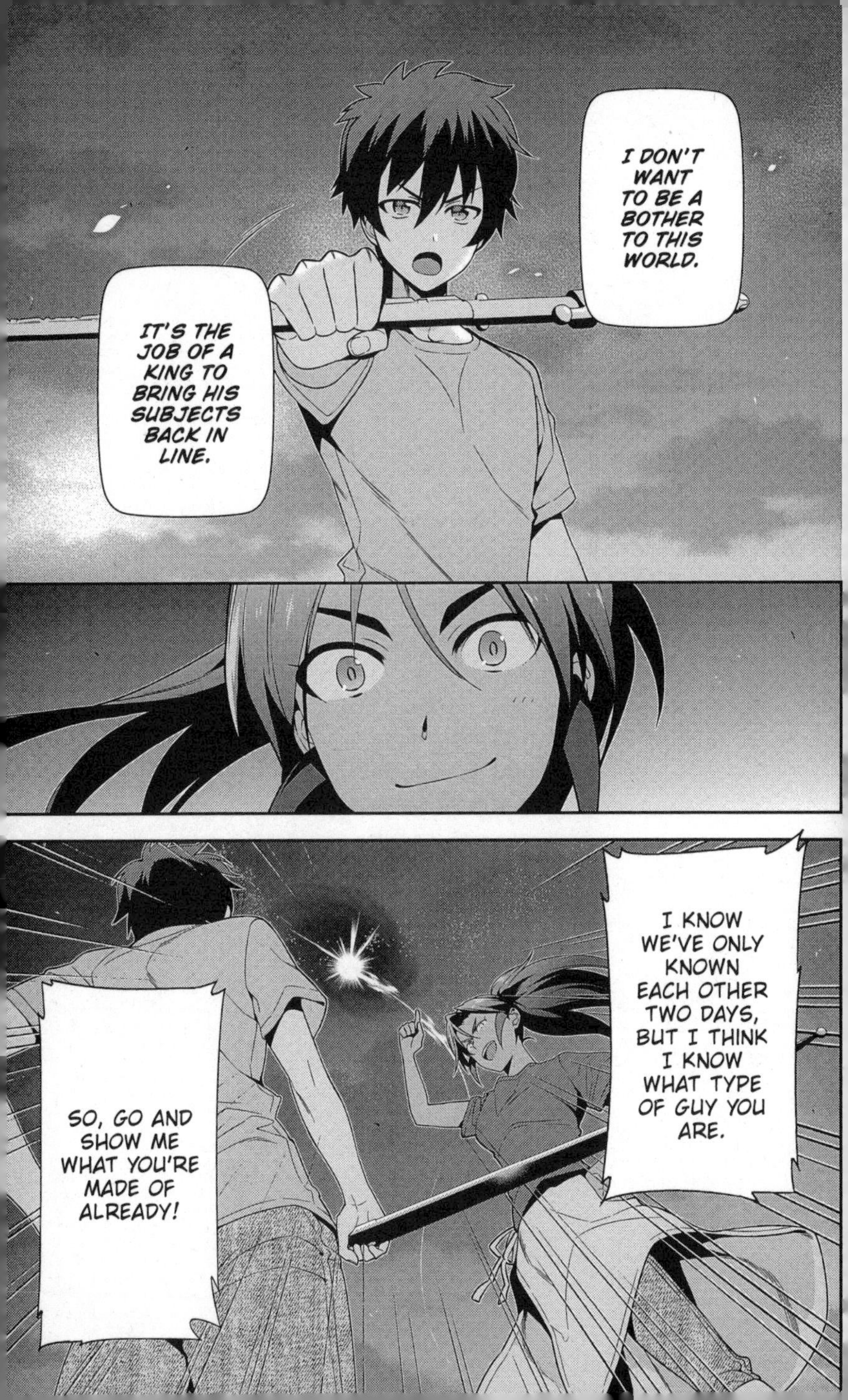
I DON'T WANT TO BE A BOTHER TO THIS WORLD.
IT'S THE JOB OF A KING TO BRING HIS SUBJECTS BACK IN LINE.
I KNOW WE'VE ONLY KNOWN EACH OTHER TWO DAYS, BUT I THINK I KNOW WHAT TYPE OF GUY YOU ARE.
SO, GO AND SHOW ME WHAT YOU'RE MADE OF ALREADY!

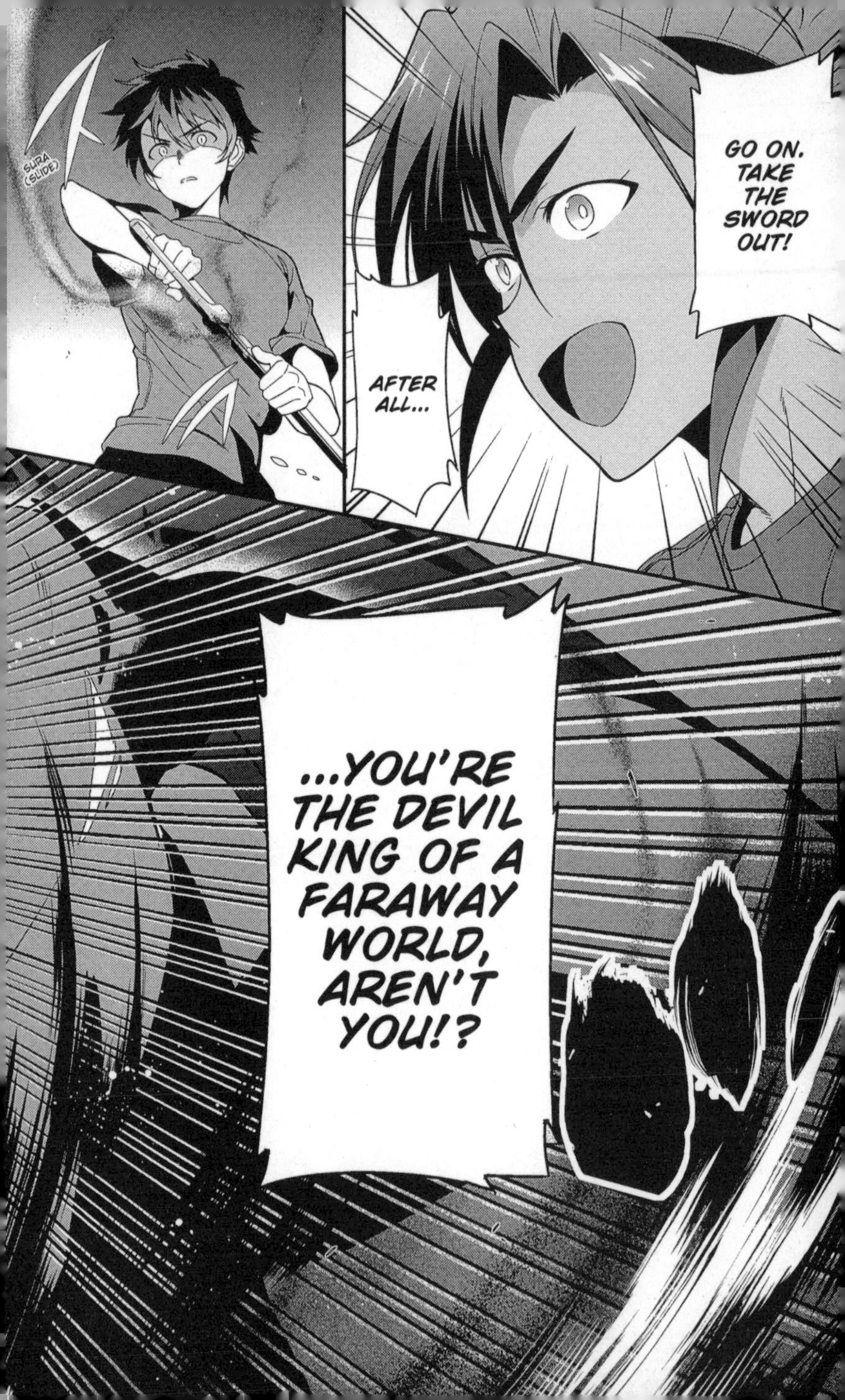
GO ON. TAKE THE SWORD OUT!
AFTER ALL...
SUPA (SLIDE)
...YOU'RE THE DEVIL KING OF A FARAWAY WORLD, AREN'T YOU!?

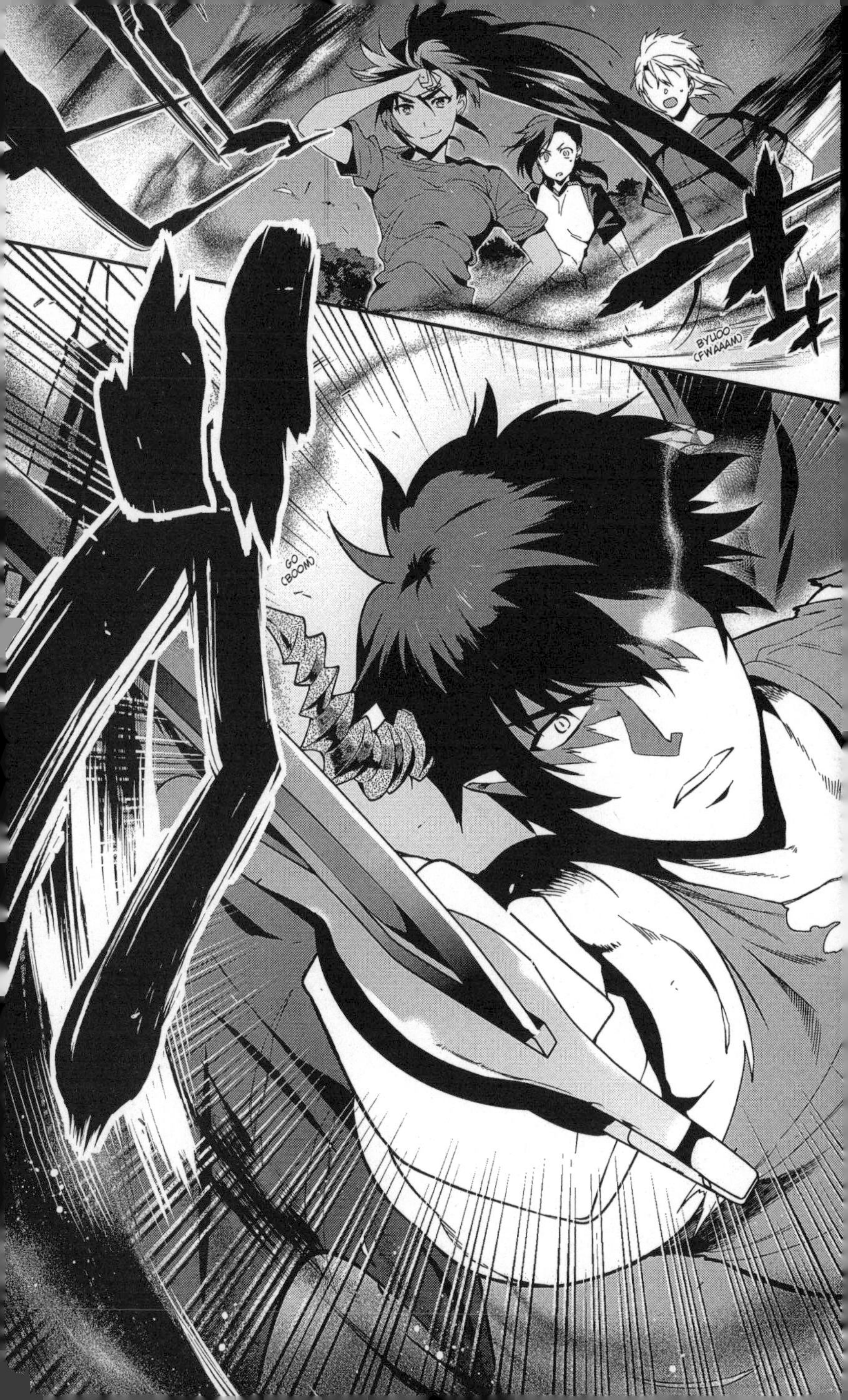
BYUOO (FWAAAM)
GO (BOOM)

THE DEVIL IS A PART-TIMER!

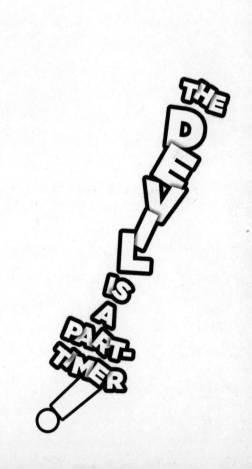

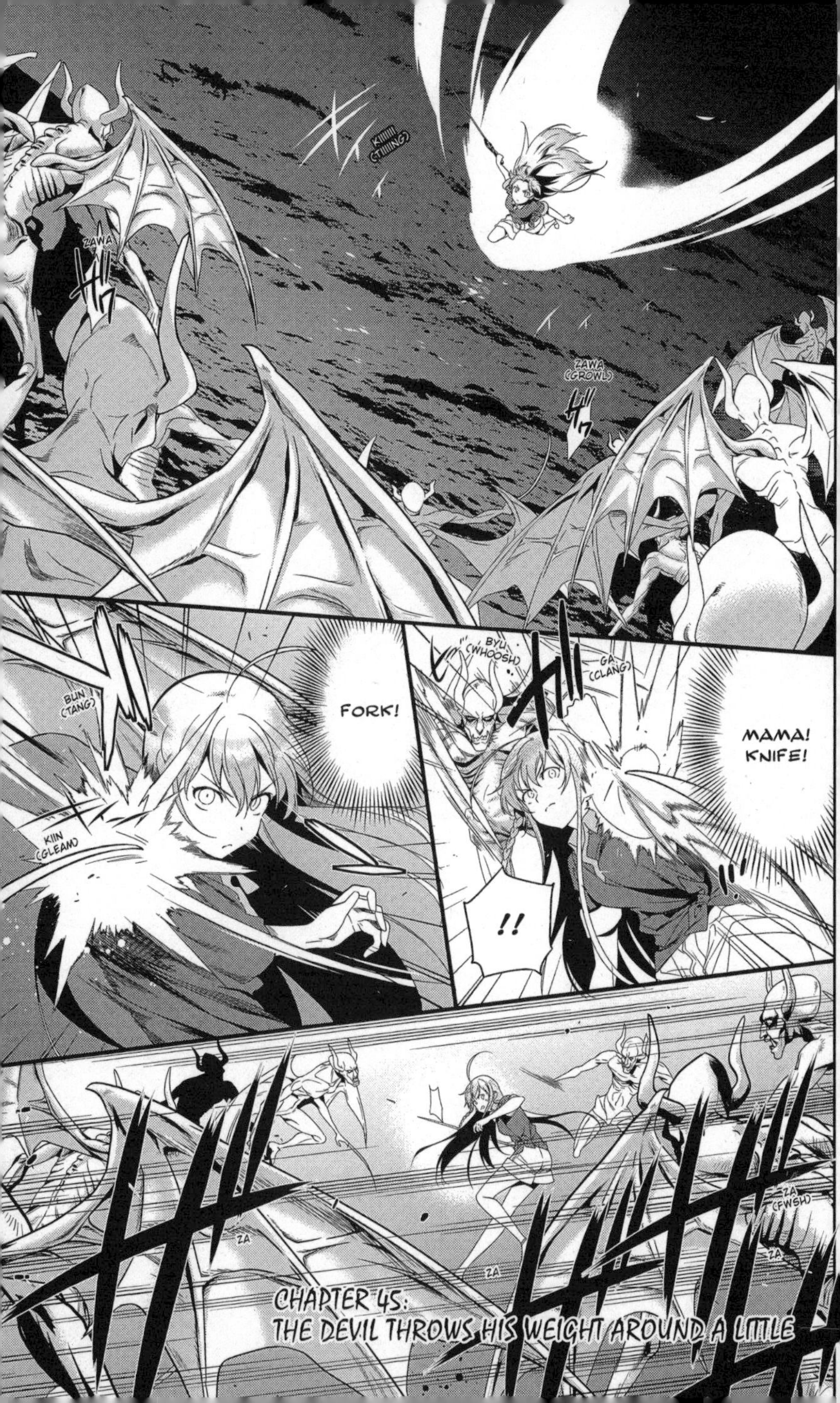
KIIIIIN (TIIIING)
ZAWA
ZAWA (GROWL)
BYU (WHOOSH)
GA (CLANG)
MAMA! KNIFE!
!!
FORK!
BUN (TANG)
KIIN (GLEAM)
ZA (FWSH)
ZA
ZA
ZA
CHAPTER 45:
THE DEVIL THROWS HIS WEIGHT AROUND A LITTLE

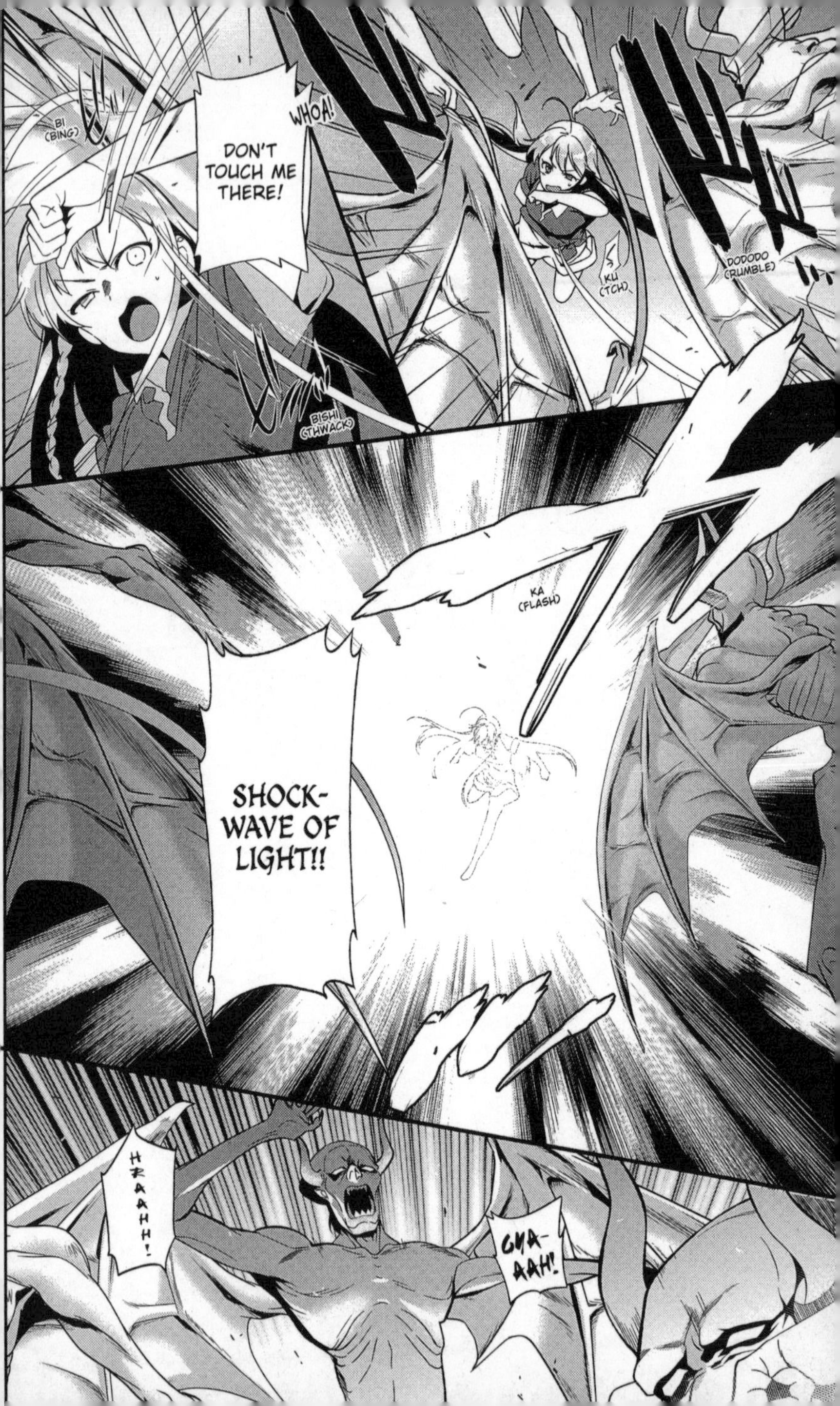
DODODO (RUMBLE)
KU (TCH)
WHOA!
DON'T TOUCH ME THERE!
BI (BING)
BISHI (THWACK)
KA (FLASH)
SHOCK-WAVE OF LIGHT!!
GYA-AAH!
HRAAAHH!

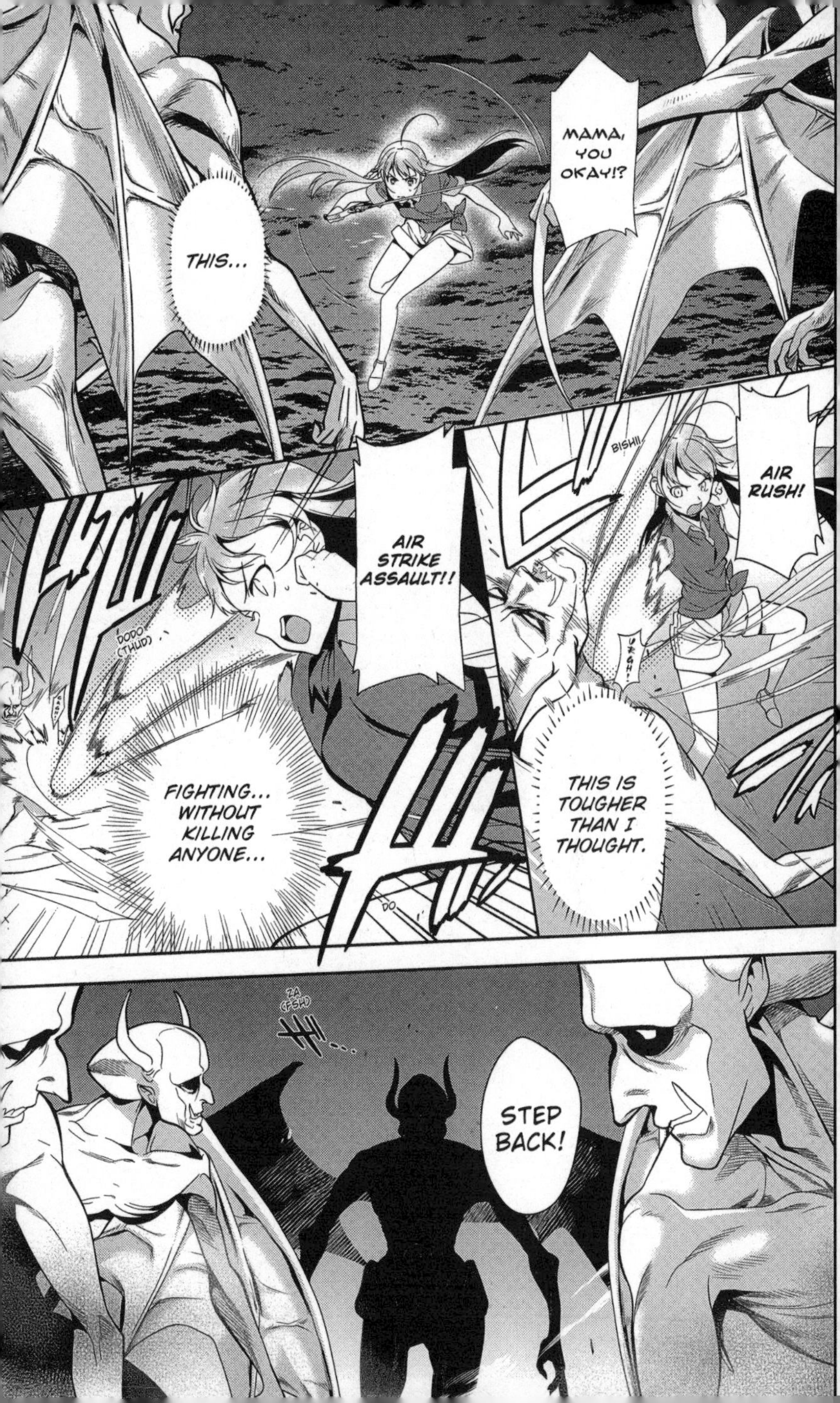
MAMA, YOU OKAY!?
THIS...
BISHI!
AIR RUSH!
URGH!
THIS IS TOUGHER THAN I THOUGHT.
DO
AIR STRIKE ASSAULT!!
DODO (THUD)
FIGHTING... WITHOUT KILLING ANYONE...
STEP BACK!
ZA (FSSH)

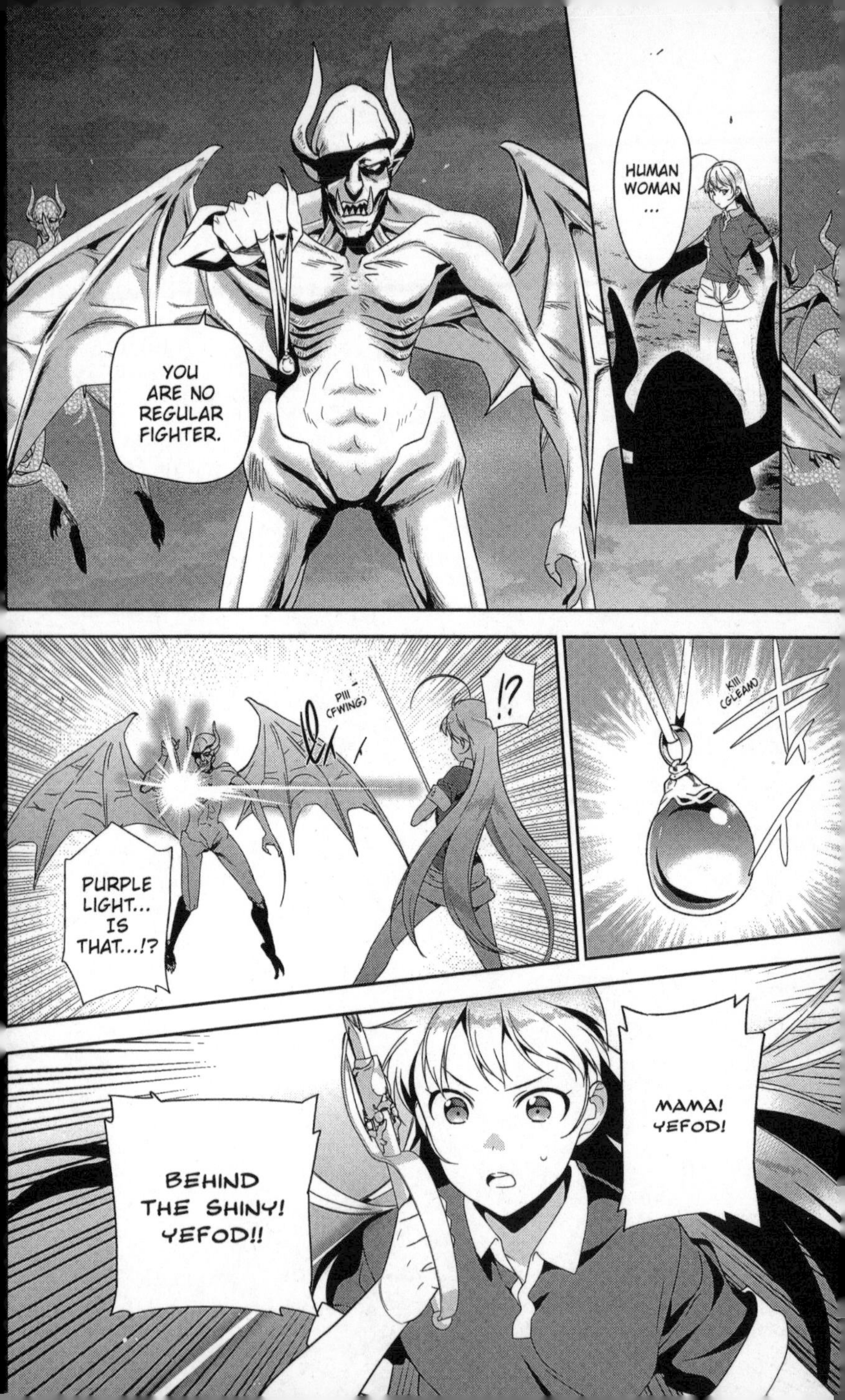
HUMAN WOMAN ...
YOU ARE NO REGULAR FIGHTER.
KIII (GLEAM)
!?
PIII (FWING)
PURPLE LIGHT... IS THAT...!?
MAMA! YEFOD!
BEHIND THE SHINY! YEFOD!!

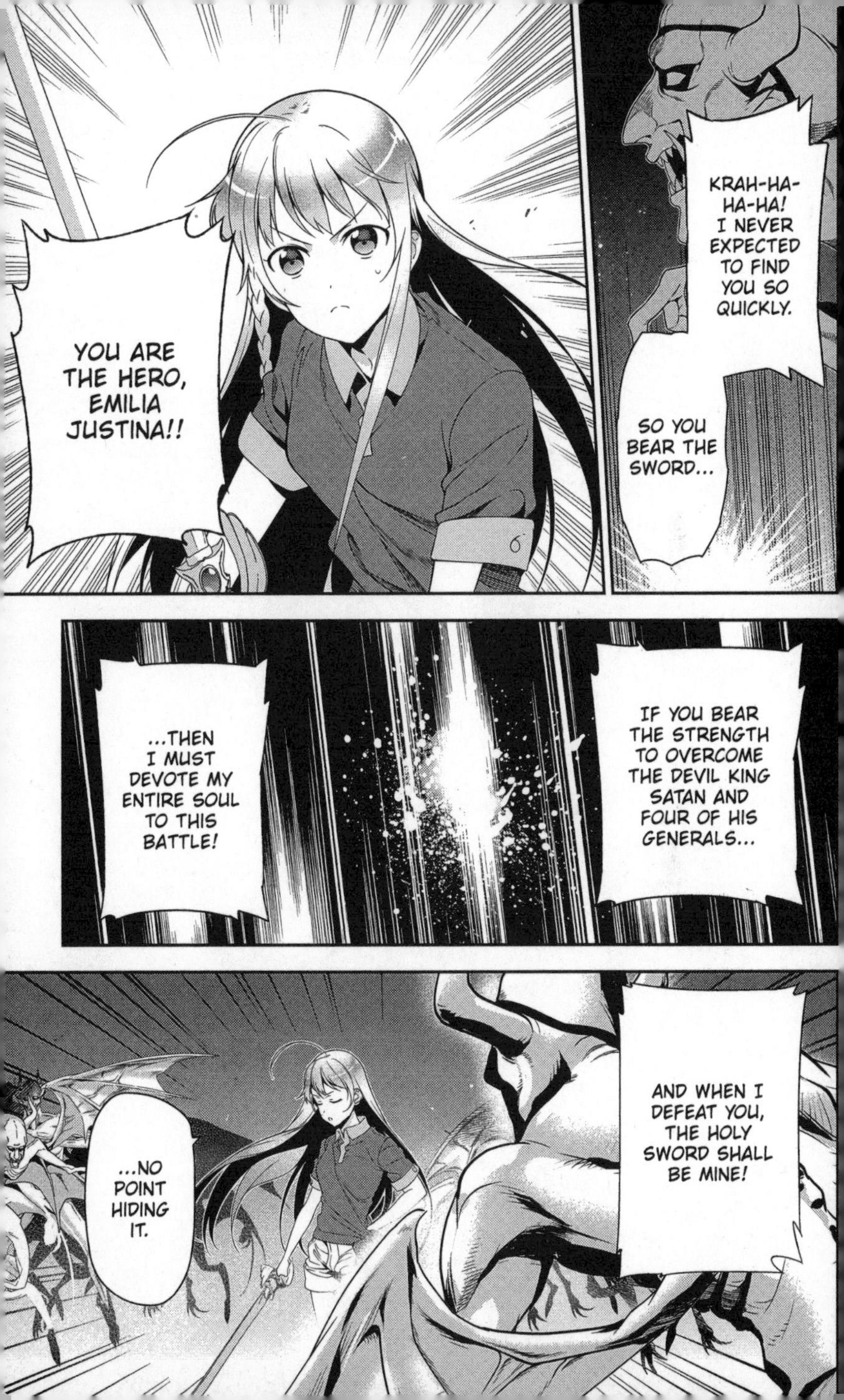
KRAH-HA-HA-HA! I NEVER EXPECTED TO FIND YOU SO QUICKLY.
SO YOU BEAR THE SWORD...
YOU ARE THE HERO, EMILIA JUSTINA!!
IF YOU BEAR THE STRENGTH TO OVERCOME THE DEVIL KING SATAN AND FOUR OF HIS GENERALS...
...THEN I MUST DEVOTE MY ENTIRE SOUL TO THIS BATTLE!
AND WHEN I DEFEAT YOU, THE HOLY SWORD SHALL BE MINE!
...NO POINT HIDING IT.

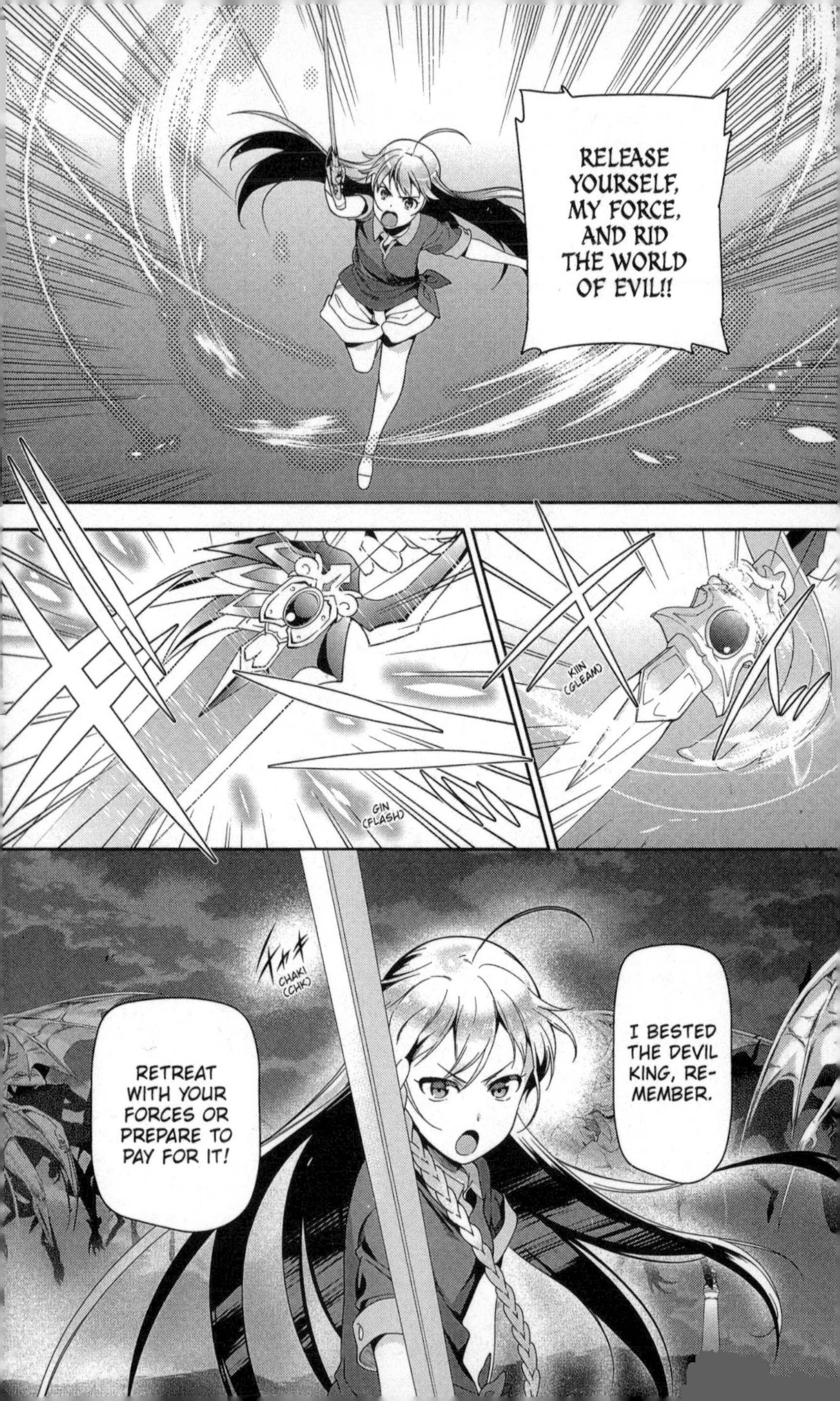
RELEASE YOURSELF, MY FORCE, AND RID THE WORLD OF EVIL!!
KIIN (GLEAM)
GIN (FLASH)
I BESTED THE DEVIL KING, RE-MEMBER.
CHAKI (CHK)
RETREAT WITH YOUR FORCES OR PREPARE TO PAY FOR IT!

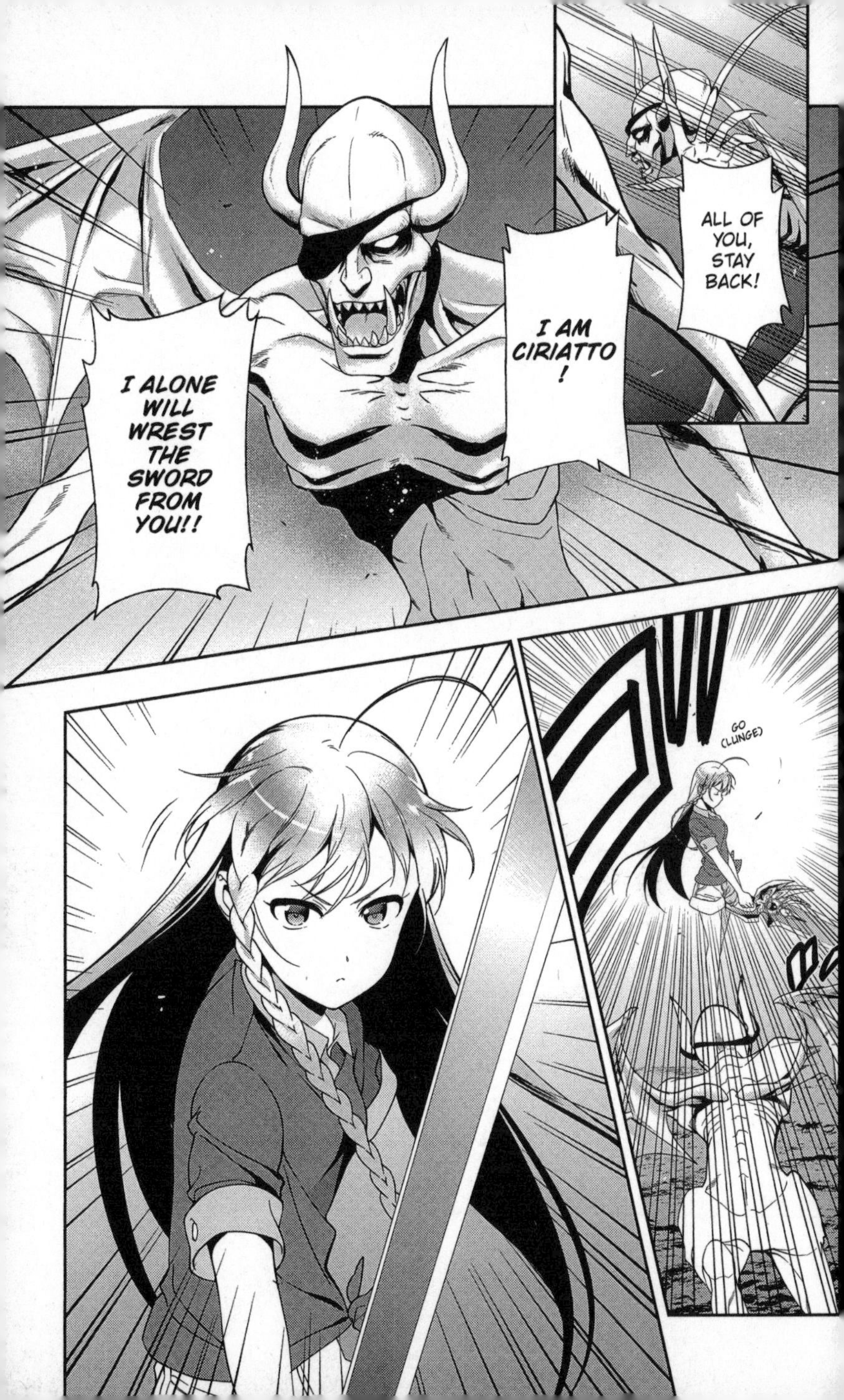
ALL OF YOU, STAY BACK!
I AM CIRIATTO!
I ALONE WILL WREST THE SWORD FROM YOU!!
GO (LUNGE)

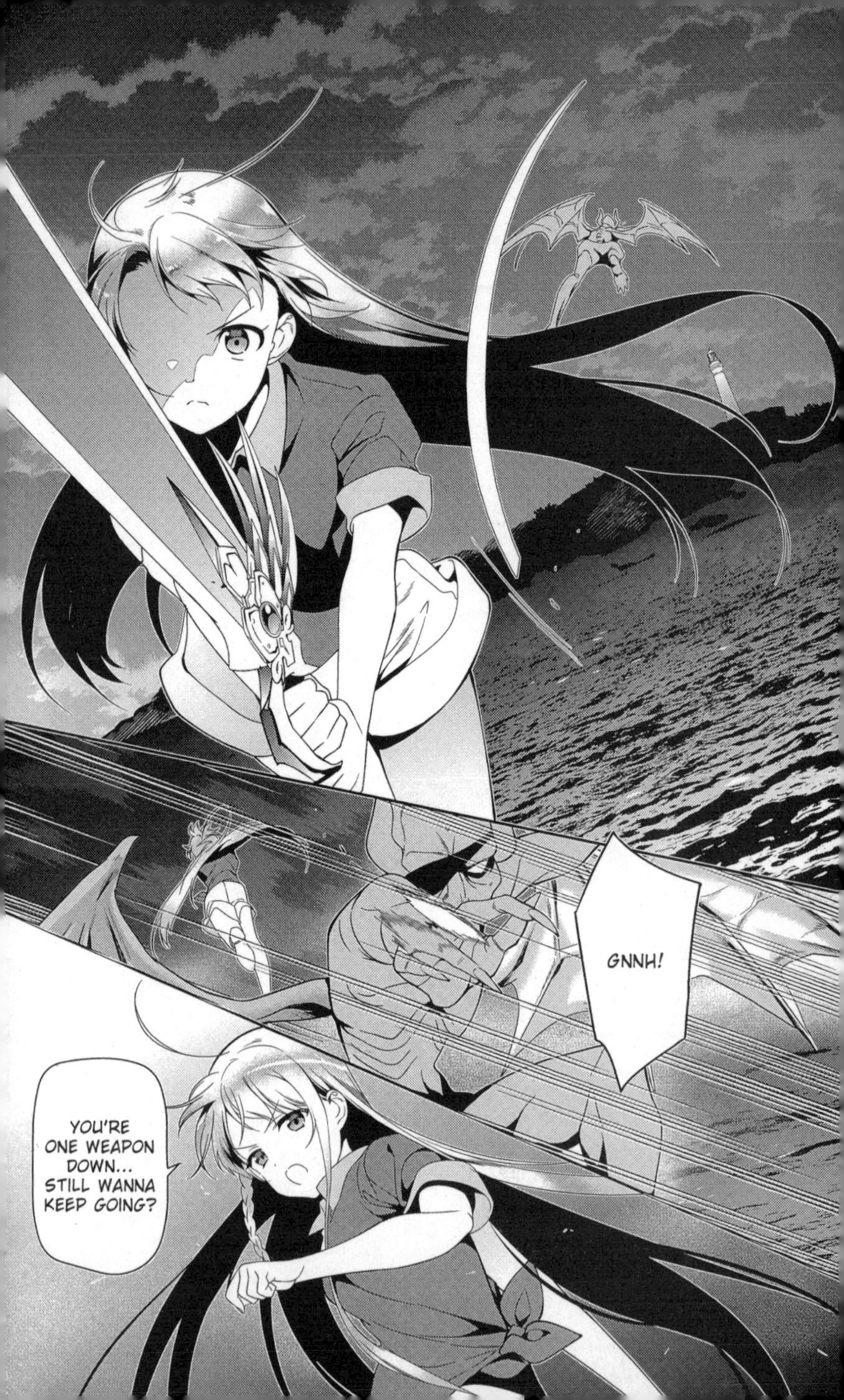
GNNH!
YOU'RE ONE WEAPON DOWN... STILL WANNA KEEP GOING?

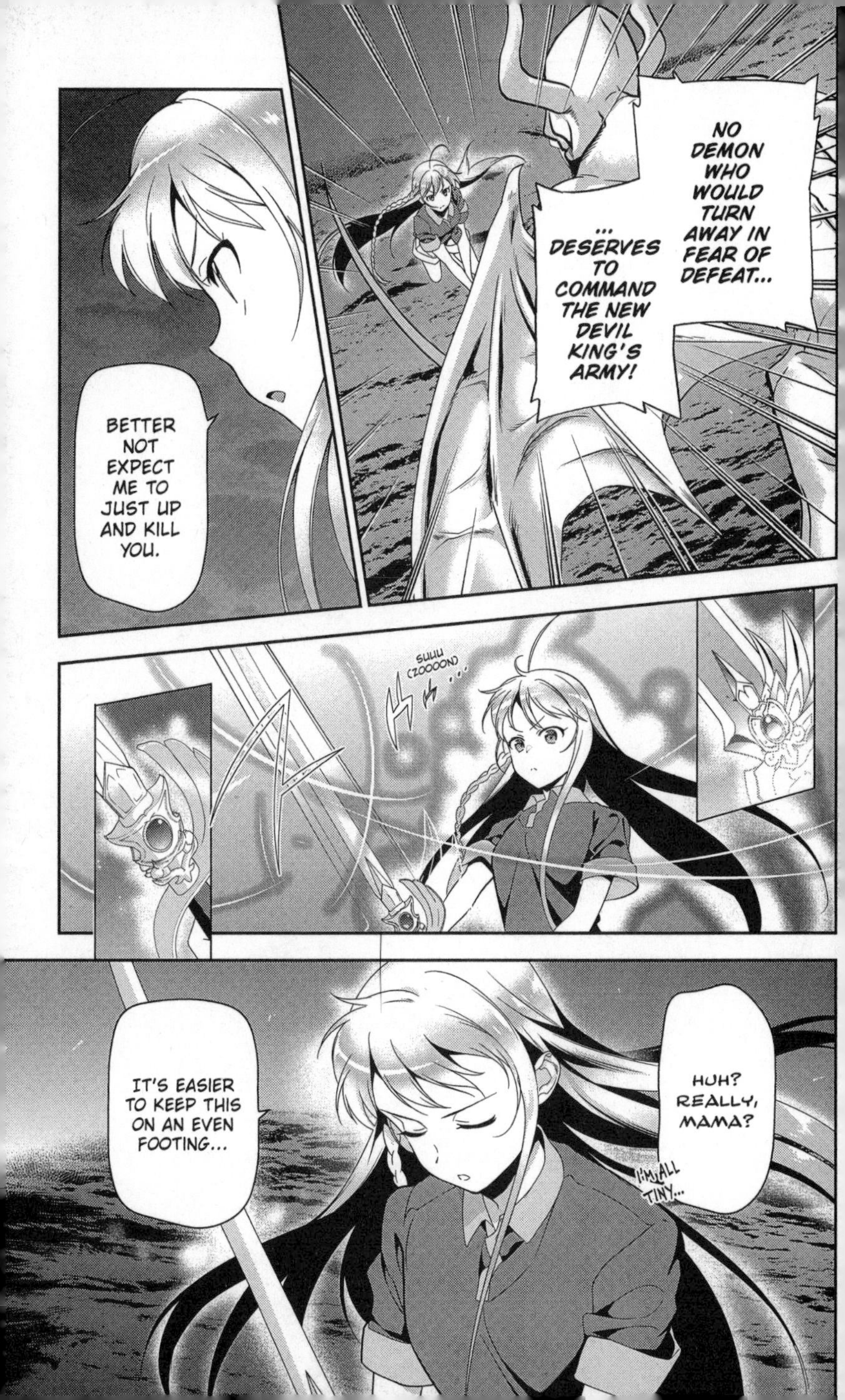
NO DEMON WHO WOULD TURN AWAY IN FEAR OF DEFEAT...
...DESERVES TO COMMAND THE NEW DEVIL KING'S ARMY!
BETTER NOT EXPECT ME TO JUST UP AND KILL YOU.
SUUU (ZOOOON)...
HUH? REALLY, MAMA?
I'M ALL TINY...
IT'S EASIER TO KEEP THIS ON AN EVEN FOOTING...

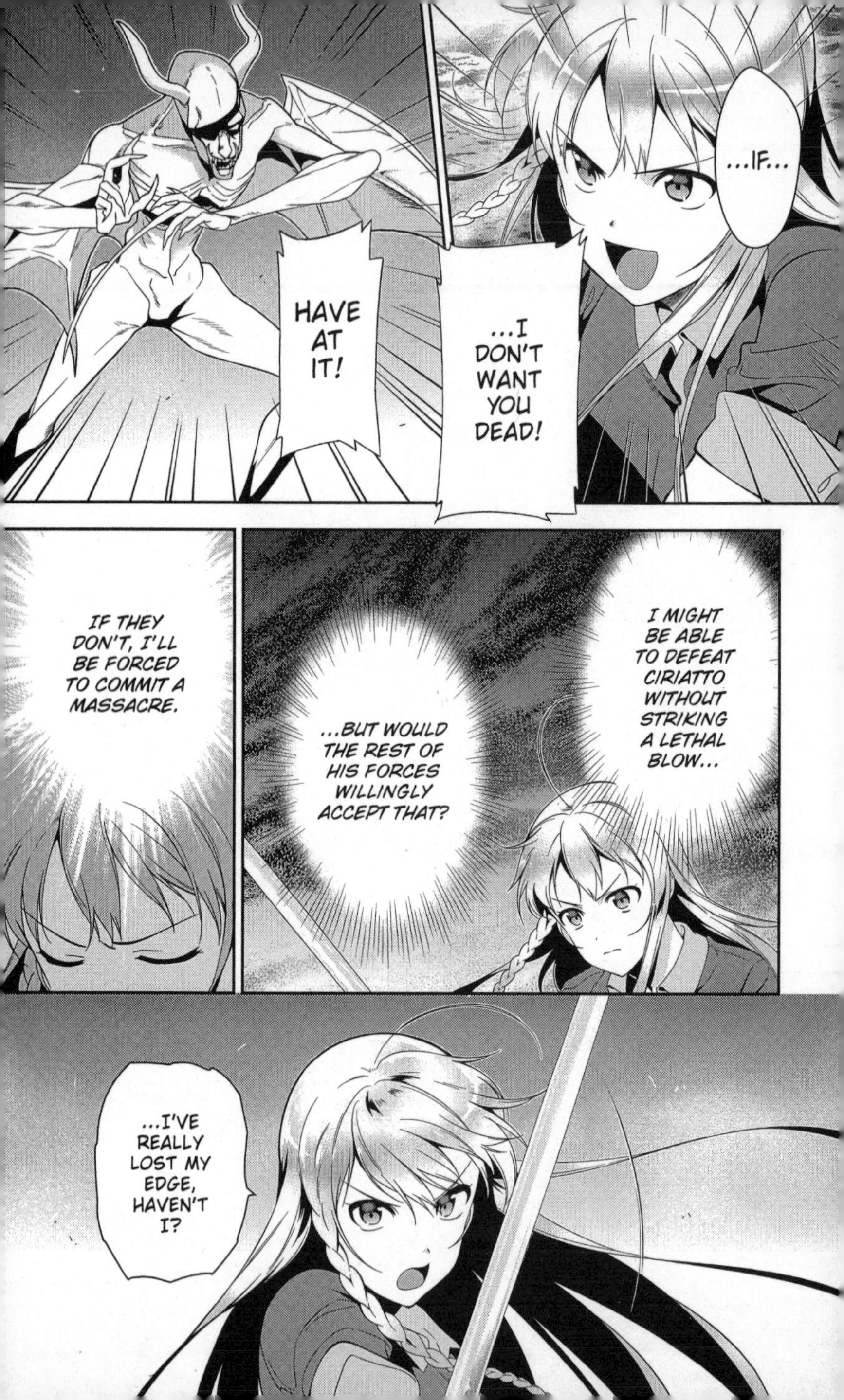
...IF...
...I DON'T WANT YOU DEAD!
HAVE AT IT!
I MIGHT BE ABLE TO DEFEAT CIRIATTO WITHOUT STRIKING A LETHAL BLOW...
...BUT WOULD THE REST OF HIS FORCES WILLINGLY ACCEPT THAT?
IF THEY DON'T, I'LL BE FORCED TO COMMIT A MASSACRE.
...I'VE REALLY LOST MY EDGE, HAVEN'T I?

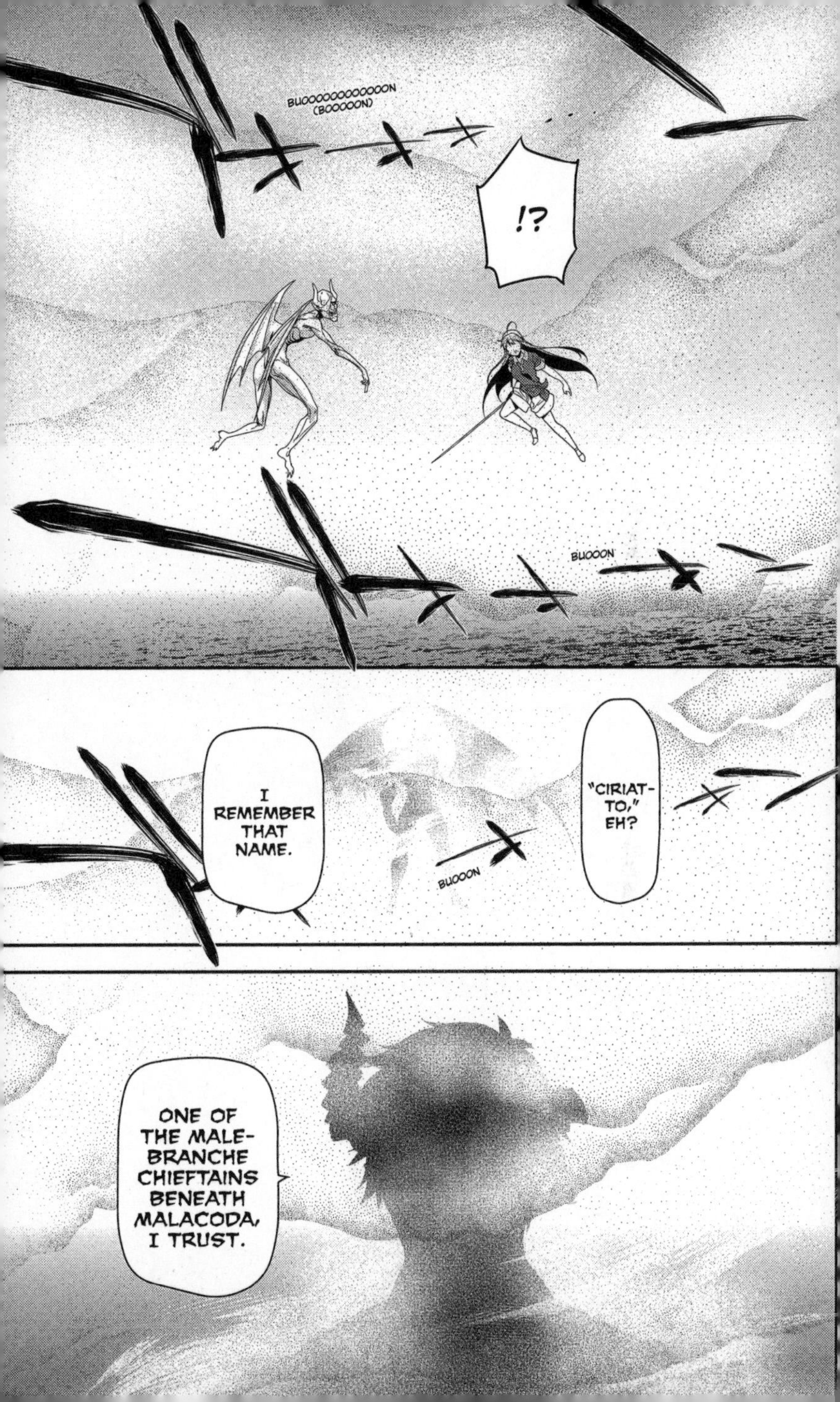

BUOOOOOOOOOOOON
(BOOOOON)
!?
BUOOON
"CIRIAT-TO," EH?
BUOOON
I REMEMBER THAT NAME.
ONE OF THE MALE-BRANCHE CHIEFTAINS BENEATH MALACODA, I TRUST.

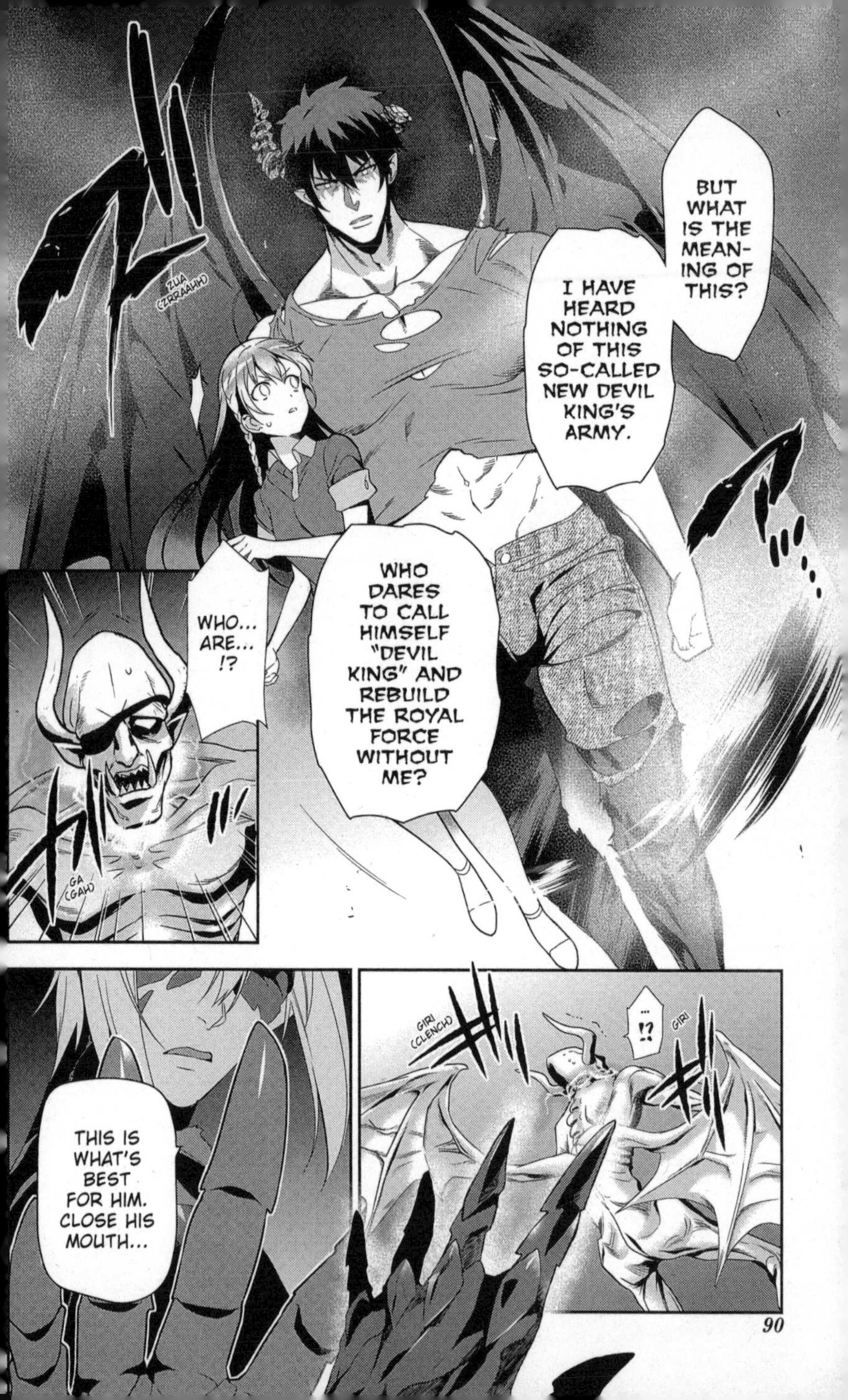
BUT WHAT IS THE MEAN-ING OF THIS?
I HAVE HEARD NOTHING OF THIS SO-CALLED NEW DEVIL KING'S ARMY.
ZUA (ZRRAAHH)
WHO DARES TO CALL HIMSELF "DEVIL KING" AND REBUILD THE ROYAL FORCE WITHOUT ME?
WHO... ARE... !?
GA (GAH)
GIRI
... !?
GIRI (CLENCH)
THIS IS WHAT'S BEST FOR HIM. CLOSE HIS MOUTH...

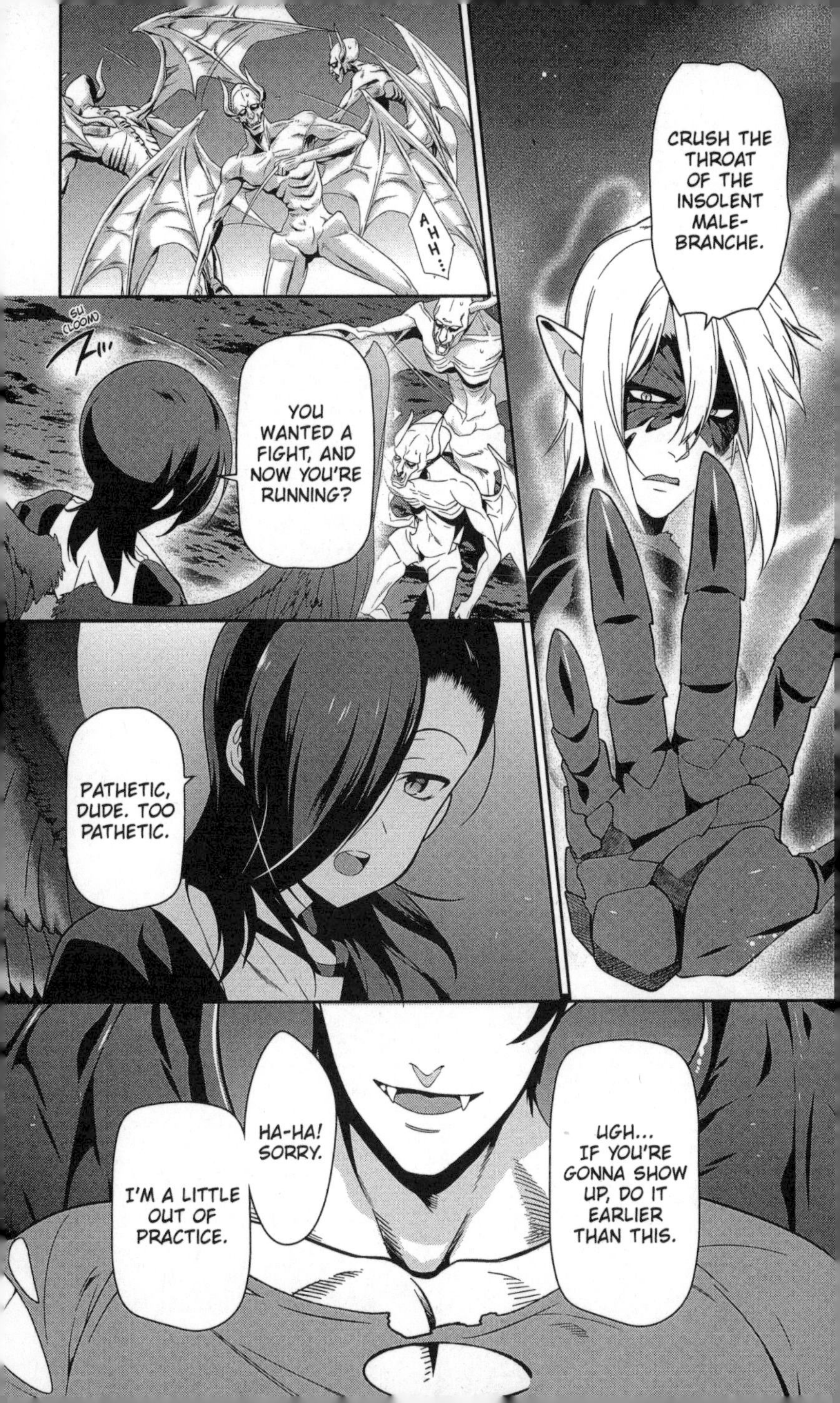
CRUSH THE THROAT OF THE INSOLENT MALE-BRANCHE.
AHH...
SU (LOOM)
YOU WANTED A FIGHT, AND NOW YOU'RE RUNNING?
PATHETIC, DUDE. TOO PATHETIC.
UGH... IF YOU'RE GONNA SHOW UP, DO IT EARLIER THAN THIS.
HA-HA! SORRY.
I'M A LITTLE OUT OF PRACTICE.

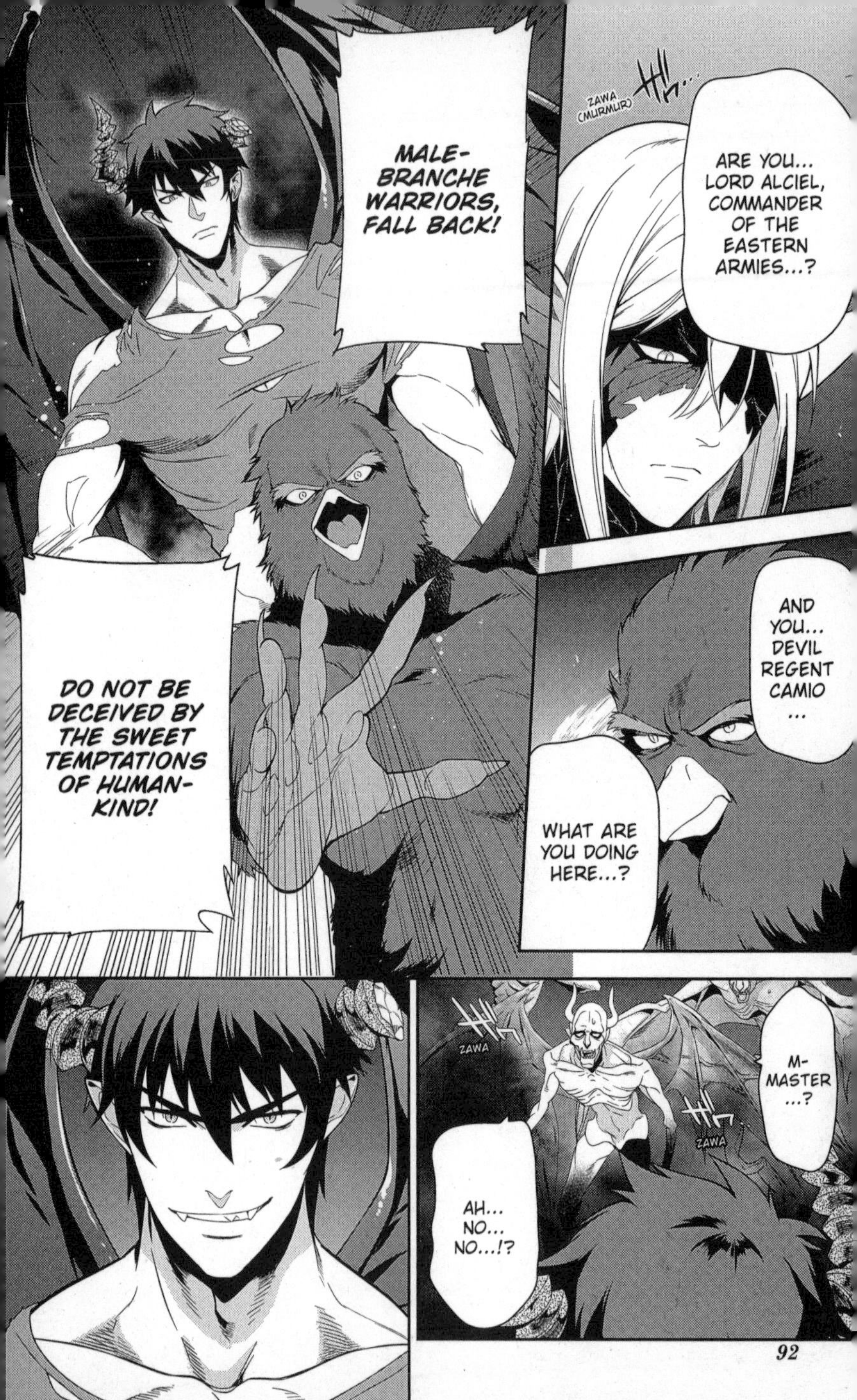
ZAWA (MURMUR)
ARE YOU... LORD ALCIEL, COMMANDER OF THE EASTERN ARMIES...?
AND YOU... DEVIL REGENT CAMIO...
WHAT ARE YOU DOING HERE...?
MALE-BRANCHE WARRIORS, FALL BACK!
DO NOT BE DECEIVED BY THE SWEET TEMPTATIONS OF HUMAN-KIND!
ZAWA
M-MASTER...?
ZAWA
AH... NO... NO...!?

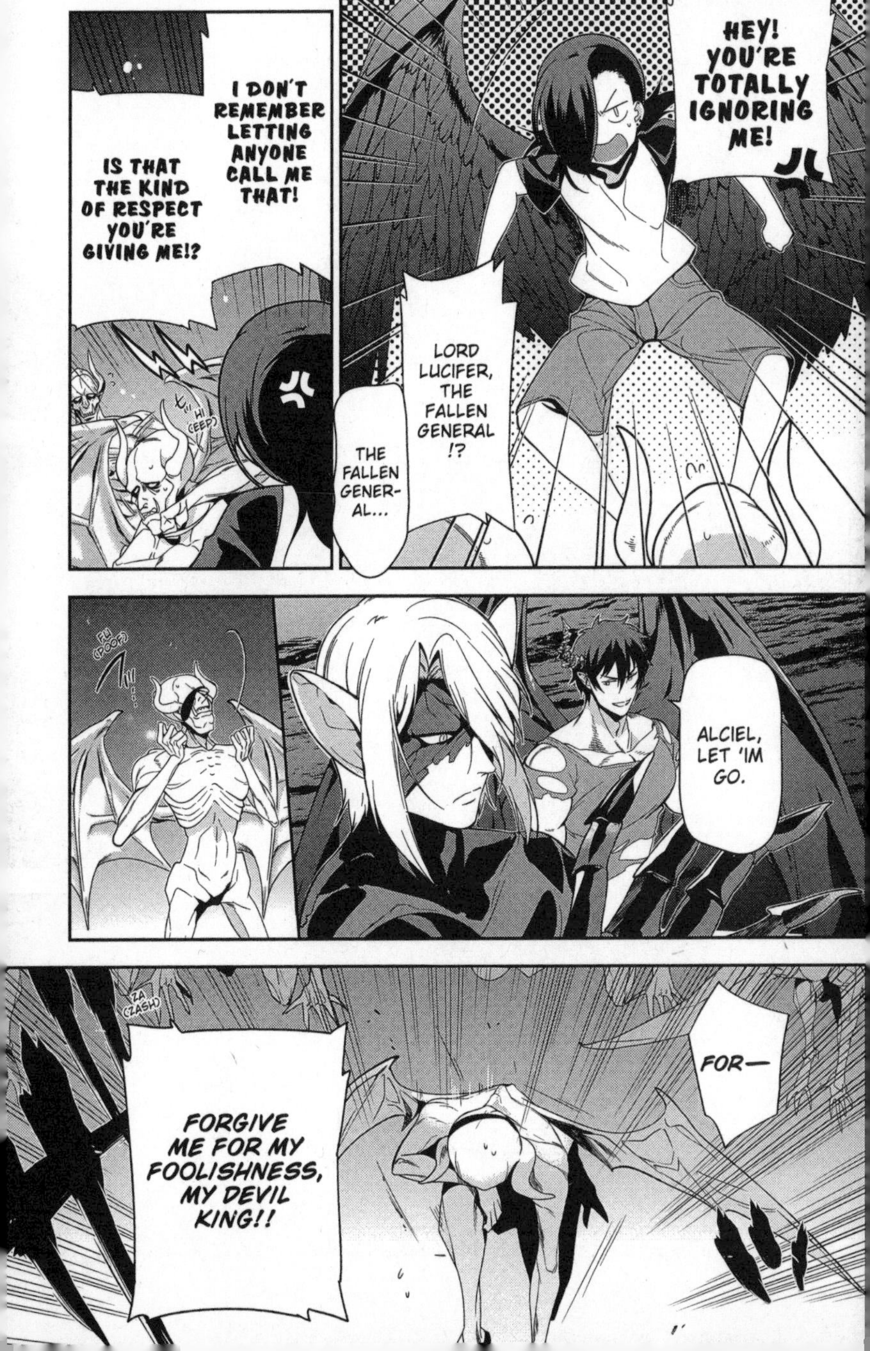
HEY! YOU'RE TOTALLY IGNORING ME!
LORD LUCIFER, THE FALLEN GENERAL!?
THE FALLEN GENER-AL...
I DON'T REMEMBER LETTING ANYONE CALL ME THAT!
IS THAT THE KIND OF RESPECT YOU'RE GIVING ME!?
HI (EEP)
ALCIEL, LET 'IM GO.
FU (POOF)
FOR—
ZA (ZASH)
FORGIVE ME FOR MY FOOLISHNESS, MY DEVIL KING!!

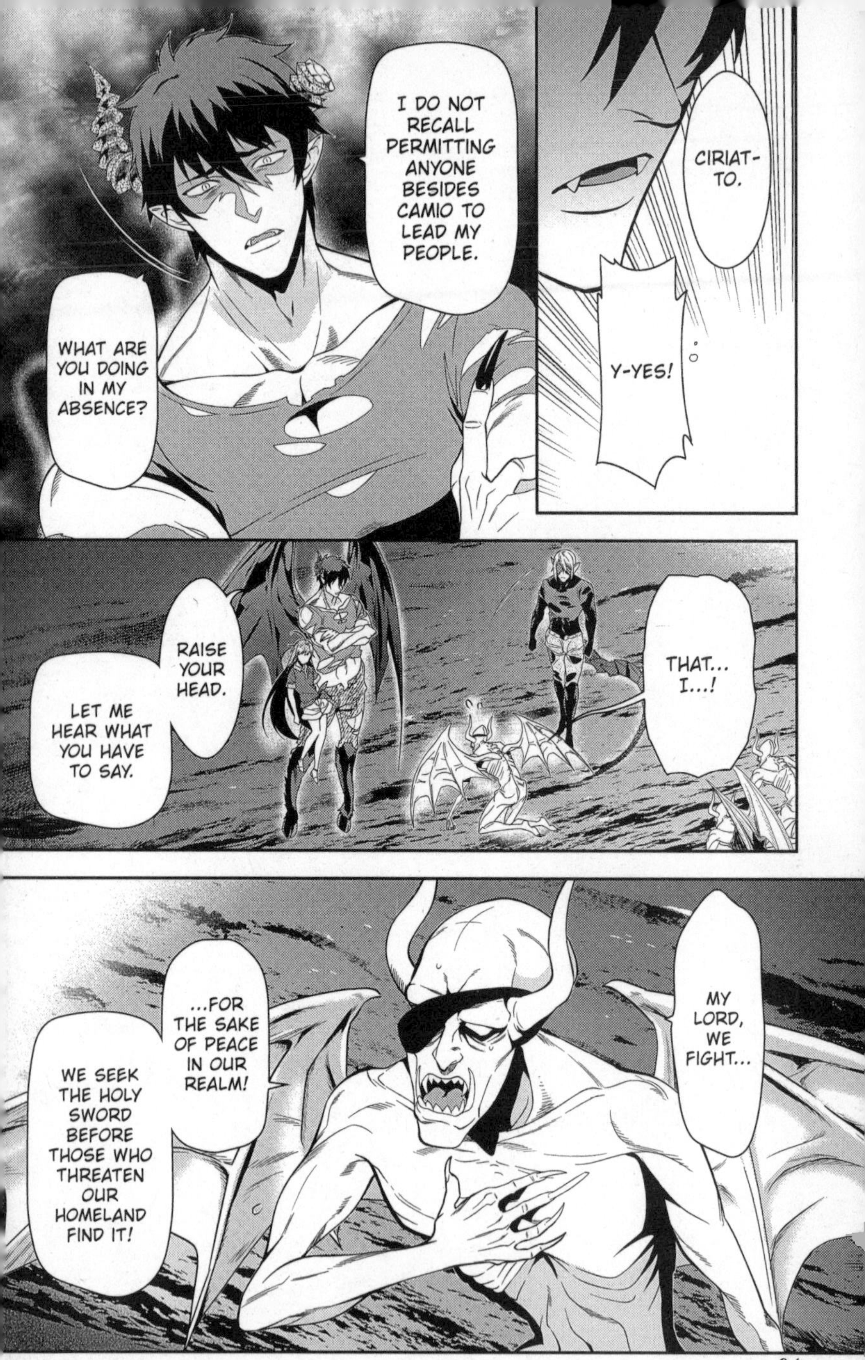
CIRIAT-TO.
Y-YES!
I DO NOT RECALL PERMITTING ANYONE BESIDES CAMIO TO LEAD MY PEOPLE.
WHAT ARE YOU DOING IN MY ABSENCE?
THAT... I...!
RAISE YOUR HEAD.
LET ME HEAR WHAT YOU HAVE TO SAY.
MY LORD, WE FIGHT...
...FOR THE SAKE OF PEACE IN OUR REALM!
WE SEEK THE HOLY SWORD BEFORE THOSE WHO THREATEN OUR HOMELAND FIND IT!

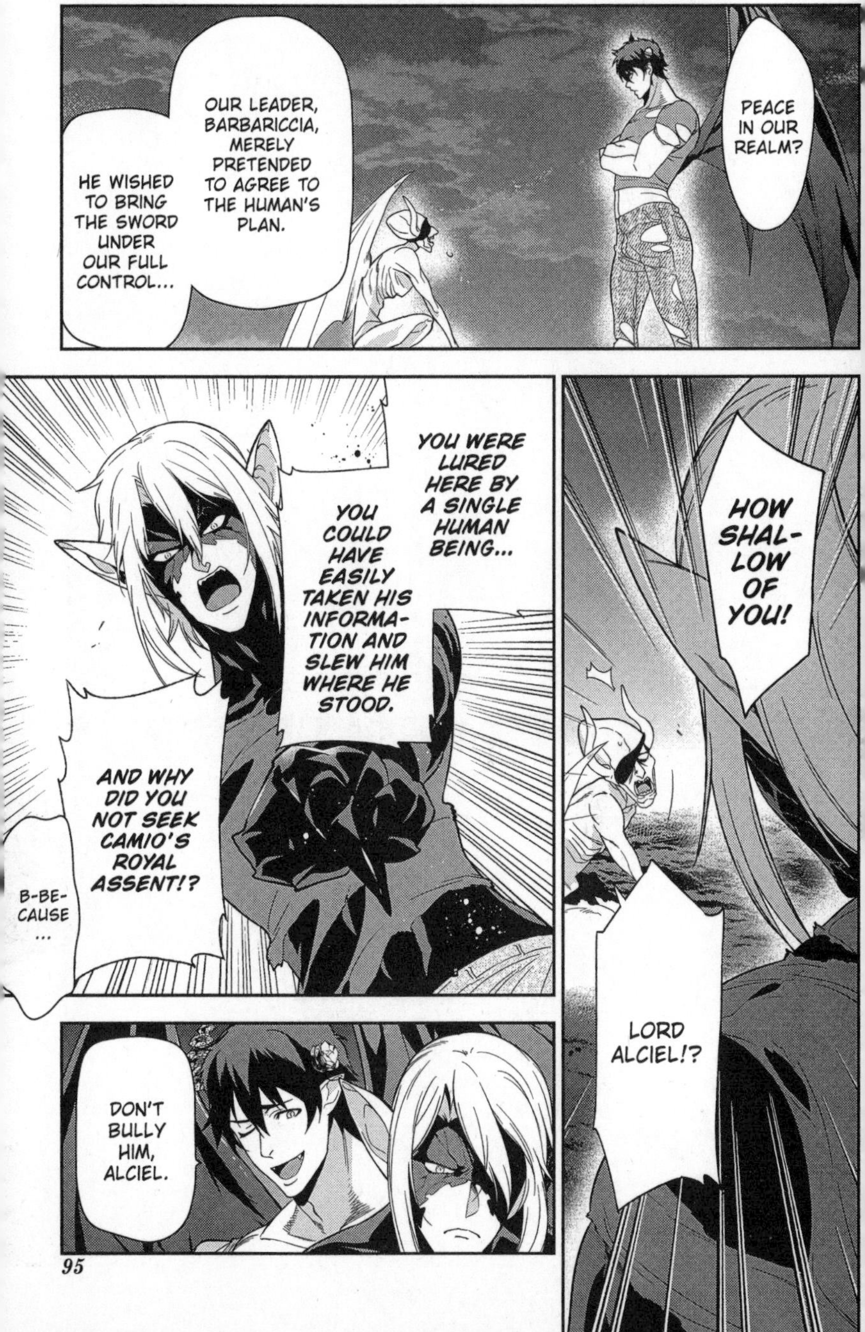
PEACE IN OUR REALM?
OUR LEADER, BARBARICCIA, MERELY PRETENDED TO AGREE TO THE HUMAN'S PLAN.
HE WISHED TO BRING THE SWORD UNDER OUR FULL CONTROL...
HOW SHAL-LOW OF YOU!
LORD ALCIEL!?
YOU WERE LURED HERE BY A SINGLE HUMAN BEING...
YOU COULD HAVE EASILY TAKEN HIS INFORMA-TION AND SLEW HIM WHERE HE STOOD.
AND WHY DID YOU NOT SEEK CAMIO'S ROYAL ASSENT!?
B-BE-CAUSE ...
DON'T BULLY HIM, ALCIEL.

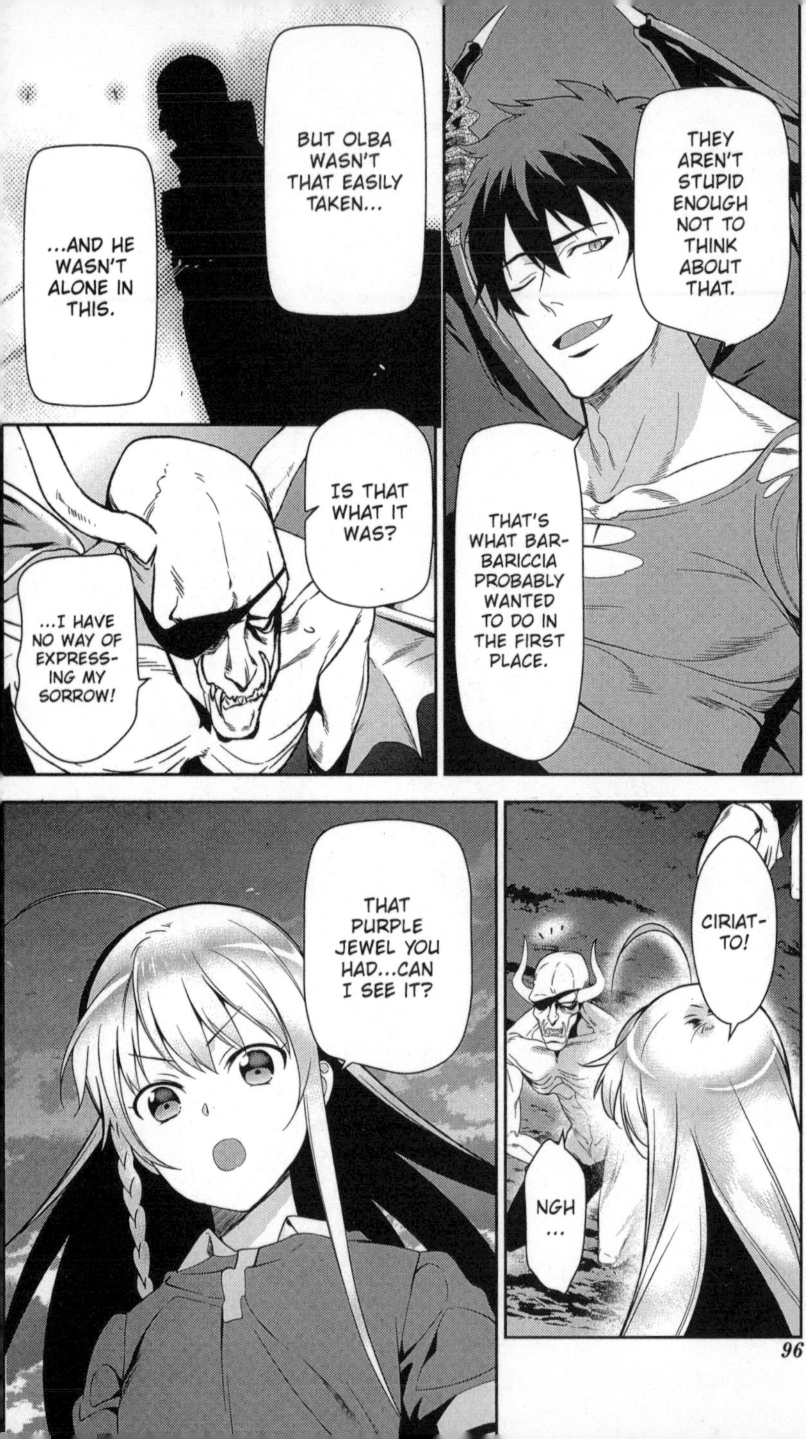
THEY AREN'T STUPID ENOUGH NOT TO THINK ABOUT THAT.
THAT'S WHAT BAR-BARICCIA PROBABLY WANTED TO DO IN THE FIRST PLACE.
BUT OLBA WASN'T THAT EASILY TAKEN...
...AND HE WASN'T ALONE IN THIS.
IS THAT WHAT IT WAS?
...I HAVE NO WAY OF EXPRESS-ING MY SORROW!
CIRIAT-TO!
NGH...
THAT PURPLE JEWEL YOU HAD...CAN I SEE IT?

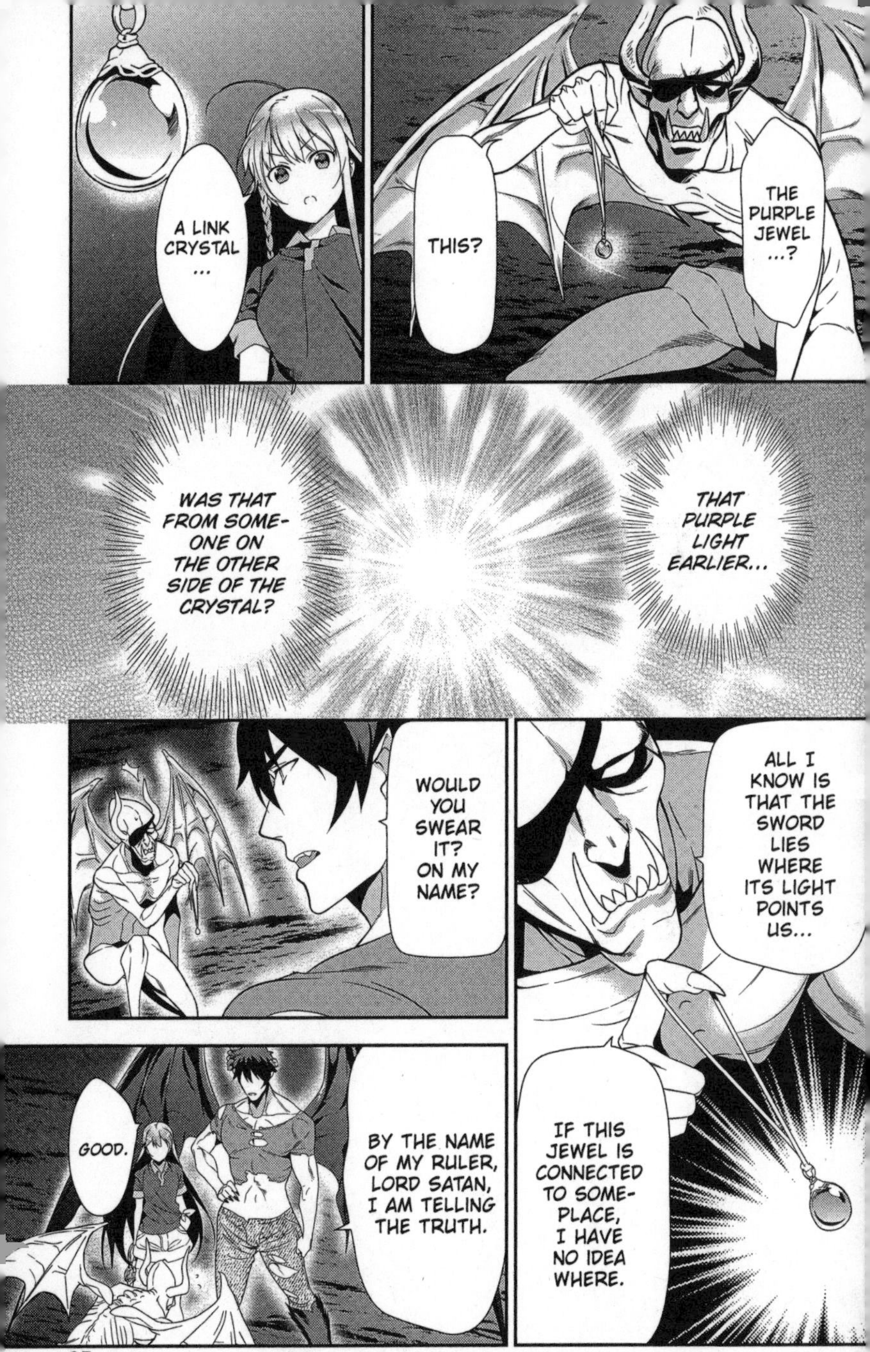
THE PURPLE JEWEL ...?
THIS?
A LINK CRYSTAL ...
THAT PURPLE LIGHT EARLIER...
WAS THAT FROM SOME-ONE ON THE OTHER SIDE OF THE CRYSTAL?
ALL I KNOW IS THAT THE SWORD LIES WHERE ITS LIGHT POINTS US...
IF THIS JEWEL IS CONNECTED TO SOME-PLACE, I HAVE NO IDEA WHERE.
WOULD YOU SWEAR IT? ON MY NAME?
BY THE NAME OF MY RULER, LORD SATAN, I AM TELLING THE TRUTH.
GOOD.

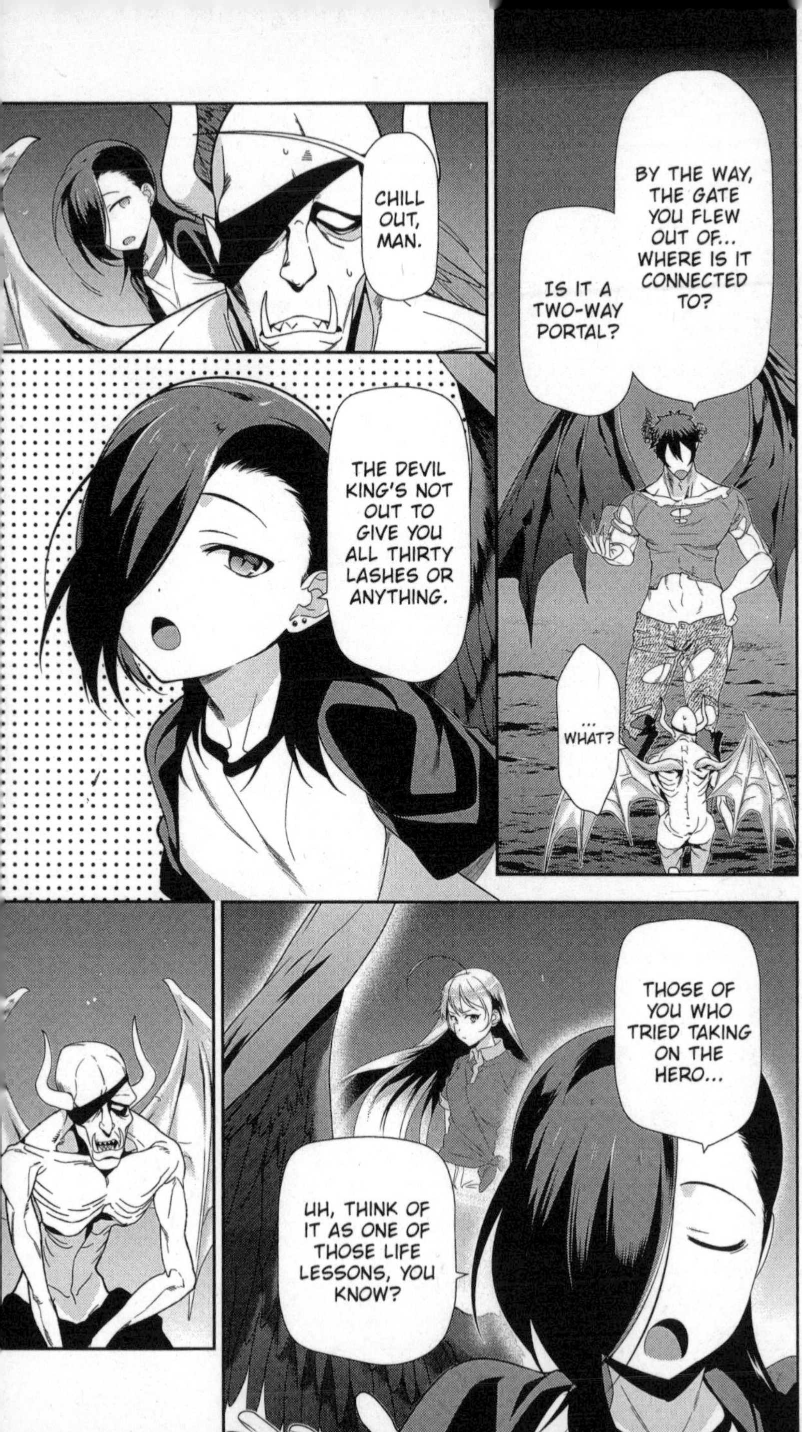
BY THE WAY, THE GATE YOU FLEW OUT OF... WHERE IS IT CONNECTED TO?
IS IT A TWO-WAY PORTAL?
...WHAT?
CHILL OUT, MAN.
THE DEVIL KING'S NOT OUT TO GIVE YOU ALL THIRTY LASHES OR ANYTHING.
THOSE OF YOU WHO TRIED TAKING ON THE HERO...
UH, THINK OF IT AS ONE OF THOSE LIFE LESSONS, YOU KNOW?

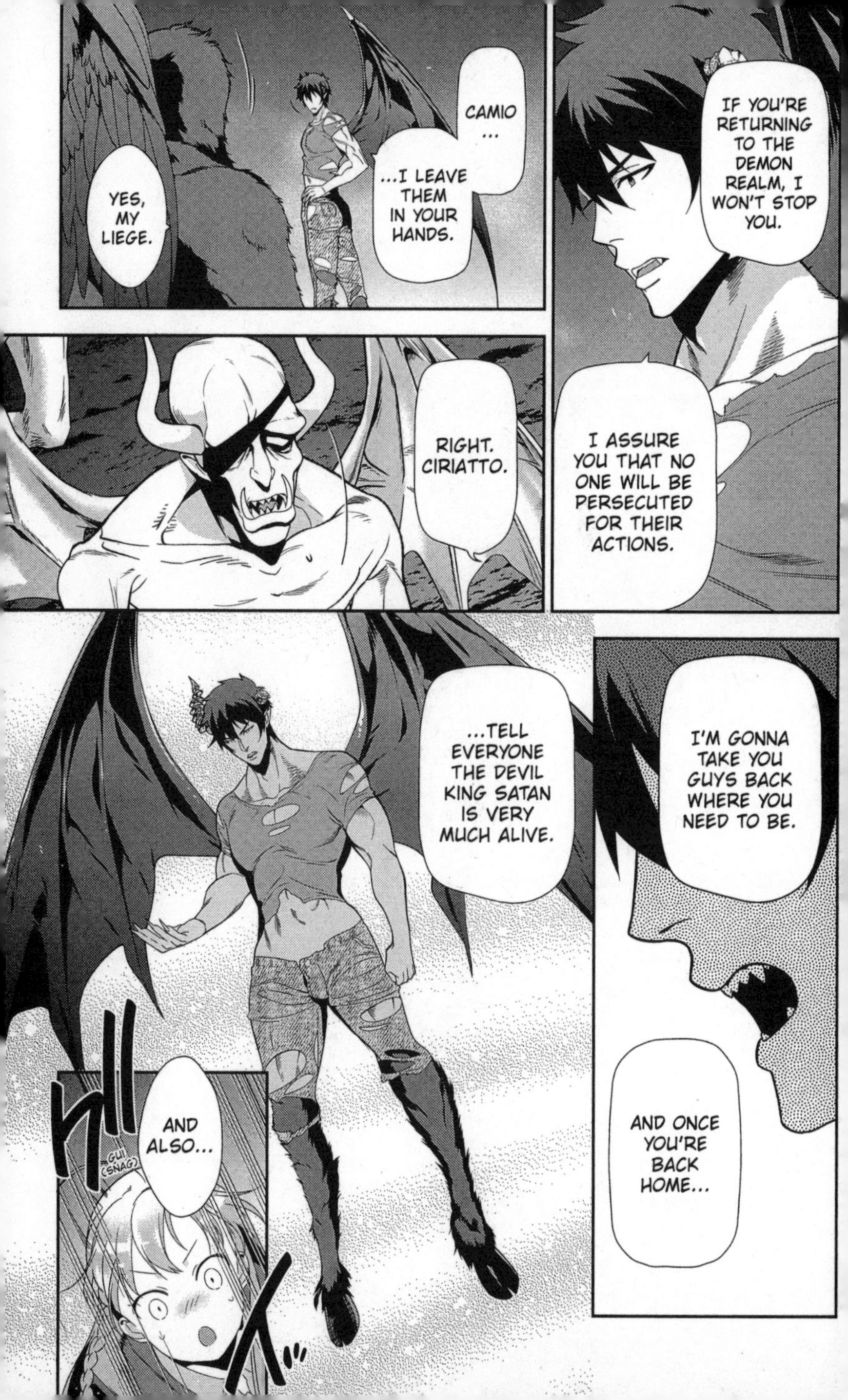
IF YOU'RE RETURNING TO THE DEMON REALM, I WON'T STOP YOU.
CAMIO ...
...I LEAVE THEM IN YOUR HANDS.
YES, MY LIEGE.
I ASSURE YOU THAT NO ONE WILL BE PERSECUTED FOR THEIR ACTIONS.
RIGHT. CIRIATTO.
I'M GONNA TAKE YOU GUYS BACK WHERE YOU NEED TO BE.
AND ONCE YOU'RE BACK HOME...
...TELL EVERYONE THE DEVIL KING SATAN IS VERY MUCH ALIVE.
AND ALSO...
GUI (SNAG)

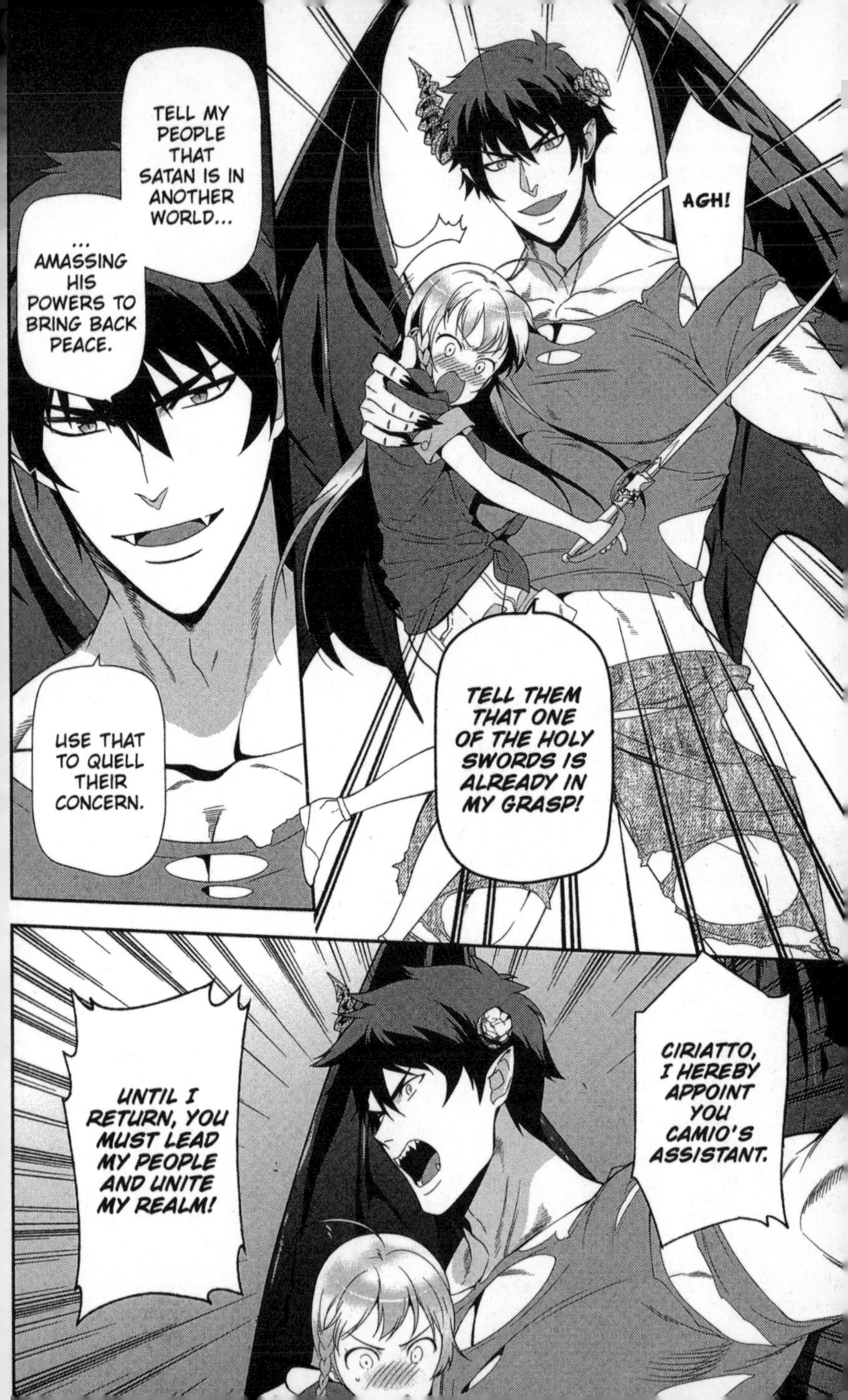
TELL MY PEOPLE THAT SATAN IS IN ANOTHER WORLD...
... AMASSING HIS POWERS TO BRING BACK PEACE.
USE THAT TO QUELL THEIR CONCERN.
AGH!
TELL THEM THAT ONE OF THE HOLY SWORDS IS ALREADY IN MY GRASP!
CIRIATTO, I HEREBY APPOINT YOU CAMIO'S ASSISTANT.
UNTIL I RETURN, YOU MUST LEAD MY PEOPLE AND UNITE MY REALM!

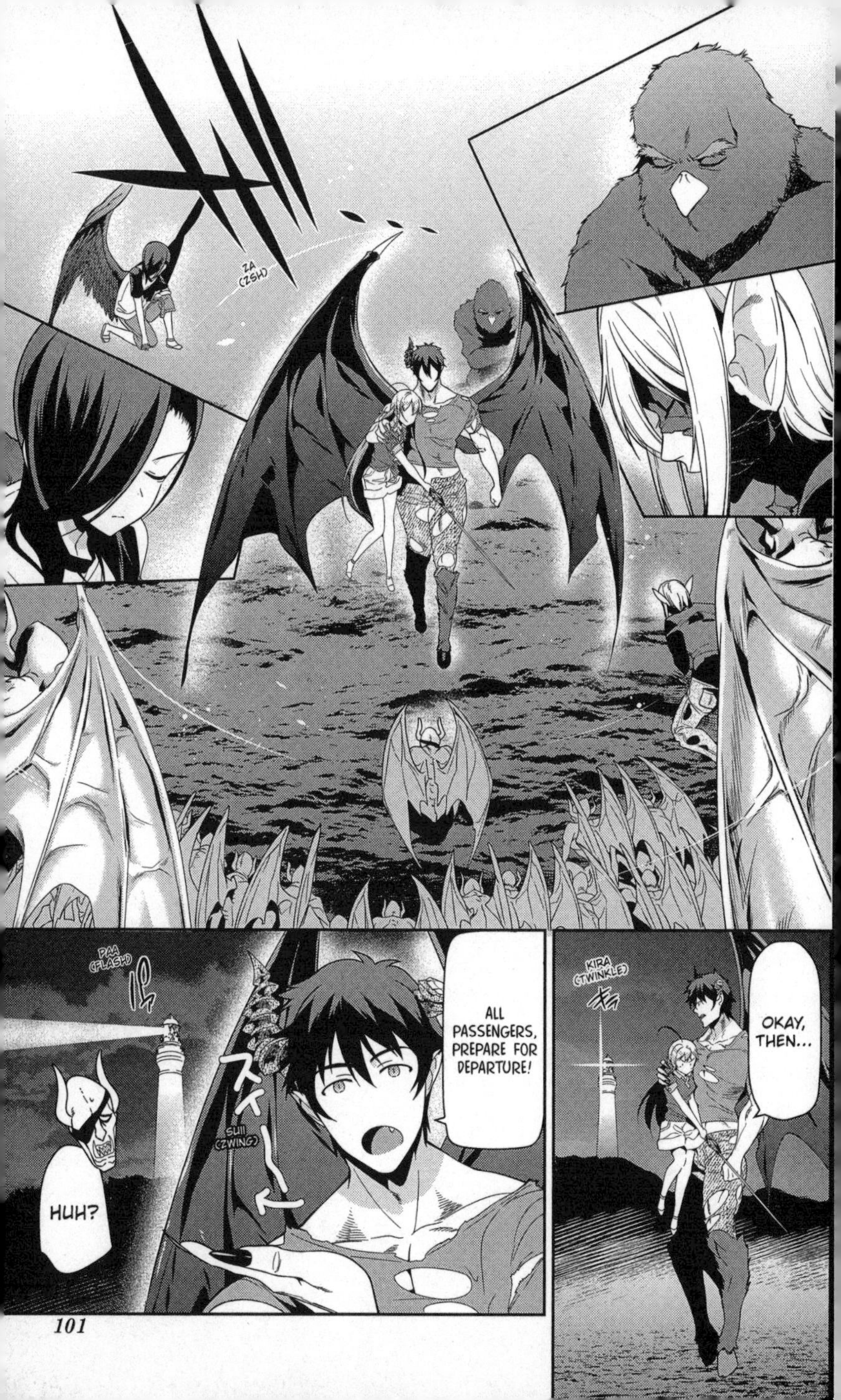
ZA (ZSH)
KIRA (TWINKLE)
OKAY, THEN...
ALL PASSENGERS, PREPARE FOR DEPARTURE!
PAA (FLASH)
SUII (ZWING)
HUH?

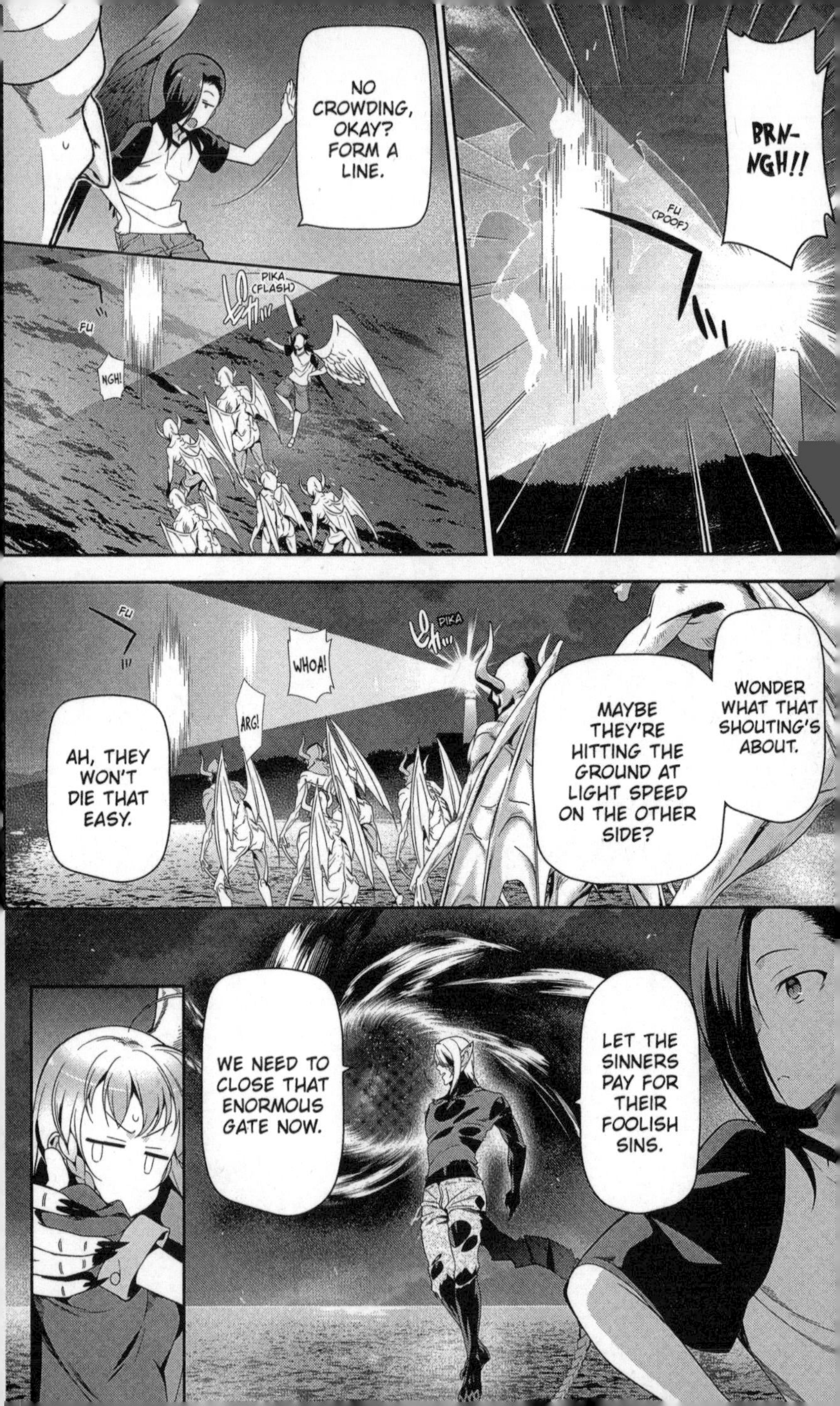
BRN-NGH!!
FU (POOF)
NO CROWDING, OKAY? FORM A LINE.
PIKA (FLASH)
FU
NGH!
WONDER WHAT THAT SHOUTING'S ABOUT.
PIKA
MAYBE THEY'RE HITTING THE GROUND AT LIGHT SPEED ON THE OTHER SIDE?
WHOA!
ARG!
FU
AH, THEY WON'T DIE THAT EASY.
LET THE SINNERS PAY FOR THEIR FOOLISH SINS.
WE NEED TO CLOSE THAT ENORMOUS GATE NOW.

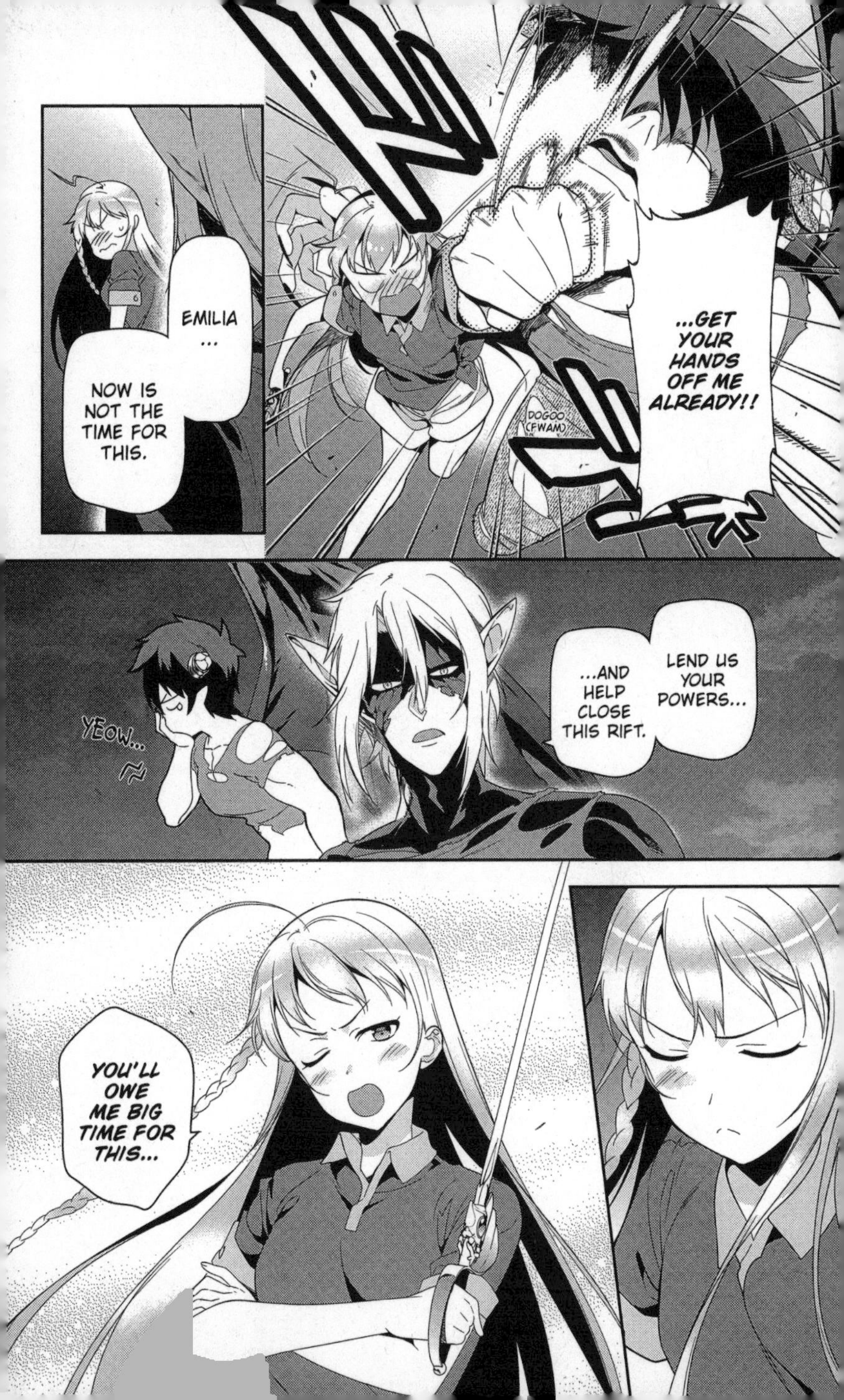
...GET YOUR HANDS OFF ME ALREADY!!
DOGOO (FWAM)
EMILIA ...
NOW IS NOT THE TIME FOR THIS.
LEND US YOUR POWERS...
...AND HELP CLOSE THIS RIFT.
YEOW...
YOU'LL OWE ME BIG TIME FOR THIS...

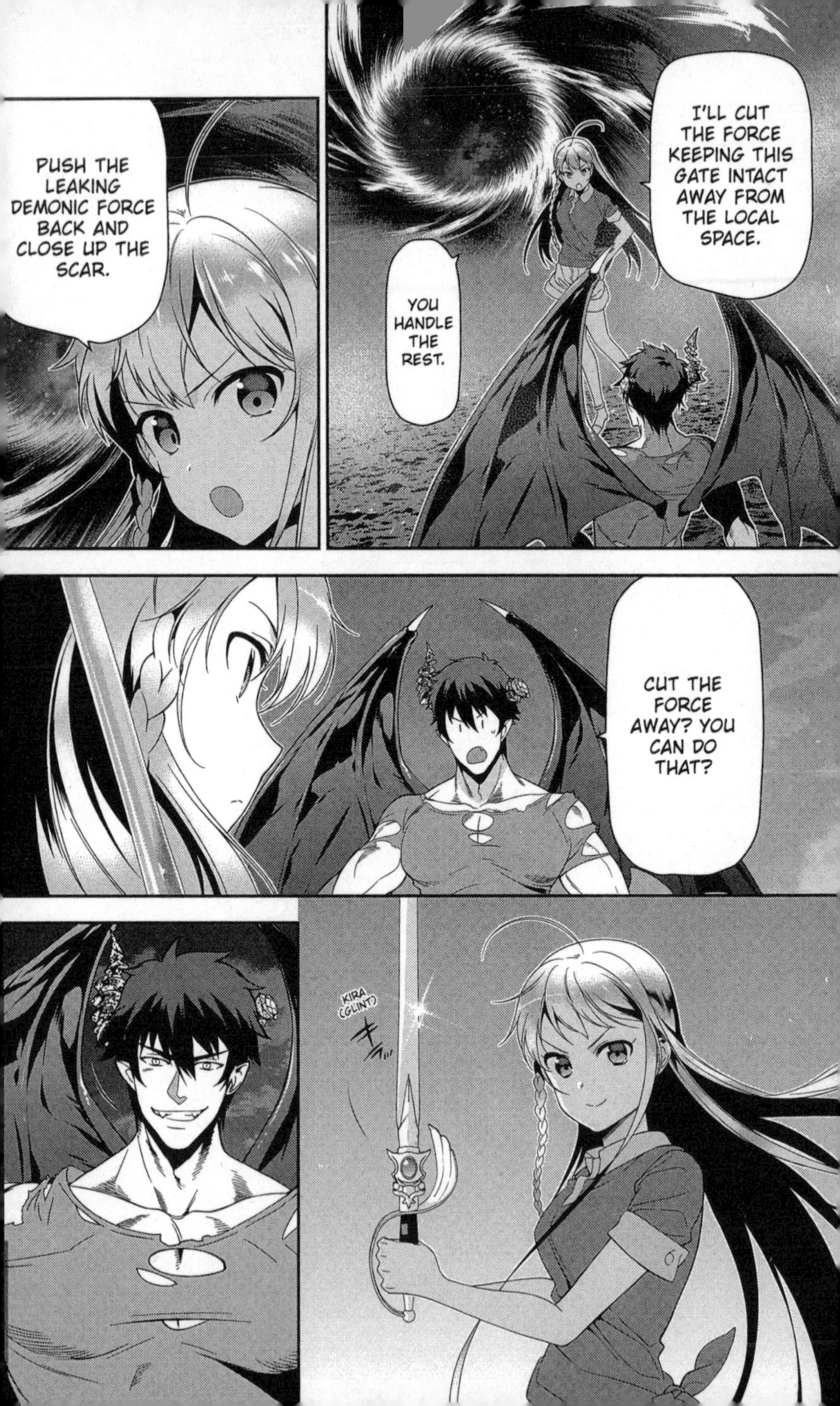
I'LL CUT THE FORCE KEEPING THIS GATE INTACT AWAY FROM THE LOCAL SPACE.
YOU HANDLE THE REST.
PUSH THE LEAKING DEMONIC FORCE BACK AND CLOSE UP THE SCAR.
CUT THE FORCE AWAY? YOU CAN DO THAT?
KIRA (GLINT)

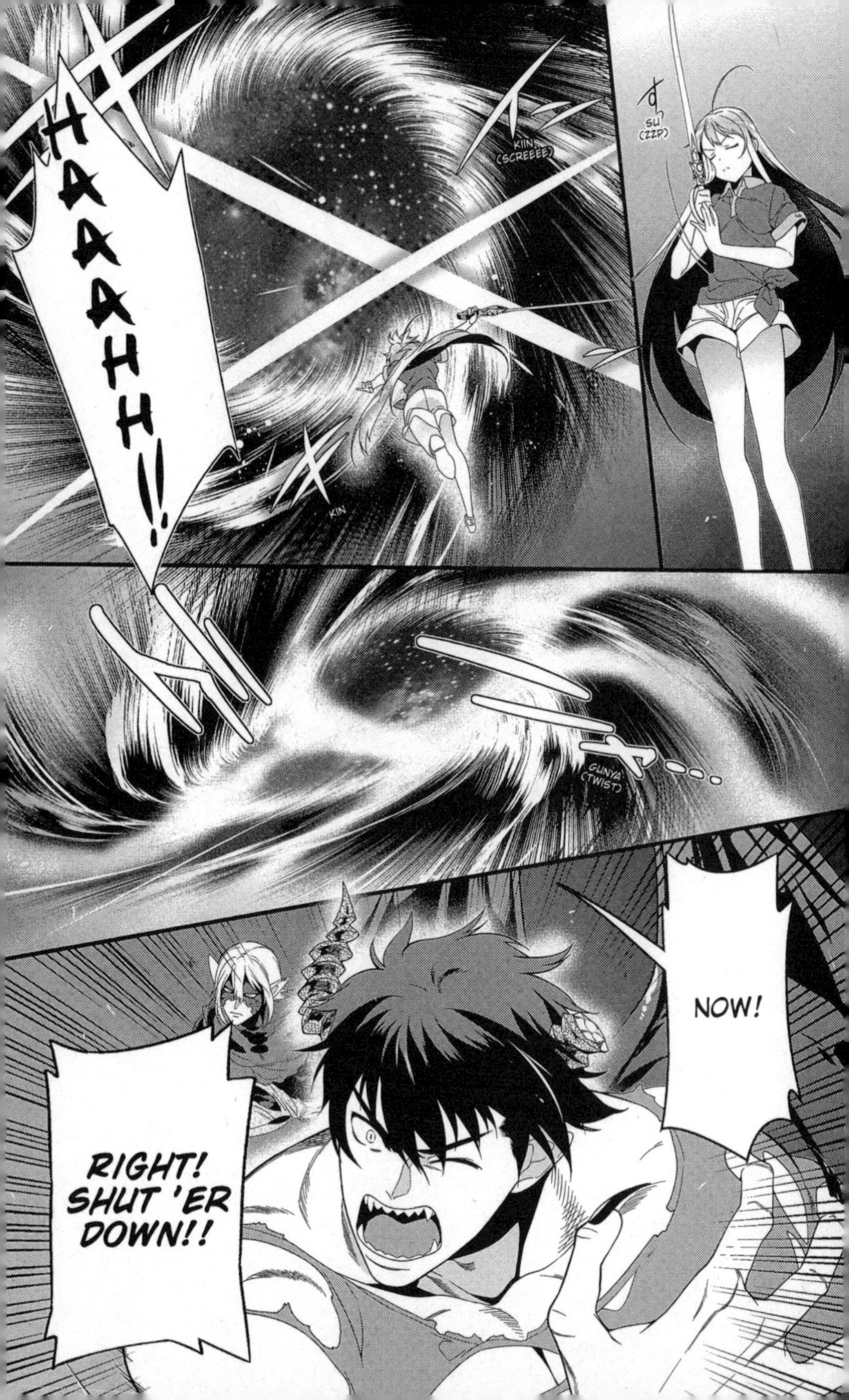

す
SU
(ZZP)
HAAAAH!!
KIIN
(SCREEEEE)
KIN
GUNYA
(TWIST)
NOW!
RIGHT! SHUT 'ER DOWN!!

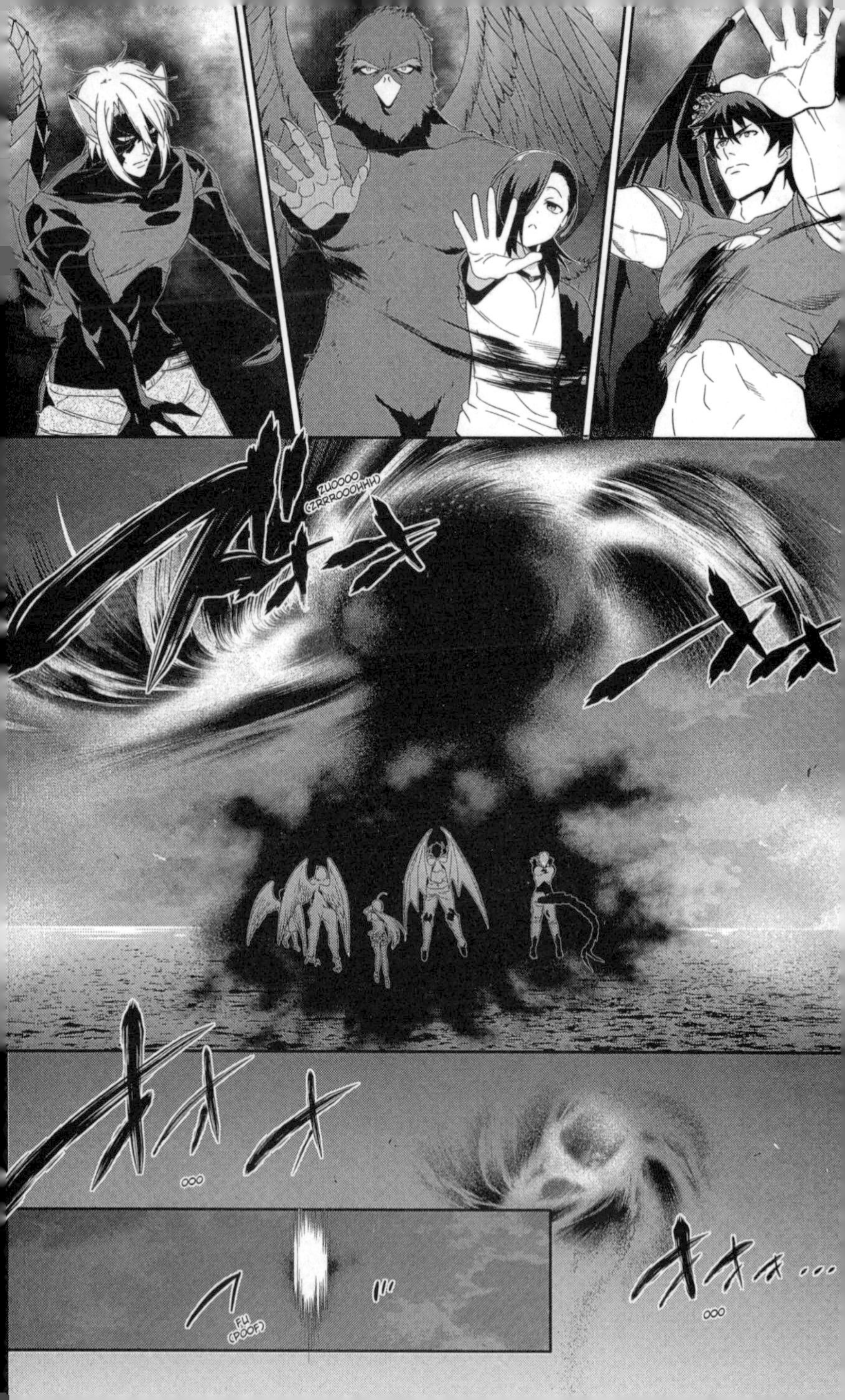
ZUOOOO
(ZRRROOOHHH)
ooo
ooo
FU
(POOF)

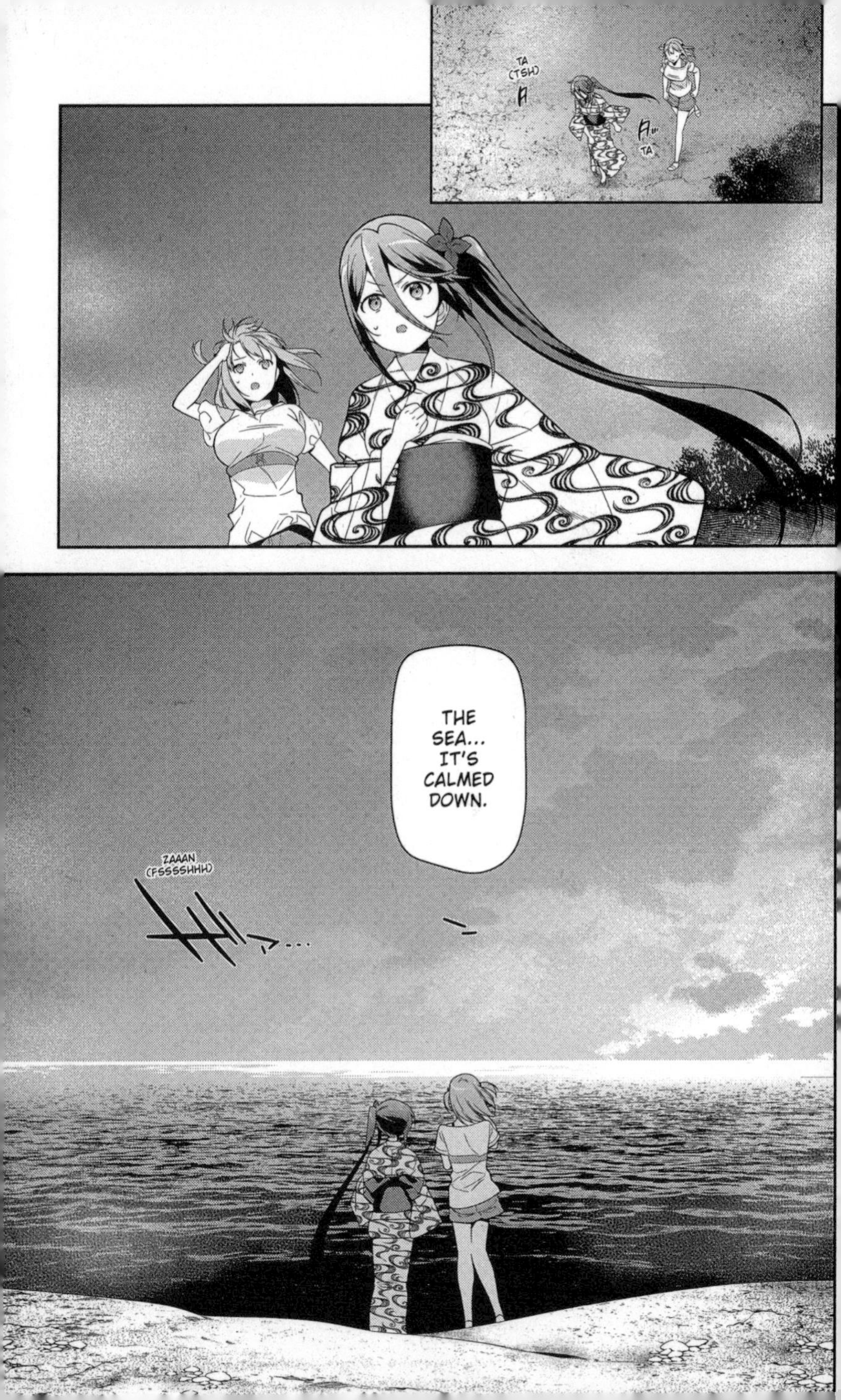
TA (TSH)
TA
THE SEA... IT'S CALMED DOWN.
ZAAAN (FSSSSHHH)

THE DEVIL IS A PART-TIMER!

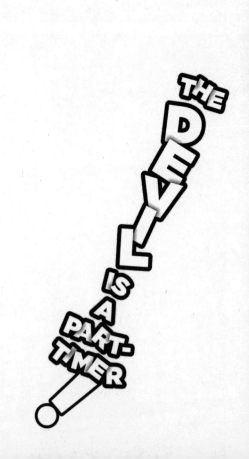

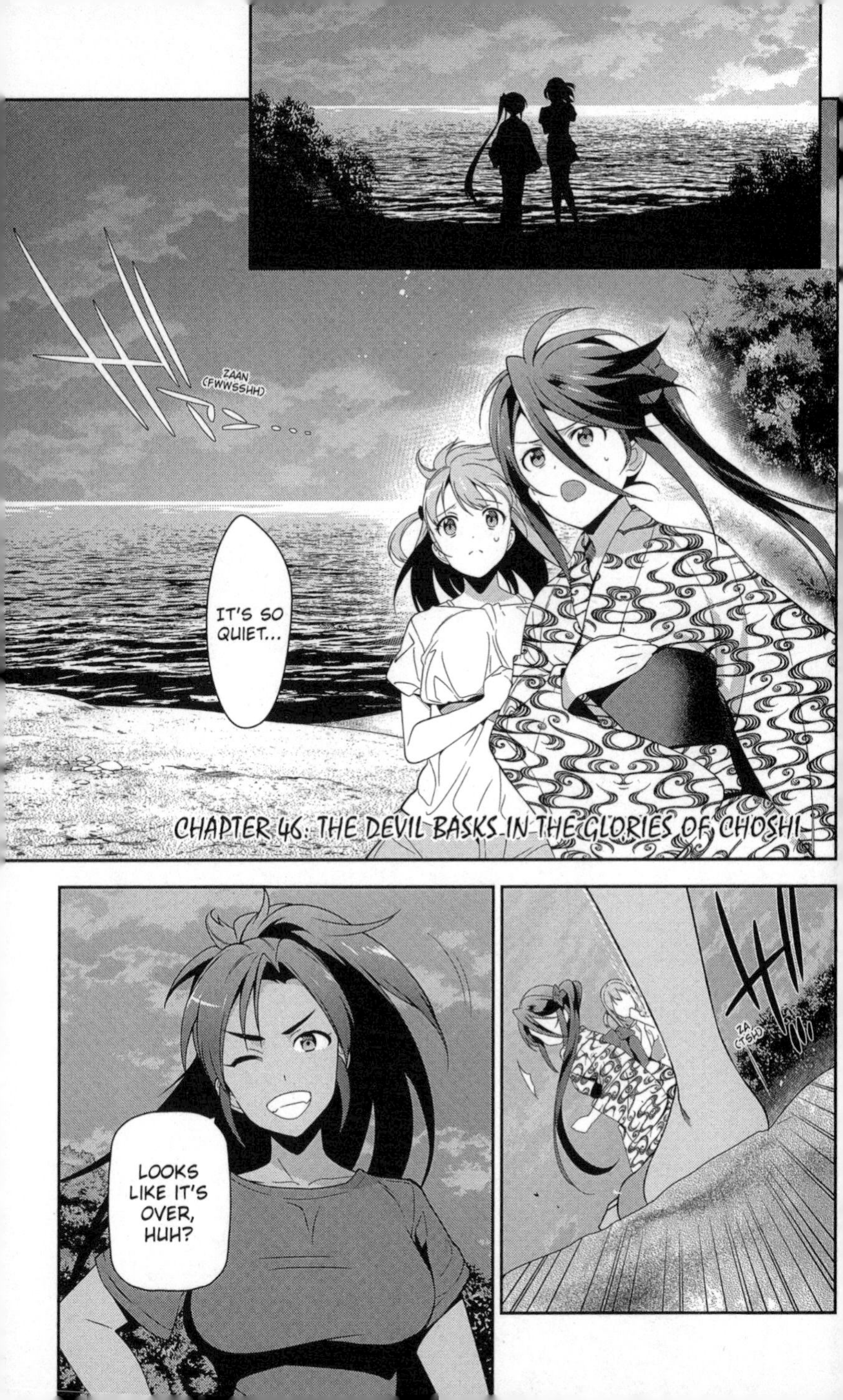
ZAAN (FWWSSHH)
IT'S SO QUIET...
CHAPTER 46: THE DEVIL BASKS IN THE GLORIES OF CHOSHI
ZA (TSH)
LOOKS LIKE IT'S OVER, HUH?

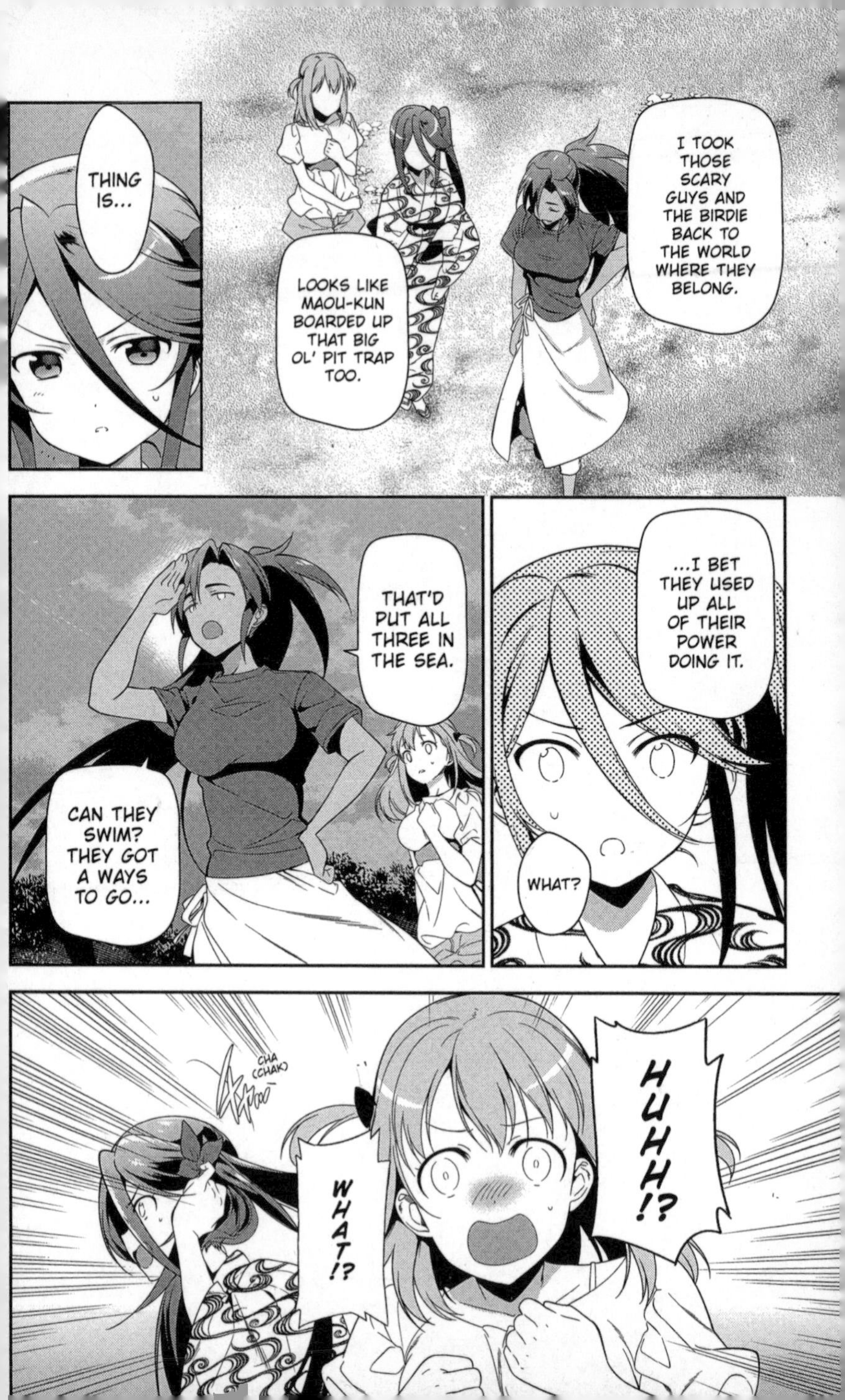
I TOOK THOSE SCARY GUYS AND THE BIRDIE BACK TO THE WORLD WHERE THEY BELONG.
LOOKS LIKE MAOU-KUN BOARDED UP THAT BIG OL' PIT TRAP TOO.
THING IS...
...I BET THEY USED UP ALL OF THEIR POWER DOING IT.
WHAT?
THAT'D PUT ALL THREE IN THE SEA.
CAN THEY SWIM? THEY GOT A WAYS TO GO...
HUHH!?
WHAT!?
CHA (CHAK)

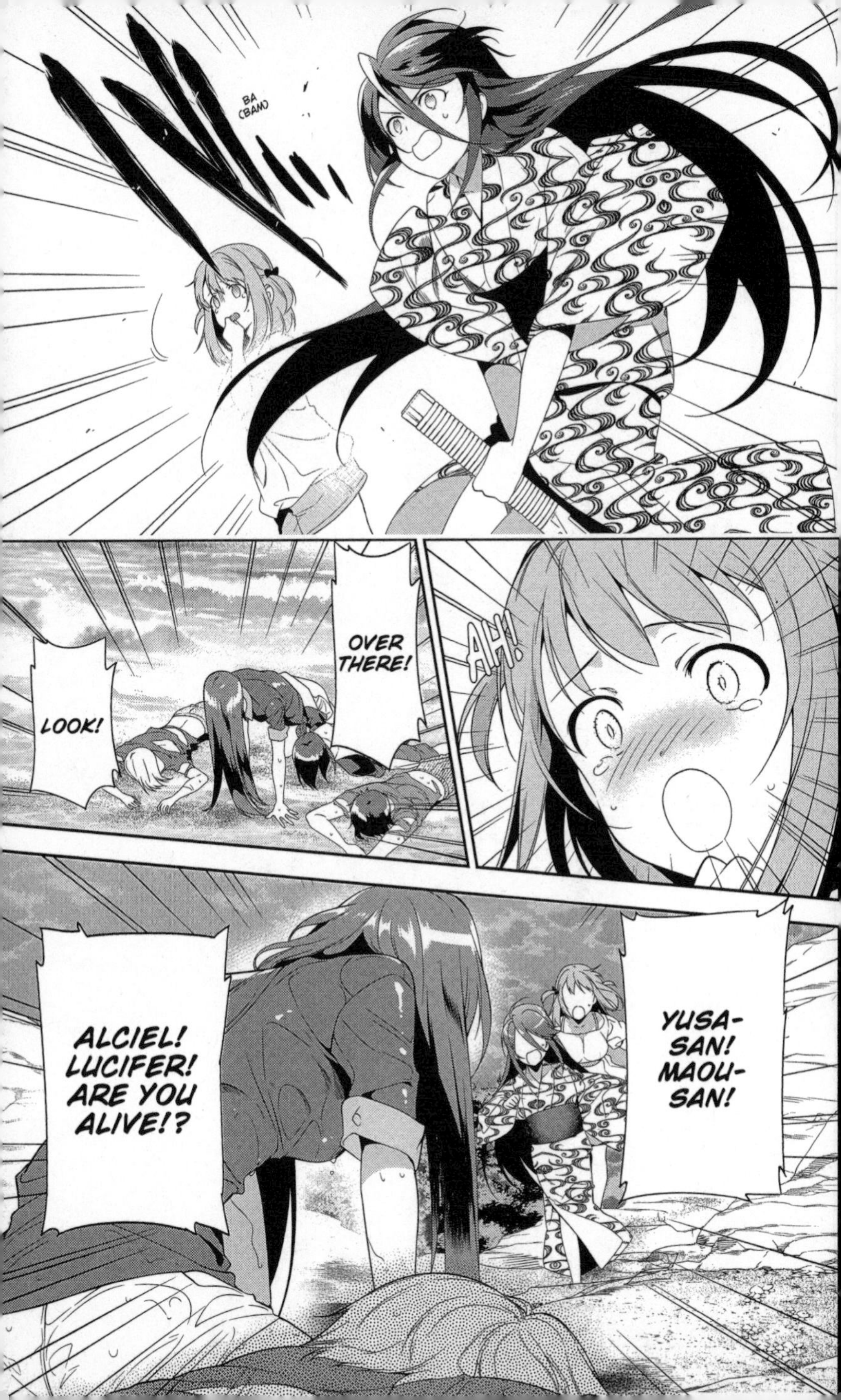
BA
(BAM)
AH!
OVER THERE!
LOOK!
YUSA-SAN! MAOU-SAN!
ALCIEL! LUCIFER! ARE YOU ALIVE!?

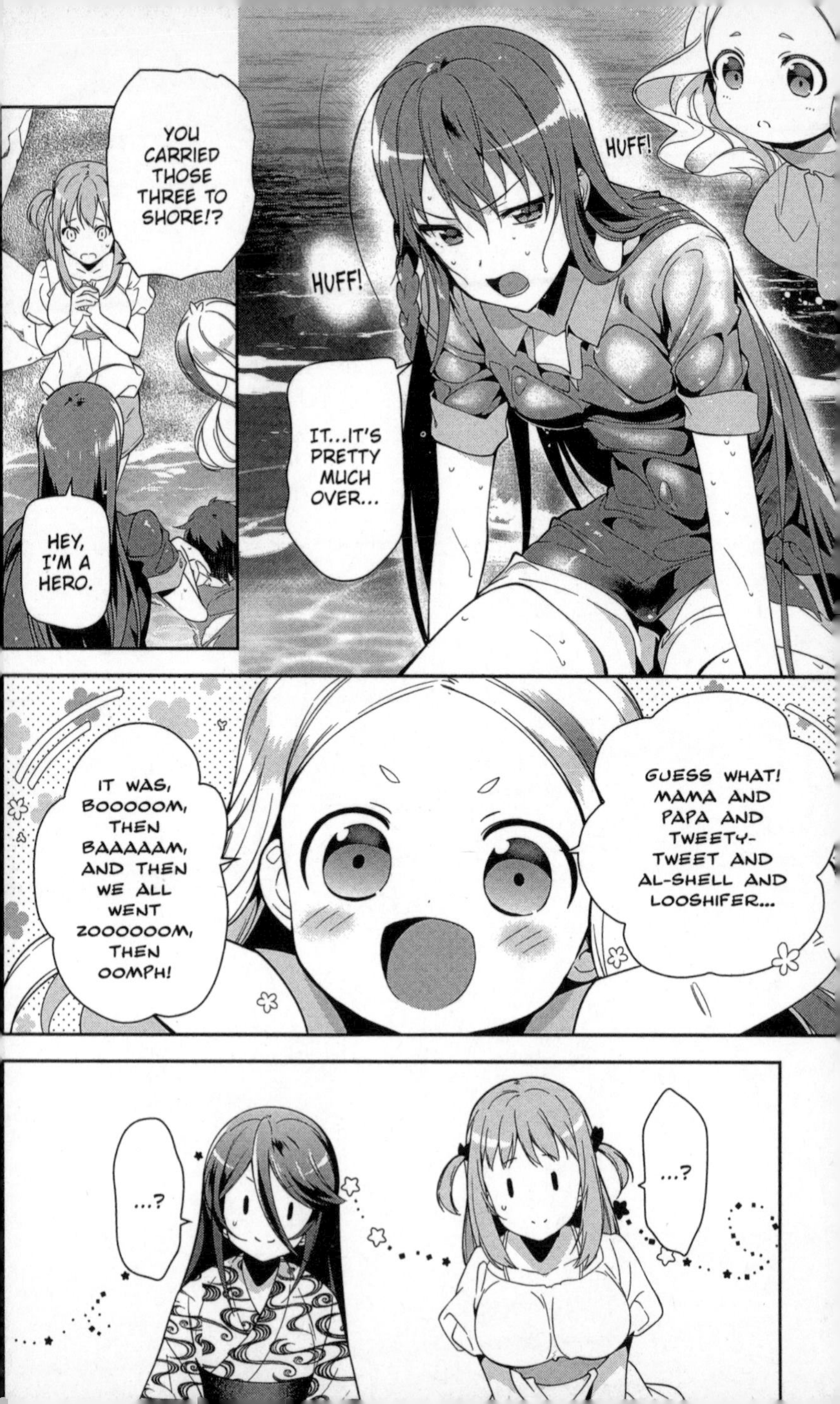
HUFF!
HUFF!
IT...IT'S PRETTY MUCH OVER...
YOU CARRIED THOSE THREE TO SHORE!?
HEY, I'M A HERO.
GUESS WHAT! MAMA AND PAPA AND TWEETY-TWEET AND AL-SHELL AND LOOSHIFER...
IT WAS, BOOOOOM, THEN BAAAAAM, AND THEN WE ALL WENT ZOOOOOOM, THEN OOMPH!
...?
...?

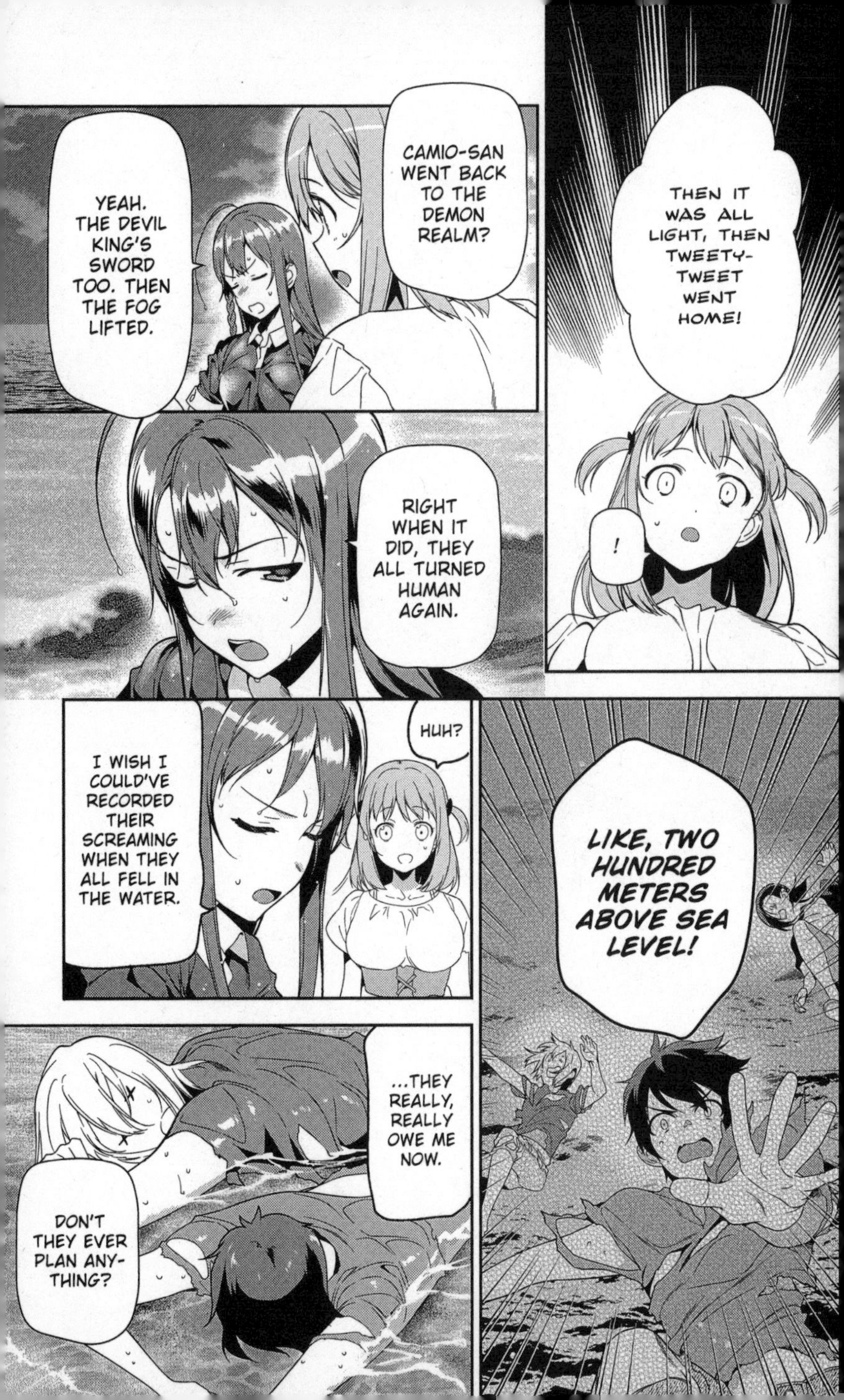
THEN IT WAS ALL LIGHT, THEN TWEETY-TWEET WENT HOME!
!
CAMIO-SAN WENT BACK TO THE DEMON REALM?
YEAH. THE DEVIL KING'S SWORD TOO. THEN THE FOG LIFTED.
RIGHT WHEN IT DID, THEY ALL TURNED HUMAN AGAIN.
LIKE, TWO HUNDRED METERS ABOVE SEA LEVEL!
HUH?
I WISH I COULD'VE RECORDED THEIR SCREAMING WHEN THEY ALL FELL IN THE WATER.
...THEY REALLY, REALLY OWE ME NOW.
DON'T THEY EVER PLAN ANY-THING?

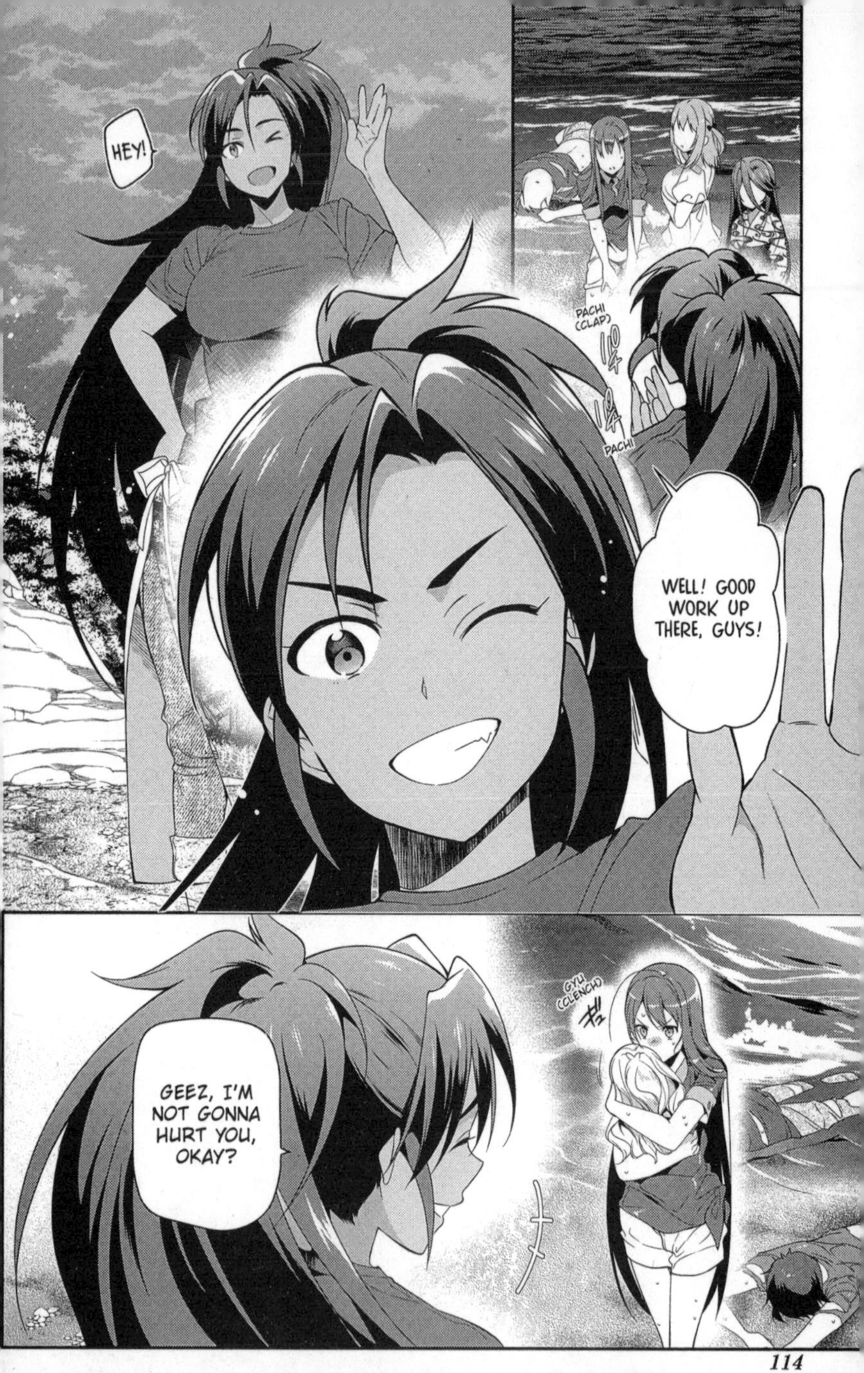
PACHI (CLAP)
PACHI
HEY!
WELL! GOOD WORK UP THERE, GUYS!
GYU (CLENCH)
GEEZ, I'M NOT GONNA HURT YOU, OKAY?

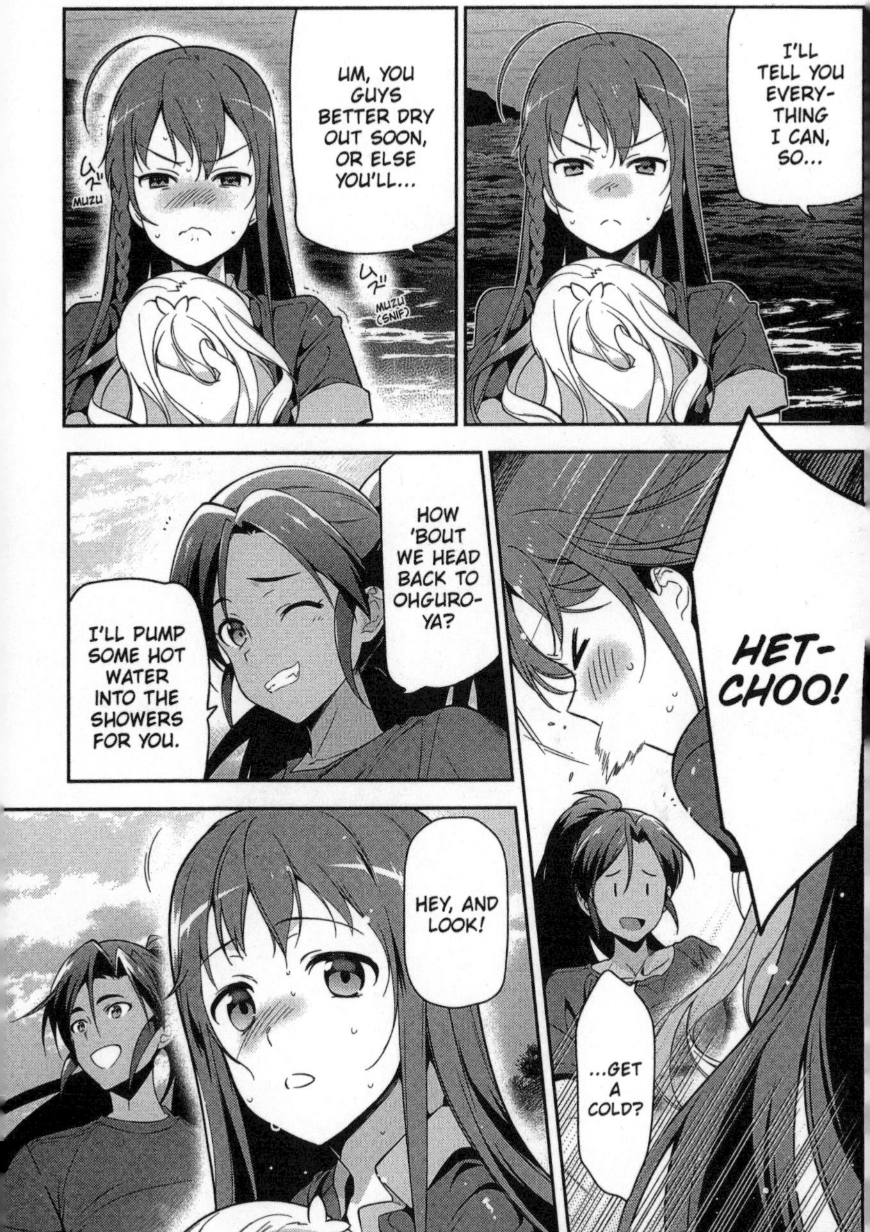
I'LL TELL YOU EVERY-THING I CAN, SO...
UM, YOU GUYS BETTER DRY OUT SOON, OR ELSE YOU'LL...
ムズ
MUZU
ムズ
MUZU (SNIF)
HET-CHOO!
...GET A COLD?
HOW 'BOUT WE HEAD BACK TO OHGURO-YA?
I'LL PUMP SOME HOT WATER INTO THE SHOWERS FOR YOU.
HEY, AND LOOK!

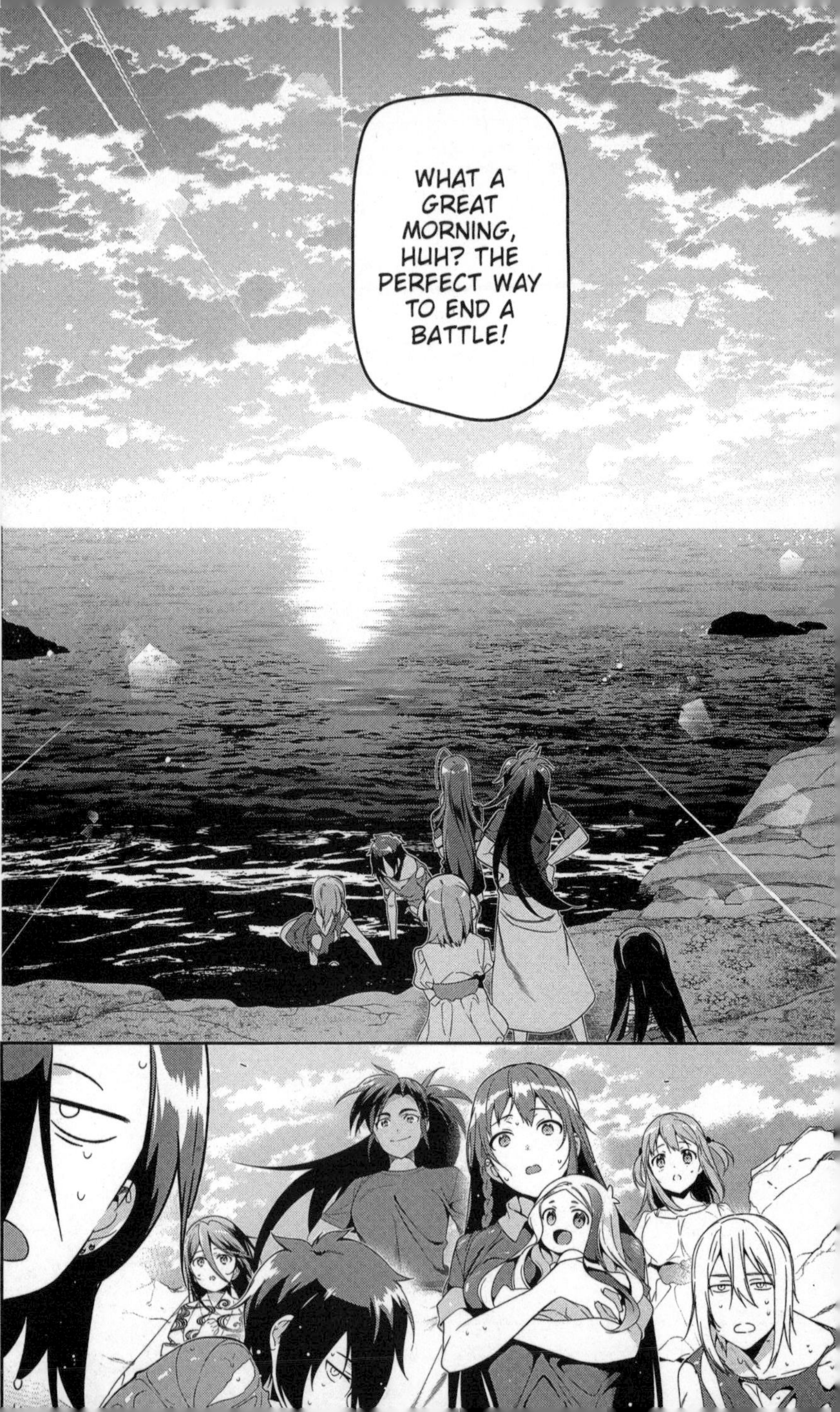
WHAT A GREAT MORNING, HUH? THE PERFECT WAY TO END A BATTLE!

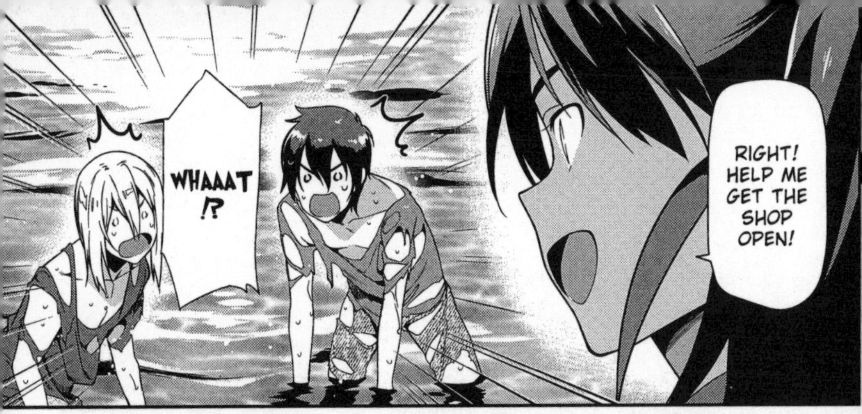
RIGHT! HELP ME GET THE SHOP OPEN!
WHAAAT !?
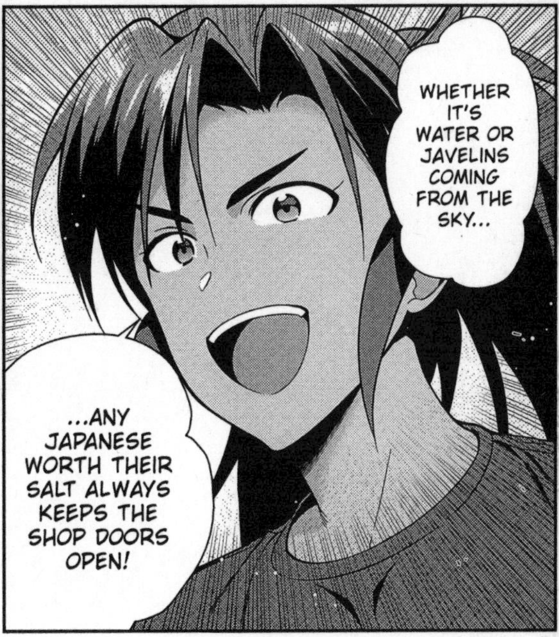
WHETHER IT'S WATER OR JAVELINS COMING FROM THE SKY...
...ANY JAPANESE WORTH THEIR SALT ALWAYS KEEPS THE SHOP DOORS OPEN!
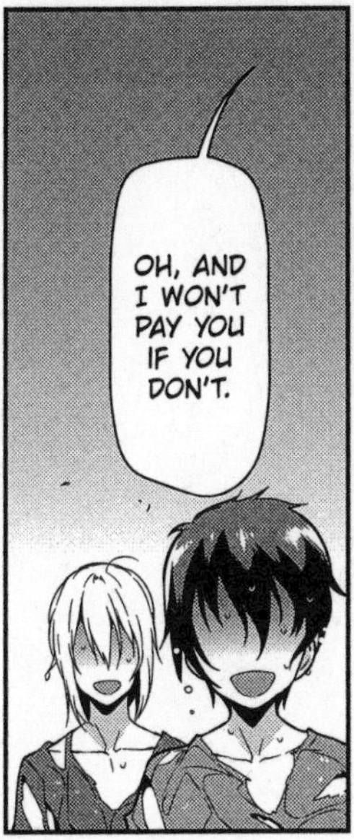
OH, AND I WON'T PAY YOU IF YOU DON'T.
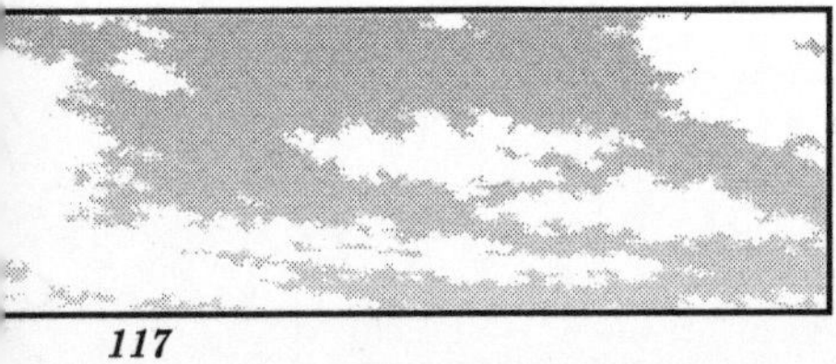

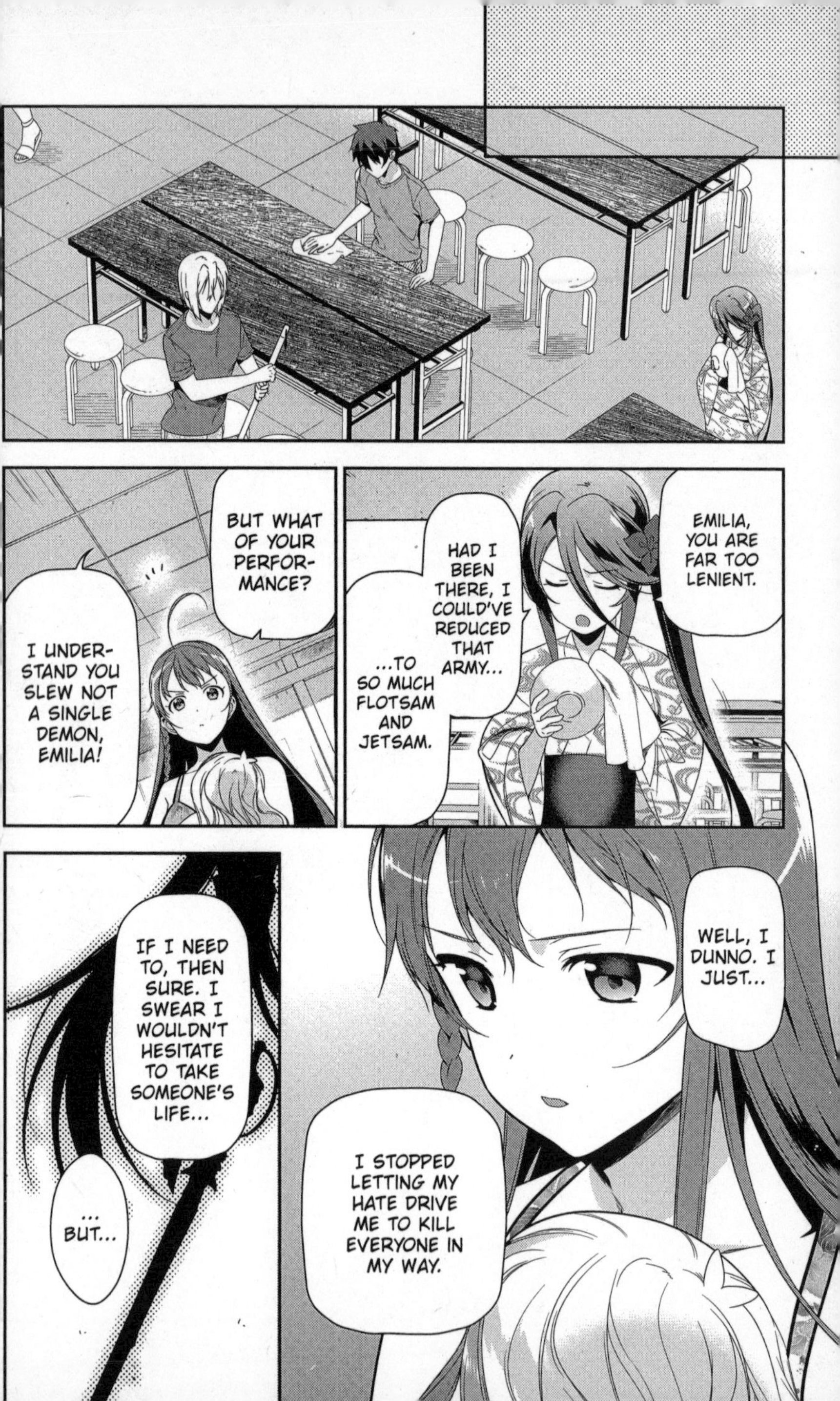
EMILIA, YOU ARE FAR TOO LENIENT.
HAD I BEEN THERE, I COULD'VE REDUCED THAT ARMY...
...TO SO MUCH FLOTSAM AND JETSAM.
BUT WHAT OF YOUR PERFORMANCE?
I UNDERSTAND YOU SLEW NOT A SINGLE DEMON, EMILIA!
WELL, I DUNNO. I JUST...
I STOPPED LETTING MY HATE DRIVE ME TO KILL EVERYONE IN MY WAY.
IF I NEED TO, THEN SURE. I SWEAR I WOULDN'T HESITATE TO TAKE SOMEONE'S LIFE...
...BUT...

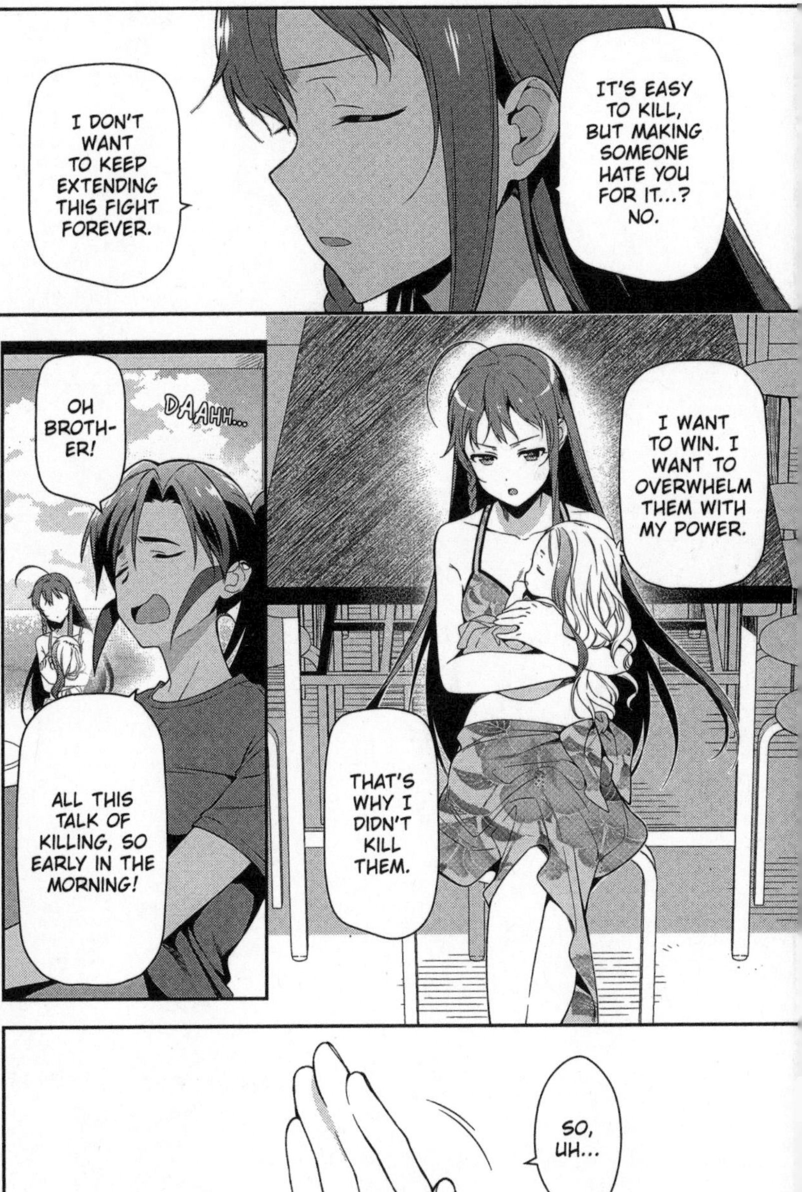
IT'S EASY TO KILL, BUT MAKING SOMEONE HATE YOU FOR IT...? NO.
I DON'T WANT TO KEEP EXTENDING THIS FIGHT FOREVER.
I WANT TO WIN. I WANT TO OVERWHELM THEM WITH MY POWER.
THAT'S WHY I DIDN'T KILL THEM.
OH BROTHER!
DAAHH...
ALL THIS TALK OF KILLING, SO EARLY IN THE MORNING!
SO, UH...

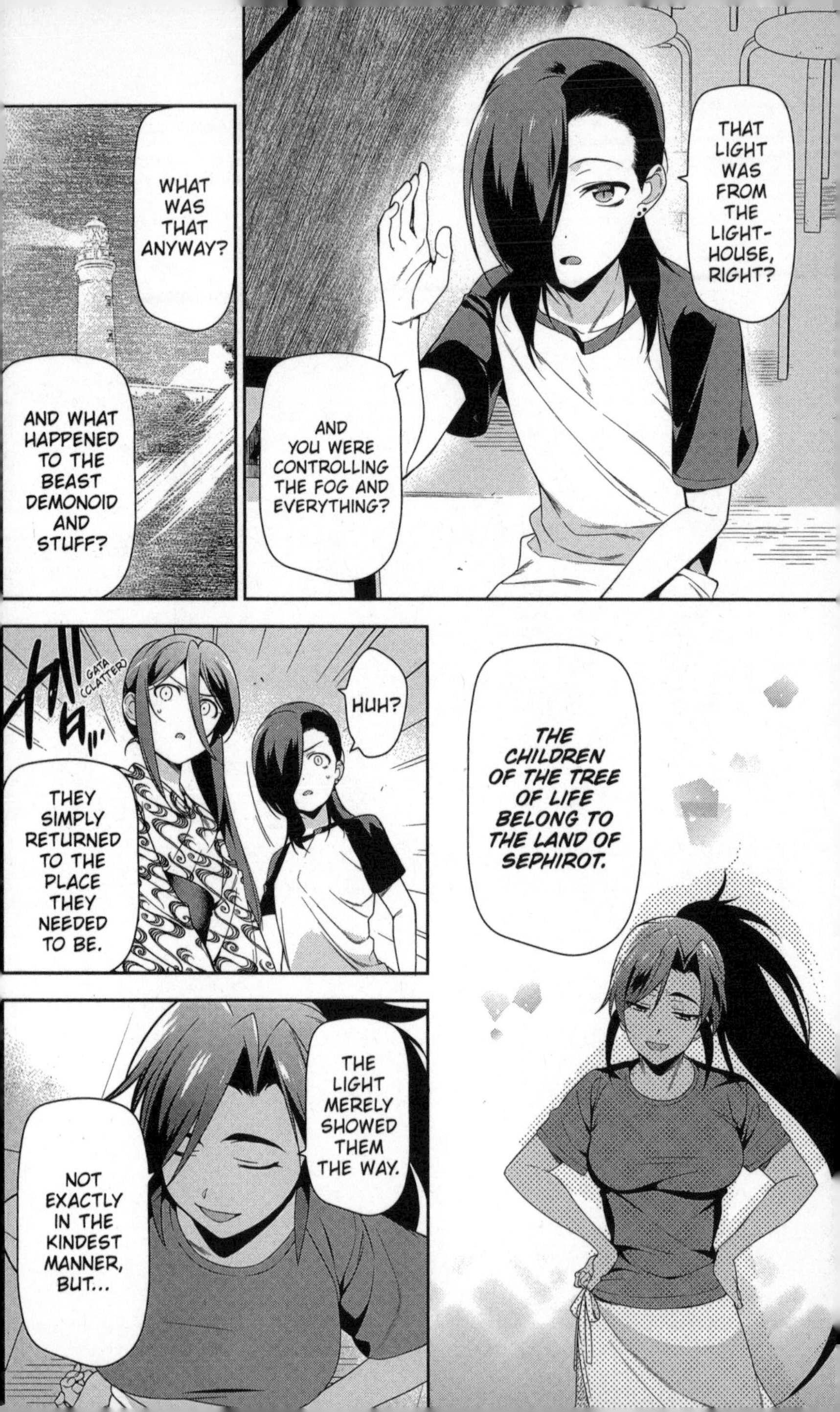
THAT LIGHT WAS FROM THE LIGHT-HOUSE, RIGHT?
AND YOU WERE CONTROLLING THE FOG AND EVERYTHING?
WHAT WAS THAT ANYWAY?
AND WHAT HAPPENED TO THE BEAST DEMONOID AND STUFF?
THE CHILDREN OF THE TREE OF LIFE BELONG TO THE LAND OF SEPHIROT.
HUH?
GATA (CLATTER)
THEY SIMPLY RETURNED TO THE PLACE THEY NEEDED TO BE.
THE LIGHT MERELY SHOWED THEM THE WAY.
NOT EXACTLY IN THE KINDEST MANNER, BUT...

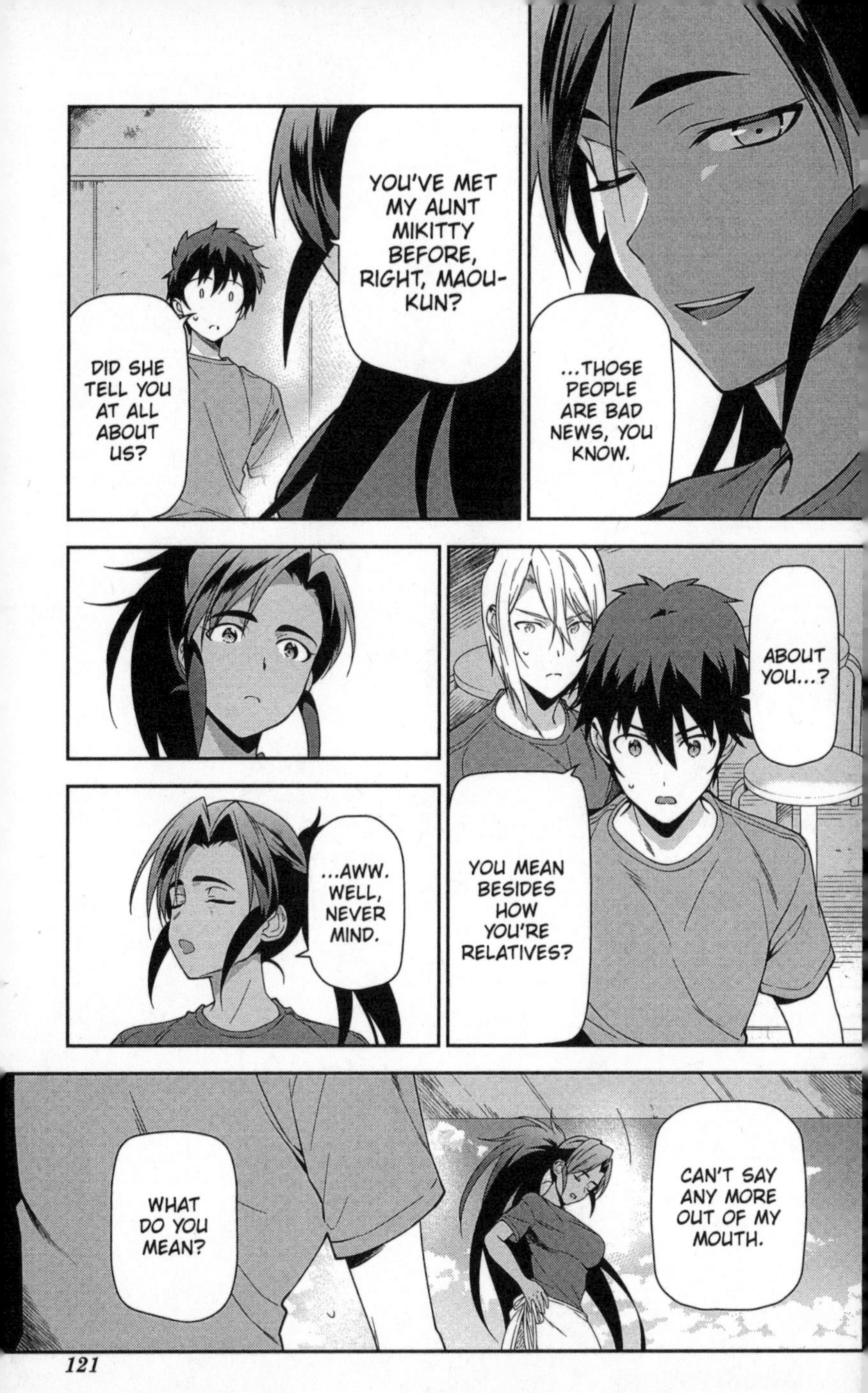
...THOSE PEOPLE ARE BAD NEWS, YOU KNOW.
YOU'VE MET MY AUNT MIKITTY BEFORE, RIGHT, MAOU-KUN?
DID SHE TELL YOU AT ALL ABOUT US?
ABOUT YOU...?
YOU MEAN BESIDES HOW YOU'RE RELATIVES?
...AWW. WELL, NEVER MIND.
CAN'T SAY ANY MORE OUT OF MY MOUTH.
WHAT DO YOU MEAN?

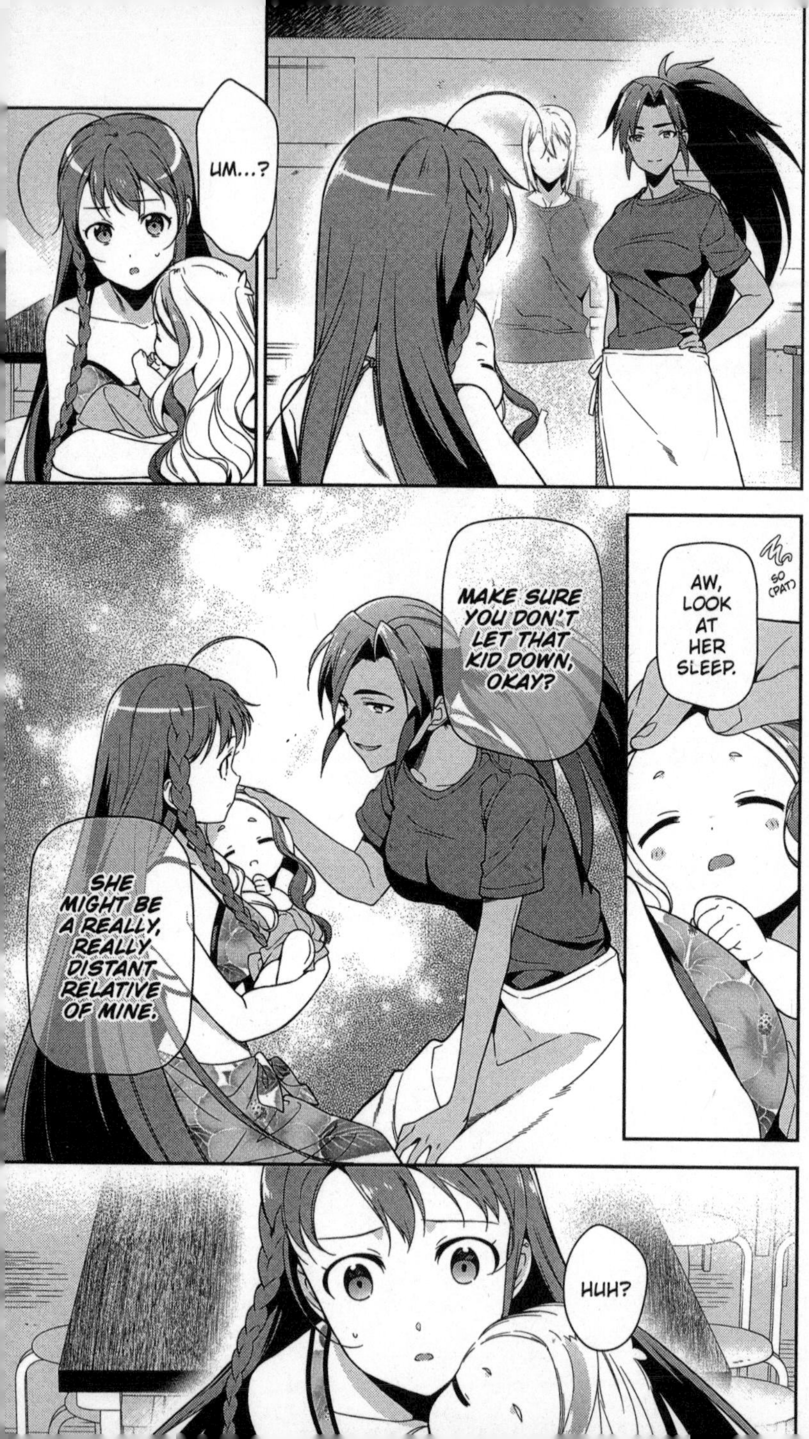
UM...?
SO (PAT)
AW, LOOK AT HER SLEEP.
MAKE SURE YOU DON'T LET THAT KID DOWN, OKAY?
SHE MIGHT BE A REALLY, REALLY DISTANT RELATIVE OF MINE.
HUH?

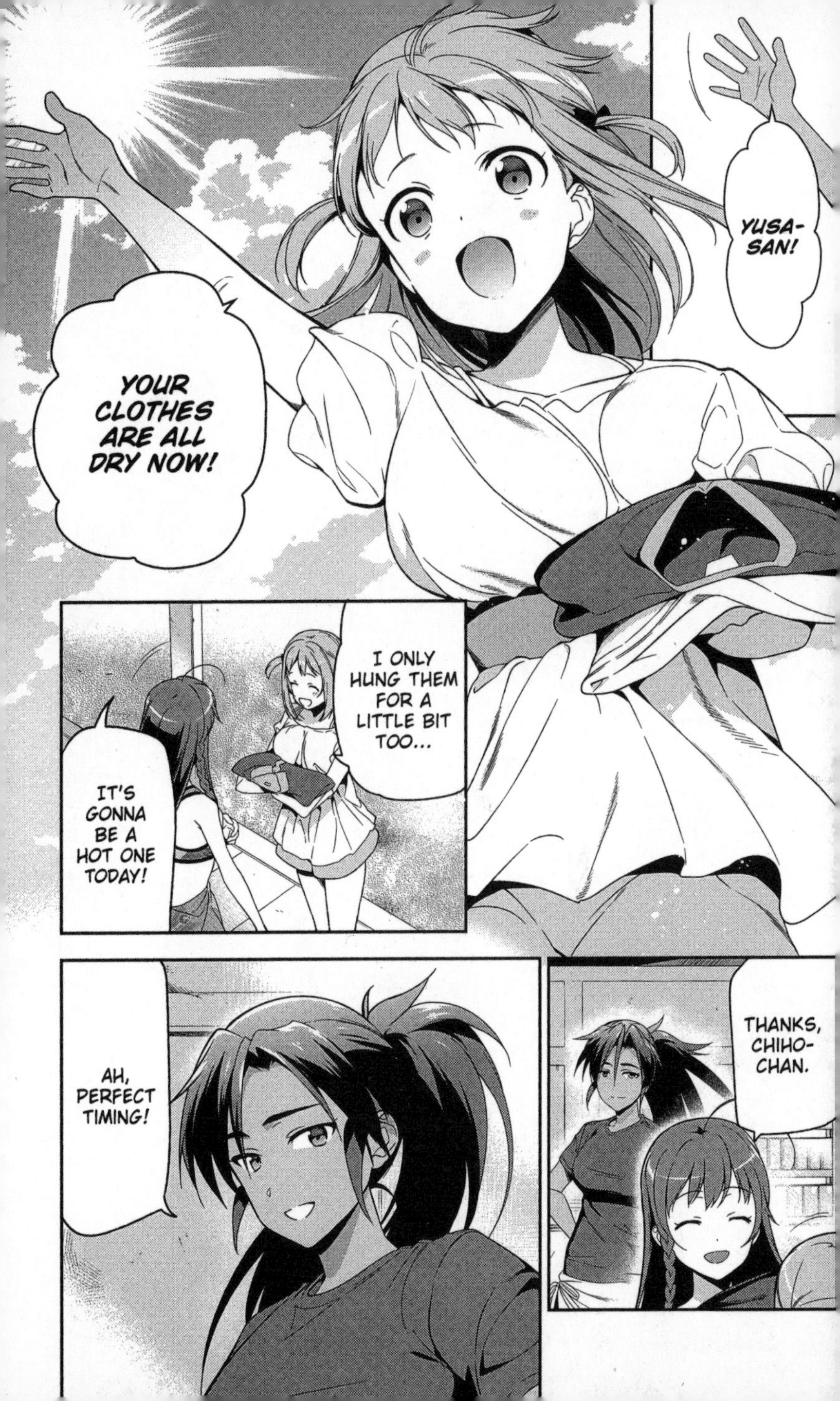
YUSA-SAN!
YOUR CLOTHES ARE ALL DRY NOW!
I ONLY HUNG THEM FOR A LITTLE BIT TOO...
IT'S GONNA BE A HOT ONE TODAY!
THANKS, CHIHO-CHAN.
AH, PERFECT TIMING!

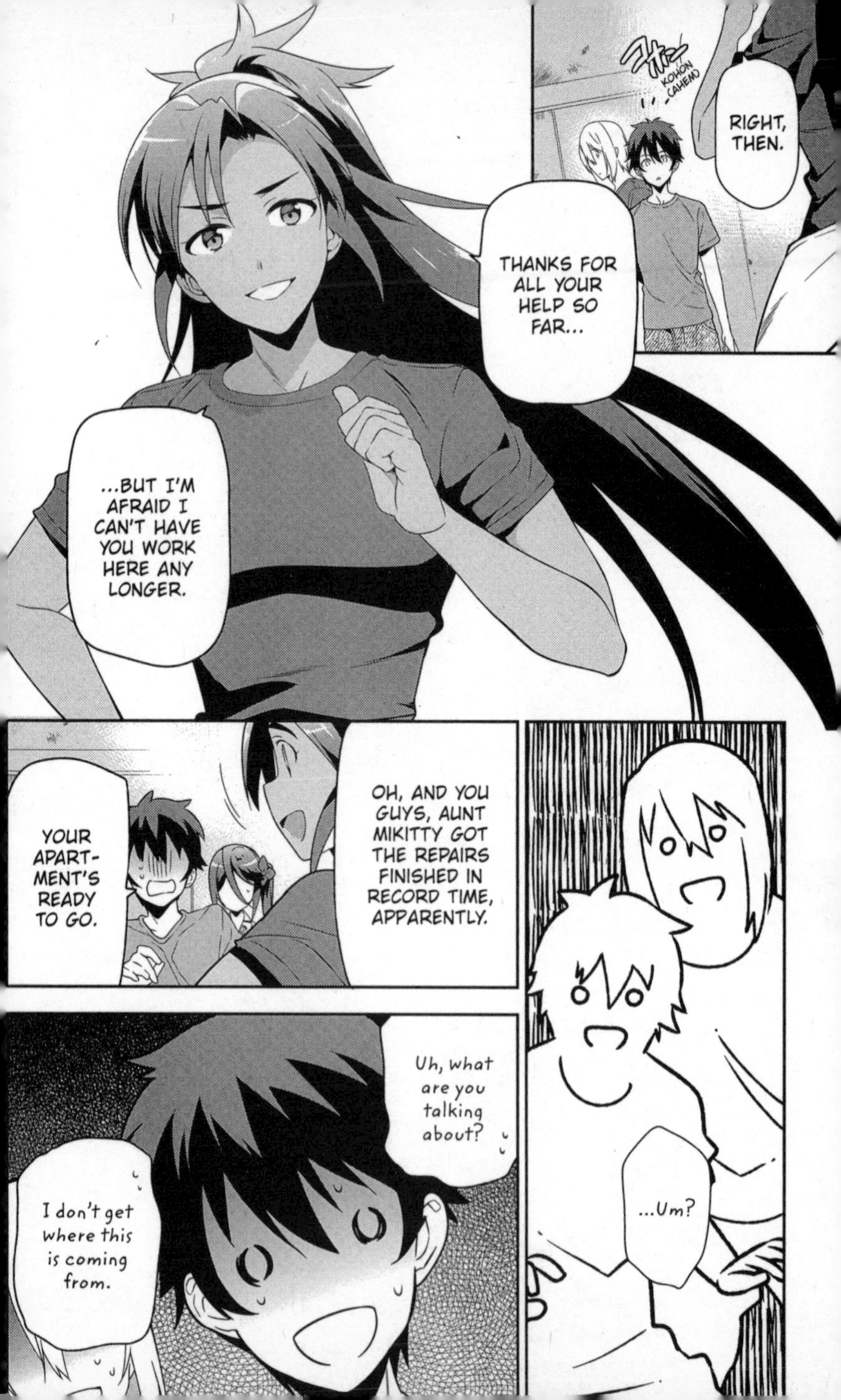
KOHON
CAHEM
RIGHT, THEN.
THANKS FOR ALL YOUR HELP SO FAR...
...BUT I'M AFRAID I CAN'T HAVE YOU WORK HERE ANY LONGER.
...Um?
OH, AND YOU GUYS, AUNT MIKITTY GOT THE REPAIRS FINISHED IN RECORD TIME, APPARENTLY.
YOUR APART-MENT'S READY TO GO.
Uh, what are you talking about?
I don't get where this is coming from.

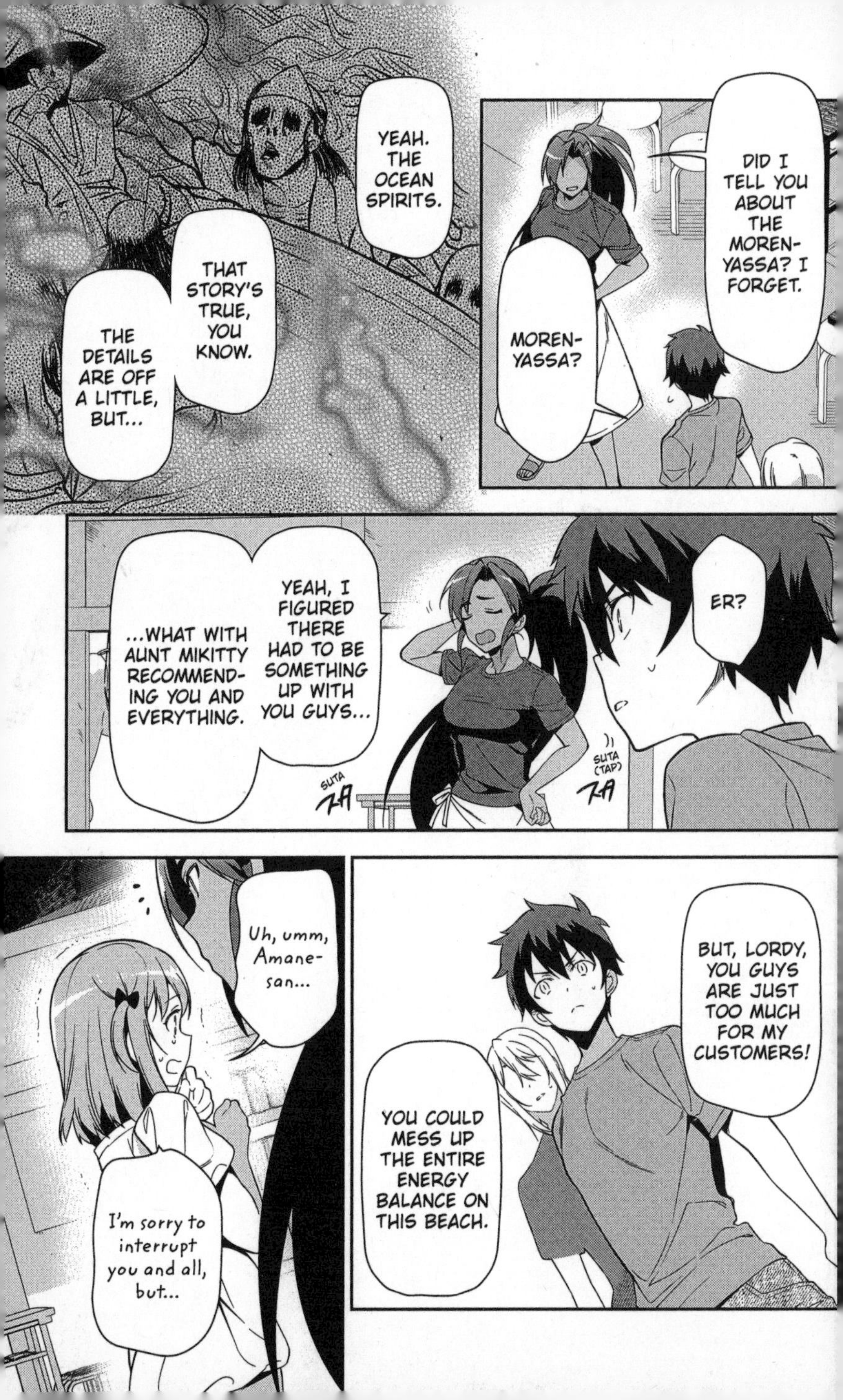
DID I TELL YOU ABOUT THE MOREN-YASSA? I FORGET.
MOREN-YASSA?
YEAH. THE OCEAN SPIRITS.
THAT STORY'S TRUE, YOU KNOW.
THE DETAILS ARE OFF A LITTLE, BUT...
ER?
SUTA (TAP)
YEAH, I FIGURED THERE HAD TO BE SOMETHING UP WITH YOU GUYS...
...WHAT WITH AUNT MIKITTY RECOMMEND-ING YOU AND EVERYTHING.
SUTA
BUT, LORDY, YOU GUYS ARE JUST TOO MUCH FOR MY CUSTOMERS!
YOU COULD MESS UP THE ENTIRE ENERGY BALANCE ON THIS BEACH.
Uh, umm, Amane-san...
I'm sorry to interrupt you and all, but...

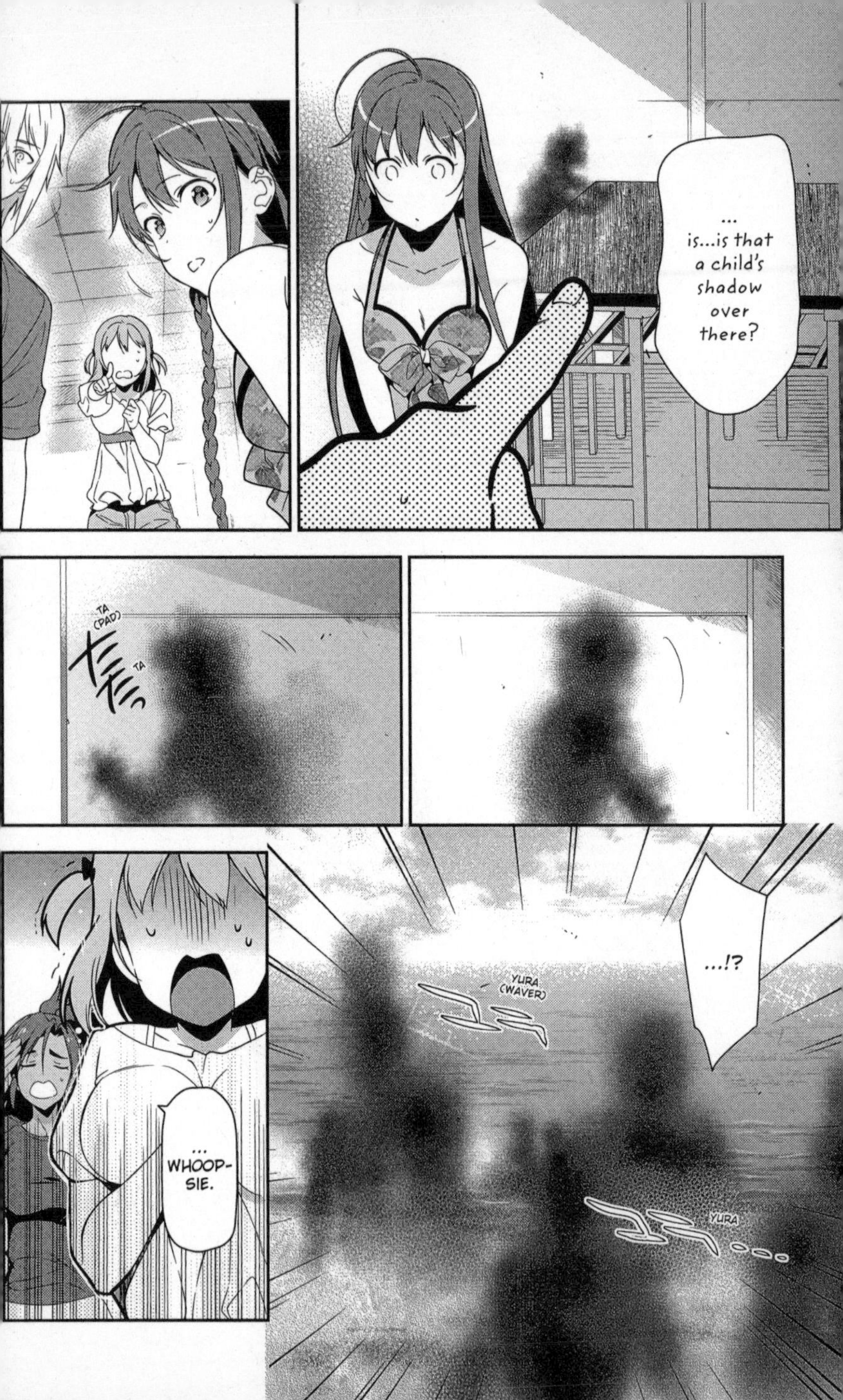

... is...is that a child's shadow over there?
TA (PAD)
TA
...!?
YURA (WAVER)
YURA
... WHOOP-SIE.

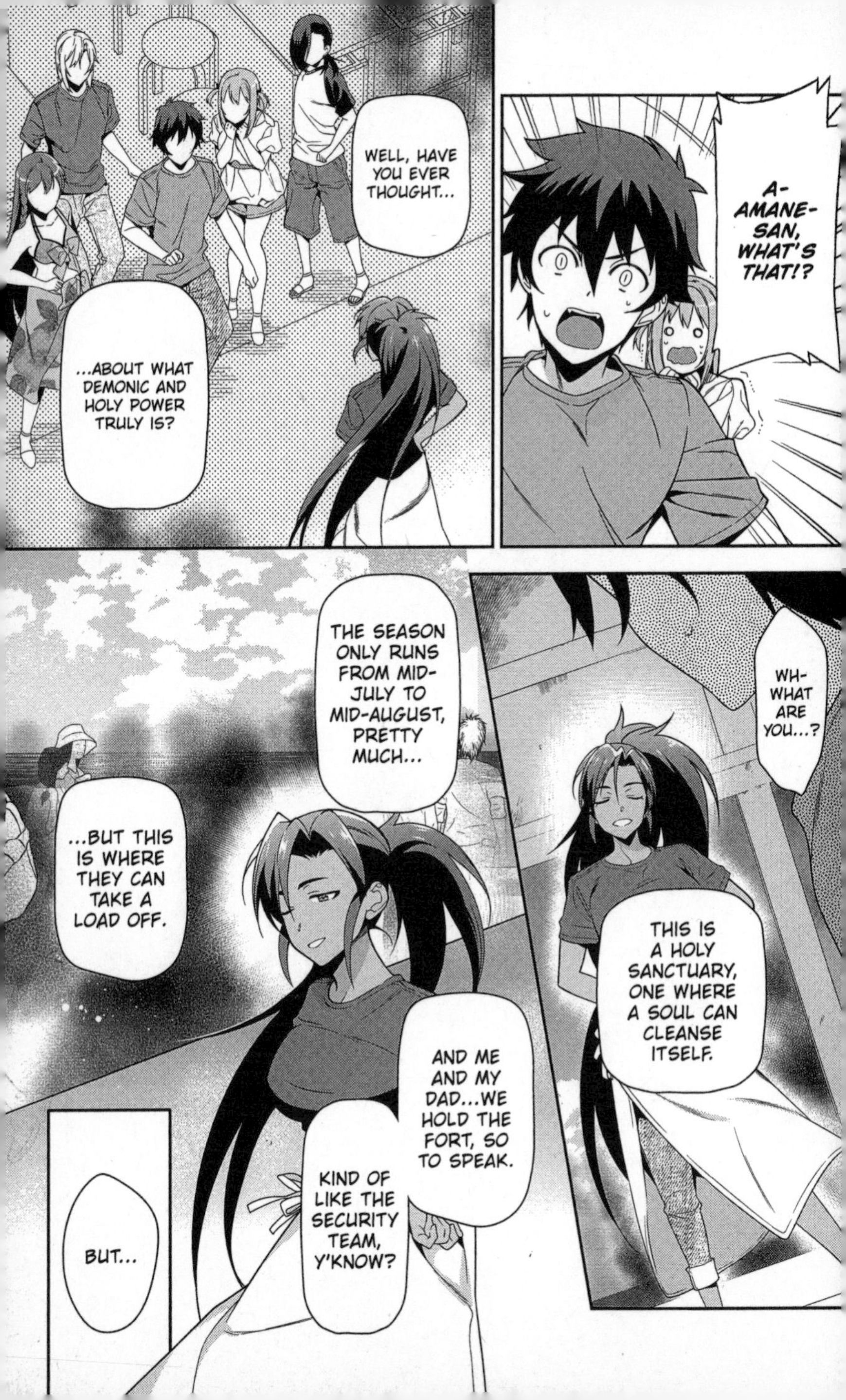
A-AMANE-SAN, WHAT'S THAT!?
WELL, HAVE YOU EVER THOUGHT...
...ABOUT WHAT DEMONIC AND HOLY POWER TRULY IS?
WH-WHAT ARE YOU...?
THIS IS A HOLY SANCTUARY, ONE WHERE A SOUL CAN CLEANSE ITSELF.
THE SEASON ONLY RUNS FROM MID-JULY TO MID-AUGUST, PRETTY MUCH...
...BUT THIS IS WHERE THEY CAN TAKE A LOAD OFF.
AND ME AND MY DAD...WE HOLD THE FORT, SO TO SPEAK.
KIND OF LIKE THE SECURITY TEAM, Y'KNOW?
BUT...

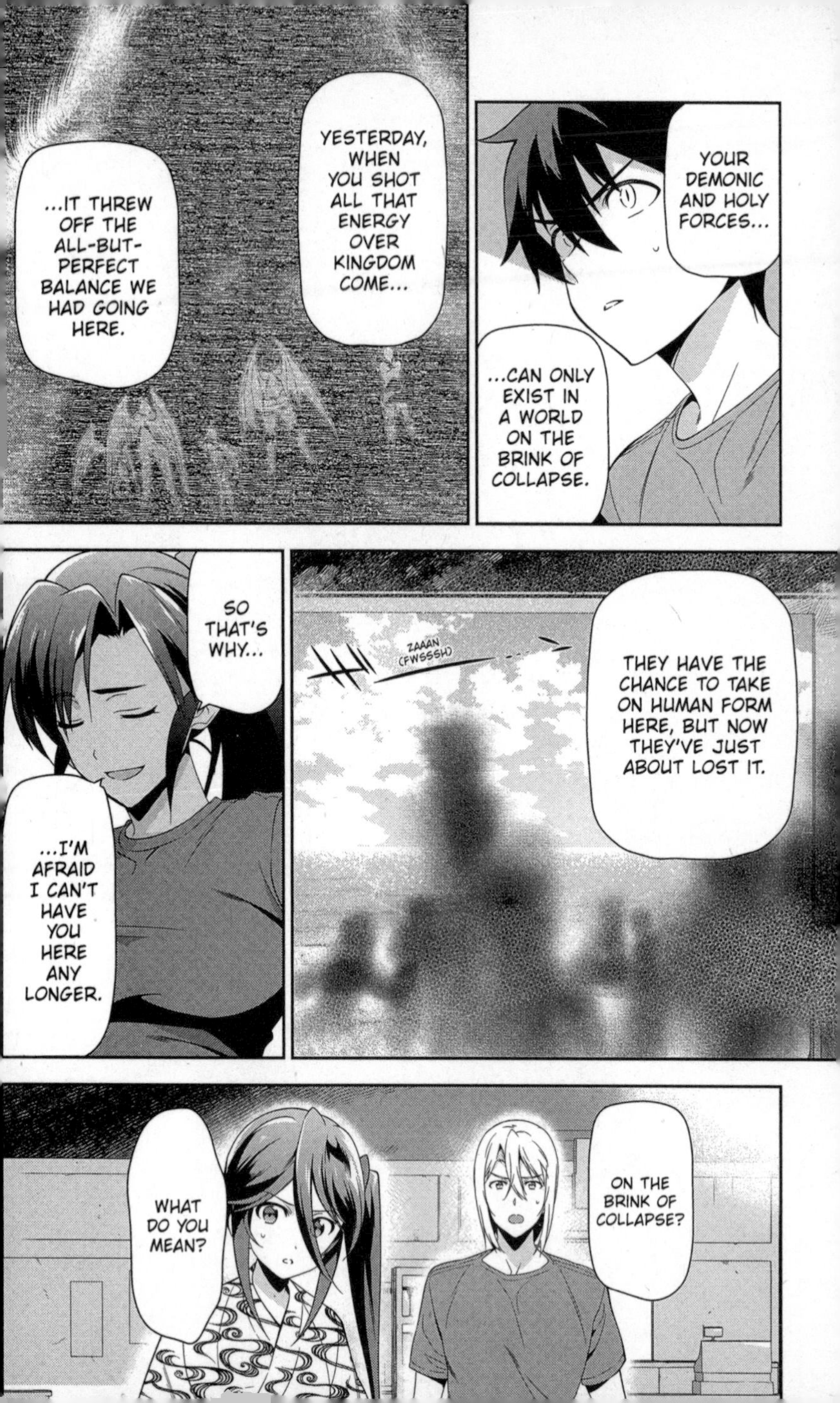
YOUR DEMONIC AND HOLY FORCES...
...CAN ONLY EXIST IN A WORLD ON THE BRINK OF COLLAPSE.
YESTERDAY, WHEN YOU SHOT ALL THAT ENERGY OVER KINGDOM COME...
...IT THREW OFF THE ALL-BUT-PERFECT BALANCE WE HAD GOING HERE.
ZAAAN (FWSSSH)
THEY HAVE THE CHANCE TO TAKE ON HUMAN FORM HERE, BUT NOW THEY'VE JUST ABOUT LOST IT.
SO THAT'S WHY...
...I'M AFRAID I CAN'T HAVE YOU HERE ANY LONGER.
ON THE BRINK OF COLLAPSE?
WHAT DO YOU MEAN?

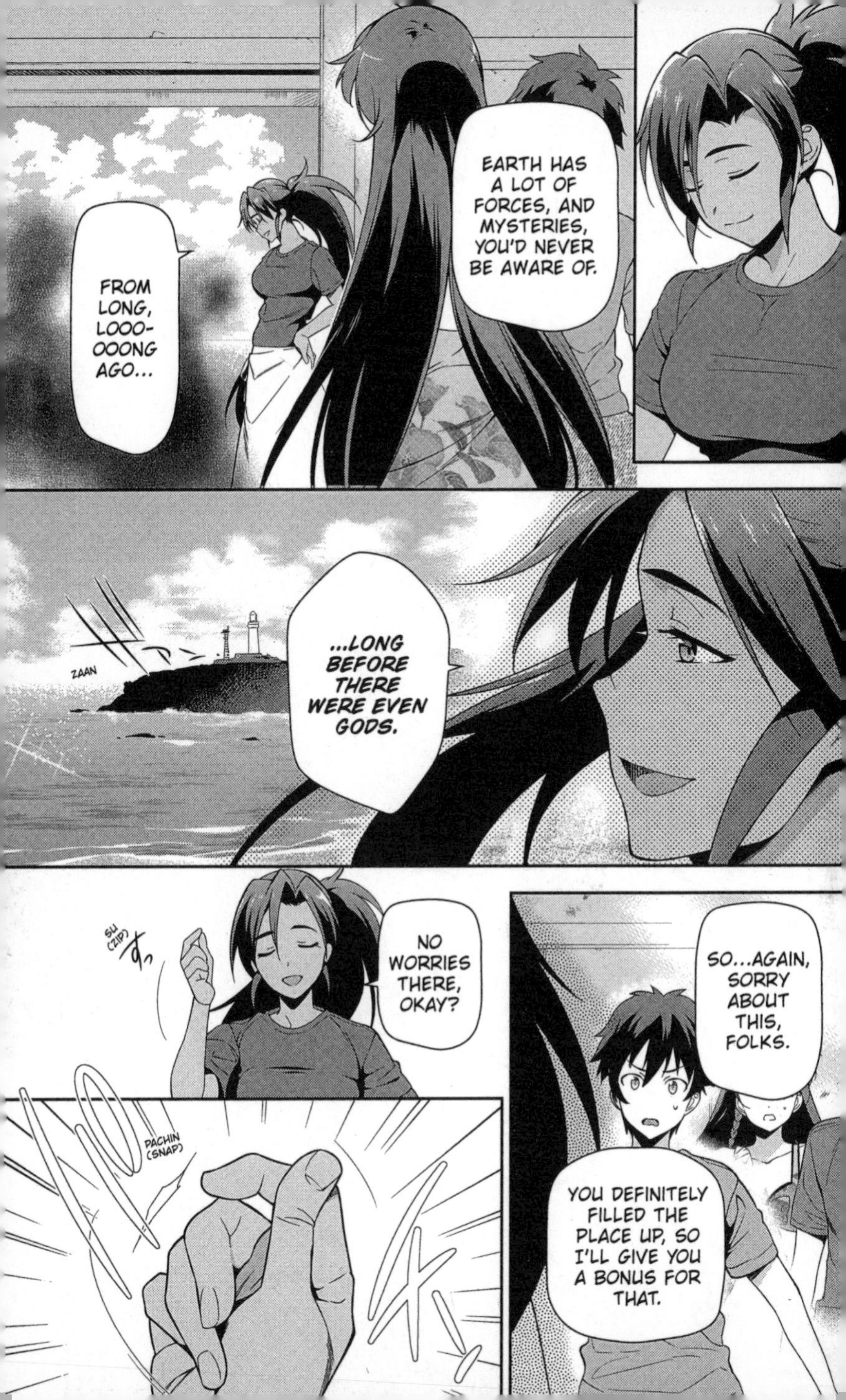
EARTH HAS A LOT OF FORCES, AND MYSTERIES, YOU'D NEVER BE AWARE OF.
FROM LONG, LOOOOOONG AGO...
...LONG BEFORE THERE WERE EVEN GODS.
ZAAN
SO...AGAIN, SORRY ABOUT THIS, FOLKS.
YOU DEFINITELY FILLED THE PLACE UP, SO I'LL GIVE YOU A BONUS FOR THAT.
NO WORRIES THERE, OKAY?
SU (ZIP)
PACHIN (SNAP)

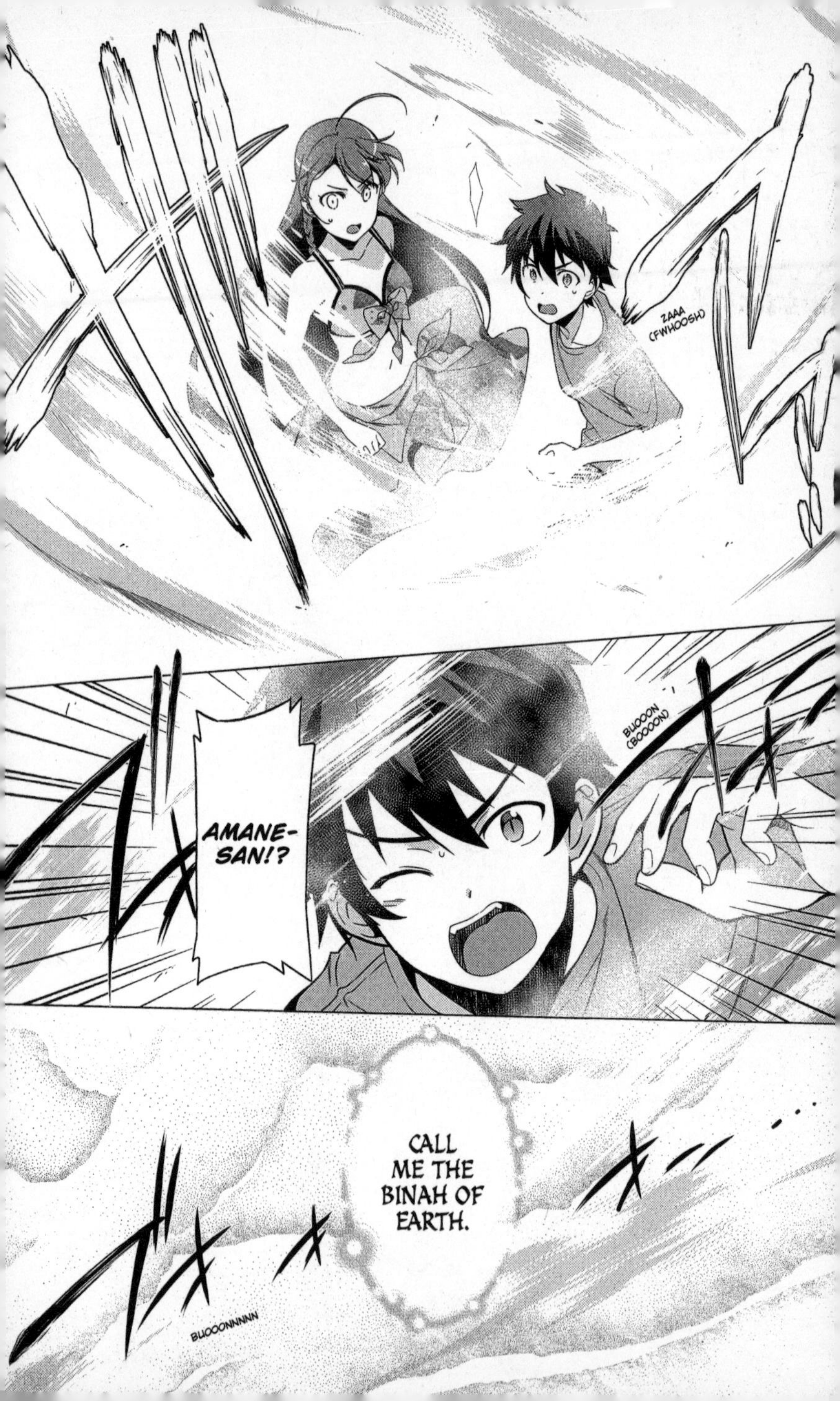
ZAAA (FWHOOSH)
BUOOON (BOOOON)
AMANE-SAN!?
CALL ME THE BINAH OF EARTH.
BUOOONNNNN

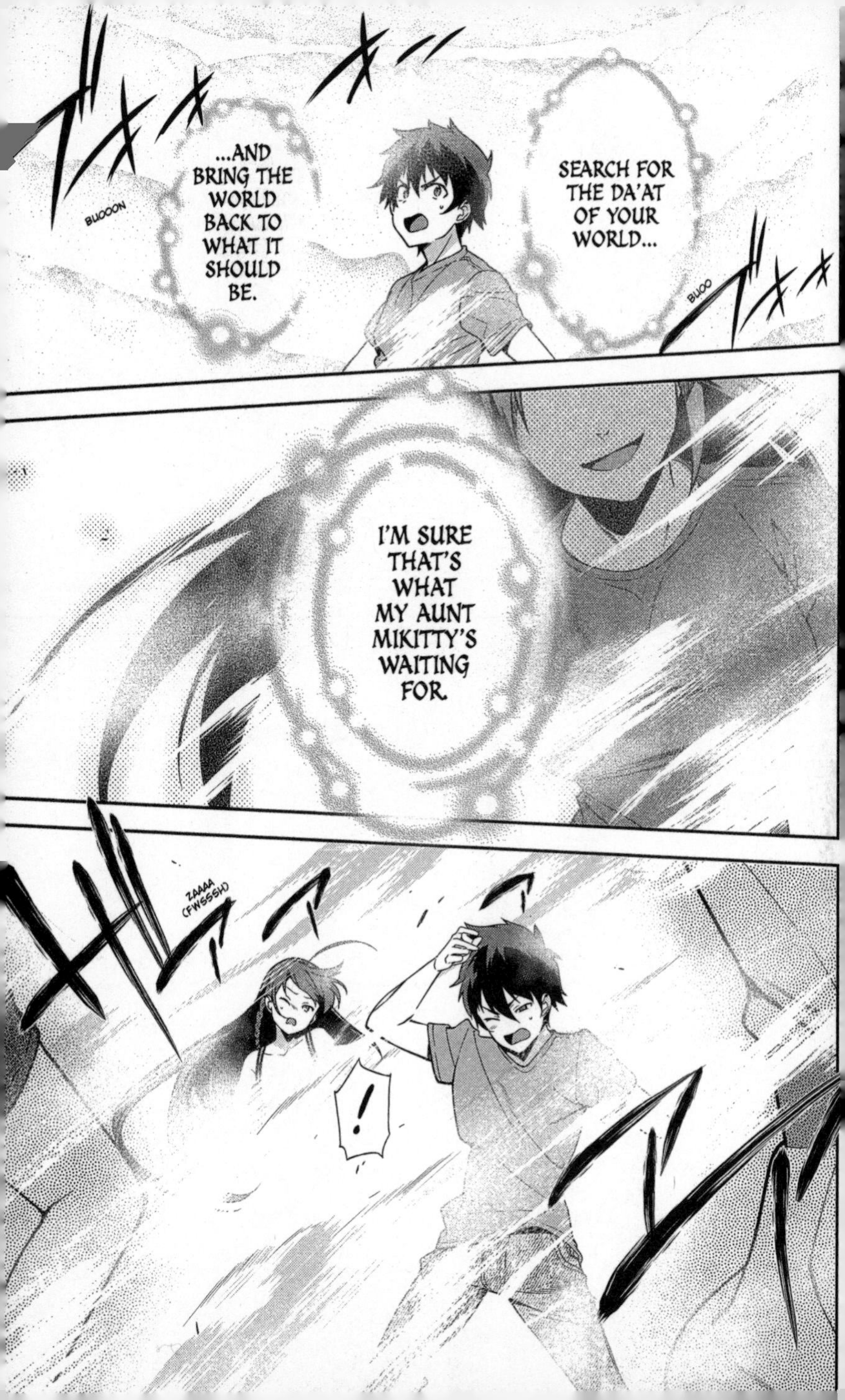
BUOO
SEARCH FOR THE DA'AT OF YOUR WORLD...
...AND BRING THE WORLD BACK TO WHAT IT SHOULD BE.
BUOOON
I'M SURE THAT'S WHAT MY AUNT MIKITTY'S WAITING FOR.
ZAAAA (FWSSSH)
!

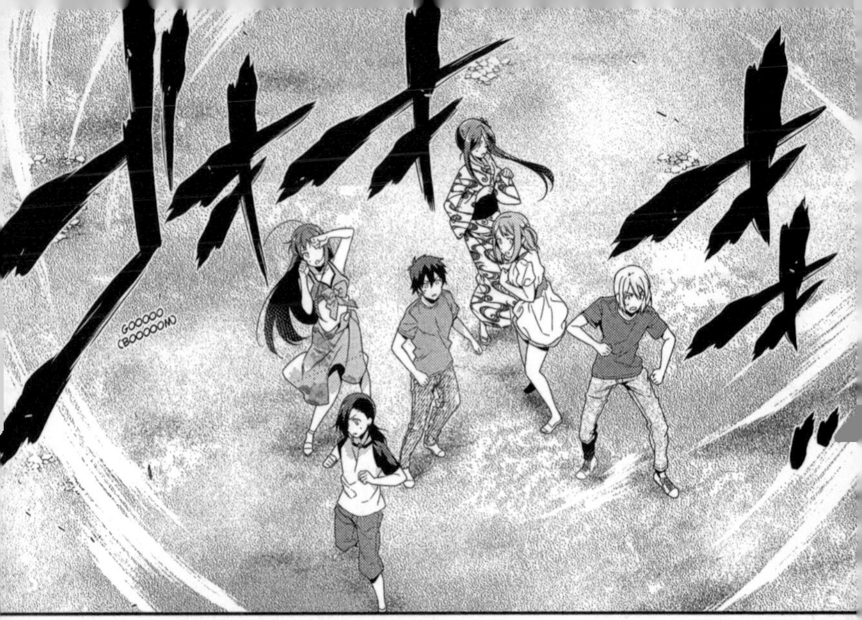
GOOOOO
(BOOOOOM)

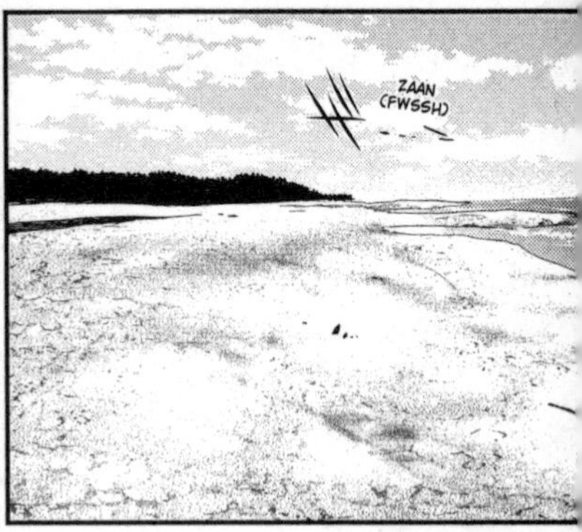
ZAAN
(FWSSH)

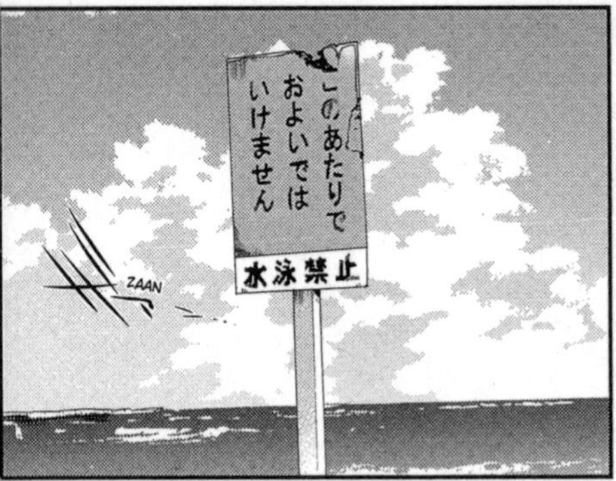
このあたりで
およいでは
いけません
水泳禁止
ZAAN

SIGN: NO SWIMMING ALLOWED IN THIS AREA, WARNING

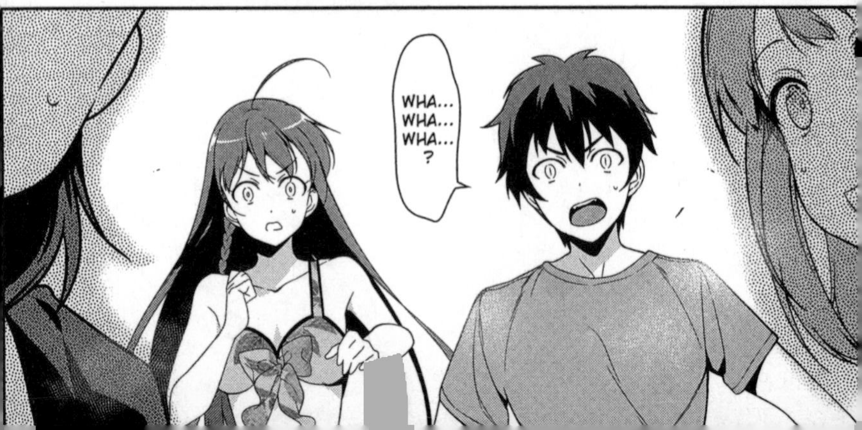
WHA... WHA... WHA...?

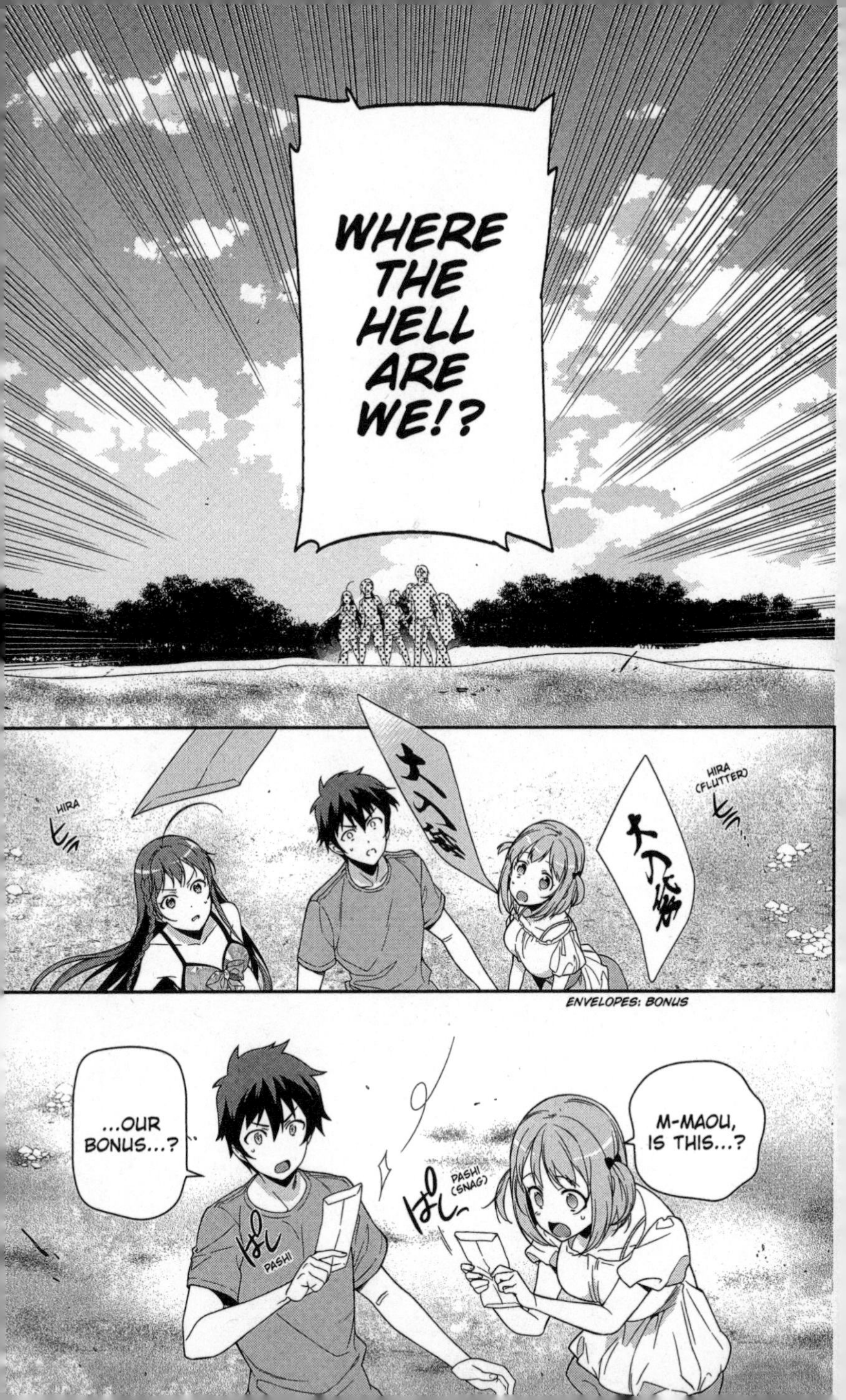
WHERE THE HELL ARE WE!?
HIRA (FLUTTER)
HIRA
ENVELOPES: BONUS
M-MAOU, IS THIS...?
PASHI (SNAG)
...OUR BONUS...?
PASHI

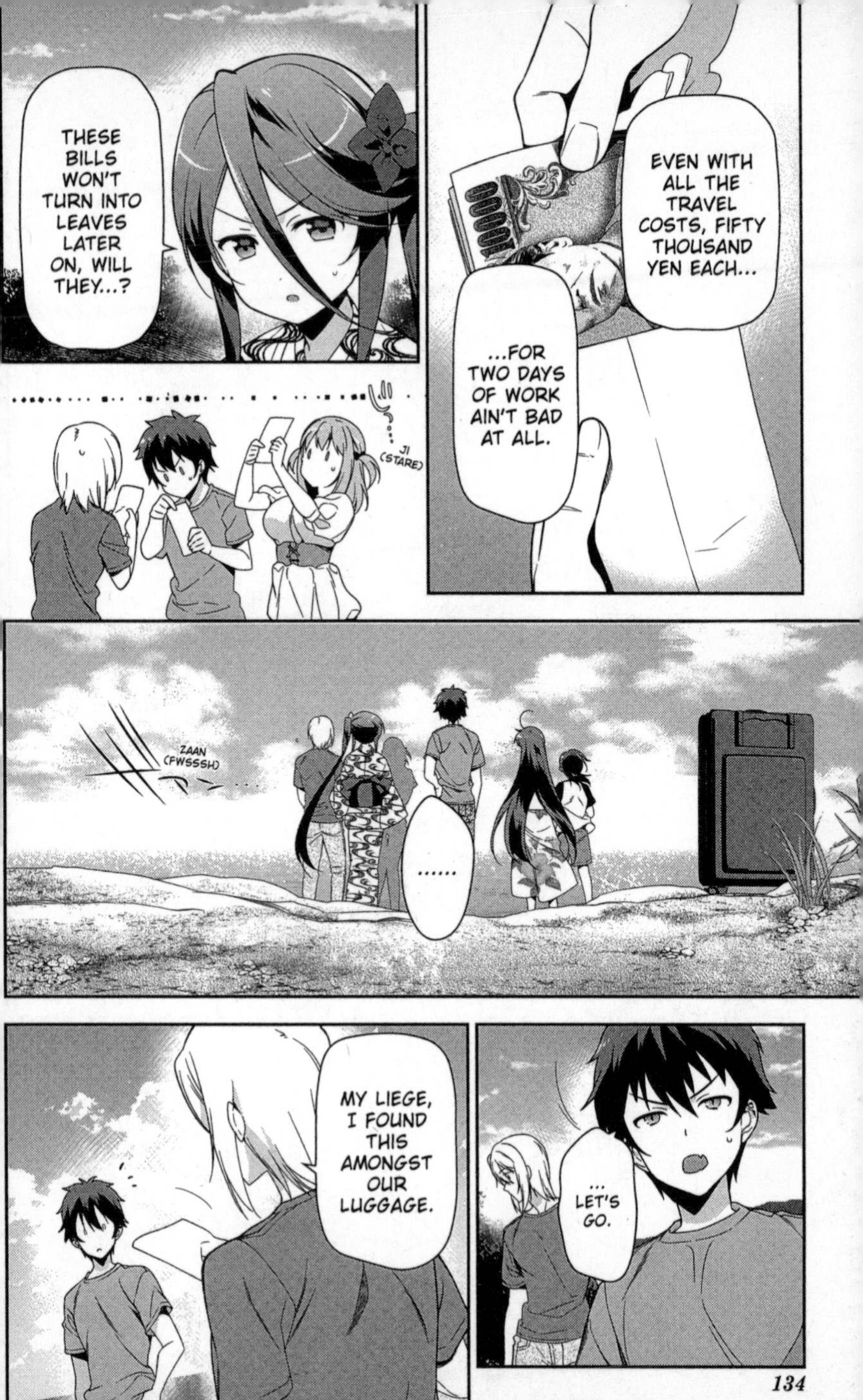
EVEN WITH ALL THE TRAVEL COSTS, FIFTY THOUSAND YEN EACH...
...FOR TWO DAYS OF WORK AIN'T BAD AT ALL.
THESE BILLS WON'T TURN INTO LEAVES LATER ON, WILL THEY...?
JI (STARE)
ZAAN (FWSSSH)
......
... LET'S GO.
MY LIEGE, I FOUND THIS AMONGST OUR LUGGAGE.

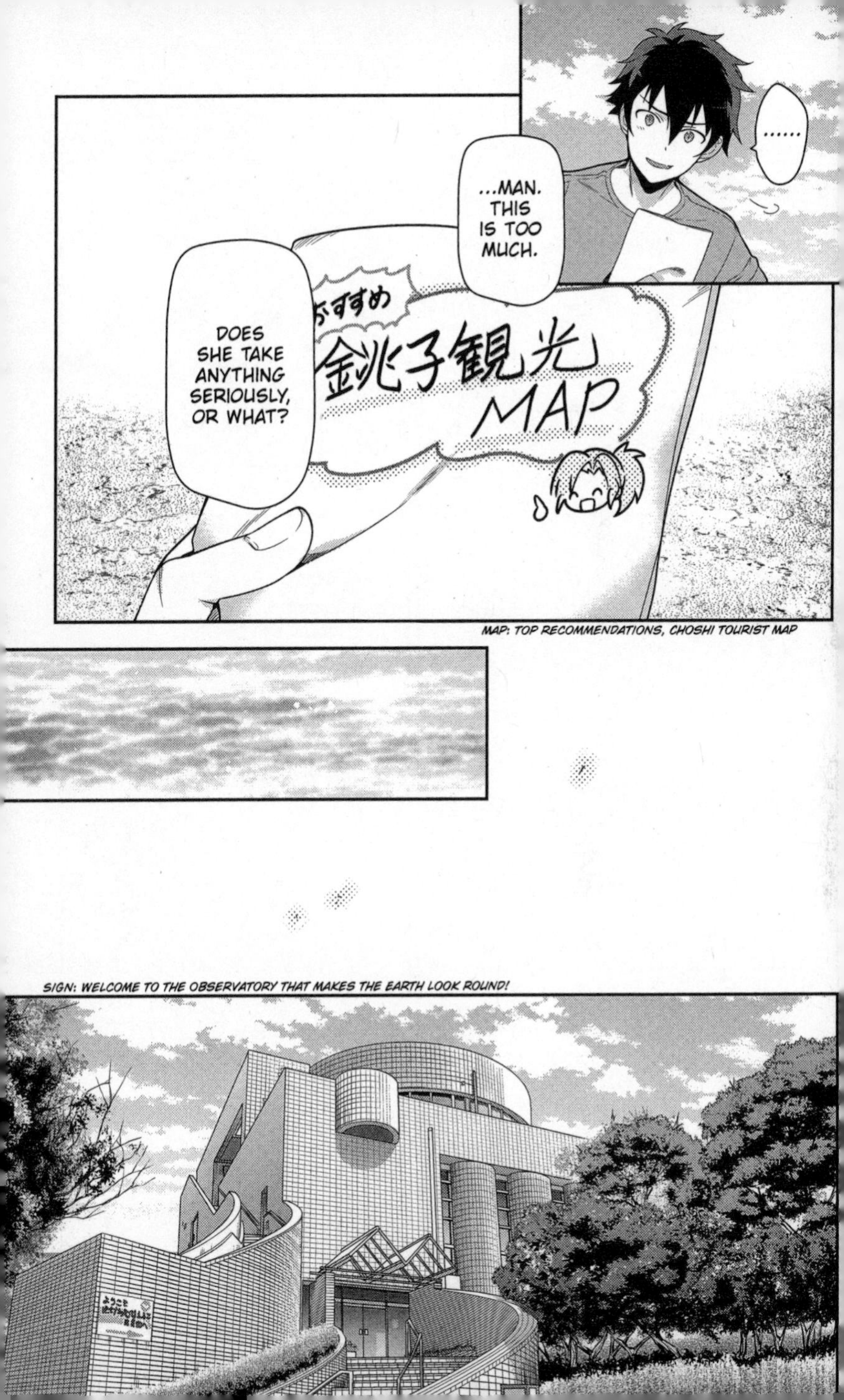
......
...MAN. THIS IS TOO MUCH.
DOES SHE TAKE ANYTHING SERIOUSLY, OR WHAT?
銚子観光 MAP
MAP: TOP RECOMMENDATIONS, CHOSHI TOURIST MAP
SIGN: WELCOME TO THE OBSERVATORY THAT MAKES THE EARTH LOOK ROUND!

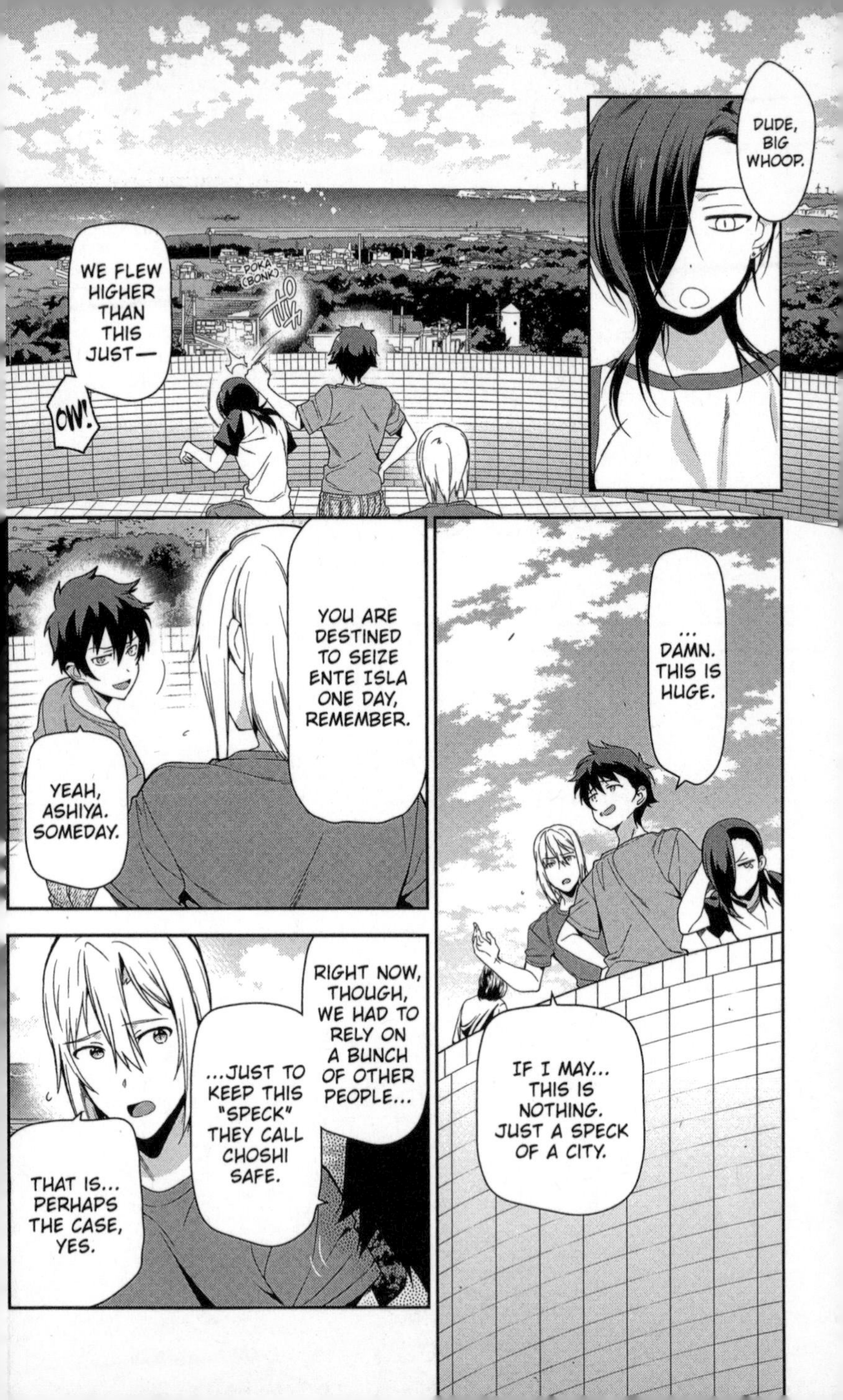
DUDE, BIG WHOOP.
WE FLEW HIGHER THAN THIS JUST—
POKA (BONK)
OW!
... DAMN. THIS IS HUGE.
IF I MAY... THIS IS NOTHING. JUST A SPECK OF A CITY.
YOU ARE DESTINED TO SEIZE ENTE ISLA ONE DAY, REMEMBER.
YEAH, ASHIYA. SOMEDAY.
RIGHT NOW, THOUGH, WE HAD TO RELY ON A BUNCH OF OTHER PEOPLE...
...JUST TO KEEP THIS "SPECK" THEY CALL CHOSHI SAFE.
THAT IS... PERHAPS THE CASE, YES.

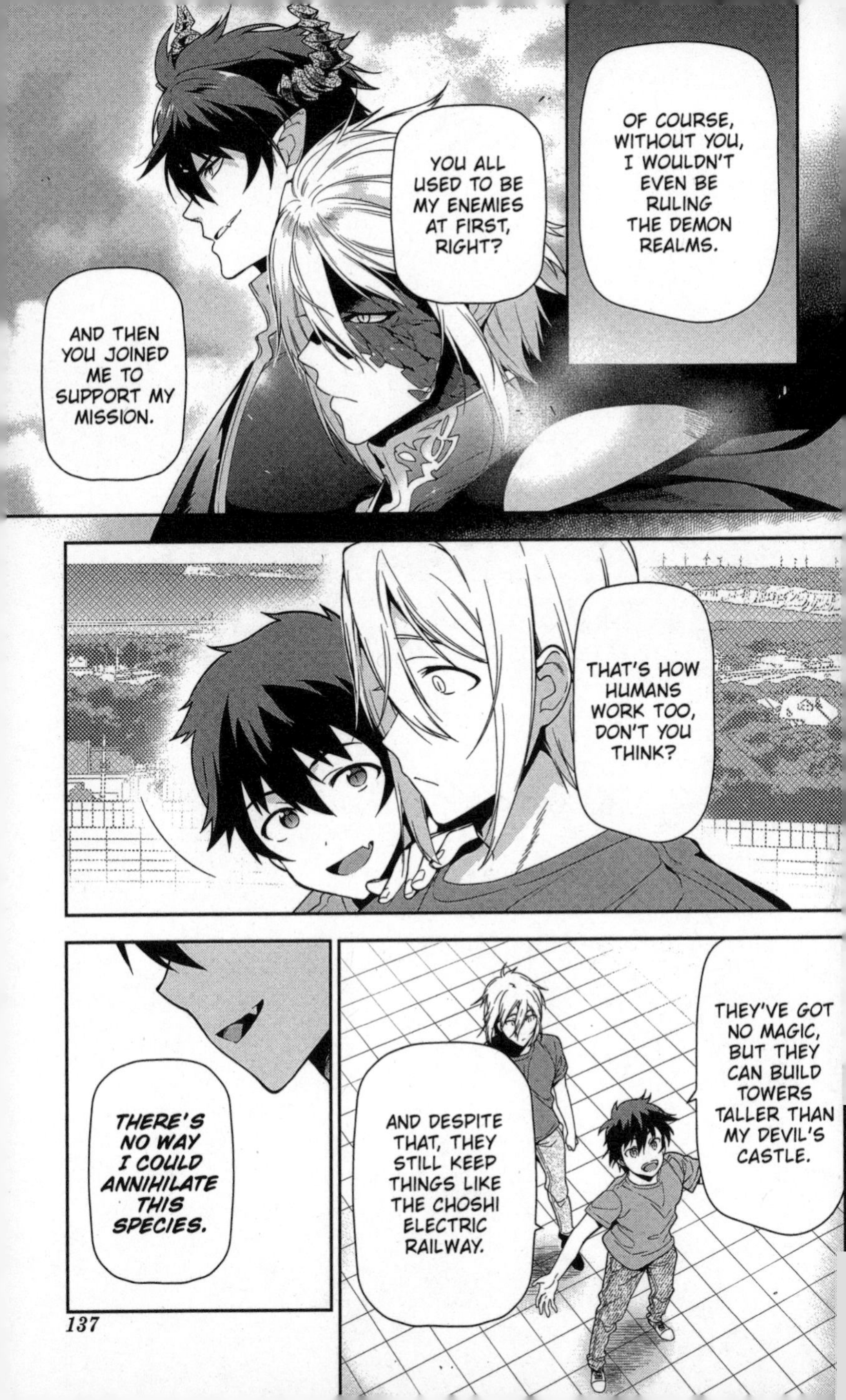
OF COURSE, WITHOUT YOU, I WOULDN'T EVEN BE RULING THE DEMON REALMS.
YOU ALL USED TO BE MY ENEMIES AT FIRST, RIGHT?
AND THEN YOU JOINED ME TO SUPPORT MY MISSION.
THAT'S HOW HUMANS WORK TOO, DON'T YOU THINK?
THEY'VE GOT NO MAGIC, BUT THEY CAN BUILD TOWERS TALLER THAN MY DEVIL'S CASTLE.
AND DESPITE THAT, THEY STILL KEEP THINGS LIKE THE CHOSHI ELECTRIC RAILWAY.
THERE'S NO WAY I COULD ANNIHILATE THIS SPECIES.

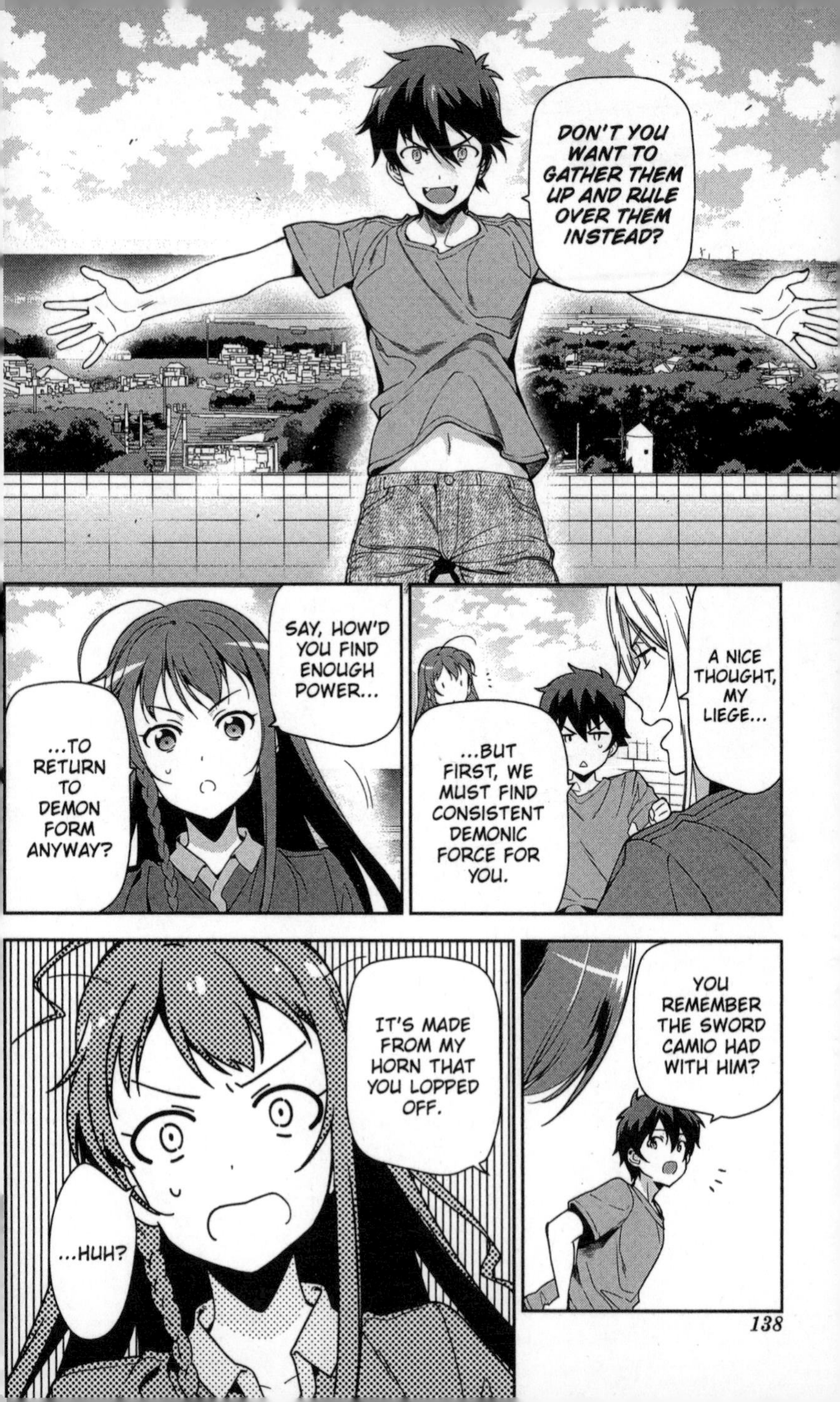
DON'T YOU WANT TO GATHER THEM UP AND RULE OVER THEM INSTEAD?
A NICE THOUGHT, MY LIEGE...
...BUT FIRST, WE MUST FIND CONSISTENT DEMONIC FORCE FOR YOU.
SAY, HOW'D YOU FIND ENOUGH POWER...
...TO RETURN TO DEMON FORM ANYWAY?
YOU REMEMBER THE SWORD CAMIO HAD WITH HIM?
IT'S MADE FROM MY HORN THAT YOU LOPPED OFF.
...HUH?

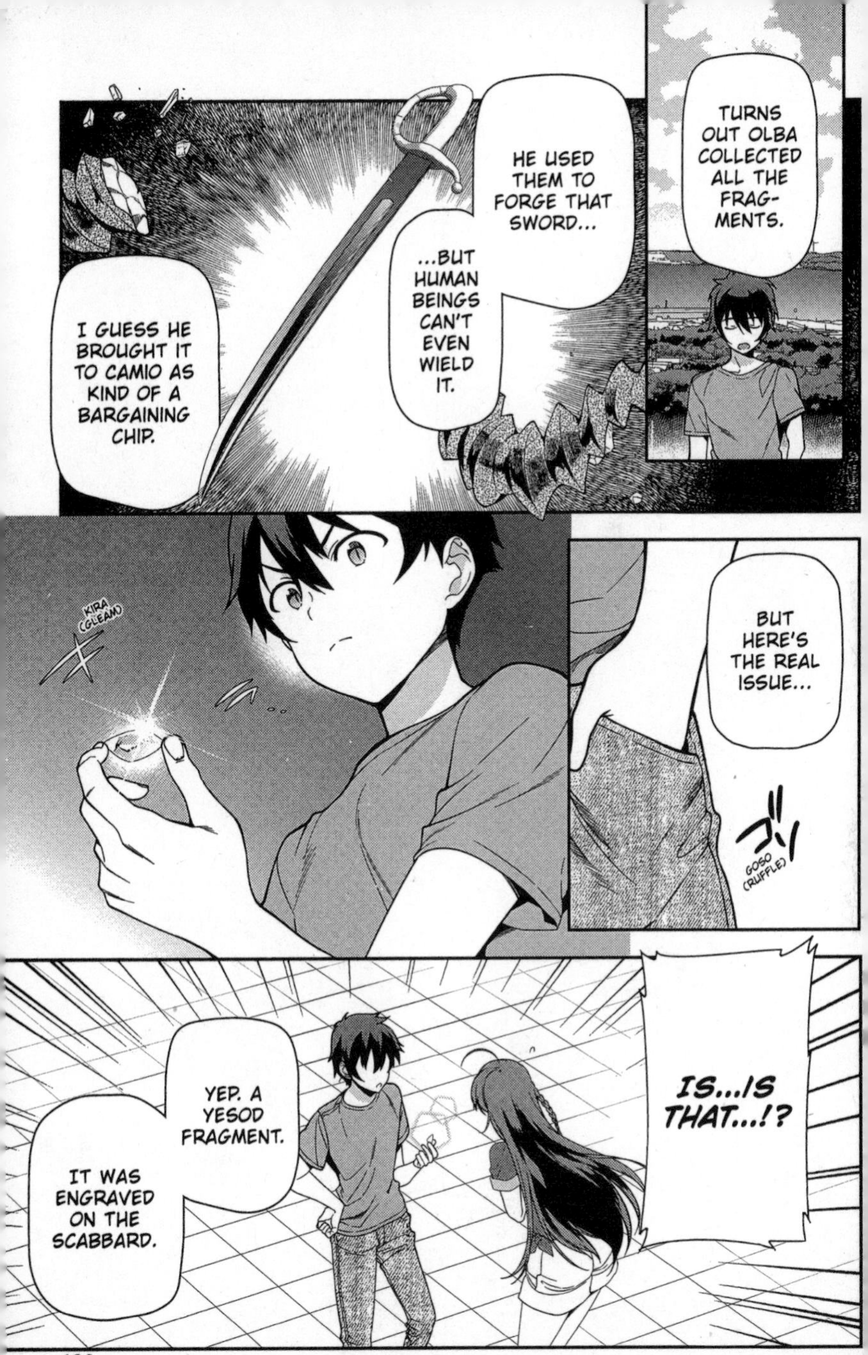
TURNS OUT OLBA COLLECTED ALL THE FRAG-MENTS.
HE USED THEM TO FORGE THAT SWORD...
...BUT HUMAN BEINGS CAN'T EVEN WIELD IT.
I GUESS HE BROUGHT IT TO CAMIO AS KIND OF A BARGAINING CHIP.
BUT HERE'S THE REAL ISSUE...
GOSO (RUFFLE)
KIRA (GLEAM)
IS...IS THAT...!?
YEP. A YESOD FRAGMENT.
IT WAS ENGRAVED ON THE SCABBARD.

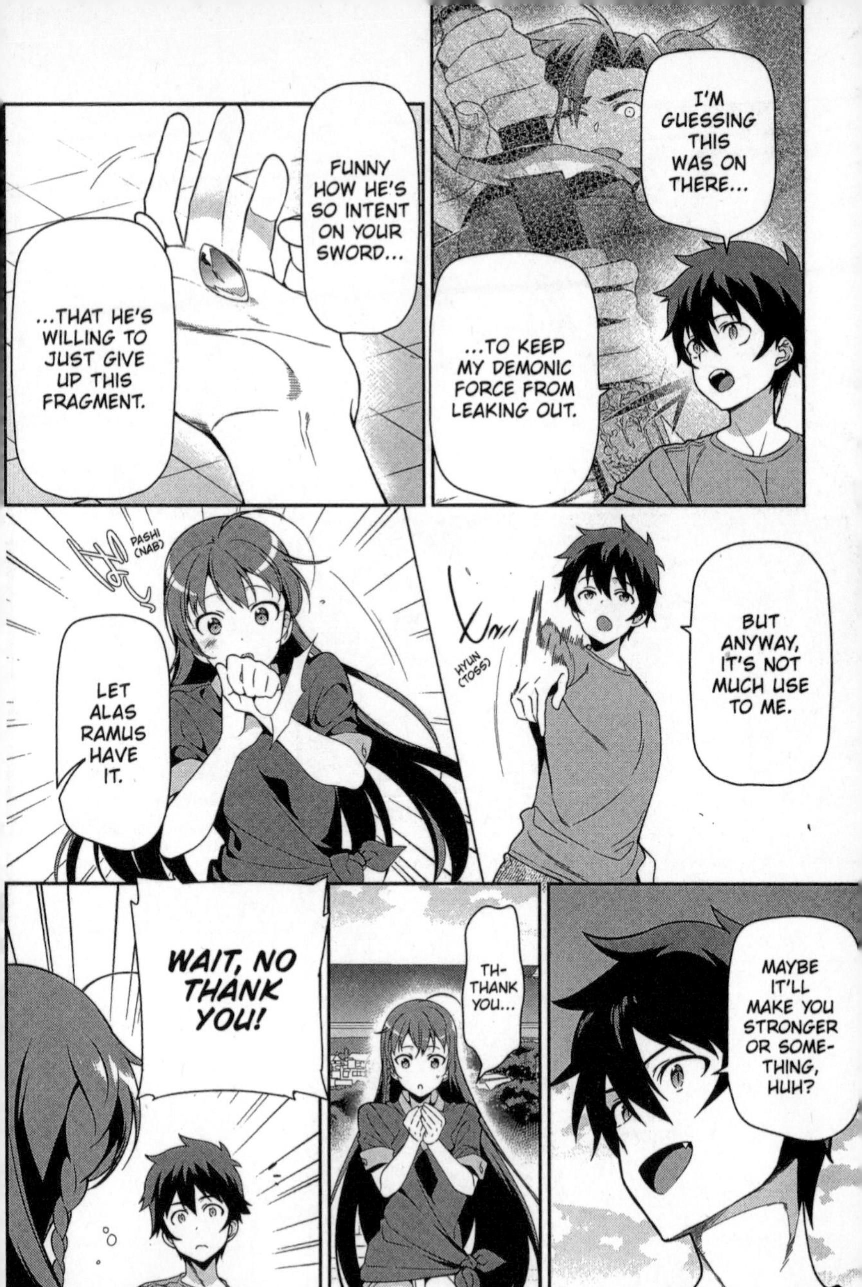
I'M GUESSING THIS WAS ON THERE...
...TO KEEP MY DEMONIC FORCE FROM LEAKING OUT.
FUNNY HOW HE'S SO INTENT ON YOUR SWORD...
...THAT HE'S WILLING TO JUST GIVE UP THIS FRAGMENT.
BUT ANYWAY, IT'S NOT MUCH USE TO ME.
HYUN (TOSS)
LET ALAS RAMUS HAVE IT.
PASHI (NAB)
MAYBE IT'LL MAKE YOU STRONGER OR SOME-THING, HUH?
TH-THANK YOU...
WAIT, NO THANK YOU!

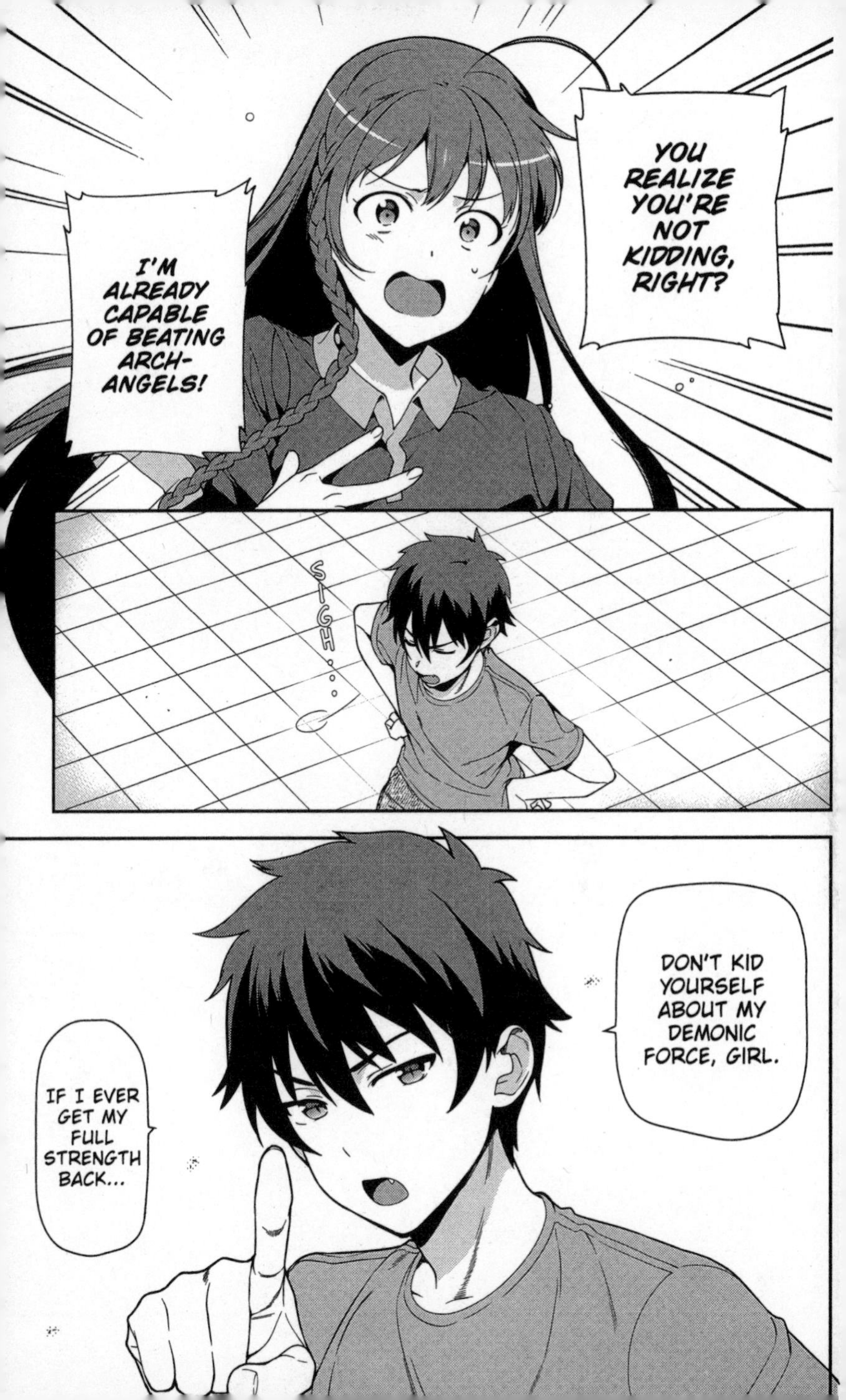
YOU REALIZE YOU'RE NOT KIDDING, RIGHT?
I'M ALREADY CAPABLE OF BEATING ARCH-ANGELS!
SIGH...
DON'T KID YOURSELF ABOUT MY DEMONIC FORCE, GIRL.
IF I EVER GET MY FULL STRENGTH BACK...

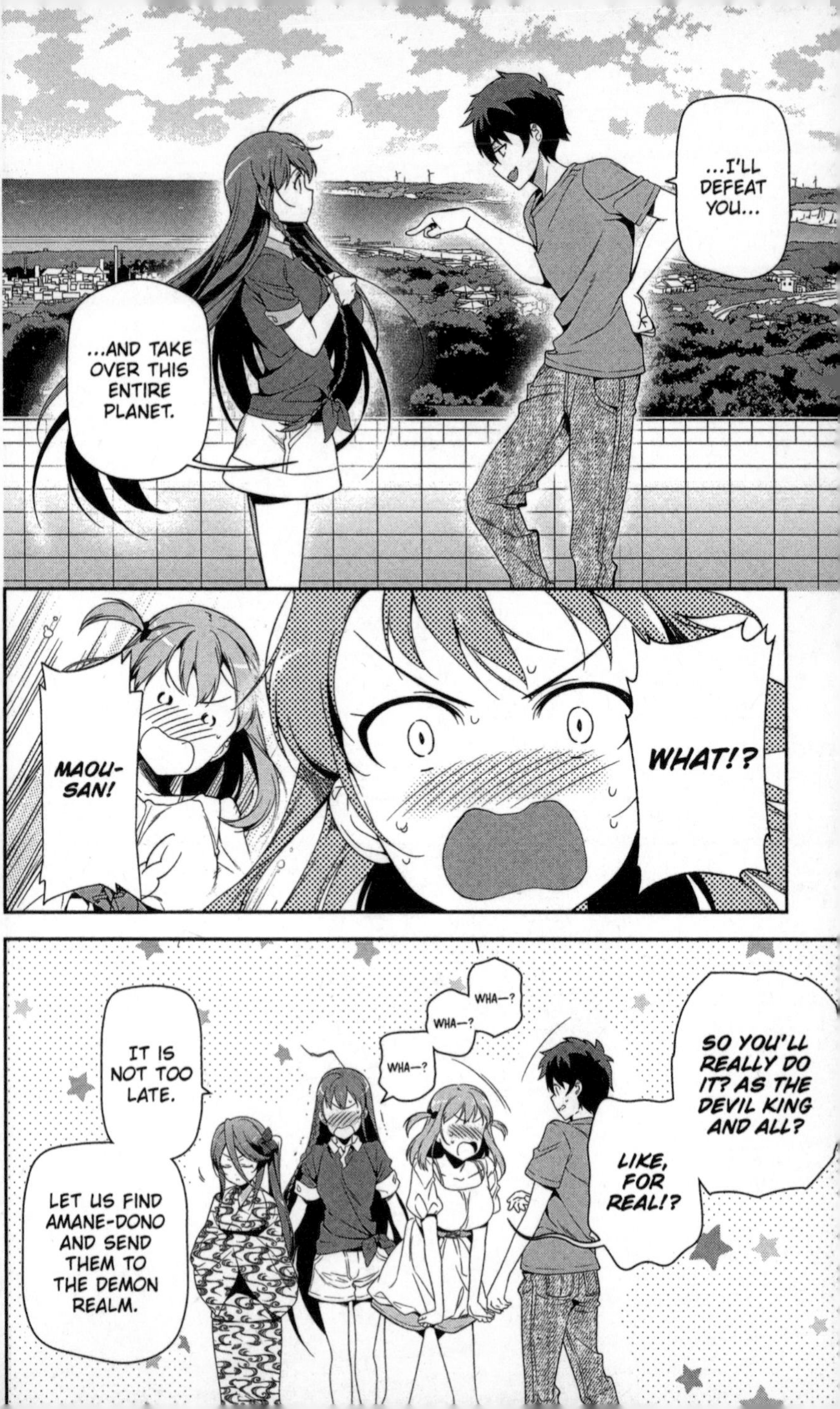
...I'LL DEFEAT YOU...
...AND TAKE OVER THIS ENTIRE PLANET.
WHAT!?
MAOU-SAN!
SO YOU'LL REALLY DO IT? AS THE DEVIL KING AND ALL?
LIKE, FOR REAL!?
WHA—?
WHA—?
WHA—?
IT IS NOT TOO LATE.
LET US FIND AMANE-DONO AND SEND THEM TO THE DEMON REALM.

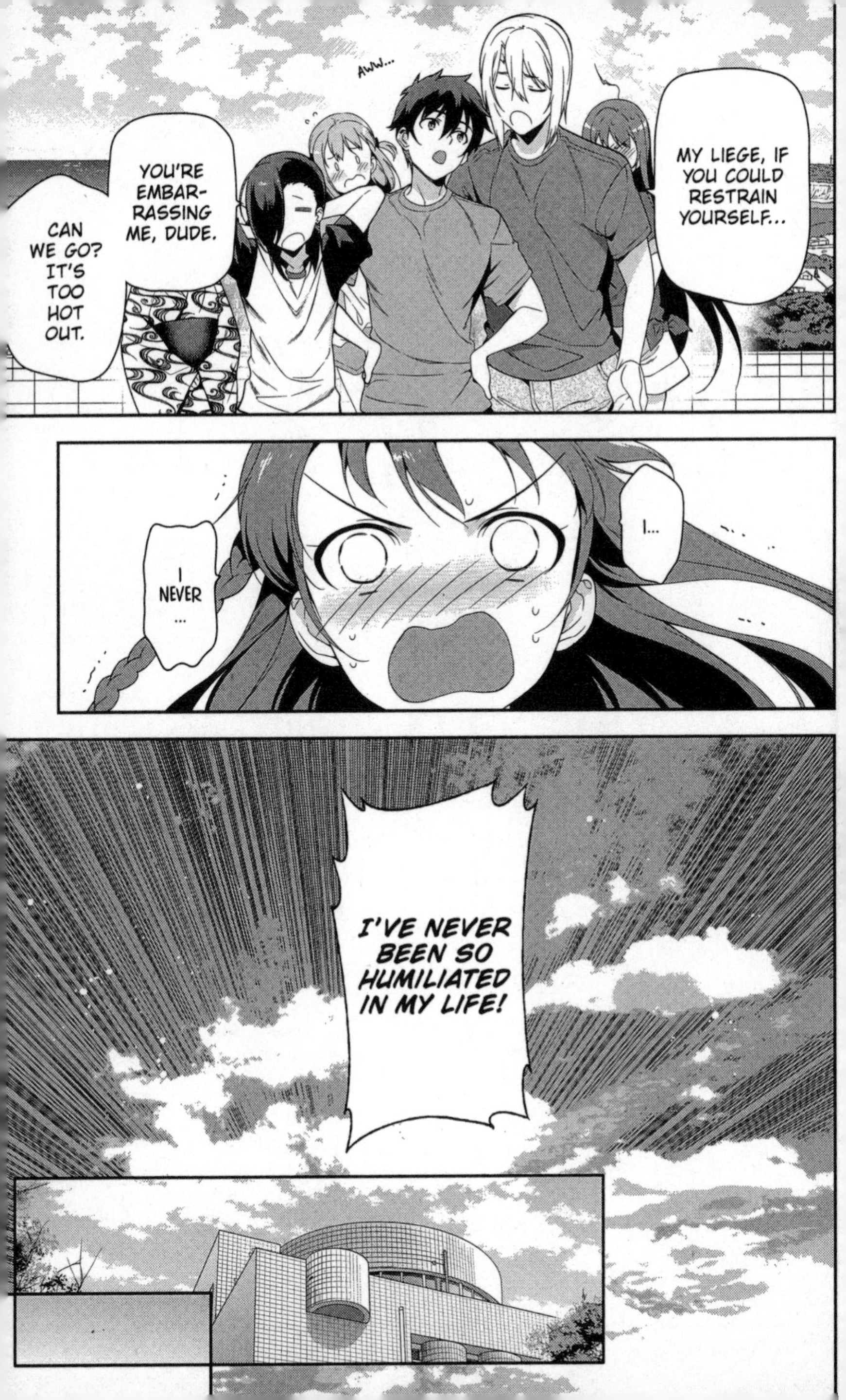
MY LIEGE, IF YOU COULD RESTRAIN YOURSELF...
AWW...
YOU'RE EMBAR-RASSING ME, DUDE.
CAN WE GO? IT'S TOO HOT OUT.
I...
I NEVER...
I'VE NEVER BEEN SO HUMILIATED IN MY LIFE!

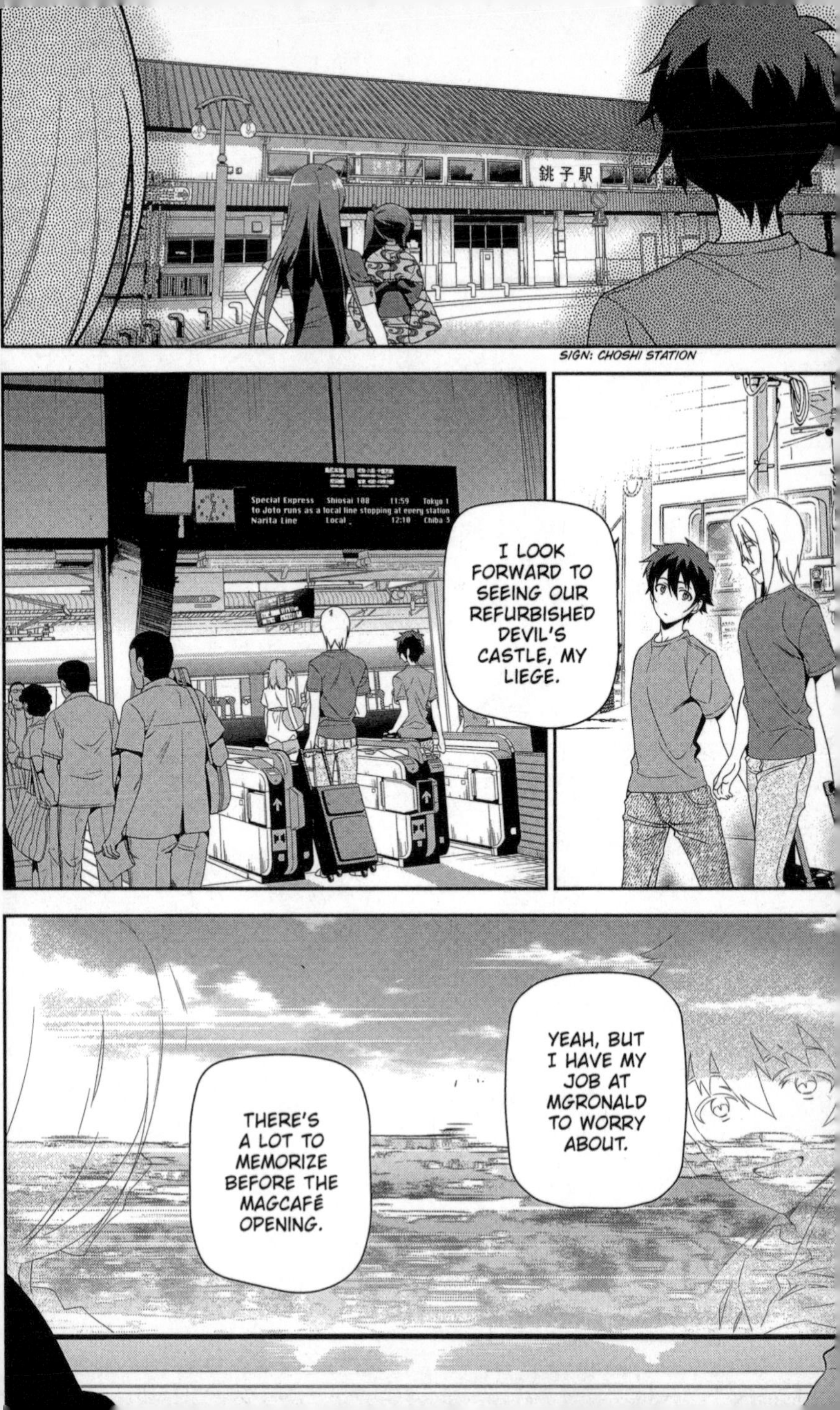
銚子駅
SIGN: CHOSHI STATION
I LOOK FORWARD TO SEEING OUR REFURBISHED DEVIL'S CASTLE, MY LIEGE.
Special Express Shiosai 108 11:59 Tokyo 1
to Joto runs as a local line stopping at every station
Narita Line Local 12:10 Chiba 3
YEAH, BUT I HAVE MY JOB AT MGRONALD TO WORRY ABOUT.
THERE'S A LOT TO MEMORIZE BEFORE THE MAGCAFÉ OPENING.

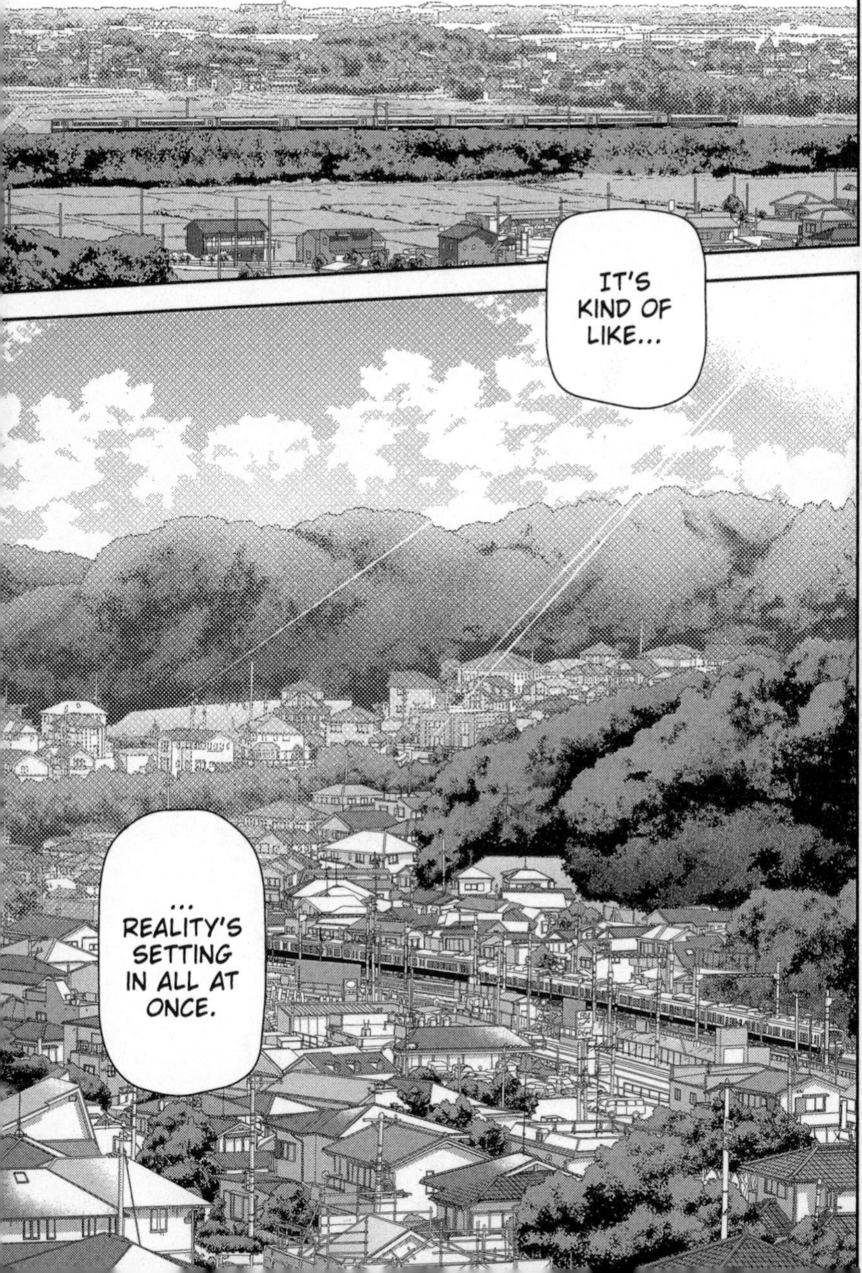
IT'S KIND OF LIKE...
... REALITY'S SETTING IN ALL AT ONCE.

THE DEVIL IS A PART-TIMER!

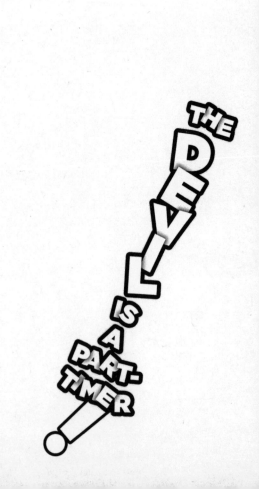

CHAPTER X: THE CLERIC BECOMES A SAMURAI-DRAMA RONIN

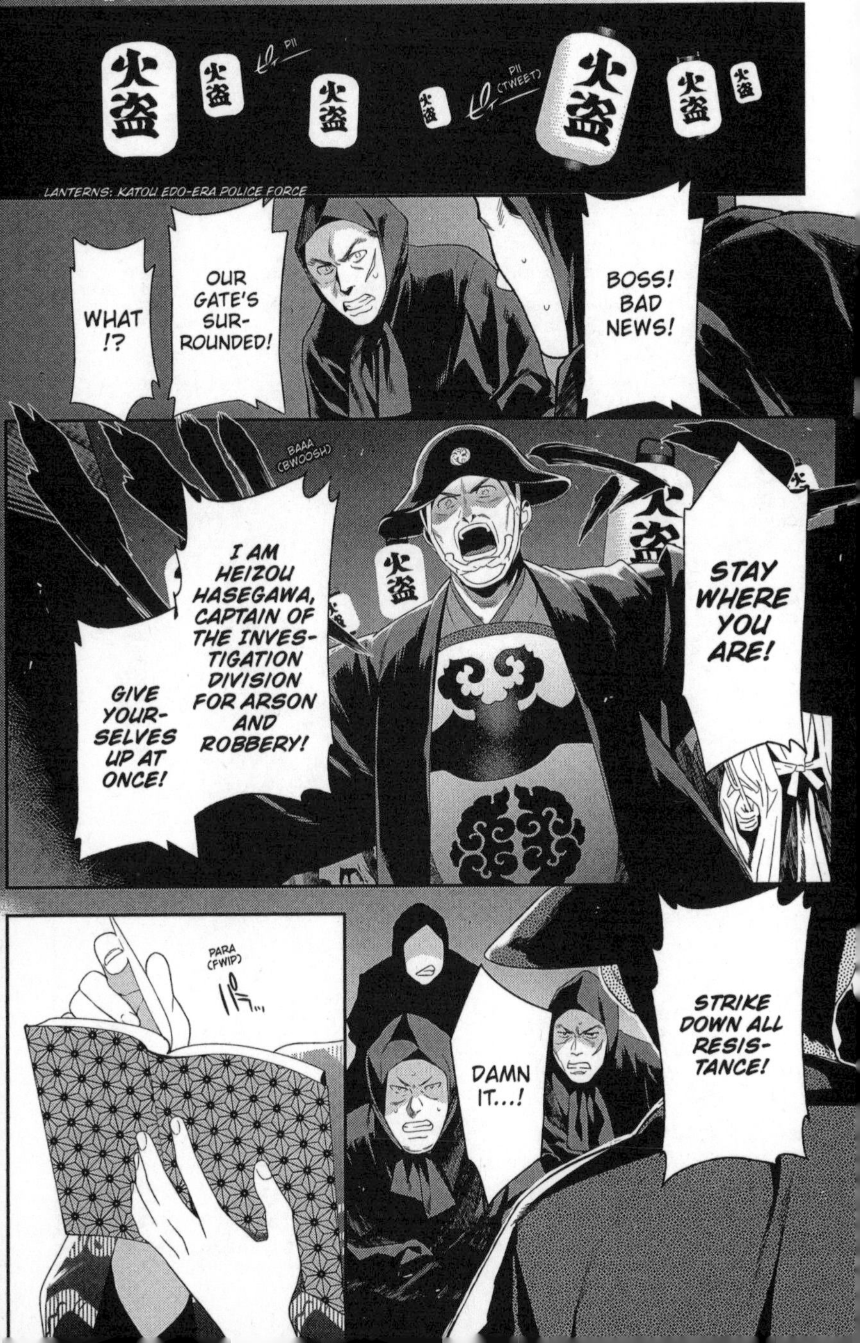

PII (TWEET)
PII
火盗
LANTERNS: KATOU EDO-ERA POLICE FORCE
BOSS! BAD NEWS!
OUR GATE'S SUR-ROUNDED!
WHAT!?
BAAA (BWOOSH)
STAY WHERE YOU ARE!
I AM HEIZOU HASEGAWA, CAPTAIN OF THE INVES-TIGATION DIVISION FOR ARSON AND ROBBERY!
GIVE YOUR-SELVES UP AT ONCE!
STRIKE DOWN ALL RESIS-TANCE!
DAMN IT...!
PARA (FWIP)

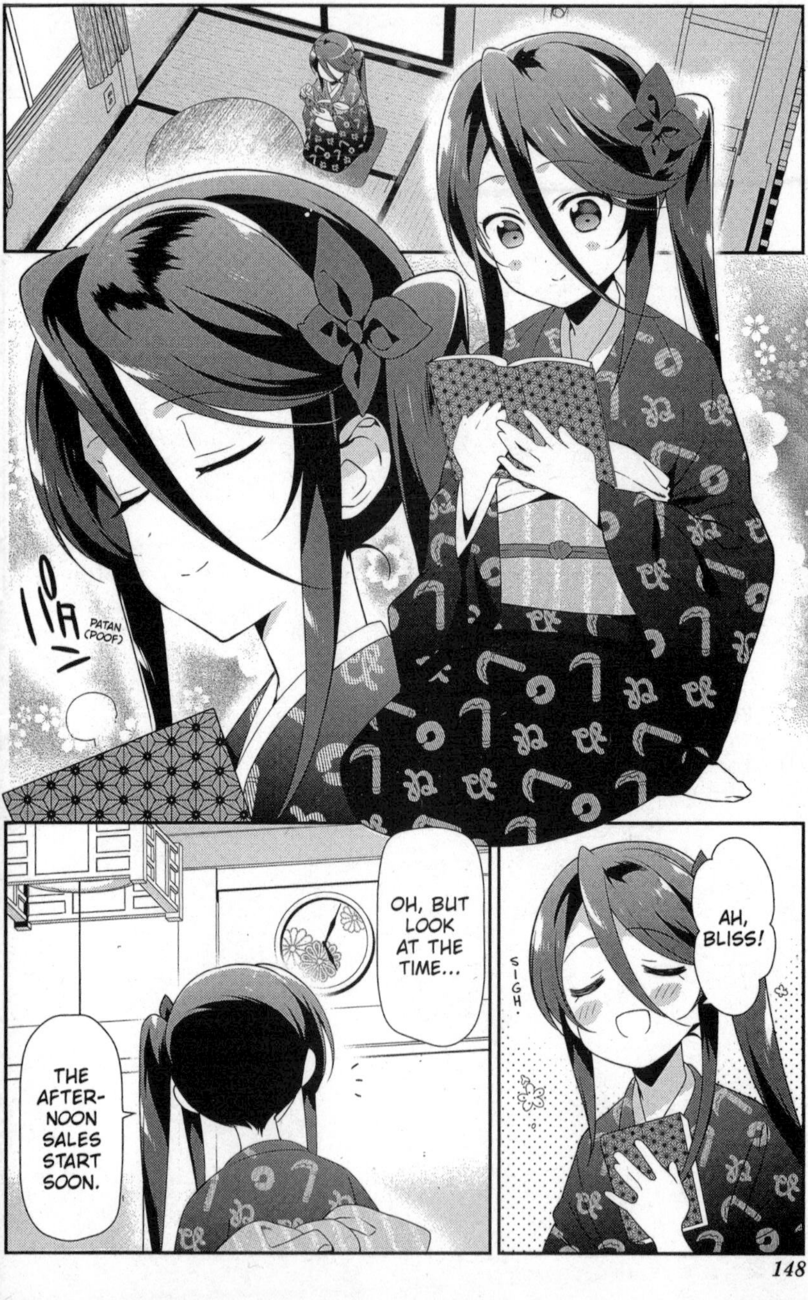
PATAN (POOF)
AH, BLISS!
SIGH
OH, BUT LOOK AT THE TIME...
THE AFTER-NOON SALES START SOON.

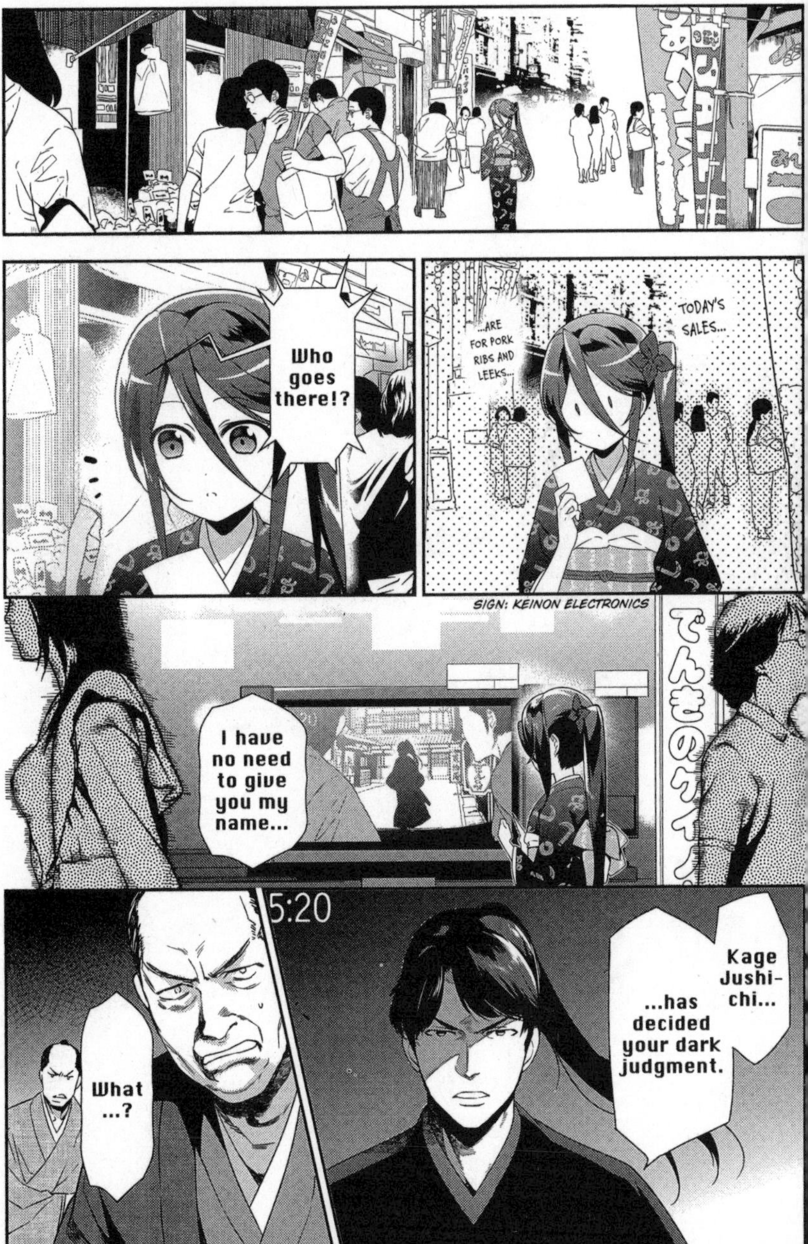
TODAY'S SALES...
...ARE FOR PORK RIBS AND LEEKS...
Who goes there!?
SIGN: KEINON ELECTRONICS
I have no need to give you my name...
5:20
Kage Jushi-chi...
...has decided your dark judgment.
What...?

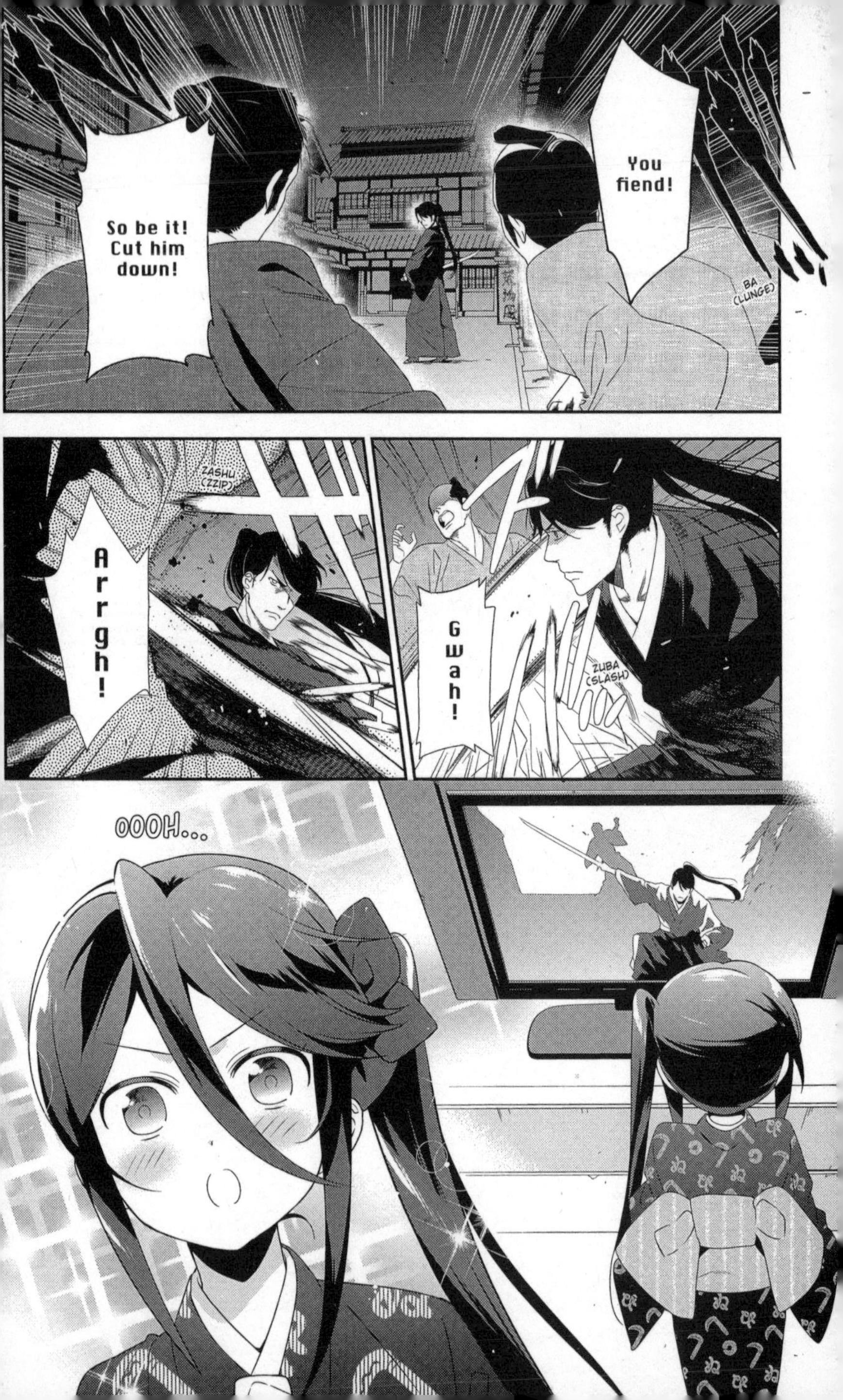
You fiend!
BA (LUNGE)
So be it! Cut him down!
Gwah!
ZUBA (SLASH)
ZASHU (ZZIP)
Arrgh!
OOOH...

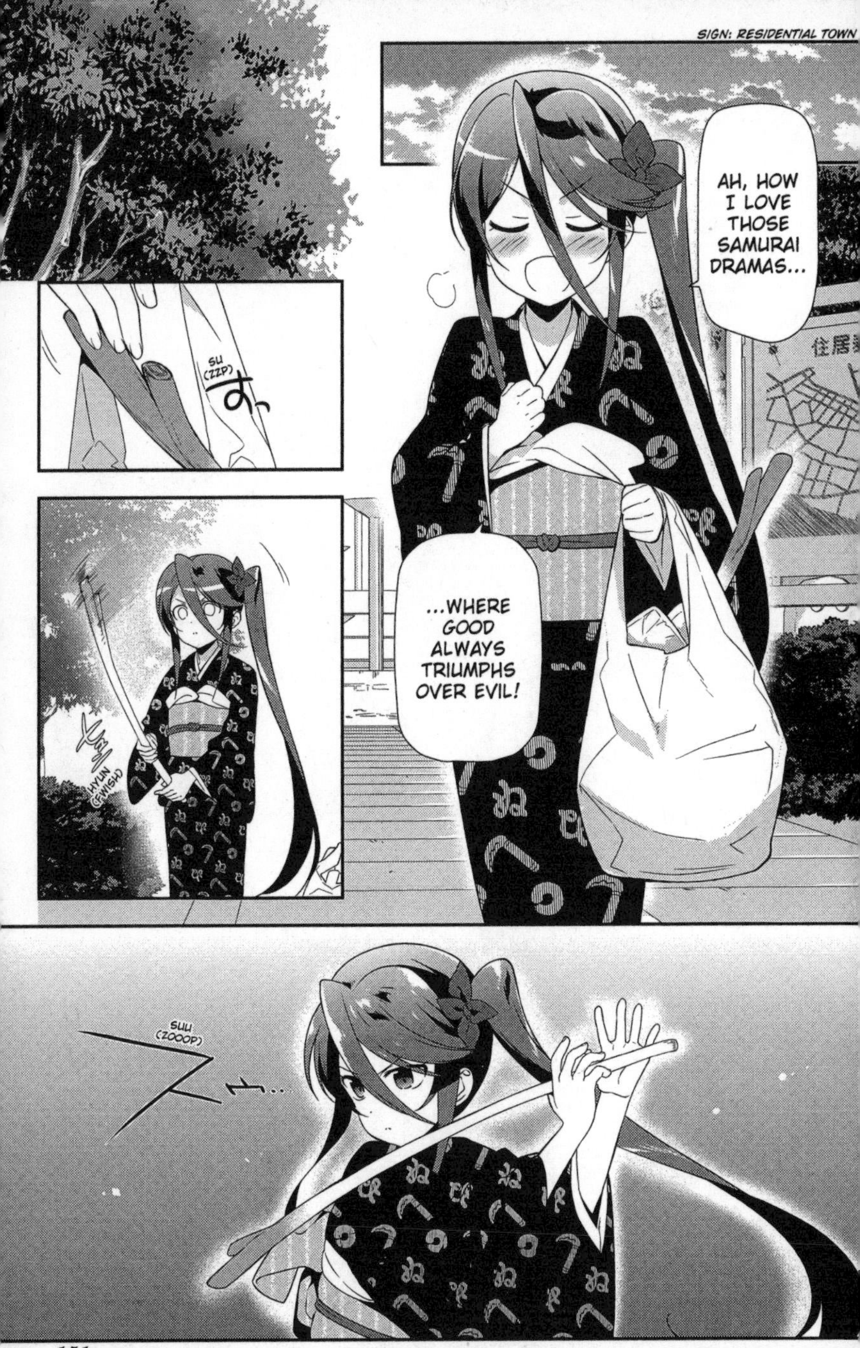
SIGN: RESIDENTIAL TOWN
AH, HOW I LOVE THOSE SAMURAI DRAMAS...
...WHERE GOOD ALWAYS TRIUMPHS OVER EVIL!
SU (ZZP)
HYUN (SWISH)
SUU (ZOOOP)

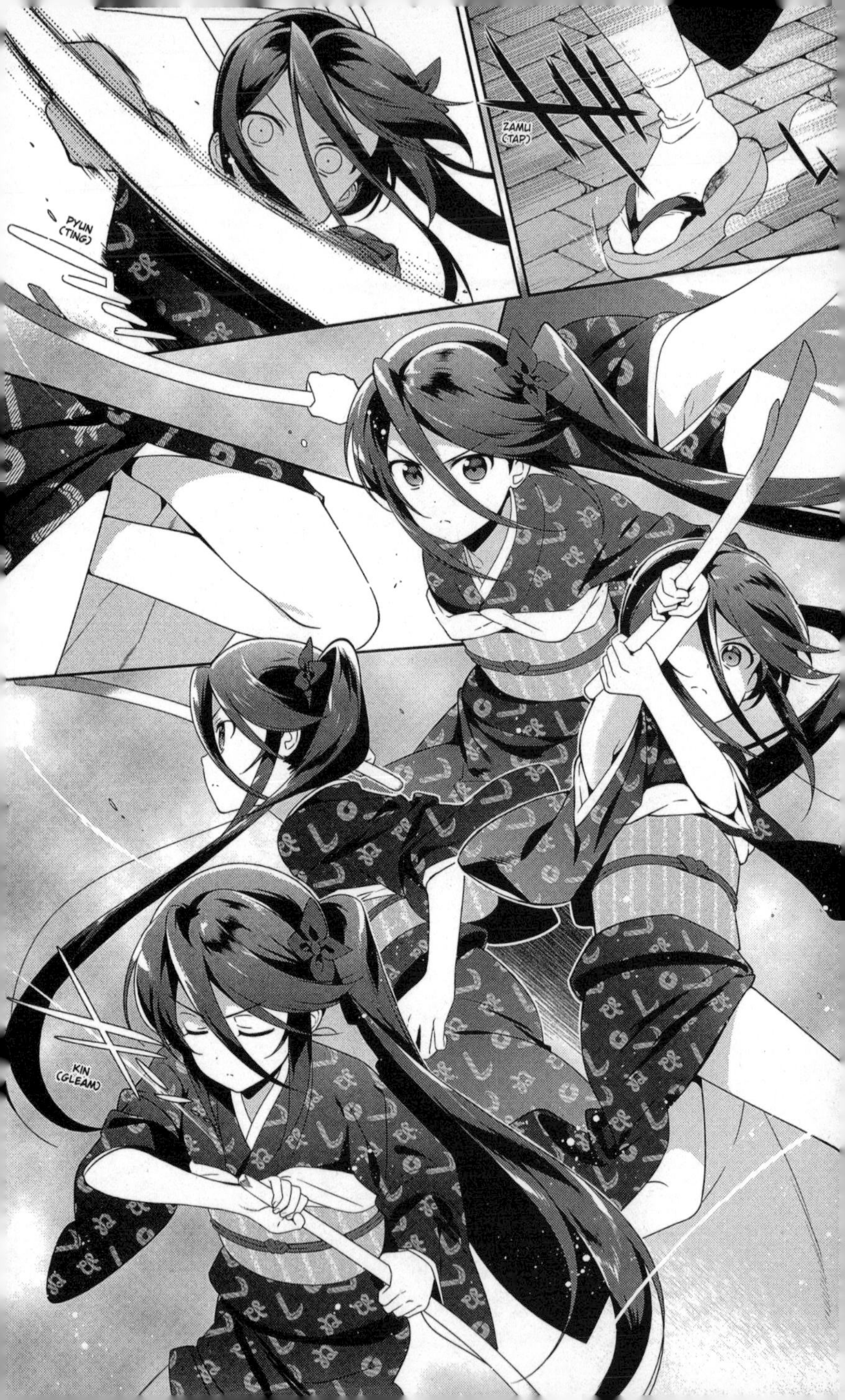
ZAMU
(TAP)
PYUN
(TING)
KIN
(GLEAM)

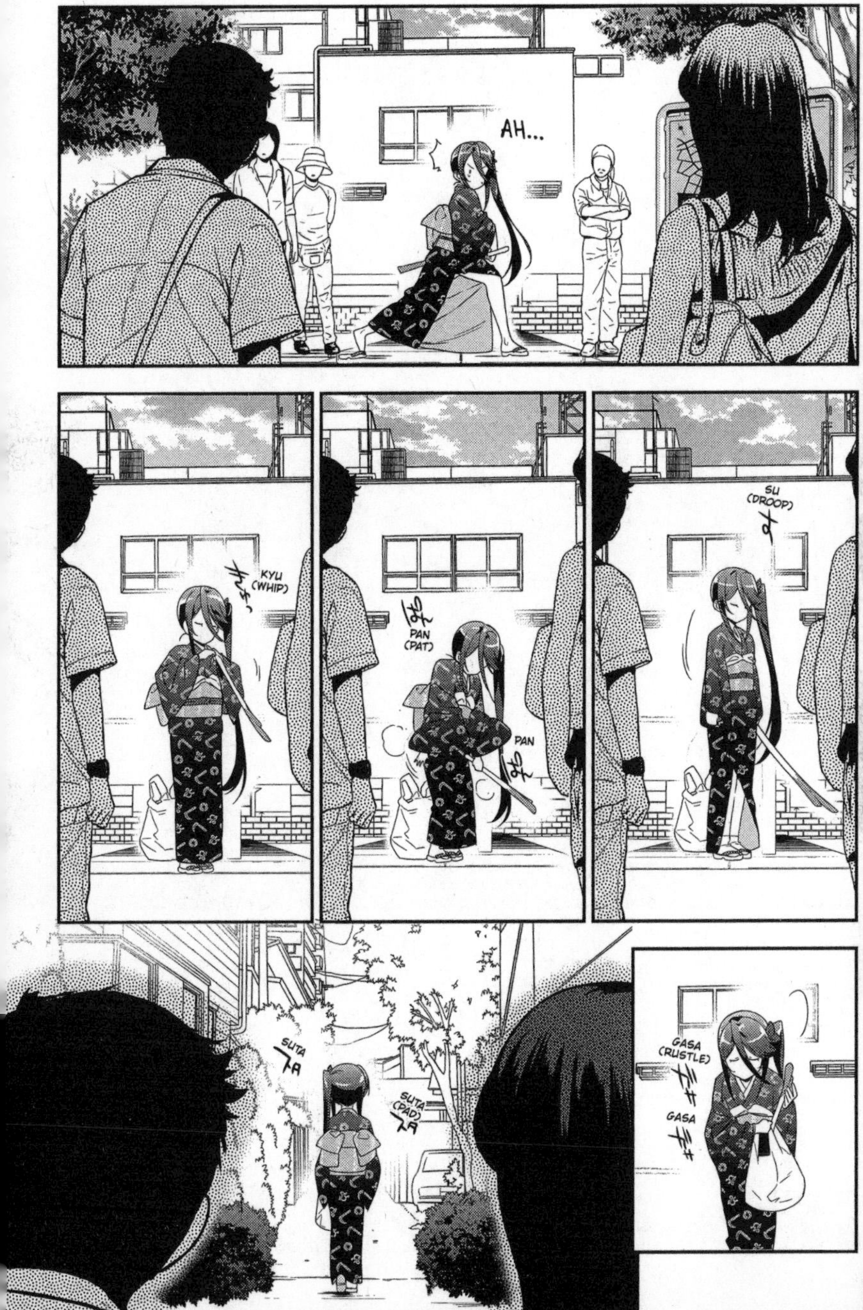
AH...
SU (DROOP)
PAN (PAT)
PAN
KYU (WHIP)
GASA (RUSTLE)
GASA
SUTA
SUTA (PAD)

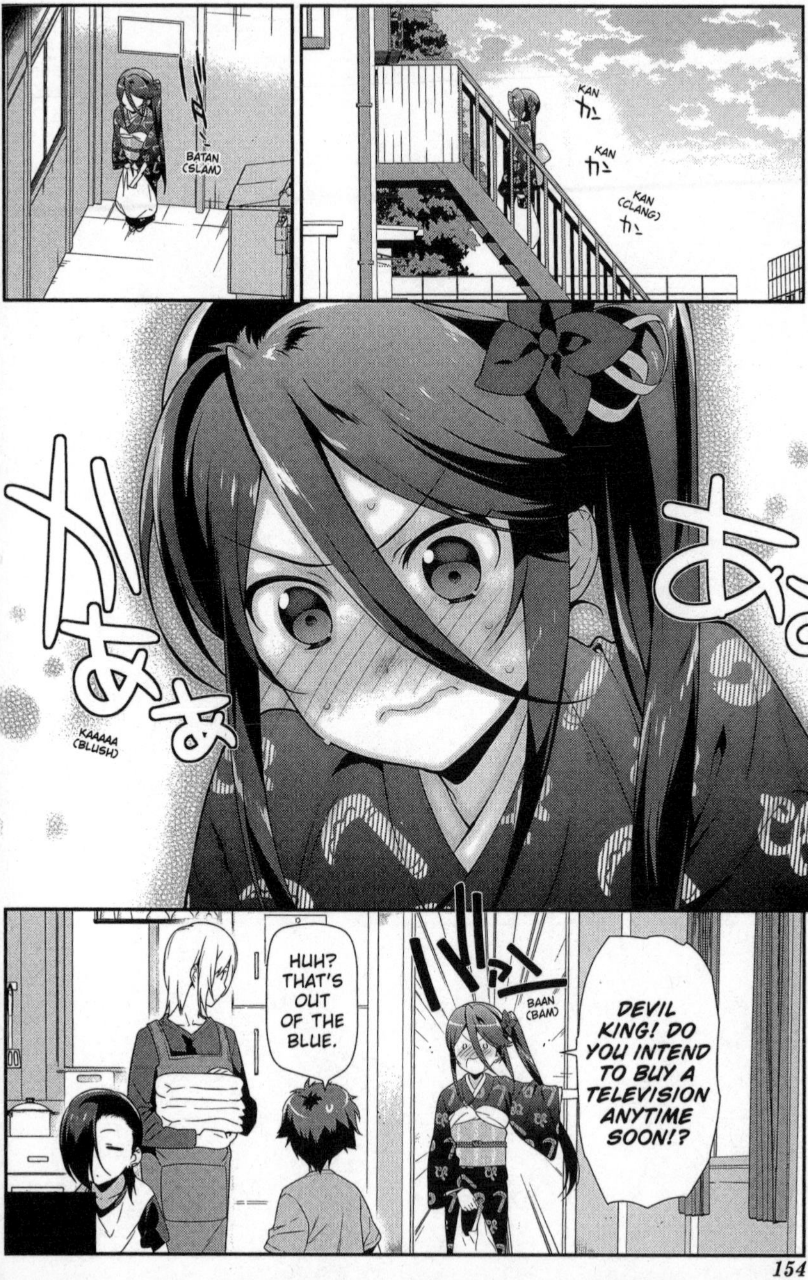
KAN
KAN
KAN (CLANG)
BATAN (SLAM)
KAAAAA (BLUSH)
DEVIL KING! DO YOU INTEND TO BUY A TELEVISION ANYTIME SOON!?
BAAN (BAM)
HUH? THAT'S OUT OF THE BLUE.

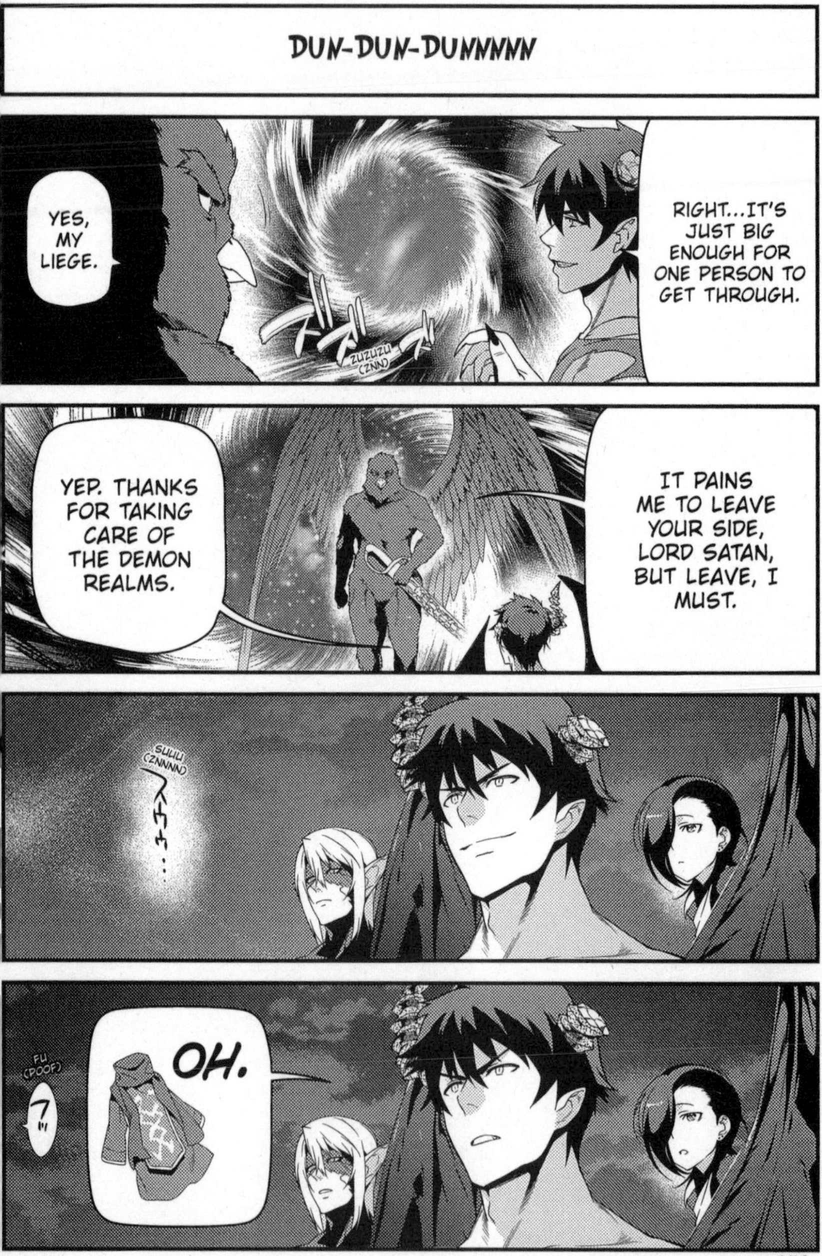
DUN-DUN-DUNNNNN
RIGHT...IT'S JUST BIG ENOUGH FOR ONE PERSON TO GET THROUGH.
ZUZUZU (ZNN)
YES, MY LIEGE.
IT PAINS ME TO LEAVE YOUR SIDE, LORD SATAN, BUT LEAVE, I MUST.
YEP. THANKS FOR TAKING CARE OF THE DEMON REALMS.
SUUU (ZNNNN)
OH.
FU (POOF)

BLESSINGS FOR A BRIGHT FUTURE

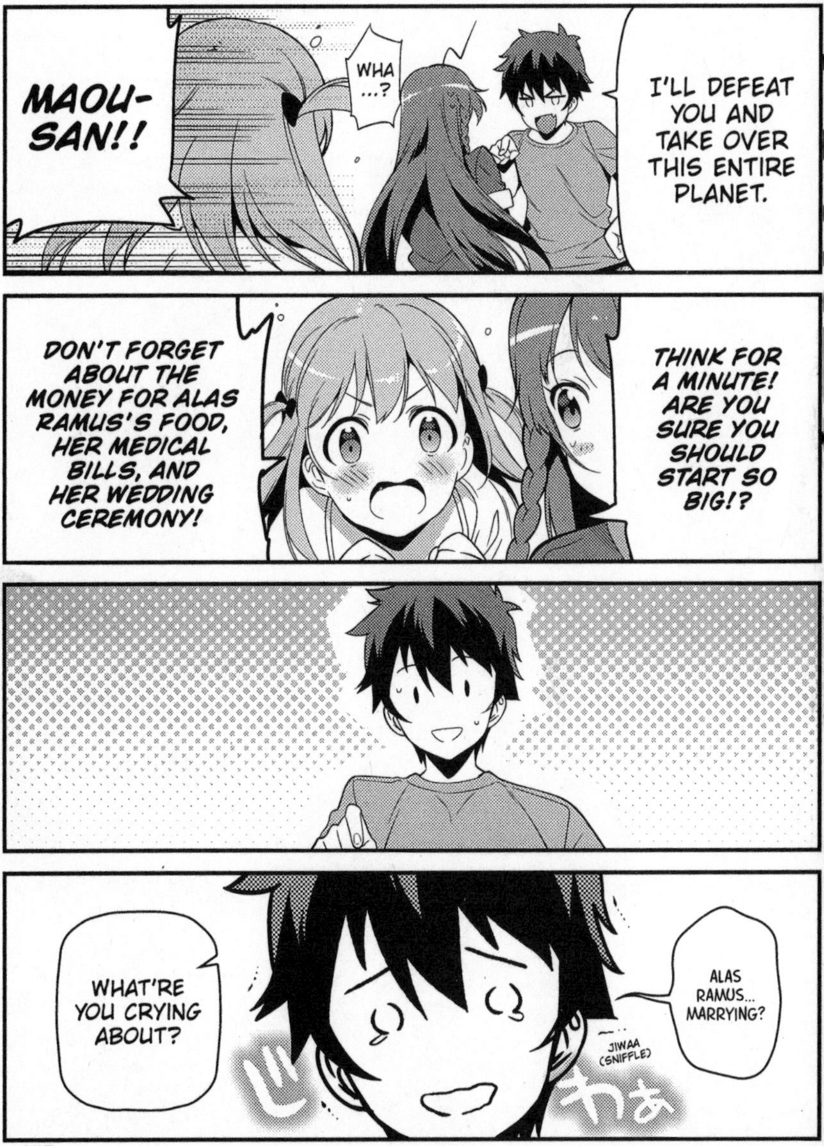
I'LL DEFEAT YOU AND TAKE OVER THIS ENTIRE PLANET.
WHA ...?
MAOU-SAN!!
THINK FOR A MINUTE! ARE YOU SURE YOU SHOULD START SO BIG!?
DON'T FORGET ABOUT THE MONEY FOR ALAS RAMUS'S FOOD, HER MEDICAL BILLS, AND HER WEDDING CEREMONY!
ALAS RAMUS... MARRYING?
JIWAA (SNIFFLE)
WHAT'RE YOU CRYING ABOUT?

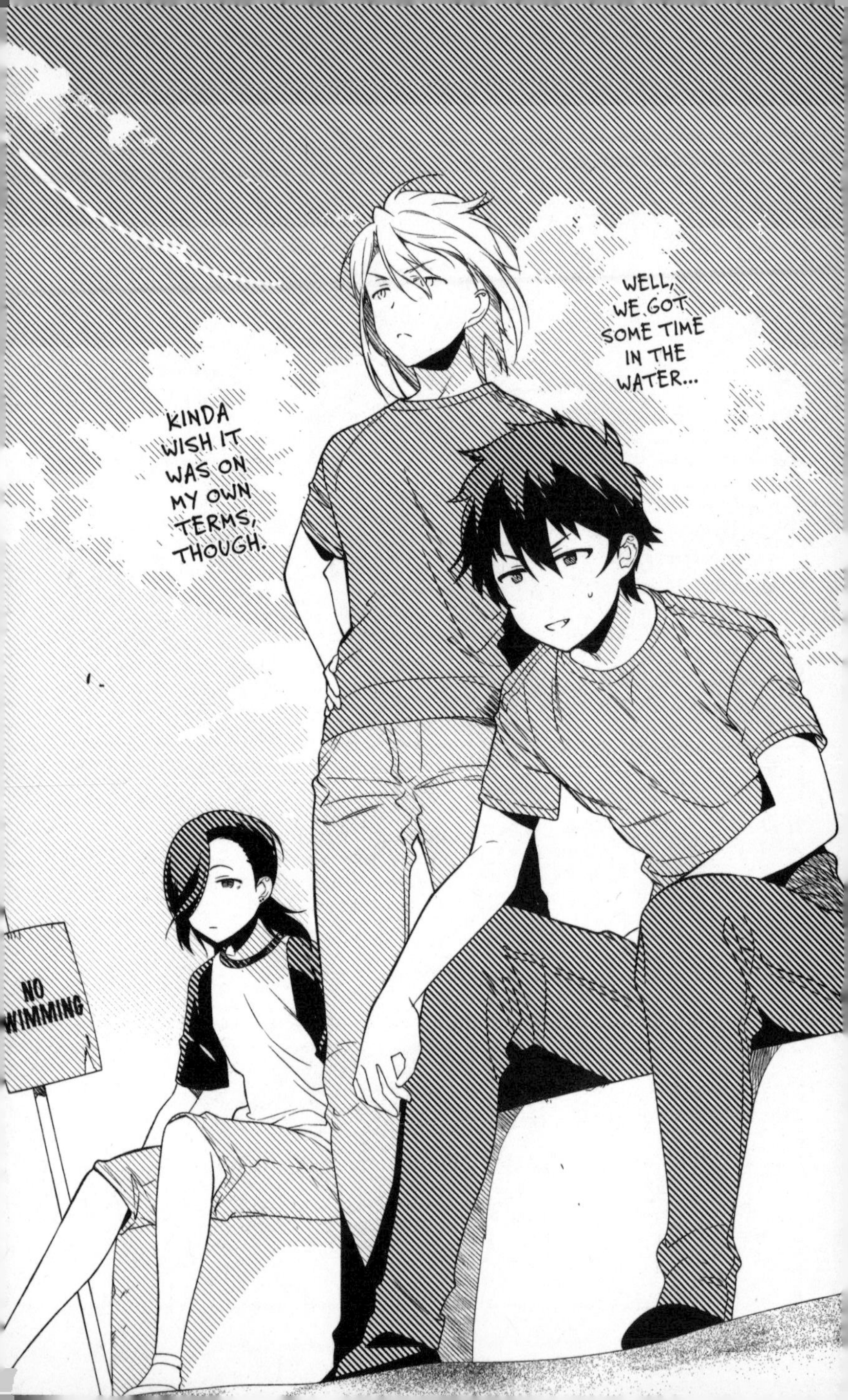
WELL, WE GOT SOME TIME IN THE WATER...
KINDA WISH IT WAS ON MY OWN TERMS, THOUGH.
NO WIMMING

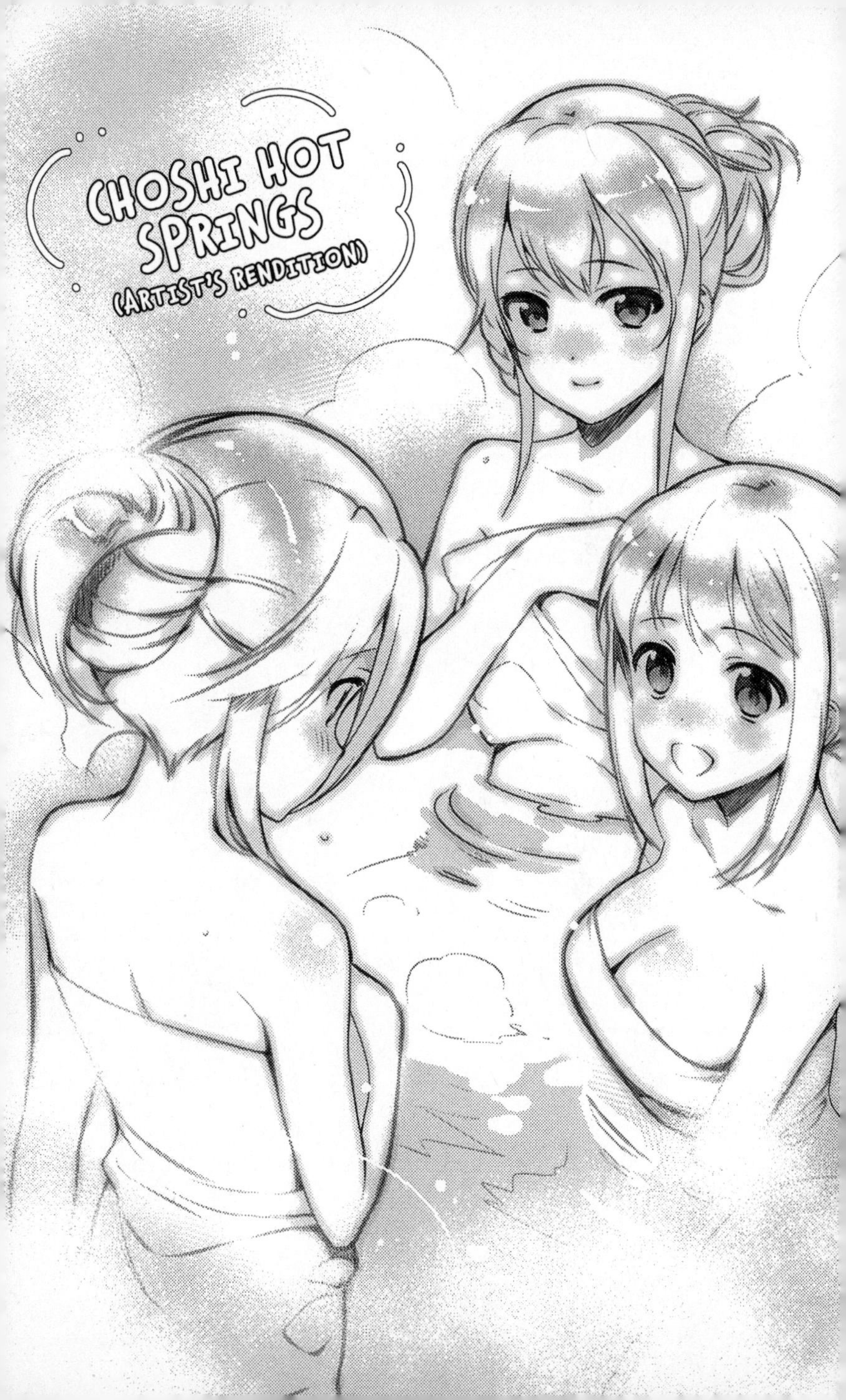
CHOSHI HOT SPRINGS
(ARTIST'S RENDITION)

HERE WE ARE AT VOLUME 9!
I'VE BEEN ABLE TO DRAW THIS FAR INTO THE STORY ENTIRELY THANKS TO THE SUPPORT OF WAGAHARA-SENSEI, 029-SENSEI, ALL THE OTHER STAFF INVOLVED, AND OF COURSE, ALL OF MY READERS. THANK YOU ALL SO MUCH FOR EVERYTHING.

I'VE ALWAYS HAD TO RELY ON THE SUPPORT OF OTHERS' VISUAL DESIGNS, BUT THIS PART OF THE STORY'S SUCH A FAVORITE OF MINE THAT I FOUND MYSELF DEALING WITH BOTH ARTIST'S BLOCK AND MY OWN WORRIES A LOT. LOOKING BACK, THERE ARE TONS OF THINGS I WOULD'VE TACKLED DIFFERENTLY, BUT IT'S ALSO GIVEN ME A CHANCE TO TAKE WHAT I'VE LEARNED AND USE IT TO CREATE AN EVEN BETTER MANGA VERSION IN THE FUTURE.

AND TO THINK, WE'RE GOING INTO DOUBLE DIGITS STARTING WITH THE NEXT VOLUME! I GET BUTTERFLIES IN MY STOMACH JUST THINKING ABOUT IT. I HOPE I'LL CONTINUE TO ENJOY YOUR SUPPORT GOING FORWARD!

SPECIAL THANKS!
SHIBA / TAKASHI YAMANO / AND YOU!
IMAGE SUPPORT: I-MAX / PHOTORIO

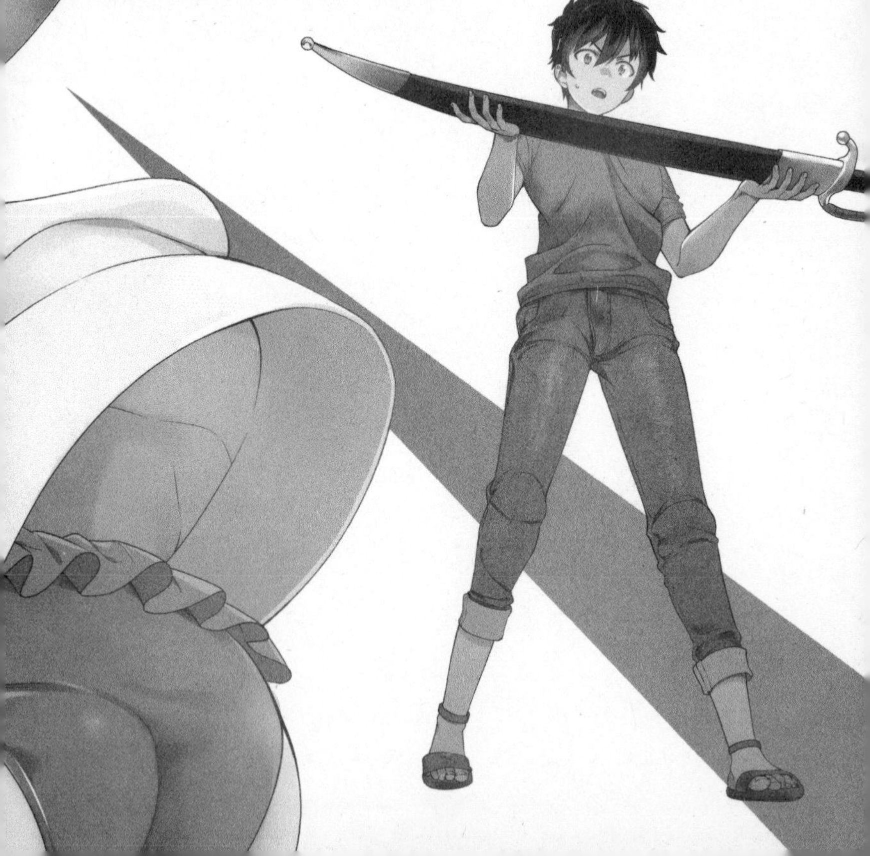

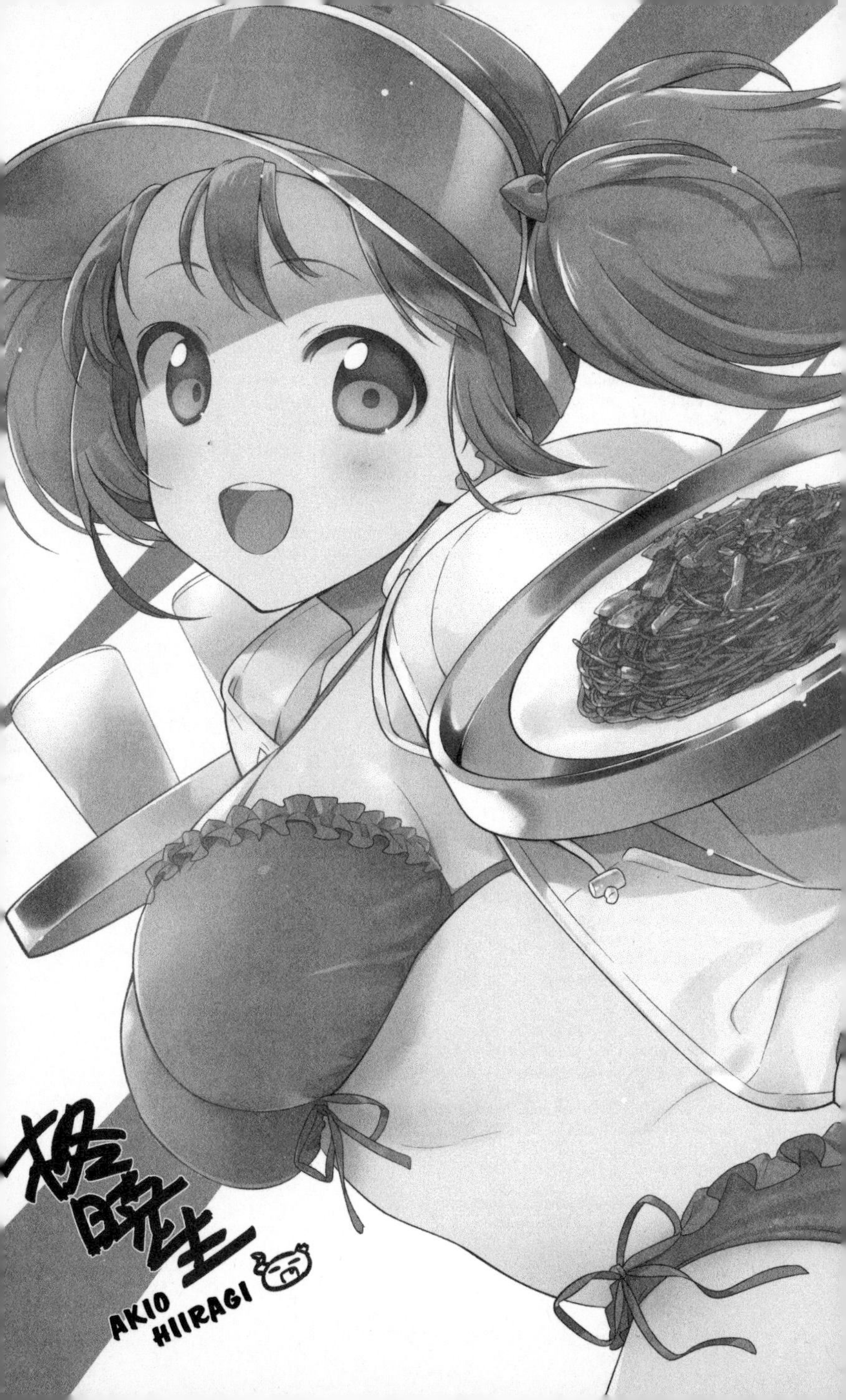
AKIO
HIIRAGI

THE DEVIL IS A PART-TIMER! ⑨

ART: Akio Hiiragi
Original Story: Satoshi Wagahara
Character Design: 029 (Oniku)

Translation: Kevin Gifford

Lettering: Brndn Blakeslee

HATARAKU MAOUSAMA! Vol. 9
© SATOSHI WAGAHARA / AKIO HIIRAGI 2016
All rights reserved.
Edited by ASCII MEDIA WORKS
First published in Japan in 2016 by KADOKAWA CORPORATION, Tokyo.
English translation rights arranged with KADOKAWA CORPORATION, Tokyo, through Tuttle-Mori Agency, Inc., Tokyo.

English translation © 2017 by Yen Press, LLC

Yen Press
1290 Avenue of the Americas
New York, NY 10104

Visit us at yenpress.com
facebook.com/yenpress
twitter.com/yenpress
yenpress.tumblr.com
instagram.com/yenpress

First Yen Press Edition: June 2017

Yen Press is an imprint of Yen Press, LLC.
The Yen Press name and logo are trademarks of Yen Press, LLC.

The publisher is not responsible for websites (or their content) that are not owned by the publisher.

Library of Congress Control Number: 2014504637

ISBNs: 978-0-316-55848-8 (paperback)
       978-0-316-43913-8 (ebook)

10 9 8 7 6 5 4 3 2 1

BVG

Printed in the United States of America